THE HOLOCAUST AS HISTORICAL EXPERIENCE

Essays and a Discussion

Edited by
YEHUDA BAUER
NATHAN ROTENSTREICH

Associate Editor
MALCOLM LOWE

HOLMES & MEIER PUBLISHERS, INC.

NEW YORK   LONDON

"The Ghetto as a Form of Government: An analysis of Isaiah Trunk's *Judenrat*" by Raul Hilberg was originally printed under the title "The Ghetto as a Form of Government" in volume no. 450 of THE ANNALS of The American Academy of Political and Social Science." Copyright © 1980 by The American Academy of Political and Social Sciences. All rights reserved.

First published in the United States of America 1981 by
Holmes & Meier Publishers, Inc.
30 Irving Place
New York, N.Y. 10003

Great Britain:
Holmes & Meier Publishers, Ltd.
131 Trafalgar Road
Greenwich, London SE10 9TX

Library of Congress Cataloging in Publication Data

Main entry under title:

The Holocaust as historical experience.

   1.   Holocaust, Jewish (1939–1945)—Congresses.
2. World War, 1939–1945—Underground movements—Jews—
Congresses. I. Bauer, Yehuda. II. Rotenstreich, Nathan, 1914–
D810.J4H6433   1980   943.086   80-23136
ISBN 0-8419-0635-1
ISBN 0-8419-0636-X (pbk.)

The publication of this book and the research that went into it were made possible by the generosity of Mr. Frank N. Lautenberg.

Manufactured in the United States of America

THE HOLOCAUST
AS
HISTORICAL
EXPERIENCE

CONTENTS

Introduction

YEHUDA BAUER and MALCOLM LOWE

The Holocaust of European Jewry under Nazi rule is swiftly becoming what some contributors to this book suspected it must become: one of the central traumas of our generation, and probably not ours alone. Publications dealing with the Holocaust are multiplying at an increasing rate. There are novels and poems. There are plays and even some operatic works. There are personal memoirs and popular histories. There are learned books and articles in the fields of most of the social sciences and humanities. Indeed, the Holocaust is increasingly becoming a subject for film and television productions. Many universities now offer at least a basic course on the Holocaust, the high attendance of Jewish and non-Jewish students testifying to both the universal implications of the subject and its uniquely Jewish significance.

Faced with the flood of material available, the average reader, student or even teacher, may well feel bewildered. He wants accurate information on a subject where historical judgment is easily clouded by emotion, but on which emotion must find expression. He wants a full picture, but cannot read more than a small part of the numerous publications. His anxiety is well-founded: those who are working in the field are still in the process of sifting facts and groping for interpretations and explanations. Some of the early facile generalizations—like the myth of Jewish "passivity"—have been demolished, but we are still far from having reached overall conclusions that are generally accepted. Whereas the first major studies were based largely on material drawn from German archives, today more and more attention is being paid to the vast number of documents left behind by the Jewish victims, which naturally give a different picture of the same events.

Even when the "facts" are seemingly placed before us, there arises the problem of comprehension for those of us who were not there. We are seared in our very being by the testimony of the survivors, who are trying to make us understand things that are almost impossible to grasp. The historical problems lead to the moral, philosophical, and theological ones, which continue to grow the more they are investigated. Nonetheless, the situation today is no longer what it was in the years immediately following World War II. Whereas what had happened seemed then so unprecedented as to be hardly believable, today the historical dimensions of the Holocaust have begun to emerge. In this sense, it may be said that the original raw experience of the survivors is now turning into a "historical experience." How this is coming about may be seen in the present book, which includes two powerful personal memoirs (as well as the quoted statements of other witnesses), while constructing a framework in which the historical connections of such testimonies can be discussed.

The material for the book originated at a conference entitled "The Holocaust—a Generation After," which was attended by many of the best-known scholars in the field when it was held in New York in March 1975. From the contributions submitted to the conference, a number were selected for the purpose of presenting a broad general picture of the state of historical research on the Holocaust. The breadth of the selection is also reflected in the variety of approaches represented: the direct personal witness of the survivor, the detailed case study of a specific community, the comprehensive historical synthesis drawing upon data from many times and places. The authors concerned were given the opportunity to develop their ideas further, so the versions of their papers that are published here could mostly take into account research that appeared after the 1975 conference.

While no single book can cover all of the issues, the present volume offers a first orientation to the kind of reader or student mentioned earlier. It gives him firm ground on which to form his own judgments and a basis on which to proceed further. Those who wish to learn more will find ample guidance in the works referred to by our authors, starting with the two great classics of Holocaust historiography: Raul Hilberg's *The Destruction of the European Jews* (Chicago, 1961) and Isaiah Trunk's *Judenrat: The Jewish Councils in Eastern Europe under Nazi Occupation* (New York, 1972). They may then find that their appreciation of these books has been deepened by the present volume, which contains contributions by Professors Hilberg and Trunk, including an evaluation of the latter's work by Hilberg.

In editing the volume for publication, we have considered two audiences in addition to the scholars who will want copies of these studies. One is the student who decides to take a basic course on the Holocaust as part of his university studies, and the teacher who offers such a course. The latter will find both a variety of starting points for class discussions and a source of topics and bibliography for student assignments. The other audience includes everyone deeply concerned about the issues, whether or not they are students in the academic sense. We mean people who have had a general training in what passes for "Western civilization," who are seeking information—and hopefully some enlightenment—about the Holocaust, and who cannot be satisfied with popularizations.

At the New York conference there were contributions on philosophical and theological implications of the Holocaust, as well as a seminar on the guises that antisemitism has adopted *since* World War II. A selection from these contributions on "reactions and responses to the Holocaust" will be published separately by the editors of the present volume. We believe that it will interest a similar readership.

Of the three sections into which this book is divided, the first on "Background," as it is called, sets the scene for everything that follows. It begins with a comprehensive survey by Saul Friedländer, which appeared in a briefer form soon after the 1975 conference, but has been expanded through the incorporation of much material from a subsequently published French version. In it Friedländer shows, first, that the attempts by some historians to "explain" the destruction of European Jewry have all failed, and that—at least for the moment—no full "explanation" can be given. This leads him to ask the more modest question of what made the Holocaust *possible* and whether we can at least identify factors that made it easier for those events to occur. Like lesser crimes, the Holocaust had its perpetrators (the Nazis), its victims (the Jews) and its onlookers (the remainder of the Western world). Professor Friedländer examines the behavior and inherited attitudes of those three groups in order to pinpoint various factors that made the Holocaust possible and whose recurrence would be danger signals in any future situation.

Next comes a profound study by Jacob Katz on the question of whether anyone could have predicted that the Holocaust was going to take place. An earlier version of the paper appeared in *Commentary* (May 1975), but in that format Professor Katz found himself unable to deal with the problems in their full depth. The paper has consequently been completely rewritten for this book, some of its central sections never having appeared in the original version. Katz explains that inasmuch as decisive historical events depend upon human choices, a historical development that seems inevitable *after* it happened may not have been inevitable at the time. He also shows that nobody predicted the physical destruction of European Jewry, not even the Revisionist leader Vladimir Ze'ev Jabotinsky, who is often said to have foreseen it. All that he anticipated, in fact, was an increase in the pressure on East European Jewry, not the mass murder of millions.

This first section of the book concludes with a study by Uriel Tal, which was hailed as an important breakthrough at the 1975 conference and whose publication has been eagerly awaited ever since. And no wonder. Where others have simply likened some modern ideologies to religions in a general way, Professor Tal has shown just how extensively Nazi ideologists borrowed, transformed, and perverted notions of Christian theology in order to present themselves as a redemptive movement headed by an eschatological savior. He has shown, too, that in Germany this tendency to move back and forth between theological and political modes of thought was not unique to the Nazis, since related phenomena can be found in the statements of other nationalistic thinkers as well as some Protestant and Catholic churchmen.

The second section of the book moves to the events of the Holocaust themselves. Two different approaches are used, both of which help the reader to come closer to those events than a general survey: the personal memoir of a survivor and the detailed case study by an experienced historian.

The first memoir is by Abba Kovner, who was a leader of the resistance in the Vilna Ghetto, and who has since become one of Israel's best-known poets and the moving spirit behind the creation of the Museum of the Jewish Diaspora in Tel Aviv. The setting of his reminiscences is a return to the shattered streets of the Vilna Ghetto in the wake of the German defeat. When Kovner recounts how the Jewish resistance was built through initiatives whose heroism often consisted in performing the most dangerous acts under the very eyes of the German guards, one feels inclined to agree with those who claim that only a poet can convey what it meant to be caught up in the Holocaust. And yet this feeling is contradicted almost immediately by the second memoir: Michel Mazor's account of how the House Committees were set up and operated in the Warsaw Ghetto. Mazor relates the origin and development of this popularly based social movement in a simple matter-of-fact tone, until suddenly one is gripped by the anguish of a stubborn battle for life against the hunger, overcrowding, and lack of elementary facilities deliberately inflicted upon the Jewish population by the Nazi occupation authorities, who hoped (as German documents have revealed) that these conditions alone would decimate the Jews. Mazor's memoir, like Kovner's, is a commentary on the vital strength of the Jewish people in the midst of tragedy.

The two case studies on Hungary and Romania are by acknowledged experts on the Jewish communities in those countries. The subject of Randolph L. Braham's paper is the controversy known in Israel as "the Kasztner case": to what extent was the destruction of most of Hungarian Jewry due to the failure of Kasztner and other Jewish leaders to warn them, how much did these leaders know, and at what times? This leads on to the broader question of how much the outside world knew about the mass killings and why the Allied governments did not do more to halt the process of destruction. It also leads to a question that is raised again later in the book, which is what does it mean to say people "know"? That is, when does the weight of evidence become such as to *force* people to believe the incredible, and indeed to act upon that belief?

Bela Vago's study, which contrasts the behavior of Jewish leaders in Hungary with those in Romania, forms a valuable complement to Professor Braham's paper. While recognizing that Romanian Jewry survived mainly because German power was less effective in Romania than Hungary, Professor Vago points out that Romanian Jewish leaders were also more resourceful and better prepared by their prewar experience and activity.

The contributions of Kovner, Mazor, Braham, and Vago prepare the way for the last section of the book, which is devoted to what has become perhaps the most controversial question in the whole field: the issue of Jewish leadership in Nazi-dominated Europe. The Germans had a policy of setting up a "Jewish Council" (*Judenrat,* plural *Judenräte*) in any area that fell under their control. Jewish leadership, however, covers not only these officially recognized Jewish Councils, but also the alternative leaderships produced by Jewish resistance movements and other organized groups of Jews, such as the semi-autonomous system of House Committees described by Mazor.

The issue has been a live and bitter one since the Kasztner case in the 1950s, especially after the publication of Hannah Arendt's *Eichmann in Jerusalem: A Report on the Banality of Evil* (New York, 1963), which portrayed members of the Jewish Councils as collaborators almost without exception and suggested that more Jews would have survived had the Councils not existed. All these earlier discussions, however, were carried on with very little knowledge of the facts. Enormous numbers of documents produced by members of the Jewish Councils and other Jewish leaders had survived the war, but they were scattered in numerous archives and written in a variety of languages. Relatively few had been studied and even fewer had been published.

That is, until 1972 when the situation was changed by the publication of Isaiah Trunk's monumental book, *Judenrat,* already mentioned. In view of the preceding controversies, Trunk sought to present merely facts. He examined the various functions exercised by the Jewish Councils as municipal or regional "authorities." For each topic—health services, to name only one—he gave examples of the policies and actions of various Councils in a large area of Nazi-occupied Eastern Europe. These were "the facts." Although Trunk offered a few conclusions at the end of the book, he expressly avoided the kind of broad generalizations unhesitatingly made by Hannah Arendt and others.

Some commentators have questioned Trunk's approach. To take an example from another field, in the nineteenth century some natural scientists were fond of describing their activity as one of gathering hard facts by way of experiment and observation; scientific laws, they claimed, were in no way speculative, but simply a summary of the mass of facts they had collected. In the twentieth century, however, philosophers of science have pointed out that this was in large measure an illusion. A scientist does not collect and record facts at random. He collects only those that seem "relevant" to him; and their "relevance" is decided by some overall world-view or general hypothesis. Facts and theories cannot be completely separated, the formulation of theories and the search for facts alternately influencing one another. So that Trunk, in compiling facts for his book, was influenced by the hypotheses that had been tossed about in earlier discussions.

This, at any rate, is the implication of Raul Hilberg's paper, which opens our section on "The *Judenrat* and the Jewish Response." Professor Hilberg argues that quite definite conclusions can be drawn from Trunk's book; that generalizations lie hidden under the flow of Trunk's facts; and that they can be brought to light and set forth. He concentrates on the Warsaw Ghetto, supplementing Trunk's book occasionally from his own reading of the diary of Czerniakov, who was the head of the Jewish Council there until his suicide on the eve of the mass deportations of Jews from Warsaw to the death camps.

The next paper, by Yehuda Bauer, presents an alternative view, arguing that different conclusions can be drawn from Trunk's book and from other material now published. The essay suggests that the concepts of both "leadership" and "resistance" need to be construed in a broad sense if we are to understand the real situation. Resistance need not mean simply armed resistance, but can also be applied to all acts of defiance that enabled Jews to go on living despite German attempts to destroy them by attrition, and go on maintaining some quality of life despite the attempts to deprive them of all human dignity. Leadership, on the other hand, means not only the Jewish Councils and the leaders of armed resistance, but also a range of organizations "intermediate" between those poles, which were not always clearly defined. Indeed, many Jewish Councils were engaged in covert resistance of one kind or another, including collaboration with armed resistance groups. Bauer's paper also makes available to the English reader the findings of a number of studies which have so far appeared only in Hebrew.

The last paper, by George M. Kren and Leon Rappoport, also broadens the debate about the notion of resistance. It offers a particularly valuable analysis of the psychology involved, drawing upon a range of examples of resistance to occupying or colonial powers. This framework enables them to isolate three essential factors which make such resistance possible and to explain why, in various cases, Nazi oppression was sometimes met by Jewish resistance and sometimes not. Like Bauer, they show that displays of resistance or non-resistance were a general and not a peculiarly "Jewish" phenomenon.

The book closes with a discussion that took place at the 1975 conference and that encompasses issues raised in the earlier sections of this volume. The discussion at the conference was actually much longer; for we have selected only those contributions that seem especially valuable and that preserve something of the lively atmosphere of the conference. The contributors are here exchanging ideas in the language of everyday conversation rather than the more formal style of learned publications.

The discussion begins with a lucid presentation of the issues by Henry L. Feingold, recounting how the earlier dispute between Arendt and her critics was altered by the publication of Trunk's book, and giving his own evaluation of the significance of the latter. Hilberg and Bauer follow with further remarks on the arguments in their papers, the former relating, as well, his personal role in getting Trunk's book published. The floor was then open to all present. Professor Trunk's closing statement forms a fitting conclusion to the discussion.

Most of the work published since 1975 has reflected the framework delineated in this discussion and at the conference as a whole. This book reflects it as well. But there are a number of studies to which we should like to draw special attention. To begin with, two short but valuable studies are Raul Hilberg's article, "German Railroads—Jewish Souls," in *Transaction, Social Science and Modern Society* XIV (1976), 60–74, and Uriel Tal's lecture, *"Political Faith" in Nazi Ideology and Policy Prior to the Holocaust* (Tel Aviv, 1978). Two symposia have been published by Yad Vashem, the organization whose Holocaust Museum in Jerusalem makes a deep impression on every visitor, from foreign heads of state to the ordinary tourist. One is Y. Gutman and E. Zuroff eds., *Rescue Attempts During the Holocaust* (Jerusalem, 1977), which considers attempts from both outside and inside Nazi-occupied Europe to rescue Jews. The other is Y. Gutman and C. J. Haft eds., *Patterns of Jewish Leadership in Nazi Europe 1933–1945* (Jerusalem, 1979), which brings further evidence to bear on the arguments presented in the third section of our book.

Yitzhak Arad's book, *Ghetto in Flames* (New York, 1980), is of special relevance to both Abba Kovner's memoir and his contribution to the discussion, since it explains why the Nazis permitted some Vilna Jews to survive after the 1941 mass killings and analyses the convoluted policies of Yacob Gens, head of the Vilna Ghetto. Material for comparison with the papers of Randolph L. Braham and Bela Vago, which are concerned with how Jews fared in two countries allied to Germany, Hungary and Romania, is provided by Meir Michaelis's book on a third ally, *Mussolini and the Jews* (Oxford, 1978). Dr. Michaelis concludes that persecution of the Jews under Mussolini was due neither to German pressure nor to a clear fascist concept of antisemitism, but to Mussolini's desire to adapt himself to Nazi policies.

Among those who contributed to the discussion in this book, Helen Fein has published *Accounting for Genocide* (New York, 1979). This is a most interesting attempt at a sociological analysis of the Holocaust. Dr. Fein tries to quantify modes of behavior of non-Jewish populations toward their Jewish neighbors in order to arrive at conclusions regarding the reasons why more Jews survived in certain countries than in others. Richard Rubenstein has published *The Cunning of History: The Holocaust and the American Future* (New York, 1975) and Emil Fackenheim *The Jewish Return to History* (New York, 1978). These studies are concerned with the philosophical and theological implications of the Holocaust rather than its historiography, but readers who are interested in the contribution of these authors to the discussion in this book will find a full expression of their views in them. A forceful contribution by Professor Fackenheim will, indeed, appear in our volume of "reactions and responses to the Holocaust" along with a contribution by the theologian Franklin H. Littell, whose book, *The Crucifixion of the Jews* (New York, 1975), analyses the role of Christian antisemitism in preparing the ground for the Nazi onslaught upon the Jews, while formulating the moral implications of the massive apostasy from Christianity constituted by the failure of most European Christians to oppose the progress of the Holocaust. Finally, three books by Yehuda Bauer may be mentioned: *The Holocaust in Historical Perspective* (Seattle, 1978), *The Jewish Emergence from Powerlessness* (Toronto, 1979) and *American Jewry and the Holocaust* (Detroit, 1981).

The 1975 conference ended with a closing address by Professor Nathan Rotenstreich of the Hebrew University of Jerusalem. It is he who contributed the "Postscript" to this book, drawing together some of the threads in the volume in order to emphasize both the difficulty *and* the necessity of historical reflections upon the Holocaust, proceeding then to make an ethical statement about the whole nature of Jewish existence in the Western world. This leads him, as it did some of the other contributors, to the special importance of Israel in the post-Holocaust world. On this appropriate note the volume ends.

Jerusalem, May 1980

List of Contributors

SAMUEL ABRAHAMSEN: Professor of Jewish Studies, Brooklyn College, City University of New York; specialist on Scandinavian Jewry.

SHLOMO AVINERI: Professor of Political Science, Hebrew University, Jerusalem; has also served as Director General of Israel's Ministry of Foreign Affairs.

ZVIE BAR-ON: Professor of Philosophy, Hebrew University, Jerusalem; in World War II joined the resistance in the Kovno Ghetto and fought in the partisan movement.

YEHUDA BAUER: Professor of Holocaust Studies, Institute of Contemporary Jewry, Hebrew University Jerusalem.

RANDOLPH L.BRAHAM: Professor of Political Science, City College, City University of New York; specialist on Hungarian Jewry.

ALICE ECKARDT: Assistant Professor of Religion Studies, Lehigh University, Bethlehem, Pennsylvania.

EMIL FACKENHEIM: Professor of Philosophy, University of Toronto; specialist on the philosophy of history and the Jewish role in history.

HELEN FEIN: holds a doctorate from Columbia University; writes in the field of twentieth century history.

HENRY FEINGOLD: Professor of History, Graduate Center, City University of New York, and Baruch College; specialist on American Jewry and on the Roosevelt administration's reactions to the Holocaust.

HENRY FRIEDLANDER: Professor of Judiac Studies, Brooklyn College, City University of New York.

SAUL FRIEDLÄNDER: Professor of Modern History, Tel Aviv University, and Professor of International Relations, Graduate Institute of International Studies, Geneva; spent wartime childhood hidden from the Nazis in a monastery.

RAUL HILBERG: Professor of Political Science, University of Vermont.

HENRY HUTTENBACH: Professor of History, City College, City University of New York; specialist on German Jewry in the Nazi period.

JACOB KATZ: Professor Emeritus of Jewish Social History, Hebrew University, Jerusalem; awarded Israel Prize (1980) for his studies on Jewish history.

GEORGE M. KREN: Professor of History, Kansas State University; specialist on psychohistory and on the Holocaust.

ABBA KOVNER: a leader of the resistance in the Vilna Ghetto and in the Jewish partisan movement; spiritual creator of the Museum of the Jewish Diaspora, Tel Aviv University; for his poetry has received the Brenner Literary Prize (1968), the Israel Prize (1970), the International Remembrance Award (1971) and the Bialik Prize (1977).

BEREL LANG: Professor of Philosophy, University of Colorado; specialist on aesthetics and modern philosophy.

MICHEL MAZOR: eyewitness and historian of the Warsaw Ghetto; during 1947–1973 Director of Archives, Center of Contemporary Jewish Documentation, Paris.

GEORGE MOSSE: Professor of History, Hebrew University, Jerusalem; co-editor of the *Journal of Contemporary History*.

LEON RAPPOPORT: Professor of Psychology, Kansas State University; specialist on the psychology of personality and on psychohistory.

NATHAN ROTENSTREICH: Professor of Philosophy, Hebrew University, Jerusalem.

RICHARD RUBENSTEIN: Distinguished Professor, Department of Religion, Florida State University; specialist on theological aspects of the Holocaust; awards include Portico d'Ottavia Literary Prize (Rome, 1976).

ISMAR SCHORSCH: Professor of Jewish History, Jewish Theological Seminary of America, New York; specialist on antisemitism in Germany.

MARIE SYRKIN: Professor Emeritus of Humanities, Brandeis University.

URIEL TAL: Professor of Modern Jewish History, Tel Aviv University; specialist on the history of modern antisemitism.

ISAIAH TRUNK: Chief Archivist, YIVO Institute for Jewish Research, New York, and Professor at the Max Weinreich Center for Advanced Jewish Studies.

BELA VAGO: Professor of General History and Strochlitz Professor in Holocaust Studies, University of Haifa; specialist on the modern history of southeastern Europe.

LENI YAHIL: Professor Emeritus of Modern Jewish History, University of Haifa; specialist on rescue and resistance during the Holocaust.

I. BACKGROUND

On the Possibility of the Holocaust:
An Approach to a Historical Synthesis*

SAUL FRIEDLÄNDER

In the three decades since the Holocaust, our knowledge of the events as such has increased, but not our understanding of them. There is no clearer perspective today, no deeper comprehension than immediately after the war. Indeed, we know that any attempt to assess the historical significance of the Holocaust means trying to explain in a rational context events that cannot be encompassed in rational categories alone, or described solely in the usual style of historical analysis.

The limitations of the historian cannot, however, quell the urge to know, and the same question continually returns to haunt us: how was the extermination of the Jews of Europe possible? This question has three essential facets: the behavior of the perpetrators, the onlookers, and the victims. More specifically, can one identify and eventually explain the motivations behind the exterminatory drive of the Nazis? Can one say why the extermination did not encounter significant countervailing forces either in Western society as such (the onlookers), or even among the victims themselves, the Jews?

First, there is a preliminary issue of crucial importance for every aspect of the Holocaust: are we dealing with a phenomenon comparable with some other historical event, or are we facing something unique not only within any traditional historical context, but even within Nazism itself?[1]

*An earlier version of this analysis entitled "The Historical Significance of the Holocaust," appeared in the *Jerusalem Quarterly* 1 (Fall 1976), 36–59. A French version is "L'Extermination des Juifs d'Europe; pour une étude historique," *Revue des Etudes Juives* cxxxv (1976), 113–44.

The Specificity of the Holocaust

If the extermination of the Jews by the Nazis could be convincingly compared with other phenomena belonging to the framework of National Socialism, or to a category of contemporary political behavior encompassing Nazism, or to some type of murderous outburst known in other periods of history, then our quest for understanding the Holocaust would be made much easier. But, in my view, this is not the case.

As regards the Nazi framework itself, there is no available documentary evidence of any plan for the *total* extermination of the Poles or the Russians.[2] Even the extermination of the Gypsies (who were considered not "enemies," but rather "asocial" elements: up to July 1942 they could serve in the German army) was planned only partially after many hesitations and executed on a limited scale during one single month in the year 1944.[3] It was the absolutely uncompromising aspect of the exterminatory drive against the Jews, as well as the frantic extirpation of any elements actually or supposedly linked to the Jews or to the "Jewish spirit," that is, the identification of the Jews as absolute evil, which fundamentally distinguished the anti-Jewish actions of the Nazis from their attitude toward any other group.

This absolute character of the anti-Jewish drive of the Nazis makes it impossible to integrate the extermination of the Jews not only within the general framework of Nazi persecutions, but even within the wider aspects of contemporary ideologico-political behavior such as fascism, totalitarianism, economic exploitation, and so on. Let us examine some attempts at such an integration to see how they become ultimately inadequate.

At the beginning of his monumental study of fascism, Ernst Nolte speaks of "a Jewish interpretation . . . based on the most appalling of all human experiences . . . (which) brings the whole weight of this experience to bear in favor of a distinction between National Socialism and fascism."[4] Actually, one does not have to be a Jew to discern that the term "fascism," as a common denominator for many diverging phenomena, is of dubious value, especially when one reaches some core problems of the various movements included. George Mosse's critique of Nolte's use of the concept of "transcendence" is extremely pertinent and need not be repeated here.[5] For us, Nolte's most dubious point is his identification of fascism with anti-Marxism, so that the persecution and extermination of the Jews becomes merely a consequence of a general counter-revolutionary, counter-Marxist drive.

To begin with, the systematic destruction of a mostly "liberal" and "capitalist" Jewry should have created doubts in the minds of the Nazis, if anti-Marxism had indeed been their first and major objective. The fundamental objection to the "fascist" explanation, however, is simply that documentary evidence shows very clearly that the anti-Marxist crusade of the Nazis *derived from* their anti-Jewish position, and not the reverse. On precisely this point recent German scholarship has made essential contributions. Eberhard Jäckel's study of Hitler's world-view, for instance, demonstrates not only that antisemitism was central to Hitler's views (Nolte saw this, by the way, but acrobatically explained such antisemitism as a kind of *Ersatz* for anti-Marxism), but also that Hitler's "living-space" conception was largely influenced by his anti-Jewish views.[6] The same point is made by Andreas Hillgruber,[7] citing equally convincing documentary evidence. But why not turn to the sources themselves? Martin Bormann unambiguously explained the relationship between anti-Marxism and antisemitism in stating, at the end of 1944: "National Socialist doctrine is therefore anti-Jewish *in excelsis,* for it is both anti-Communist and anti-Christian. National Socialism is solid to the core, and the whole of its strength is concentrated against the Jews. . . ."[8] Hitler's first and last political utterances were not against Marxism, but against the Jews. Thus, the "fascist" generalization is very questionable, at least as regards the Holocaust. The link between Nazi antisemitism and anti-Marxism did, however, have crucial implications, which I shall discuss later.

The "totalitarian" generalization[9] is no more solidly founded than the "fascist" one. A close comparison between Nazi Germany and Stalinist Russia, for example, employing the accepted criteria of "totalitarianism," shows easily that the differences were greater than the similarities on almost all counts, and certainly where the conception of "the enemy" was concerned. According to the accepted understanding of totalitarianism, "enemies" are fought and persecuted in order to galvanize energies and frighten potential opponents.[10] Now, in various totalitarian regimes "the enemy" has been a functional concept that changes with time, according to circumstances. But under Nazism there was one "enemy" that never changed: the Jews. In other totalitarian regimes the persecution of enemies has been widely publicized. Even the fate of the inmates of Siberian camps was not kept secret by the Stalinist regime, any more than the executions of many so-called opponents from the very first days of the Bolshevik Revolution. The Nazis themselves made no secret of the executions of the SA leaders or of other opponents to the regime both before and during the war. But as regards the Jews, although the myth of a world Jewish conspiracy may have galvanized energies, and although the early persecutions had a frightening effect on the German population, the later stages of Nazi policy—the extermination itself—were kept as secret as possible. For the Nazis, the extermination of the Jews was a fundamental urge and a sacred mission, not a means to other objectives.

Of course, the Nazis used against the Jews the extreme forms of bureaucratic manipulation and domination that are typical of totalitarian regimes and—on a more diffuse level—of modern society in general.[11] Similarly, the complete disregard for human life and the value of the individual, so often demonstrated in our century, made the Nazi task easier.[12]

But these circumstances merely facilitated the exterminatory drive; they do not explain its most characteristic feature—its absolutely uncompromising nature.

Some historians look for explanations in a supposed "economic function" of the extermination of the Jews.[13] Yet the persecution and extermination of European Jewry destroyed an immense labor force just when the Nazi Reich was involved in the most desperate stages of total war.[14] It has been calculated that the Final Solution inflicted an enormous loss on the German war economy, one that totally dwarfed any gains drawn from despoiling the victims.[15] But here again, the Nazi sources speak for themselves. When, in 1941, Reichskomissar Lohse asked Rosenberg if all the Jews of the East were to be exterminated "without considering economic interests, for example, the needs of the Wehrmacht for specialized workers for the armaments industry," the minister answered: "On principle, one shall not take into account any economic consideration in the solution of this problem."[16]

Apparently unique within both the Nazi context and that of other contemporary politico-ideological frameworks, is the extermination of the Jews comparable with earlier murderous outbursts? Some have mentioned the great European witch-hunt of the sixteenth and seventeenth centuries.[17] Yet this comparison fails, not merely numerically (all told, some tens of thousands of "witches" were killed), but essentially. The witch's confession, although not necessarily exempting her from death at the stake, enabled her and the inquisitor to work together for the salvation of her soul.[18] That is, religious thought did not regard the witches as irredeemably damned: quite the contrary. For the Nazis, however, the Jew was irredeemably evil in his very being.

As for various previous attempts at genocide (the Armenians massacred by the Turks during World War I are usually cited), the difference is clear: those murderous attacks stemmed always from easily identifiable ethnic or political conflicts between a majority and a minority group, without invoking some fantastic myth or the "inherent evil" of the group to be exterminated. Thus, although there are precedents for an attempt at total physical eradication, the Nazi exterminatory drive was made unmistakably unique by its motivation.

Finally, the Nazis were innovators even within the context of the long history of anti-Jewish persecutions. Whereas before the Nazi era the Jews were subjected to conversion or expulsion, besides sporadic acts of violence, only the Nazis elaborated and implemented the idea of systematic extermination.

To conclude these preliminary remarks, I shall turn to a recent approach that actually eliminates the specificity of the extermination of the Jews by eliminating any specific significance of Nazism in recent German history. This is the approach of Professor Geoffrey Barraclough in a series of three articles published by the *New York Review of Books* in the Fall of 1972.[19]

His criticism is directed essentially against what he calls the "liberal view" of German history, which by stressing ideological, political, and constitutional history at the expense of social and economic trends, has attributed, he claims, an artificial specificity to the Nazi Reich.

"Post-liberal" historians, in Barraclough's terminology, are now setting things straight: a new periodization of contemporary German history reveals the progressive structural changes that began within German society in the late 1870s and have continued into the present time, thereby including the Nazi era within a general process of social and economic transformation in which it loses any outstanding specific characteristics. "For the younger historians," writes Barraclough, "the central theme is not the rise of Nazism, but the incipient class conflict . . . this is the threat which lends unity to the period 1879–1969. . . ." Or: ". . . the obsessive preoccupation of the older historians with the rise of Nazism, as though it were the main content of German history since Bismarck, is bound to result in distortion. The younger historians have restored the balance. . . ."

But what then of the particular aspects of Nazi ideology and criminal behavior that characterized Nazism for the "liberal" historian? Barraclough mentions "Nazi beastliness," but he "smooths it over" (to use the term that he himself applies to the manner in which "liberal" historians, according to him, deal with social dichotomies). In his own way, Geoffrey Barraclough stumbles over the same obstacle that so blatantly invalidates the "fascist" and "totalitarian" generalizations about Nazism. Both Hannah Arendt and Ernst Nolte were aware of the centrality and specificity of the Jewish question within Nazi ideology and practice; but they built a general theory, which instead of attempting to explain this specificity, disregarded all its main aspects. Similarly, Barraclough begins by agreeing that "our knowledge of what happened at Auschwitz has vastly increased, but not our understanding"; but then he offers, rather than a historical framework within which the factors leading to Auschwitz could be better scrutinized, one in which Auschwitz practically disappears.[20]

To put it bluntly, understanding what happened at Auschwitz is far less important to Barraclough than certain aspects of social mobility within contemporary German society. There is no ultimate objective criterion of what is important in history; each historian interprets history according to his values. My answer to Barraclough and to the "post-liberal" historians is therefore very simple: choose whatever point of view you wish for looking at the German past, but do not deny that your point of view stems from very specific values, from an explicit view of what problems of that past are important, and what are side-issues. Those values I do not share.

Thus, for me the extermination of European Jewry cannot be subsumed under generalizing explanations, much less "smoothed over" in the "post-liberal" fashion. But this immediately raises an obvious question: if those events neither fall within general socio-political categories of analysis, nor have an apparent explanation within the wider framework of German history, then is not the Holocaust a unique event, an anomaly of history that may have the utmost significance on a theological or philosophical level, but falls outside the scope of any historical interpretation? In trying to escape the inadequate generalizations or outright evasions that reduce the Holocaust to banalities, do we not arrive at the other extreme of making the Holocaust an event so unique in human history that we cannot give it any signification whatsoever?

To this dilemma one may tentatively answer that the Holocaust does not fall within the framework of explanatory categories of a generalizing kind, but was nevertheless the result of cumulative historical trends that can, in part at least, be identified and explained. These trends lead us necessarily to the major issues mentioned at the outset: the behavior of the perpetrators, of the onlookers, and of the victims.

The Perpetrators

Three main ways of explaining the behavior of the exterminators have been attempted. First, some historians of modern antisemitism have concentrated on the social and political roots of Nazi anti-Jewish policies, stressing the political exploitation of the socially-induced resentment of the Austrian and German middle classes in the late nineteenth and early twentieth centuries as a fundamental explanatory framework.[21] Others dwell upon the ideological roots of Nazi antisemitism, which make the Final Solution a result of the unfolding of ideas and theories, sometimes propagated by small esoteric groups, but seeping into increasingly wider social strata.[22] The third approach deals essentially with the organization of the extermination, with its administrative and bureaucratic processes.[23]

The first two approaches usually invoke such phenomena as the exacerbation of contemporary nationalism, the expansion of racial and neo-Darwinist thinking, the cult of violence, and the mood of cultural despair; this returns us to "fascism" as an explanation. The third approach may invoke the rise of all-powerful bureaucracies in modern society, the spread of mass phenomena, the all-pervasive impact of modern organizations and technology, mostly in respect of mass death; we are back within the general framework of "totalitarianism." A synthesis of these various approaches is also possible (in a way, Hannah Arendt's *Origins of Totalitarianism*[24] is an effort in that direction). Yet perhaps an additional dimension, that of the utterly irrational impulse, of some kind of insanity, is still missing.

Precisely in order to stress the centrality of the irrational dimension, another approach has developed. It seeks to identify the motivation of the Nazis and the pathological origins of their exterminatory drive.[25] It sees as pathological less the killing itself than the motivating obsession with the Jewish danger, the various fantasms that initiated the uncompromising drive towards the expulsion and then the extermination of the Jews. This approach need not disregard other factors; I shall indicate below how they are to be integrated with it. It does, however, raise its own questions, especially: what connection is there with any pathological element in *pre-Nazi* antisemitism?

Once the Jew had been defined as a major symbol of evil in Christian society, profound transformations of this society might bring about changes in the outward characteristics of the symbol, but not in its nature. In a way, the Jew fulfilled the essential function of a collective counter-ideal as a means of distinguishing between Good and Evil, between Pure and Impure, between what society ought to be and what it was forbidden to be. Objective social tensions between the Jews and their environment, whether due to Jewish auto-segregation or to their penetration into sensitive fields of social competition, simply intensified a situation originally created by factors independent of anything the Jews could have done or not done.

In every age, each social group projected some of its fears onto the Jew. Mostly, these culturally and socially induced projective mechanisms took a relatively mild form. For a minority, however, the attitude toward the Jew became an outlet for deep-seated emotional disturbances. The studies of Ackermann and Jahoda, of Loewenstein, of Gough, of Adorno and his group,[26] have variously established possible links between extreme antisemitism and individual pathology. I have myself[27] sought to find confirmation of these assumptions in the biographies of extreme antisemites, which indeed seem to confirm their pathological motivations.

In non-crisis periods, these studies suggest, pathological antisemitic obsessions found little echo outside limited circles; but during crises in which existing interests, norms and certainties collapsed or seemed threatened, the emotional regression experienced by masses of people, the weakening of rational controls, offered vast opportunities to the extreme antisemitic minority. In German society extreme antisemitism, including Hitler's own obsessions, expanded against such a background after World War I.[28] Yet while this very general analysis identifies conditions permitting the rise of Nazi antisemitism, it leaves open the question of the specific relationship between the antisemitic obsessions of the Nazi leadership and the huge bureaucracy industriously implementing the Final Solution. Here our starting point should be, it seems to me, a re-examination of the myth of the Jew in the Nazi world view, and particularly in Hitler's world view. A careful analysis of this myth suggests some three distinct components.

First of all, there was an almost metaphysical conception of the Jew as a kind of cosmic principle of evil. This view, a manifest transformation of the extreme trends of religious antisemitism, appears very clearly in Hitler's conversations with Eckart and in *Mein Kampf* ("if the Jew wins, his crown will be the death wreath of humanity").[29] A second component was simply the classic racialist position pushed to extremes: the Jews are a culture-destroying race which, throughout history, has attempted to eliminate the culture-creating efforts of the higher races, and is now aiming at world domination through racial defilement, internationalism (Marxism), democracy and pacifism.[30] Finally—and perhaps most importantly—the Nazis considered the Jew a *bacillus,* a source of possibly mortal infection. This "bacterial" component of the myth was quite distinct from the general racial one, and its absence from the explicit ideological framework does not diminish its importance. On the contrary, this is the image of the Jew that appeared, firstly, at the level of spontaneous expressions, but also at the level of extermination practices and rituals.

In his analysis of the image of the Jew as parasite, Alex Bein showed that for the Nazis parasite and bacillus were identical, but that the racial view and the parasitico-bacterial one were distinct. Bein quotes Rosenberg and Schickedanz to show how the conception of inferior races differed from that of the Jew as an anti-race.[31] Let me add an example taken from Himmler's notorious Posen speech, delivered on October 4, 1943 on the occasion of an SS military group-leaders meeting.

In this speech, Himmler referred to the Russians in a racial context, but to the Jews in a bacterial one. (Had the racial metaphor been carried through, Himmler might rather have compared the Russian inferior race with the Jewish destructive race.) He explained that Russians were like animals; thus, the death of tens of thousands of Russian women working on German anti-tank ditches was of no more consequence than the death of animals if it could save German lives; but since the Germans were not cruel to animals, they would not be needlessly cruel to these "human animals" (*Menschentieren*). On the other hand, the Jews were bacilli that had to be eradicated at all costs; moreover, one should avoid letting those engaged in the eradication of the bacilli become infected themselves: "We don't want, in the process of eradicating a bacillus, to be infected by that bacillus, to fall ill and die ourselves."[32]

Now let us see how the distinction between the three components of the myth makes evident a specific linkage between the pathology of the limited group (particularly that of Hitler himself) and the dedication of the huge bureaucratic machine to its murderous task. For indeed, more factors than mere "blind obedience" lay behind such dedication. First, Hitler's own "charisma" certainly contributed to the acceptance of his fantasies about the Jew. Second, Nazism constantly tended to obliterate the distinction between the symbolic plane and that of reality.[33] This tendency allowed, by definition, the interlocking of fantasms and reality assessments; it suffices in itself to explain the easy penetration of psychotic delusions into Nazi theory and practice.

Lastly, the biological framework of racialist ideology made it easy to establish a link between the microbial conception of the Jew and the general racial one. What was considered reality at the microbial level became metaphor at the general racial one. In this way, the microbial conception gave the fundamental impetus to the relentless drive for physical exclusion and later extermination while the racial ideology, whose general historical and philosophical framework was adapted to views then common amongst the German middle classes, served as the rationalizing framework for the instructions given to the vast masses of civil servants in charge of the details of the Final Solution. The fuzzy racial ideology could not have been the "prime mover," but it was the "transmission belt," the mediating element between the murderous pathological drive and the bureaucratic and technological organization of the extermination.

The racist rationalization of the microbial obsession of the Nazi "true believers" formed part of a wider ideological synthesis, whose other main elements were the anti-rationalist tradition (the neo-romantic and anti-liberal trends) and the anti-Marxist stance. Such anti-rationalism and anti-Marxism, however, were themselves merely particular Nazi expressions of much wider currents that shaped the world view of important segments of the middle classes throughout Europe. In this sense, the ideology constituted one of the links between the anti-Jewish attitudes of the Nazis and the behavior of the onlookers, that is, Western society.

The Onlookers

The structural connection between the behavior of the perpetrators and that of the onlookers is obvious: the extermination of nearly six million Jews, though emerging and proceeding virtually unchecked, took hardly three years to accomplish. Had there been countervailing action on a significant scale, whether massive attempts at hiding, constant protests and demonstrations, or violent intervention from outside occupied Europe, the course of extermination would have been made much less rapid and more difficult.[34] Thus, the virtual passivity of the onlookers directly relates their behavior to that of the exterminators themselves, whatever the differences in motivation and culpability. The question again is: why?

While the "banality of evil" is certainly insufficient to explain the murderous anti-Jewish drive of the Nazis, an initial explanation of the general passivity of the onlookers may be sought precisely in the most banal behavior, be it pure self-interest at the individual or group level, pseudo-ideological choices, or antisemitism to a greater or lesser degree. Yet even at this level of banality one point has to be stressed: such passivity—not to speak of collaboration with the Nazis—always resulted from a choice in which the Jew weighed less than any other consideration involved. This being said, the problem facing the historian remains: can one, beyond these simple arguments of common sense, which although correct, seem to remain on the surface of things, find more general and basic explanations for the passivity of the onlookers?

Any of several explanatory frameworks might contribute to our understanding of these attitudes: a general trend of indifference to mass death in modern society (especially in the midst of war), the differential impact of spiritual (religious) leadership and state collaboration on the attitude of the masses, the various degrees of integration of Jews within the surrounding social frameworks, the cohesiveness of those societies themselves, and so on.

I wish to outline an approach that lets one link the attitude of the onlookers with some aspects of that of the exterminators, but also has some relevance to that of the victims. Since, however, in Eastern and Southeastern Europe the intensity of traditional antisemitism is a sufficient answer (although many nuances are evident even there), I shall discuss almost exclusively the West, where the appraisal of motivations is more complex.

Above it was noted that Nazi anti-liberalism and anti-Marxism were part of a much wider current, a counter-revolutionary atmosphere that spread far beyond the "fascist" movements and variously affected most parts of the European middle classes. This well-known ideological background has, in our context, a crucial significance: anti-liberal feelings contributed vastly to isolating the Jew, to eliminating whatever protection he had within Western society, to making him a total "outsider," just when these same feelings, coupled with middle-class antipathy to Marxism, were encouraging the view of the Nazi as an "insider." The convergence of these two ideological trends contributed to the passivity of the onlookers, at least during the decisive period in which help could still have had a major effect, that is, up to the middle of the war. Afterwards, with the major deportations from the West completed and the extermination machine working at full speed, it was too late. Let me briefly examine both trends.

The emancipation of the Jews meant above all their acceptance within the legal frameworks of European states, as citizens equal before the law, but it hardly ever meant their undifferentiated acceptance by society in those states. The rise of antisemitism in the West during the later nineteenth century created a growing dissonance between the legal status of the Jews as citizens equal to others, and their real status in society. This process was compounded by the growth of the anti-rationalist, anti-liberal current already mentioned: the increasing rejection of the legalistic and universalistic values of rational liberalism obviously implied an increasing readiness to accept the annulment of the legal equality of the Jews. The distinction between the "legal country" and the "real country," coined by Maurras, spread far beyond the narrow limits of the "Action Française" and illuminates the situation throughout Western Europe, at least on the continent.

Some historians will call this a post-Holocaust view of the past and claim that the "symbiosis" between Jews and their surrounding society, in Germany for instance, was genuine until well after World War I. But it would be easy to amass documents proving this "symbiosis" to be an illusion—a Jewish illusion. Hannah Arendt, in my view, correctly summed up the situation in *The Origins of Totalitarianism:* "Society, confronted with political, economic and legal equality for Jews, made it quite clear that none of its classes was prepared to grant them social equality, and that only exceptions from the Jewish people would be received."[35]

The fundamental reticence of large strata of Western society toward the Jews, compounded by anti-liberal contempt for the legal framework of universalistic democracy, explains why legal exclusion of the Jews, when it returned, was widely accepted—even encouraged (certainly not strongly opposed)—in this same society. The most damning evidence is that showing how this process, promoted by the Nazis from 1933, was taken over almost autonomously by various other authorities and institutions. When in 1938 Rothmund, the Swiss chief of police, suggested to the Germans that the letter "J" be printed on the passports of German and Austrian Jews, he was not just creating further legal discrimination against those Jews, but also implicitly suggesting that the legal rights of Jews could be rescinded within the Western world in general.[36] It was, it seems, the French Foreign Minister Georges Bonnet who, during his conversation with Ribbentrop at the end of 1938, mentioned the possibility of shipping thousands of Jews to Madagascar.[37] When the Vichy government promulgated its anti-Jewish laws, in 1940 and 1941, it did so not under Nazi pressure, but rather on its own initiative; it was independently eliminating the gap between the "legal country" and the "real country."[38] And when the Vatican's reaction to these contemplated measures was sought by Léon Bérard (the Vichy ambassador there), he was encouraged to abolish a legal equality which seemed offensive to Christian society.[39]

The passengers of the S.S. *St. Louis,* wandering through the Atlantic Ocean in the spring of 1939, became symbols of the new Jewish situation, as would subsequently the passengers of the S.S. *Patria* sinking in sight of the coast of Palestine. A little earlier, the Evian Conference had shown virtually all Western countries wary of accepting more Jews and contemplating with equanimity the disappearance of legal protection for hundreds of thousands of them.[40] The 1943 Bermuda Conference adopted *de facto* the same attitude under the cover of vague formulas, but now with the knowledge of mass extermination. . . .

This whole process is epitomized by the letter sent in January 1944 by Msgr. Adolf Bertram, Archbishop of Breslau, to the Reich Minister of the Interior. The German bishops had just learned that measures previously applying only to full Jews would henceforth apply to Christians of mixed race (*Mischlinge*). The Archbishop summarized the measures already imposed upon the latter and added: "All these measures aim clearly at segregation at the end of which threatens extermination. . . ." The German Catholics would feel "deeply hurt," continued Msgr. Bertram, "if those fellow Christians now would have to meet a fate similar to that of Jews."[41] I once wrote about the "ambiguity of that sentence."[42] But there is actually no ambiguity; the Jews who remained Jews were unprotected by any law, be it human or divine— they could be exterminated.

In this description of a general trend in attitudes toward the Jews, I have omitted numerous exceptions: acts of courage and devotion, public protests, various manifestations of solidarity. Similarly, the remarks that follow about attitudes toward Nazism describe simply a trend discernable in a very complex historical situation. It is in this sense that the attitude of important groups of Western society toward Nazism is explicable by the same internal crisis as their attitude toward the Jews.

In both its propaganda and its spontaneous expression, Nazism consistently claimed to issue from the "true" values of Western, particularly European, culture. Of more importance to us, it was perceived as such by many Europeans and even Americans for the reasons already mentioned: large segments of the middle classes inclined to the anti-liberal trend and, especially, were absolutely hostile to "Bolshevism." There is no need for elaborate proof. We have, first of all, the many explicit ideological justifications of "appeasement," continuing up to the very last days before the outbreak of war. During the war itself, such attitudes were blatant in continental Western Europe. The Nazi Reich, until the middle of the war, was considered an acceptable partner; the "new order" not merely appealed to a small minority of extreme collaborationists, but rather collaboration was sought by important sectors of society in the occupied or neutral countries of Europe.[43]

Regarding France, one usually distinguishes between "state collaboration," the necessary collaboration imposed by a kind of *raison d'état,* and "collaborationism," which was emotionally motivated.[44] I wish to suggest that "state collaboration" disguised much "collaborationism" that did not dare reveal itself. Moreover, among many who kept aloof or even declared themselves favorable to a victory of the Allies, there was, up to about 1943, a sneaking admiration for the Reich as representing the true values of Western civilization.

A recent unpublished doctoral dissertation shows that after the Soviet Union entered the war, public opinion in French Switzerland was animated by fear and hatred toward the Soviet Union far more than toward the Nazi Reich.[45] Concerning the Vatican, the same thesis has been more than amply demonstrated. It seems that the general tide of European public opinion turned against the Reich only in 1943 when Germany's defeat became a likelihood.

In short, the Western middle-class revolt against the liberal tradition contributed to both the isolation of the Jews and also, when combined with extreme anti-Bolshevism, to a largely tacit acceptance—until the middle of the war—of many aspects of Nazism. By then, the major deportations of Western Jews had taken place. Thus, just when the Jews, losing their legal status, were becoming *total outsiders* again as far as Western society was concerned, that is, bereft of any protection whatsoever, the Nazis managed to appear in the eyes of many (and especially on beginning their attack against the Soviet Union) as true bearers of Western values, as *real insiders* though formal enemies. To help the outsider against the insider requires a strong motivation: indeed, the Jews had no chance of being massively helped, be it for this fundamental reason alone, until it was largely too late.

The Victims

With the behavior of the victims during the Holocaust, one reaches the unwritten part of that terrible history, the one that few historians would feel strong enough to write. There are some excellent scholarly monographs, especially Isaiah Trunk's remarkable work on the Jewish Councils,[46] and a lot of painful polemics; but there has been no attempt at a general outline, not even at a general conception of how one should approach the history of "the life and death of the Jews of Europe in the Nazi era," which would probably have to start with the end of World War I. This major task of historians of the Holocaust for years to come seems almost impossible. Not only is a particular emotional strain involved, but even reliable documentary evidence is scarce. My present question, however, is simply: did anything in the behavior of the Jews play into the hands of the exterminators or hamper them? Did anything in that behavior contribute to the passivity of the onlookers?

Defined in this way, the question immediately evokes the issue of the Jewish leadership in occupied Europe, the "Jewish Councils." I shall not, however, address myself to this topic, so extensively investigated by Trunk and others, except to emphasize the importance of distinguishing between the subjective and the objective aspects of the situation, between intentions and outcome (objectively, the Jewish Councils may have facilitated the extermination process in most cases; subjectively, their intentions were the very opposite).[47]

In my view, the attitude of the Jews of Europe between the wars is no less important and relevant than that of the wartime Jewish leadership if one wishes to understand the Jewish element in the Holocaust. The above double question then becomes: how does one explain the unawareness of the majority of European Jews concerning the nature of the unfolding events, so that many tens of thousands, who might have left continental Europe in time, stayed on passively until it was too late? And secondly: what historical interpretation can one give to a certain type of Jewish involvement in public life that encouraged, if not the hatred of extreme antisemites, at least the diffuse antisemitism of those who were to become the "onlookers"?

That European Jews during the thirties were unaware of the nature of emerging events cannot be denied today. One can argue that there is no way of foreseeing developments of so unique a character; indeed, nobody could have foreseen the Final Solution itself. But a sense of imminent danger, of possibly catastrophic changes, might have been expected from European Jews as soon as Hitler came to power. Yet most Jews remained unaware that the time of radical change had come.[48]

Recent research on the German Jews makes sad reading, indeed. One sees how each group, blinded by its own ideology and presuppositions, was wrong in its own way.[49] The emerging trend of events was hidden by pre-formulated models. In addition, however, the various types of mistakes can be explained by some general underlying motivations that are painfully simple.

Many German Jews—and European Jews in general—were unable to face the fact that assimilation, "symbiosis," had failed, that all their efforts and hopes had been largely in vain. They were not ready to evaluate the past critically and recognize that their real status differed from their legal status. To abandon their illusions would have meant drawing the most painful conclusions not only on an abstract level, but about the nature of Jewishness itself, and worse still, about their very physical existence in Europe— conclusions about the course of daily life, which few had the strength to draw. It would have meant severing strong and real roots and trying a new course repellent to most: expatriation, whatever its geographical destination.

Moreover, by seeing themselves as full-fledged members of Western society and adopting its criteria of perceptions and evaluations, the Jews had difficulty, until it was too late, in reaching conclusions concerning Nazism that the most influential strata of Western society did not share. The Jews of Europe certainly reacted with vehemence to the antisemitic measures of the Nazis; yet many of them imagined, like other Europeans, that the Nazis— members of Western civilization, after all—would eventually "settle down."[50] Indeed, not a small percentage of the German Jews who had emigrated in 1933 came back to Germany in 1934 and 1935. . . .[51]

There were also two rather typical approaches of the Jews to their surroundings that made them even more impervious to what was happening. Many tended toward an extreme and short-range pragmatism, which turned them into fundamentally apolitical citizens chiefly seeking to succeed in life and relatively oblivious to significant shifts in the political scene until too late. Others, though fewer, sought to solve their own problems through solving the general problems of humanity: the intense desire to deny the specificity of the Jewish situation led these Jews into a kind of abstract thought that was obliged to eliminate nuances and ambiguities and hide the complexity of social and political developments under the *a priori* smoothness of theoretical constructs.[52]

It was, however, rather the latter group who, through their involvement in public life, actually increased at least the diffuse antisemitism of the future "onlookers." In very general terms, the strong involvement of the Jews in the rise and expansion of modern capitalism had fueled many of the antisemitic slogans of the nineteenth century, and still maintained a strong impact after World War I.[53] But in the latter period the stereotype of the Jew as a revolutionary and, in a more general way, as a detractor of established values, became no less important.[54]

Consider Germany and Austria. The bitterest critics of the most hallowed values were Jews—Harden, Kraus, Tucholsky—critics of values, of the surrounding culture, even of misuse of the German language. What could have created more profound irritation within a deeply wounded society which felt that all its most sacred traditions were suddenly disintegrating? Even if they were correct *in abstracto*, these Jewish critics were painfully unaware of the morbid sensitivity of the groups surrounding them. Franz Kafka, in a letter written to Max Brod in May 1920, rightly condemned a tendency that did the greatest harm to the Jews themselves.[55]

What caused the most significant antagonism, needless to say, was the involvement of Jews in the revolutionary movements of World War I and afterwards. Ya'acov Talmon has recently described the intimate link between Jews and revolution throughout European history since the French Revolution and Jewish emancipation.[56] The reasons are fairly familiar: the Jews transferred into the ideological and political realms a secularized version of the messianic ideals of Jewish religion. Having rebelled against religious tradition and left the framework of their religious and social community, those Jews who sought other horizons never really integrated into non-Jewish society and, therefore, free of former bonds and unhampered by allegiances to some new traditional unit, were more open to ideas of radical change than many of their non-Jewish contemporaries.

The extensive and prominent involvement of Jews in the German revolutions at the end of World War I became the object of endless ulterior polemics.[57] It may well be, as Werner Angress's study suggests,[58] that more often than not Jewish revolutionary leaders were well-meaning and fuzzy idealists burning with messianic fervor, but having little practical idea of how really to change society. But for antisemites, and non-Jewish society in general, such fine distinctions were irrelevant. Is it not significant that Thomas Mann, the most respected representative of contemporary German liberalism, identified two of the most anti-liberal, revolutionary figures in his novels as Jews, Nafta and Breisacher, and portrayed them with particularly negative traits?[59]

The myth of the revolutionary, culture-destroying Jew, perhaps intent on world domination, penetrated into Western consciousness more strongly than ever before. The relentless revolutionary drive of a tiny proportion of Jews—actually ones who kept hardly any link with their community ("non-Jewish Jews," to use Isaac Deutscher's phrase)—gave Jews as a whole a stigma which was to have the direst consequences.

Here indeed we are closing the circle. Whatever the Jews did or failed to do, they could not prevent the existence of antisemitism as such, nor even the emergence of the murderous antisemitism of the Nazis, which was fueled by an element of true insanity and growing disintegration totally independent of the Jews themselves. Nazi antisemitism, however, was able to reach its full scope because it did not encounter strong countervailing forces within European society. The absence of these forces stemmed from a view of the Jew as an "outsider" and of the Nazi as an "insider." The Jews could not have radically altered this view, but undoubtedly the identification of Jews with world revolution made the task of Nazi propaganda easier and reinforced a pre-existing tendency of Western society to see in the Jews undesirable elements which had to be excluded, whatever might ensue for the victims of exclusion.

But then, let us ask again: why did a fraction of the Jewish community turn with such ardor toward revolution? Because after leaving the ghetto physically and spiritually, they did not find a non-Jewish society ready to integrate them beyond the mere legal equality granted them as citizens. There is a deadly logic in the dialectic of antisemitism.

Writing in 1944, Hannah Arendt analyzed the total foreignness, the loneliness of the Jews: the "pariah tradition," as she called it. She quoted a famous sentence from Kafka's novel *The Castle,* in which the hero, the symbol of the Jew, is told: "You are not of the castle, you are not of the village, you are nothing at all."[60]

The pariah tradition is not meaningful if we look at the situation of the Jews from the viewpoint of the exterminator. What most epitomizes the Holocaust in Kafka is rather the closing scene of *The Trial,* the cold-blooded execution of the hapless, defenseless man. This scene has a highly ambiguous detail: in his last moment the victim sees someone looking at him from a distant window, someone even making a movement of some kind with his hands—a movement, which from far away might appear to be commiseration, but which the victim cannot interpret and which, anyway, is of no help. The victim is then stabbed, "as a dog," he thinks, and dies.

But if we consider the wider historical setting, the relationship between the Jew and that Western society in which he sought to integrate himself and from which he was rejected—the society which left him alone in his hour of greatest need—then the symbolism of *The Castle* assumes a profound significance, though one unmentioned by Hannah Arendt.

The hero of the novel is a foreigner who believes that he has been allowed to enter the social system represented by the castle and the village. Indeed, he has been formally asked to join (is even this certain?), but on trying to fit into the system discovers that no one is really ready to accept him. He then becomes a revolutionary of sorts, trying to circumvent the traditional channels of authority, expressing opposition to injustice as he sees it, siding with the "pariahs" of the system (the Barnaby family). His revolutionary effort is ambiguous, like the ambiguity of the whole Jewish attitude to modern Western society, in which the drive for radical change alternated with an intense desire to belong to society as it was. At any rate, the more the hero of the novel attempts to belong, the more isolated he becomes and the lower he sinks. One can foresee his ultimate doom.

Kafka never finished the novel, but he mentioned to some friends its envisaged end. According to his biographer, Max Brod, Kafka planned to show the hero falling lower and lower; suddenly a message is sent from the castle: he is accepted! But the message is too late; the hero is dying or dead.

When, after the end of the war, Western society opened its arms to the

Jews and, in reaction to the discovery of the whole magnitude of the Nazi massacres, the Western antisemitic tradition was at least temporarily discarded, most of the Jews of Europe could no longer enter that new society. But the most terrible question remains to be answered, the question that will probably never find its answer, although it is the most crucial one for understanding the past and anticipating events to come: did the castle send the messenger because the injustice, the evil done, was recognized? Or was the messenger sent because the hero was dead?

Notes

1.   For Isaac Deutscher, its uniqueness is the greatest obstacle to understanding the Holocaust, so that future generations may understand it even less than we do. *The Non-Jewish Jew and Other Essays* (London, 1968), p. 163.

2.   On this subject see Jacob Robinson, *And the Crooked Shall Be Made Straight* (New York, 1965), pp. 92ff. The notorious Thierack letter of October 13, 1942 (Nuremberg Document NG-558, quoted in Raul Hilberg, *The Destruction of the European Jews* [Chicago, 1961], pp. 295–96) implies that mass killings of Poles and Russians were considered, and did take place, but says nothing about total annihilation.

3.   Hans-Joachim Döring, *Die Zigeuner im NS-Statt* (Hamburg, 1964), pp. 189ff. and 193ff.

4.   Ernst Nolte, *Three Faces of Fascism: Action Française, Italian Fascism, National Socialism* (New York, 1966), p. 19.

5.   George L. Mosse, "E. Nolte on Three Faces of Fascism," *Journal of the History of Ideas* 27 (1966), 621–25.

6.   Eberhard Jäckel, *Hitlers Weltanschauung: Entwurf einer Herrschaft* (Tübingen, 1969).

7.   In "Die 'Endlösung' und das deutsche Ostimperium als Kernstück des rassenideologischen Programms des Nationalsozialismus," *Vierteljahrshefte für Zeitgeschichte* 20 (1972), 133–53.

8.   In *Hitler's Secret Conversations* (N. Cameron and R. H. Stevens trs., intn. by H. R. Trevor-Roper, New York, 1953), p. 587 (entry for the night of November 29–30, 1944).

9.   Found above all in Hannah Arendt, *The Origins of Totalitarianism* (2nd ed., New York, 1958).

10.   Compare Max Horkheimer and Theodor W. Adorno, "Elements of Anti-Semitism," in *Dialectic of Enlightenment* (New York, 1972), pp. 168–208 (esp. p. 171). Norman Cohn, in *The Pursuit of the Millenium* (London, 1957), has drawn a brilliant comparison between the crusades of millenarian movements against "enemies" and such crusades in Nazism and Communism.

11.   Such "bureaucratic" aspects of the Final Solution are emphasized in H. G. Adler, *Der verwaltete Mensch* (Tübingen, 1974).

12. Gil Elliot, in *Twentieth Century Book of the Dead* (London, 1972), regards the Holocaust as an example of mass killings whose total so far this century is some 110 million victims.

13. For instance, O. Kraus and E. Kulka, *The Death Factory: Document on Auschwitz* (Oxford, 1966).

14. At the height of the war, more than three-quarters of the people in every Jewish transport were being exterminated on arrival at the camps, the remainder being only temporarily reprieved and intended to die from exhaustion: Joseph Billig, *Les Camps de concentration dans l'économie du reich hitlérien* (Paris, 1973), p. 66.

15. Raul Hilberg, *op. cit.* (note 2 above), pp. 645ff.

16. Nuremberg Documents PS-3663 and PS-3666. Some emphasize that economic imperatives seem occasionally to have taken priority; even Hitler, at least twice, ordered postponement of the killing of some Jews for economic reasons. Yet such examples remain exceptions. Apart from the very last months of the war—and even then only very partially— there is no documentary evidence of the exploitation of the Jews as slave labor being given precedence over their extermination.

17. As Adolf Leschnitzer, *The Magic Background of Modern Antisemitism* (New York, 1956), pp. 96ff. Leschnitzer is correct to the extent that some of the psychological motivations appear to be similar.

18. See especially Norman Cohn, *Europe's Inner Demons* (London, 1975), pp. 253–55.

19. Issues of October 9, November 2 and November 16, 1972.

20. Barraclough, in a sense, rationalizes a disturbingly widespread phenomenon: most general histories of the twentieth century give a central place to Nazism, yet mention the fate of the Jews and the Final Solution in no more than a few lines. On one aspect of this phenomenon, see Gerd Korman, "Silence in the American Textbooks," *Yad Vashem Studies* 8 (1970), 183–202.

21. For instance, Raul W. Massing, *Rehersal for Destruction* (New York, 1949); Peter G. J. Pulzer, *The Rise of Political Anti-Semitism in Germany and Austria* (New York, 1964).

22. George L. Mosse's *The Crisis of German Ideology* (New York, 1964) is a good example of this approach, which also seems to underlie Leon Poliakov's *The History of Antisemitism* (3 vols., London, 1974–1975).

23. As Raul Hilberg, *op. cit.* (note 2 above), and Adler, *op. cit.* (note 11 above).

24. *Op. cit.* (note 9 above).

25. For instance, Norman Cohn, *Warrant for Genocide* (New York, 1967); Saul Friedländer, *L'Antisémitisme nazi: Histoire d'une psychose collective* (Paris, 1971). This approach has precedents in the series "Studies in Prejudice" promoted by the American Jewish Committee and the series "Studies in the Dynamics of Persecution and Extermination" published by the Columbus Centre in Britain.

26. Nathan W. Ackermann and Marie Jahoda, *Antisemitism and Emotional Disorder* (New York, 1950); Rudolph Loewenstein, *Christians and Jews: A Psychoanalytic Study* (New York, 1952); H. G. Gough, "Studies of Social Intolerance," *Journal of Social Psychology* 33 (1951), 237–69; Theodore W. Adorno and others, *The Authoritarian Personality* (New York, 1950).

27. *Op. cit.* (note 25 above), pp. 27ff.

28. Some recent psychoanalytic studies of the pathological basis of Hitler's own anti-semitism are: Walter C. Langer, *The Mind of Adolf Hitler* (New York, 1973); Robert G. L.

Waite, "Adolf Hitler's Anti-Semitism," in B. B. Wolman ed., *The Psychoanalytic Interpretation of History* (New York, 1971). For an evaluation of these studies, see my *History and Psychoanalysis* (New York, 1978).

29.   At this level, Nazism appears not only as a transformation of Christian antisemitism, that is, as a mutation of Christian "orthodoxy," but also as a modern version of Manichean heresies or even older religious conceptions, in which an evil principle fights with the principle of good for the control of the universe.

30.   Both of these two components were reflected in Hitler's manner of understanding the "Protocols of the Elders of Zion" (about whose authenticity he had no doubts) and similar literature; see, for instance, Ernst Boepple, *Adolf Hitlers Reden* (Munich, 1933), p. 57.

31.   Alex Bein, "The Jewish Parasite," *Yearbook of the Leo Baeck Institute* 9 (1964), 3–40 (esp. pp. 21ff.).

32.   Nuremberg Document PS-1919.

33.   This point is convincingly demonstrated by Uriel Tal's contribution to this volume. See also Victor Klemperer, *Notizbuch eines Philologen* (Berlin, 1949) and Nachman Blumenthal, "On the Nazi Vocabulary," *Yad Vashem Studies* 1 (1957), 49–66.

34.   A crucial factor here, of course, is the extent to which knowledge about the extermination program spread. In Germany itself wide circles "knew" by 1942–1943: see my *Kurt Gerstein: The Ambiguity of Good* (New York, 1969). Allied governments, but also neutrals and the Vatican, were aware already in Summer 1942: see Arthur D. Morse, *While Six Million Died* (New York, 1968), and my *Pius XII and the Third Reich* (New York, 1966). The British press reported remarkably precise and extensive details: Andrew Scharf, "The British Press and the Holocaust," *Yad Vashem Studies* 5 (1963), 169–91. In occupied Eastern Europe the rumor spread from numerous eyewitnesses; in occupied Western Europe, however, precise information seems to have been scarce, though it was known that the condition of deported Jews was terrible. See also Randolph L. Braham's contribution to this volume.

35.   *Op. cit.* (note 9 above), p. 56.

36.   See Carl Ludwig, *La Politique pratiquée par la Suisse à l'égard des refugiés au cours des années 1933 à 1945* (Berne, 1958).

37.   Note of Ribbentrop of December 9, 1938: U.S. Government Printing Office, *Documents on German Foreign Policy*, ser. D, vol. IV, pp. 481–82. For the attitudes of various governments concerning the fate of the Jews during the thirties, see Eliahu Ben-Elissar, *La Diplomatie du IIIe reich et les juifs, 1933–1939* (Paris, 1969).

38.   Raul Hilberg, *op. cit.* (note 2 above), pp. 393ff.

39.   See my *Pius XII and the Third Reich, op. cit.* (note 34 above), pp. 92ff.

40.   In November 1938 Georges Rublee, head of the international committee established by the Evian Conference, wrote to the State Department that apart from the United States and Great Britain, virtually all countries (including the British dominions and colonies) had shut their doors to Jewish emigrants. See Eliahu Ben-Elissar, *op. cit.* (note 37 above), p. 363.

41.   Guenter Lewy, *The Catholic Church and Nazi Germany* (New York, 1964), pp. 290–93.

42.   In my *Kurt Gerstein, op. cit.* (note 34 above), p. 148.

43.   See, for instance, Robert O. Paxton, *Vichy France: Old Guard and New Order, 1940–1944* (New York, 1972).

44.   For this distinction, see Stanley Hoffmann, *In Search of France* (Cambridge, Mass., 1963).

45.   Jacques Meurant, "La Presse et l'opinion de la Suisse romande face à la guerre européenne et à ses repercussions en Suisse" (Ph.D. dissertation, Geneva, 1974).

46.   Isaiah Trunk, *Judenrat: The Jewish Councils in Eastern Europe under Nazi Occupation* (New York, 1972).

47.   The failure to make this distinction vitiates the analysis of Hannah Arendt in *Eichmann in Jerusalem: A Report on the Banality of Evil* (New York, 1963).

48.   Groups such as the Hasidim of Eastern Europe, who lived closely within the confines of tradition and paid little attention to developments in the gentile world, tended to regard Nazism as at most threatening fresh persecutions of a familiar kind. Yet even assimilated Jews in Nazi Germany were largely unaware that a new kind of threat was looming.

49.   Abraham Margaliot, "The Political Reaction of German-Jewish Organizations and Institutions to the Anti-Jewish Policy of the National Socialists, 1932–1935" (in Hebrew, Ph.D. dissertation, Jerusalem, 1971).

50.   A grotesque example is the declarations of support for the new regime made in 1933 and 1934 by the Reichsbund Jüdischer Frontsoldaten (an organization representing 30,000 Jewish veterans of World War I). See further George Mosse, "The Influence of the Volkish Idea on German Jewry," in *Germans and Jews* (New York, 1970), esp. pp. 105ff.

51.   Of about 600,000 German Jews, about 150,000 emigrated during 1933–1938 and a comparable number between November 1938 and the beginning of the war. See Werner Rosenstock, "Exodus 1933–1939: A Survey of Jewish Emigration from Germany," *Yearbook of the Leo Baeck Institute* 1 (1956), 373–90.

52.   An example is Rosa Luxemburg, as quoted in J. P. Nettl, *La Vie et l'oeuvre de Rosa Luxemburg* (2 vols., Paris, 1972), vol. II, p. 855.

53.   Besides the involvement of Jews in some financial scandals of the twenties and thirties (Barmat, Sklarek, Stavisky), a negative impression remained from the role that certain Jews (Walter Rathenau, Albert Ballin) had played in the German war economy (as rumored war profiteers).

54.   The attempt by Abram Léon in *The Jewish Question: A Marxist Interpretation* (New York, 1970) to give a Marxist explanation of Nazi antisemitism is therefore to be rejected. According to Léon, the crisis of capitalism had led capitalists to divert popular resentments onto the Jews as representatives of an earlier form of capitalism (Jewish-financed enterprises in the pre-capitalist period); ironically, capitalists could now do this without risking harm to themselves, because Jews (following assimilation) no longer played an indispensable economic role in this respect. Yet was not Hitler's first book, written in collaboration with Eckart, entitled "Bolshevism from Moses to Lenin"? (Léon's book was written in Belgium in 1943 without full knowledge of events; he himself died later in Auschwitz.)

55.   Franz Kafka, *Correspondence, 1902–1924* (Paris, 1965), p. 325.

56.   Ya'acov Talmon, "Jews and Revolution," in *The Age of Violence* (in Hebrew, Tel Aviv, 1974).

57.   Jews held key posts in the early Bolshevik regime, dominated transient revolutionary regimes in Hungary and Bavaria, and were prominent in the uprisings in various parts of Germany.

58.   Werner T. Angress, "Juden im politischen Leben der Revolutionszeit," in Werner E. Mosse ed., *Deutsches Judentum in Krieg und Revolution 1916–1923* (Tübingen, 1971).

59.   To accuse Thomas Mann of antisemitic tendencies is too easy an escape. For a

balanced view of the question, see Kurt Loewenstein, "Thomas Mann zur jüdischen Frage," *Bulletin des Leo Baeck Institut* 10 (1967), 1–59.

60.   Hannah Arendt, "The Jew as Pariah: A Hidden Tradition," *Jewish Social Studies* 6 (1944), 99–122 (quotation on p. 115).

Was the Holocaust Predictable?*

JACOB KATZ

Most of those who lived through the period of the Holocaust—whether they observed it from nearby or afar—will readily testify that at first the information reaching them seemed absolutely unbelievable, impossible. In retrospect, however, we all have the urge to inquire into the sequence of events that led to the tragedy and, after surveying them, tend to conceive of them as the unavoidable course of destiny. Such a complete turnabout in the attitude to an event, from while it was occurring to after it had taken place, can admittedly be observed in other instances. In the case of the Holocaust, however, the contradiction stands out as especially flagrant because of the emphatic nature of the contradictory attitudes. As information about the crime began to filter into countries outside the Nazi-occupied areas, its enormity put it beyond belief. Yet once it became evident that the unbelievable had indeed occurred, people's minds turned in the opposite direction. The question asked today, often in a self-torturous vein, is how we could ever have overlooked the signs that unmistakeably foretold the impending tragedy.

This query reaches out to different dimensions of the past. The prehistory of Nazidom, as well as the first years of Hitler's regime, have been scrutinized for signs indicating that the Nazi movement was prepared to implement its program of destroying the Jews and that Hitler was resolved to carry this out in the simple, physical sense of the word. Subsequently, the spotlight has been turned on German antisemitism in the last decades of the nineteenth century, and its forerunners in the Romantic nationalism of the early nineteenth century, there to detect the seeds of Nazism and its inherent Jew-hatred. Some have gone even further, attempting an analysis of the German mentality as reflected especially in such representatives as Luther,

*A shortened version of this essay appeared in *Commentary* May 1975.

Hegel, Wagner, and Nietzsche, and as revealing a tendency toward tyranny, totalitarianism, and intolerance.

But the inquiring mind could not stop at the German border. The proscription of Jews by the Christian churches, as well as Christian teaching since the early Middle Ages, emerged as a historical background for the terrible scene of the present. Jewish-gentile relations since antiquity have been searched for an answer to the frightening riddle of the present. Though the connection between the different phases of past history and the climax of the Holocaust has not always been explicit, it is safe to state that today scarcely any historical, sociological, or philosophical analysis of early antisemitism can remain unconscious of the symbolical presence of the six million dead of Auschwitz and Treblinka.

Was the Holocaust Predicted?

Although many unexpected events occur in history, their unexpectedness is often obscured in historical narrative by the way in which data are presented as an uninterrupted stream of events flowing from one to another. In describing the rise of Hitler, the historian can muster the trends and factors that, in their sequence of operation, seem to have predetermined the outcome—the triumph of Hitler over his adversaries. He will cite the economic crisis of the late twenties and early thirties, German national pride wounded by the Treaty of Versailles, and perhaps go back to the Thirty Years War and beyond, to find out why it was "denied to Germany" to catch up with the development of the West, why that country remained "impervious" to true democracy. His account of the Holocaust may begin by tracing the history of Jewish-gentile relations since antiquity.

For those who witnessed what happened, however, there remains the antinomy between the initial feeling of being taken by surprise and the later inclination to reconstruct the event as inevitable. The antinomy is accordingly often overcome through the proposition that some people—at least—had foreseen the event. Not everybody was blind, but most people were deaf, refusing to listen to the warnings of the clairvoyant.

In 1945, after the horrors of the Holocaust were already fully known to us, I heard Arnold Zweig quoting what he himself had told Menahem M. Ussischkin during his visit to Jerusalem in 1932 when the ascendance of Hitler seemed imminent; namely, that this would lead to the total destruction of German Jewry. But the book *Bilanz der deutschen Judenheit* (Amsterdam, 1934), written by Arnold Zweig shortly after Hitler's ascent to power, attests to his real views at that time. Zweig feared the downfall of German Jewry and saw the danger that Leftist intellectuals like himself would incur by remaining in Germany. Yet he assumed that a man like Martin Buber would still be able to fight for the ideal of religious socialism in Germany and Zweig strongly enjoined upon him to continue.

Now that the highly interesting correspondence between Arnold Zweig and Sigmund Freud during the years 1927–1939 has been published,[1] we have first-hand evidence of what Zweig's prognosis of the future amounted to in the ensuing years. Having escaped from Berlin, Zweig settled in Haifa in 1934. Though a Zionist since his early years, he failed to take root in the Hebrew-speaking and emphatically Jewish-nationalist environment of Mount Carmel. From there he commented on events in Europe, taking every sign of setback in Hitler's advance as an omen of his pending downfall. I am far from suggesting that Zweig, in quoting what he said to Ussischkin, was concealing the truth. What does occur in such cases is that statements uttered under certain circumstances that lent them their meaning assume, in retrospect, a weight that they were far from having carried in their original setting.

Vladimir Jabotinsky is often quoted by his followers as having coined the phrase: "Liquidate the Galuth or the Galuth will liquidate you." Indeed, rereading Jabotinsky's speeches in the years preceding World War II, one comes across sentences that sound like an apprehension of the coming doom. But what did those warnings mean in their original context? This great Jewish patriot tried to prod his people to a more active Zionism than the leadership in charge thought possible or even contemplated. In the late thirties he propagated the "evacuation" of Polish Jewry, and would not have hesitated to enlist the assistance of the Polish government, regardless of its antisemitic motivations, to implement this plan. To convince the Jewish public of the urgency of his scheme, Jabotinsky pointed to the plight of German Jewry, which was emigrating under the pressure of anti-Jewish legislation. It was in this connection that Jabotinsky used the phrases that to us assume the frightening connotation of the Holocaust.[2]

What he had in mind, however, was an aggravation of economic, social, and political measures against the Jewish community in Poland itself. He had no apprehension of a possible conquest of other countries by the Nazis. He shared the illusion of many Jewish intellectuals about the fragility of Nazi rule, believing that it would crumble, either through internal difficulties or at the first clash with any external power. How unaware he remained of what was in store for the world in the near future is clearly demonstrated by his conception of the evacuation. His suggestion was to transfer one and a half million Polish Jews to Palestine in the course of the next ten years. Neither the scope nor the imminence of the tragedy was foreseen in this suggestion. Jabotinsky's vision, inspired though he was by a deep passion for the welfare of his people, was as limited by the impenetrability of the future as the vision of anybody else.

What transpires from the analysis of these two instances is that the alleged predictions, intended to bridge the hiatus between past and future, on the contrary reflect the intrinsic dichotomy that keeps them apart. Only in retrospect (and when interpreted in the context of later events) did those statements made about the future assume the nature of prophecy. Instead of solving our problem, however, this observation puts it into a sharper focus. For if logic regards the course of development in retrospect as compelling, why could human reason not have reached the proper conclusion in advance? Applied to the case under consideration, why was the doom of European Jewry, which on looking back seems to have been predestined by foregoing events, not realized? Are contemporaries to be blamed for some failure?

This last question hovers over most of the deliberations relating to the history of the period. The blame has often been explicitly put upon certain groups or individuals who, supposedly, could have foreseen events and have acted accordingly. Such blame is also implicit in many historical descriptions that seemingly do nothing but record the events in their chronological sequence, except that occasionally they cast a pitying glance on the contemporaries who "ignored" what is so crystal clear to the historian. Many of these strictures would be seen to be ill-conceived if the accusers would first face the problem of historical prediction, realizing its intrinsic epistemological and psychological limitations.

Was a Nazi Government Foreseeable?

The impediments to foreseeing future developments are of two kinds, the one deriving from the limitations of human perception and judgment, the other inherent in the objective nature of historical events themselves. To explain the latter kind of impediment, let us return to the disparity between the conception of an event before and after it has occurred. If the event *depended upon the decision of one or more persons,* it would, in advance of its occurrence, always be regarded as an open-ended possibility—the decision may fall this way or that. Human beings live in the consciousness of acting freely; accordingly, they assume that other people, too, on whom their destiny depends, are able to choose this or that step in any crucial decision. Only *after* such an event has occurred can it look as if it was predetermined by the given data, including the psychological disposition of the person or persons involved.[3]

In other words, when estimating the future and coming to a decision on how to act, a person is generally in an open-ended situation, in that the outcome of certain decisions of others cannot yet be known. Consequently, those who reproach people for not having adopted, in an open-ended situation, the action that now seems to have been obvious and mandatory in the light of subsequent events, though it was *only the latter* that made the situation a closed one, project something that emerged in a later stage of development into an earlier phase. They ignore, in fact, the very nature of historical development, characterized as it is by a creation and growth that, through the *decisions and actions* of living people, *adds* to the store of already existing layers of data. Such demands make the objects of their reproach into potential prophets first, so as to turn them into villains later.

Every historian, including historians of the Holocaust, is therefore in a certain psychological predicament. When a historian undertakes to describe a certain phase of the past, he is equipped with knowledge of the later phases—the result of countless subsequent decisions. Still, when he is about to present the choices and dilemmas of people acting within the first phase, he has to ignore his own knowledge and instead depict, interpret, and judge their actions exclusively on the basis of motives that could enter their consciousness. In the words of the great Dutch historian Johan Huizinga, it is "to imagine the past as if it were still only present."

A case in point is the emergence of a Nazi government in Germany. Up to January 1933 people could only know that Hitler might come to power; they did not know that he would, even though, in retrospect, the historian may present the *Führer's* rise as a chain of events following one another with the force of inevitable necessity. Everybody who lived through the period knows that those who had the most to fear his ascendance were the most hopeful that it would not come about. But even those who wished to see him succeed did not yet know whether he would. In November 1932 his fate still seemed to depend on the votes of the millions, and the elections of that month indicated a diminishing trend in popular support for him. For this it was easy to find an explanation, since the economic crisis, one of the main issues through which Nazi propaganda tried to draw people into its camp, had passed its peak; the number of unemployed was clearly decreasing. There were defections from the party and Hitler had difficulties in keeping it solvent and retaining his authority over different groups conflicting with each other over the course to be followed in the future.

That power nonetheless fell into Hitler's hands was due to the plight of the other political parties, which, split between the Left and the Right, were incapable of establishing a working majority. It was at this juncture that President Hindenburg, on the advice of his coterie, invited Hitler to form a coalition government with the non-Nazi Right. The latter, believing in their capacity to tame him, accepted the deal.

Here we have an example of what we may wrongly expect of people when we say they ought to have foreseen what was still in the making. As Hitler's assumption of power was contingent on the decisions of others (Hindenburg and various Right-wing politicians), who themselves were hesitant as to what course to take, any prediction would have been mere guesswork.

Was Nazi Policy Predictable?

In retrospect, Hindenburg's decision to call upon Hitler to form a government is rightly regarded by historians as one of the most fateful decisions, not only in the history of Germany and in Jewish history, but also in the history of the world. Yet the very expression "fateful" indicates that the full significance of the step was to emerge only in the future. Contemporaries felt it to be a decisive step, but in assessing its possible consequences they could only speculate on the basis of the given data and analogies derived from historical experience.

Much of the speculation was admittedly very mistaken. The non-Nazi

Right completely failed to tame Hitler, while those Leftist intellectuals who had recommended for many months that Hitler be allowed to come to power, assumed he would fail and seal his own doom.[4] Nonetheless, it remains true that the significance of the event could have been assessed then only according to what it demonstrably implied at the time. This was momentous enough. It meant the domination of the country by a party that denied the principles on which the former government and the established order had been founded: democracy, parliamentarianism, racial tolerance, and equality before the law. Instead the party avowed the principle of leadership, i.e., government by a self-appointed elite that owed allegiance to one man whose command was to be law—a man who had given indication enough of his irrational visions and his passionate hatred of his enemies, among whom the Jews loomed most conspicuously.

Still, the declarations of even the most revolutionary parties have never been taken by people as guidelines to be used in implementing practical policies. In this case too, even those who supported Hitler very often did so under the tacit assumption that though he would indeed reverse some of the trends of postwar Germany—such as acquiescence in the Treaty of Versailles, the semi-socialist economy, or the permissiveness of Weimar culture—he would relinquish his other radical tendencies when faced with harsh realities and responsibility for the conduct of the affairs of the state.

How could people have been so foolish, thus the question very often runs, not to have seen what was in store for them at the hands of Hitler, when he did nothing but carry out what he had promised in so many words in his book *Mein Kampf?* The answer is not that people did not read the *Führer's* voluminous treatise. They had ample opportunity to become aware of his declared intentions both during his rise to power and during the first years of his rule. The real answer is not even in the selective acceptance and partial awareness of what reaches one's senses and understanding—although this goes a long way to explain the seemingly faulty response to received stimuli. There is, rather, an essential difference between announcing an intention and the resolution to act upon it on the part of the actor *himself.* Nobody, including Hitler himself, could know whether he would ever have the opportunity to carry out his intentions, and how far he would go in adhering to them. Only in retrospect is there a tendency for the time lag, as well as for the essential difference between intention and execution, to be blurred and become one of the main sources of misjudging the past.

This whole complex of problems can be well demonstrated through an episode in the story of Hitler's bid for power. An exclusive club of well-to-do conservative-minded citizens in Hamburg, accustomed to listening to lectures and speeches by active politicians, decided in the winter of 1926 to invite Adolf Hitler to address them. Hitler was in the first stages of reorganizing his party after the failure of his 1923 Putsch, which had taken him to prison and caused him to undergo a temporary political eclipse. He was not yet free to make public speeches in all places in Germany, but succeeded in attracting attention as a consistent opponent of the ruling parties of the country and indeed as a radical detractor of the Weimar Republic itself, conforming in that respect to the principles avowed by the members of the Nationalklub in Hamburg.

His two-and-a-half hour speech was taken down in stenogram, but was published only in 1960 by the Research Center for the History of National Socialism in Hamburg. As was observed by Professor Werner Jochmann, director of the center, who edited this text, the speech is a most revealing document, not only for the tactics of Hitler's propaganda but even more for the way in which this propaganda was absorbed.[5]

Hitler concentrated in his speech on the weakness of postwar Germany, attributing it exclusively to the influence of Marxism, which had undermined the former strength of the country. This trend, basically foreign to the nature of the German people, was made responsible for all the woes of the present. Hitler declared its eradication to be the highest national goal, for which he wished to enlist the support of his listeners. In this approach, Jochmann assures us, he succeeded at least partially. The Hamburg patricians of 1926 resented the ascendance of the new ruling class with its social-democratic background—though, indeed, not with the idea in mind of replacing it by an even more radical order of an even less aristocratic character. They longed instead for the reestablishment of the prewar order in which they had played a key role in state and society. Still, the resentment against the prevailing order that they shared with Hitler created a common ground between them, enabling the speaker to inspire his audience and even secure the future support of some of them.

Now, Jochmann's historical analysis of Hitler's speech has shown that it clearly reveals all the radical elements of his program and the manner of its execution, which, properly understood, would no doubt have frightened away the conservative audience of the Nationalklub. Puzzled by the divergence between what the audience apparently absorbed from the speech as against what it in fact contained, the editor offers the explanation that the listeners paid attention only to what was in harmony with what they themselves felt and thought, but neglected and overlooked what would have repelled them if properly understood.

This explanation may be correct as far as it goes. But in order to resolve the contradiction between what the contemporary listener gauged from this address and what the reader of today would derive from reading it, one has to consider not only the psychology of the listener in 1926 but also that of the reader of 1960 or of today. Knowing what occurred in between prompts the *post-facto* reader to attribute to those words the weight absorbed, so to say, from later history.

This can best be shown through the association with the Holocaust that would certainly arise in the mind of every present-day reader of Hitler's speech, in spite of the Jews not being mentioned in it *at all.* Of course, radical antisemitism belonged to the Nazi program from its very beginning, but

Hitler thought it more opportune in the Hamburg club to speak about the Marxists and the adversaries of national Germany in general, to destroy whom, he declared, was his party's irresistible resolve. In describing the process of destruction, he resorted to expressions of the Darwinian struggle going on in nature between the strong and the weak, deriving from it the appropriate lesson for the human sphere. It was the natural right of the stronger to overpower the weak and eliminate them.

Reading such utterances, one cannot help thinking gruesomely of Auschwitz and Treblinka. This is, however, clearly a predating of notions and events, from which the historian is duty bound to refrain. He may well recognize in the Hamburg speech the potentiality of Hitler's deeds as far as his intentions were concerned. But he is not permitted to disregard the contingence on which the realization of those intentions depended. The historian's assignment is rather to follow the evolving of events step by step, keeping in mind at every juncture the open-ended possibilities inherent in the situation. He has to lead up to the culmination of events, but not to anticipate it.

Contemporary Assessments and Historical Judgment

The denial of the possibility of foreseeing the course of events does not imply that there was no way for contemporaries to assess the situation and its dangers in a more or less intelligent fashion. As in any human situation open-ended toward the future, the appraisal had to be made by surveying the factors at work in the present and weighing the chances of possible shifts and changes in the future. Obviously, no universal agreement could be reached either on the diagnosis of the present or on the prognosis of the future.

Accordingly, when Hitler came to power, contradictory recommendations for action were made and conflicting decisions were taken by different people on the basis of their respective evaluations of the situation. Some Jews chose to emigrate, while others chose instead to weather the storm at home until the Nazis moderated their attitude toward Jews or met their downfall. Some chose to cooperate with the regime in order to facilitate emigration and save as much as possible of Jewish possessions through the transfer of German products to Palestine—the line taken by the official leadership of the Jewish Agency; others instead supported the boycott of German wares all over the world in order to bring upon Hitler an economic debacle—the passionately defended position of the Revisionists. The records of the later Nazi period, especially the phase of ghettoization and deportation, are full of even more frightful dilemmas. This is amply documented especially by the history of the *Judenräte,* where in extreme cases the sending of people to death in the hope of saving the lives of others was dependent upon the assessment of what was in store for all concerned in the future.

The historian who wishes faithfully to record the external and internal struggle of those involved in the dilemma, and even more if he desires to pass moral judgment upon the decisions taken, is not permitted to use the knowledge he has gained by hindsight. He has to explain people's behavior on the basis of what they themselves knew at that time, weighing—in the light of accessible information and possible insight—whether the decision was rational, judicious, and moral by whatever yardsticks were conceivably available to *the actors themselves.* Naturally, people will be found to have acted on different levels of rationality and, where moral considerations are involved, they will be found to have revealed different degrees of courage and character. Any such moral judgment, however, must be preceded by the reconstruction of the situation as exactly as the historical sources will permit.

That is why such judgments must remain the prerogative of the historian. Not because he has a sharper moral sense than others, but because he alone is equipped with the critical acumen and training to do the preparatory work of reconstruction. And moral judgment of this kind can be pronounced on individuals only when we are able to imagine the plight they were in. We have no way of judging the *Judenräte* as a collective, but only this or that representative of them whose circumstances are sufficiently familiar to us.[6]

To be sure, the behavior of individuals is not the only object toward which the historian may direct his judgment, nor is the yardstick always a moral one. Even in the extreme situation in the ghettos, when the plight of the inmates had been clearly realized by all, it was not only the character of the individuals that determined whether they would join the underground that chose to go down fighting. It was also the mentality derived from education, religiosity, and social and political aspirations that made the difference between passivity and quietism on the one hand and activism and initiative on the other. The more so at the earlier stages, when the decision about what to do was dependent on insight into the nature of the situation. Different sets of concepts were applied to the process of interpretation and the conclusions differed accordingly. Whether these were appropriate to the situation can be judged only without resorting to the hindsight derived from later events. Moreover, the judgment does not concern merely the character of individuals, but rather the mentality of the groups to which they belonged.

Of course, some such sets of concepts can be seen to have been strikingly inappropriate. The attempts of Max Naumann and Hans Joachim Schoeps to be accepted by the Nazis in virtue of their adherence to a Germanic *Weltanschauung* can be dismissed as autistic self-deception, disregarding the results or, for that matter, the disloyalty implied toward other Jewish groups. At the other end of the scale stood the Leftist intellectuals, well represented by the now famous Frankfurt proponents of the critical theory who, committed to a Marxist interpretation of history, could conceive the ascendance of the Nazis only in terms of an aberration in the social forces, and were entirely impervious to the role played by the defamation of the Jews in Nazi ideology and the Nazi political program.

In documenting this last observation, I can contribute something from my own recollection. In 1932 I was preparing my doctoral thesis at Frankfurt University under the guidance of Karl Mannheim, the sociologist. Mannheim did not formally belong to Max Horkheimer's institute of social research, but was personally and ideologically an integral part of Horkheimer's group. Two months after the Nazi takeover Mannheim, apprehensive that my studies at the university might be terminated because of my being a Jewish foreigner, urged me to complete my thesis and take the examination before the end of the academic year in June. As to his own position, he remarked that the Nazis would not dare touch the incumbents of full professorial chairs in the universities. In April that year, when the purging of academic institutions began, Mannheim was one of the first to be thrown out.[7]

Of the sets of concepts available, to be rooted in Jewish consciousness and to have deeper Jewish commitments certainly helped people in orientating toward the new situation. At least it protected one from despair; the cases of suicide occurred conspicuously in the radically assimilated circles who, seeing their world in a shambles, found the burden of life unbearable. Having overcome the first shock, Orthodox and Zionist circles tried to make the best of it. German Jewry experienced a kind of cultural regeneration, documented in literary and adult educational activity, that dwindled only when continuous emigration sapped the available forces and when, after November 1938, the Nazis paralyzed even these signs of Jewish public life. The Zionist movement in particular drew a good deal of formerly indifferent Jews into its orbit, not only because it offered a way of escape to Palestine, but mainly because its ideological concepts came nearest to accounting for the situation that had evolved. The exclusion of the Jews from German society seemed to support unequivocally the erroneousness of assimilationist trends and ideologies.

The congruency between the Zionist interpretation of Jewish history and existing circumstances lasted, however, only as long as Nazi persecutions were kept *within the limits of historically paralleled patterns.* An example is J. F. Baer, who left Germany for the Hebrew University in Jerusalem as early as 1930 and had an opportunity to ponder from a distance on the significance of what was happening in the country of his origin. The result was the short book *Galut,* written in the first two years of the Nazi regime: a deep-going analysis of the concept of Exile that had encompassed the Jewish people on its path since early antiquity. Baer concluded his analysis with the observation that "we today can read each coming day's events in ancient and dusty chronological tables, as though history were the ceaseless unrolling of a process proclaimed once and for all in the Bible."[8] There was, therefore, after all a significant meaning to what was going on and Baer, as the historian of the Jews in Spain, may well have had in mind the fate of the Spanish Jews that foreshadowed the tragedy of his own Ashkenazi tribe. Such an analogy was painfully moving, but at the same time it also had a soothing effect. One could have the feeling of entering the path of the historically prescribed course inherent in the Jewish essence and destiny.

This was a possible mental response to the events in the mid-thirties, when the forced displacement of the German Jews from their positions raised at most the apprehension of their ultimate expulsion. In the ensuing years, however, when the waves of persecution mounted, and especially when the frightful information about the ghettos and death camps reached the world from behind the borders of the warring Third Reich, the events transcended *all* the wonted concepts derived from historical experience.

For Auschwitz and Treblinka there was no earlier historical analogy and there was no philosophical, or for that matter theological, frame of mind that could possibly integrate them into any system of thought. The Holocaust was an absolute *novum* lacking accountability in any rational terms at the disposal of the generation that experienced it. It lacks it to this very day, in spite of the tremendous effort that has been devoted to investigating the Holocaust in its three aspects: the historical, the philosophical, and the theological. It remains to be seen whether subsequent generations will be more successful in evolving some line of thought adequate to deal with what, for the generation that lived through it, can only be characterized as a trauma, a wounding experience beyond the reach of intellectual conceptualization.

In the light of the radically transcendent character of the Holocaust, one is led to ask what significance there can be in attempting to lay bare its roots in the more or less remote past, or even in composing a historical record of how it proceeded. What enlightenment can we possibly derive from tracing the prehistory of the Holocaust, the history of antisemitism, or Jewish-Christian relations in past centuries, if indeed the Holocaust has to be conceived as an absolute *novum* unparalleled in previous generations? And what is the use of going through the details of the horrors in historical retrospect? Is it not just a kind of masochism imposing upon ourselves some form of atonement for not having shared the fate of the victims?

An answer to these perplexing questions can be given only on the basis of a clearly conceived idea of what the capabilities of historiography are in general. If one expects the historian to show how later events were produced by previous ones as an inevitable chain of cause and effect, the expectation must be declared unrealistic. No such connection between past and present can ever be established.

Still, the fact that a later event was not a necessary result of previous ones does not mean that there were no relations between them. When the Holocaust was set in motion, it absorbed many earlier elements of both German and Jewish history, elements without the previous existence of which the later phases of the Holocaust would have been impossible. This presents historiography with a sufficiently significant task: to describe the process of absorption and transformation of the earlier in the later, and thereby to illuminate the present situation. The merest indication of how the task can be carried out will be offered in the remaining sections of this essay.[9]

From Medieval to Modern Antisemitism

In ancient times the Jewish community outside the homeland of Palestine lived in separation from its social surroundings, since its exclusive religious concepts and commitments kept it apart from its polytheistic neighbors. It paid for this exclusiveness by incurring misconceptions and hatred in the outside world. When the polytheistic world that surrounded the Jewish community became itself indebted to Jewish tradition, through accepting this tradition in the Christian reinterpretation unacceptable to Jews, the mutual exclusiveness and denial of the two societies assumed a singular, historically almost unparalleled character. Christians tolerated the existence of the Jewish minority among them on condition that, politically and socially, it remained on the level of the pariah. It could continue to exist as a negative witness to the victory of Christianity. Jews, for their part, submitted outwardly to Christian dominance, but maintained at the same time a kind of mental reservation against its validity and awaited its termination, at least insofar as it involved a Jewish sojourn in foreign countries of exile.

Under the wings of such ideologies, Jews could continue a precarious existence, fulfilling a sometimes not unimportant, but never highly regarded, economic role. They were, at any rate, never permitted to transcend the status of strangers who, once their service was deemed unnecessary or their usefulness became outweighed by other, notably religious considerations, could be dispensed with, expelled or physically destroyed. The perennial role as an outcast gave the Jew the image of an almost inhuman being, an image reflected in the connotations of the name "Jew" in all European languages by the later Middle Ages.

An end seemed to be promised to this pariah status of the Jews when, in the wake of rationalism and enlightenment, Jews were extricated from their peculiar position and brought into the category of citizens. As the underlying intellectual upheaval also implied the subversion of the traditional concepts of Christianity, the theological prop supporting Jewish exclusion seemed to be broken. In a secularized state and society, so the prognosis sounded, not only would the barriers to the economic, social and political integration of the Jews be removed, but the vestiges of prejudice would also evaporate.

This prognosis, though supported by rational considerations, was only partially fulfilled. If integration depended on the disappearance of Jewish particularities in the choice of profession, in family and communal cohesion, and in special cultural traits, the prophets of total assimilation had good reason to be disappointed. The Jewish minority, even where it had been granted formal emancipation at one stroke (as in France and Holland), remained a clearly recognizable subgroup even after the elapse of three or four generations. It was still distinguished by concentration in certain fields of economic activity, marriage within itself, communal solidarity and, of course, religious nonconformism and a certain cultural proclivity.

Jewish social existence, therefore, still called for ideological concepts that could account for it. How the Jews themselves took care of this need is not our concern here. But Jewish existence continued to occupy the minds of others as well. Jews presented a problem possibly more perplexing than in the pre-emancipation period, when the accepted theological conception had explained the Jews' origin and character, justified their current apartness and social status, and prognosticated their future as an ultimate conversion to the Christian truth. When the cognitive elements of that conception had been confuted by rationalism, a novel theory was needed to account for Jewish peculiarities.

Such a theory was provided by rationalism in the same period as the undermining of theological concepts that paved the way for Jewish emancipation. The new theory based itself on the ethnological concept of history—spelled out most eloquently by Voltaire—according to which the conduct and fate of tribes and nations can best be understood through the way in which their character is reflected in their literary and other cultural products.[10] Jewish religion, and especially its literary fountainhead the Bible, remained the clue to understanding Judaism and Jewish history, though no longer in the traditional Christian vein of seeing the Jewish nation as the chosen people forsaken because of their religious failure, but rather as the documentation of Jewish character, propensities, and peculiarities. Although a desire to undermine the historical foundation of the Christian church was Voltaire's primary motive for vilifying the Bible, he was at the same time convinced that, by exposing the immoral and indeed barbaric character of biblical figures, he had found the clue to the behavior and conduct of Jews in his time as well as through the ages. That the Jewish character is bad and Jewish national traits are despicable remained unquestioned; the negative evaluation of Jews was simply taken over from the Christian tradition and the rationalist had to find an explanation for it which accorded with his philosophical outlook.

Here we apparently come across the crucial point of transition in time and essence from Christian to post-emancipation antisemitism. Jews entered the modern world under the auspices of rationalism, insofar as it predicted a state of affairs where neither national origin nor religious affiliation would bar the way of the individual in State and society. It looked as if Jews would be given a good chance to rehabilitate themselves, moving away from the marginal position they occupied and dispelling the prejudices that clung to their image and their very name.

Such rehabilitation indeed took place more or less completely in some countries. In Holland, no less than in other Christian countries, Jewish emancipation was regarded apprehensively and strong arguments, based mostly on the traditional image of the Jews, were marshalled against it in the course of the public debate that preceded it in 1796. Yet, once achieved, it has scarcely been questioned; the unfavorable image of the Jew has been mitigated at least to the extent that Jews could find their place in the social structure, while retaining a good deal of their ethnic-cultural physiognomy. In

Britain the social reservation against Jews remained stronger, yet their status as legitimate citizens became firmly established and reflections upon Jewish status and character and the role of Jews in society, though sometimes strongly voiced, never gained momentum.

In France, Austria, and Hungary, and most conspicuously in Germany, on the other hand, the initial misgivings about Jewish emancipation were almost never silenced. From the very beginning, public opinion wavered between the utopian expectation of absolute assimilation, amounting to the utter effacement of the Jewish physiognomy, and disbelief in the Jews' willingness or capacity to shed any of their real or alleged character traits. The first generation of emancipated French Jews, and the half-emancipated Jews in the other countries where emancipation was achieved only gradually, were exposed to permanent scrutiny to see whether they had lived up to expectations or had proved the skeptics' thesis that the social experiment was futile.

It is the skeptics' attitude that is of historical interest to us. It can correctly be characterized as the taking over of the traditional Christian denial of the validity of Jewish existence, denial to Jews of the right to equality and to full human dignity, an archaic, possibly irrational commitment, for which the most varied sets of ideological arguments were mustered. The Voltairian approach, which equated the critically evaluated personalities of biblical Judaism with its modern representatives, was merely one variation of these ideologies. Indeed, Voltaire's anti-Jewish sallies were only a concommitant of his anti-Christian campaign; yet this combination became a prototype for a kind of pagan antisemitism that made Judaism responsible even for the evils attributed to Christianity. At the opposite pole were combinations of Jew-hatred with any of the neo-Christian outlooks, the common denominator of which was the salvaging of Christianity in spite of a partial acceptance of historical and rationalistic criticism of its scriptures. All such reconstruction of Christianity as a religious *Weltanschauung* or system of morality took its historical predecessor, Judaism, as a foil to demonstrate the superiority of Christianity.

Thus, even where Christian dogmas and traditions were denied or ignored, the inferiority of Judaism was taken for granted. This inferiority, with all its possible consequences, could then be transferred to those who were attached to Judaism be it only through their racial origin. Diluted Christianity indeed served as one of the most fertile grounds for antisemitic theories. As it has been well said, even Christian scholars who maintained that Jesus never existed concurred that Jews crucified him.

The main scene of antisemitism deriving from a diluted Christianity was Protestant Germany, but there was no lack of examples in Catholic countries as well. Indeed Eduard Drumont, the central figure of French antisemitism, adhered to the tenets and symbols of Catholicism not out of conviction of their religious truth, but rather as a part of the French mentality—a frame of mind to which he declared Jews incapable of conforming even if they converted to Christianity.[11] Thus, overt traits of a racial conception were infused into a seemingly Christian texture—a not uncommon process of confluence evident in many other theoreticians of modern antisemitism. Any such theory gave ideological support to the tacit assumption that the Jewish character was defective and the Jewish mentality depraved, tenets implied in the theological tradition of Christianity and infused by it into the popular concepts of European culture.[12]

From Modern to Nazi Antisemitism

The primary role of modern antisemitic theories, consequently, was not to create new animosity against Jews, but to impede the recession of inherited emotions, distortions, and prejudices. Once preserved under the cover of modern ideologies, however, anti-Jewish bias and passion tended to become *more* radical than in the original theological setting.

For though Christian doctrines had implied justification for the pariah position of the Jew, they at the same time accounted for and even warranted his existence. Because Christian theology held out the hope for the individual Jew to be saved by baptism, and anticipated the ultimate conversion of the whole of Jewry at the end of days, it had theoretically preserved a place for them in the scheme of things. Their mere existence at least was ideologically vindicated. The supplanting of Christian teachings by rationalistic ideologies changed the whole perspective. The idea of Jewish regeneration had been retained, but it had shifted from the sphere of spiritual transition into the realm of social reality. Jews were expected to regenerate by adopting new social norms and patterns.

The pro-Jewish trend maintained that Jews could and would attain this objective. The antisemites, however, denied the possibility of Jewish re-generation, thus barring Jews absolutely from any prospect for the future. Once the "interim" spiritual impurity ascribed to Jews by Christians had been turned into an indelible and incurable character defect, the presence of Jews in a non-Jewish society appeared to be intolerable. Indeed, the more consistent among the antisemites, like Gyözo Istoczy in Hungary, Eduard Drumont in France and Eugen Dühring in Germany, did not limit their recommendations, like some of their less radical associates, to the restriction of Jewish rights. They spoke openly about expatriation and extermination.

Because of the similarity between the conclusions of these ideologues and the ideology of the Nazis, they are often presented as precursors and forerunners of Nazism. The Nazis themselves indeed recognized their indebtedness to antisemites of earlier generations in attempting to build up a pedigree that would ensure the historical continuity of their movement in German national history. But we may well ask about the concrete meaning of such a tracing back of a later development to earlier phenomena, by either those involved in the development or the observing historian. The connection between the two phases of development certainly did not have the character of historical causation. The Nazi ideologues surveyed the German past and, while rejecting trends at variance with their intentions, adopted others that seemed to fit them. Because of their support for Jewish emancipation Dohm, Humboldt, and Hardenberg were decried as un-German; Luther, Fichte, Dühring, and others were declared to be legitimate representatives of the German spirit. The fact that a *choice* had to be made between prototypes of conflicting attitudes in the German past clearly demonstrates that, far from the past having wholly determined the present, it was inhabitants of the present who *constructed* the connection with the past by selectively adopting those figures and trends with which they felt they had an affinity.

Moreover, between the activity of the Nazis and the utterances of those whom they chose as their spiritual mentors, or those whom the historian picks out as their forerunners, there lies the hiatus of time. This is so not only in the case of Luther, the connection between his anti-Jewish outbursts and the Nazi atrocities being a mere analogy, but even in the case of political antisemites of the late nineteenth century like Dühring, whose thinking may have had a demonstrable bearing on the emergence of Nazism. True, Dühring revealed an almost morbid hatred against Jews and a radical denial of anything remiscent of Judaism. Committed as he was to a Darwinian concept of human history, he affirmed the right of the strong and biologically healthy to destroy the weak and feeble, lest the latter undermine the strength of the former with whom it lives in parasitic symbiosis.[13] Conceptually the ideas of Dühring are indeed far-reaching in their anticipation of Nazi ideology. But who could say in 1880 that fifty years hence the ideas of the lonely philosopher would be adopted as a practical program by a political party, and that this party would acquire the apparatus of a mighty state to implement those ideas?

Between Dühring and Hitler there was not only the hiatus of fifty years of fateful history, but also the psychological difference between the man of pure thought who, being detached from the plane of action, gave free reign to his ideas and fantasies, and the man of uninhibited will who was ready to act on such ideas and fantasies. It was the relentless determination of Hitler and his gang to put the might of the State behind the ideas of the antisemitic tradition in its most radical version that produced the Holocaust. The relationship between the forerunner and the successor is established only after the event. Dühring, in short, did not turn into a forerunner of Hitler until Hitler appeared on the scene, or rather until the latter revealed through his actions what kind of a person he was. Once this happened, the designation of Dühring as Hitler's forerunner was a legitimate one, for he indeed harbored sentiments similar to Hitler's. As it turned out, Dühring's sentiments could be fatefully effective in the context of another time and through the actions of another person.

The perplexing interdependence between past and future can perhaps be illuminated by a thought experiment, portraying something that could have happened but did not. Had France produced a French Hitler, or Hungary a Hungarian one, Drumont and Istoczy would have easily assumed the role of Dühring as the precursors who foreshadowed the catastrophe. There is nothing frivolous in portraying such a contingency. France as well as Hungary had an antisemitic tradition from which such a radicalization could have emerged. Though these countries did not produce a Hitler, when the Nazi regime gained control of them the local tradition of antisemitism became clearly evident through the assistance Hitlerites received and the tacit consent of many to what they were perpetrating. To elucidate the problem even more, let us carry the mental experiment a step further. Is a Dutch Hitler imaginable? The very idea sounds absurd. Such a man would have had to create the antisemitic ideology and the anti-Jewish impulses *ex nihilo*. The absence of these elements in Holland is not only documented by the history of Jewish-gentile relations in the nineteenth century, but also by Dutch behavior toward Jews and Germans during the Nazi rule of their country.

The Present Uncertainty

The portraying of fictitious events is a legitimate methodological tool for setting reality in perspective. History, however, consists of hard facts, things that occurred and, having once occurred, became irreversible. One may be convinced that a Hitler could have arisen in France or Hungary, or for that matter that his ascendance could have been avoided in Germany. Nonetheless, what might have happened in France or Hungary does not belong to history; what happened in the wake of Hitler's rule there and anywhere else does. It is indelibly incarnate in the recorded past of all the European nations, first and foremost in the history of the German people. On an altogether different plane, the Hitler period became a part of Jewish history not to be deleted or forgotten.

It is the allotted task of historiography to record the events as completely as it can, but not to predict the future, which is anyhow a futile expectation. Those who warn us of a possible repetition of the Holocaust simply project the past into the future—a way of prognostication that has always turned out to be false. What we can derive from knowledge of the past is rather the right question to be put in the diagnosis of the present.

We could define the predicament of Jewry when it emerged from the ghetto as that of a community in need of rehabilitation, the objective of emancipation in its broad historical meaning. Antisemitism, on the other hand, represented a tremendous effort to impede the process of rehabilitation. This counterblast having reached a frightful climax in the Holocaust, the question to be asked is: in what direction are we now moving? For meanwhile the process of rehabilitation, too, has taken a momentous step forward through the auto-emancipatory act, the establishment of the Jewish State. A connection between the Holocaust, with all that it signified, and the establishment of Israel and the readiness of the majority of the Jewish people to protect it, is more than obvious. But what about the resistance to rehabilitation? Has it spent its vigor in the frightful act of the Holocaust, or is it only dormant and ready to awake on a future occasion?

To put the question differently, we may ask about the lasting effect of the Holocaust. Will it operate as cathartic agent paving the way to a final reconciliation between Jewry and its adversaries, or will it serve as a paradigm to prove that the Jew as Jew, either as an individual or as a collective, has a lower claim to existence and dignity than the members of any other human group on earth? Indications of both these tendencies could be pointed out in the history of the post-Holocaust decades. Which tendency will prevail in the long run is the fateful question hovering over our generation. The doubt implied in the question arises out of the context of past events. The answer to it is still hidden.

Notes

1.   Ernst L. Freud ed., *Sigmund Freud-Arnold Zweig, Briefwechsel* (Frankfurt am Main, 1968).

2.   Jabotinsky, *Ketavim* (Jerusalem, 1947–1959), vol. V, pp. 187–88; vol. XI, p. 238; vol. XII, p. 190; etc.

3.   How the individual's conception of himself as a freely acting personality, who often takes his decision after much hesitation and heart-searching, squares with the fact that subsequently it looks as if, given the external and internal circumstances, the decision could not have been different, is a question for philosophers to resolve. It is the perennial question of human free will, that can, as philosophers will agree, be argued and believed either way, but can never be conclusively demonstrated in the affirmative or negative.

4.   Amongst such intellectuals Jews were conspicuously represented, such as Leopold Schwarzschild, the editor of the influential *Tagebuch.*

5.   Werner Jochmann ed., *Im Kampf um die Macht: Hitlers Rede vor dem Hamburger "Nationalklub von 1919"* (Frankfurt am Main, 1960).

6.   Therein lay the basic fault of Hannah Arendt's arguments in her book *Eichmann in Jerusalem* (New York, 1963). More a philosopher than a historian, she skipped the stage of reconstruction and rushed on to pass judgments. Lacking a concrete conception of what happened, she revealed no real insight into the situation of the people whose behavior she was ready to judge. Exploiting the wisdom of hindsight, she unwittingly, perhaps, but conspicuously, assumed a stance of moral superiority to which nobody who was not tested could possibly have a claim.

7.   With no intention of irony, I may add that some years later Mannheim, having found refuge in the London School of Economics, wrote his "Zur Diagnose unserer Zeit," *Mass und Wert,* September–October 1937, pp. 100–121, which laid bare the underlying forces that led to

the Nazi takeover and its consequences. An extended version of this analysis occurs in his collection *Diagnosis of Our Time* (London, 1943).

8. J. F. Baer, *Galut* (Berlin, 1936), p. 103.

9. See Jacob Katz, *From Prejudice to Destruction/Anti-semitism, 1700–1933* (Cambridge, Mass., 1980).

10. See especially Voltaire's *Essai sur les moeurs et l'esprit des nations.*

11. Especially in his *La France juive devant l'opinion* (Paris, 1886).

12. In this respect it is worth distinguishing between two kinds of secularization. One is when a domain previously under the jurisdiction of religion becomes independent. For instance, today economists are not concerned with whether the Pope permits or forbids the payment of interest on loans. The other is when religion loses its control over a certain domain, but all its successors perpetuate something of its attitude and content, so that religion continues to operate in an implicit way. This is what happened with attitudes toward the Jews. See Hermann Lübbe, *Säkularisierung, Geschichte eines ideenpolitischen Begriffes* (Freiburg, 1965).

13. Beginning with his *Die Judenfrage als Racen-, Sitten- und Culturfrage* (Karlsruhe and Leipzig, 1881).

On Structures of Political Theology and Myth in Germany Prior to the Holocaust*†‡

Uriel Tal

From the outset of his political career, as well as in *Mein Kampf,* Hitler defined Nazism as a "political article of faith."[1] Shortly before the Nazis seized power, Hendrik de Man realized that the strength of the Nazi party resided in its ability to respond to the political and emotional needs of the masses, especially during the critical days of the Weimar Republic. One such need was "the longing for myth and utopia . . . the demand for leadership personalities"; it was the very lack of a unified view within Nazi ideology that accounted for its strength, according to de Man, for it was thus able to respond to different and even opposing social classes "by the vagueness of its ideas and the many contradictions in its mythology."[2] Toward the end of

*This study has been supported in part by the Memorial Foundation of Jewish Culture, New York.

† I am indebted to Mr. Moshe Halevy, research assistant at Tel Aviv University for his skillful assistance; also I should like to thank Mrs. Penina Howarth, Philadelphia, USA, for her helpful cooperation

‡ The following publications by Uriel Tal include additional and parallel studies on the topic of this article: *"Political Faith" of Nazism Prior to the Holocaust,* Annual Lecture of the Schreiber Chair of Contemporary Jewish History, Tel Aviv University: 1978, 53 pp., *Structures of German "Political Theology" in the Nazi Era,* Second Annual Lecture of the Schreiber Chair of Contemporary Jewish History, Tel Aviv University: 1979, 58 pp., "Civil Rights and Theological Status of German Jewry at the Beginning of the 'Third Reich' (1933/34)" in: *Chapters in the History of Jewish Society in the Middle Ages and in Modern Times,* the Jacob Katz Anniversary Volume, Hebrew University, Jerusalem: 1980, pp. 125–145 (in Hebrew).

World War II, at the very height of the Holocaust, Heinrich Himmler repeated one of the basic doctrines of his faith and proclaimed that "this Reich will now be a sacred myth."[3]

Thus, from the beginning until the end of the Nazi movement and party, the efforts of a number of Nazi leaders on various levels in the hierarchy were directed to imparting a redemptive character both to the *Führer* and to the Reich.[4] Regarding the policy of Hitler himself, it may seem as though Hitler ascribed to himself the authority and character of a savior only in the first years of the Nazi movement, during the years of struggle in the days of the Weimar Republic, but no longer did so after he assumed power. In reality he presented himself simultaneously in the role of an eschatological savior and as a modern, sober political leader during both the Weimar period and the days of the Third Reich.

The redemptive character given to *Führer* and Reich was derived from the realm of theology and then transfigured into forms of secularism and politics.[5] It is in this sense that the present work will speak of "political theology"; that is, without any connection with the use of the term *politische Theologie* in recent theological and socio-political disputes.[6] Many instances can be given of how statements by Nazi party leaders and heads of state during the Third Reich used concepts taken from theology and religious tradition to ascribe a supra-human quality to Hitler.[7] One may also cite the contemporary statement of a distinguished scholar of constitutional law, Carl Schmitt: "All pregnant concepts of modern political science are secularized theological concepts."[8] Schmitt, however, as George Schwab has correctly pointed out, is not to be regarded as one of the spiritual fathers of Nazism—despite his support of Hitler between 1933 and 1936—or as one who simply "paved the way for the *Führerstaat.*"[9]

Rational Means and Supra-Rational Goals

Nazism functioned in a political and administrative framework, and within this framework it had to employ rational criteria and instruments (although even in this rational, systematic and efficient area the Nazi regime did not completely achieve its goals, leading some scholars to call it "the authoritarian anarchy").[10] At the same time, many of its objectives were regarded by a number of its leaders as supra-rational. Those who were involved in the Holocaust directly and indirectly, whether as administrators or ideologists, as well as intellectuals, thinkers, artists, and educators who actively supported the Nazi *Weltanschauung,* attempted to build a bridge over this contradiction between rational forms of function on the one hand, and the supra-rational goals or motivations on the other.

These goals included racial purity, the supremacy of the Aryan or Nordic race in Europe, the resettlement of conquered territories by Germans of pure blood, the subjugation of the peoples of Eastern Europe, and the weakening and liquidation of the forces that opposed Nazism, namely, the so-called "powers transcending the State" *(überstaatliche Mächte).* Among the last were the churches especially the Roman Catholic, whose nature and status was a concern of Martin Bormann amongst others.[11] Christianity was criticized and even negated as a product of Judaism.[12] About this, however, there was perpetual argument; Nazi policy toward Christianity was also constantly influenced by internal and international considerations. These ambivalences between the immediate aims and ultimate goals of the Nazi regime, and especially the contradictions between Nazi declarations about Christianity and the policies actually adopted, caused great personal vexation and disciplinary problems among members of the clergy, as among laymen who might simultaneously belong to a church, the party and even the SA.[13]

The focus of all these goals, from the rise of Nazism until the end of the war, was the Jew, who served as both a symbol and a concrete embodiment. As the irrationality and impracticability of many of these goals became clearer, the antisemitic policies of the Nazis became more virulent, going from the persecution of the Jews to their expulsion and finally their annihilation.

The goals of Nazism, as understood by many of its leaders, were considered necessary for the economy yet at the same time superior to the economy;[14] they took on the character of myths in which romantic or mystical motives were intermingled with sober political considerations. The mixture of these views and policies was one of the reasons for the intense Nazi preoccupation with questions of *Weltanschauung.* A considerable number of governmental bureaus and party departments, various security agencies (principally the SS), as well as intellectuals and scientists, became increasingly active in an attempt to come to grips with questions such as: *Weltanschauung* and science, politics and belief, rationalism and inwardness, intellectualism and the racial affirmation of life.[15]

There was, in fact, a Nazi dread and even contempt of intellectuals, as illustrated by Alfred Rosenberg's difficulties in attracting them.[16] The roots of this attitude are already found in the ideology of the fathers of political antisemitism in the later nineteenth century[17] and even earlier;[18] they continue to be detectable in the Weimar period.[19] An early speech of Hitler (April 27, 1923) correspondingly set up an opposition between the "instinct and will" and the "corrosive, all-leveling intellect,"[20] while an instance of the connection between Nazi anti-intellectualism and antisemitism is the statement of Karl Beyer (1933): "Jewish intellect and German faith are here conceived radically. And when we really think radically, our attitude on the Jewish question will be one of absolute estrangement."[21] Rational criticism seems to have been one of the chief bugbears of Nazism because of the rational autonomy and freedom inherent in reasonable criticism ever since the rise of the Enlightenment in the eighteenth century, but also because of the political danger that would be incurred by a state striving for totality.

With the rise of the Third Reich, Hitler went further and formulated that

Weltanschauung in forms borrowed from religion, for he believed it to be a substitute for religion, being both pragmatic and sacral. Here also, as in so many other instances, the Jew served as a focus, as the symbol, the embodiment and the causal reason for what was called the enfeebled will of the nation in its struggle for existence.[22]

The attainment of irrational goals by rational means was clearly stated by Alfred Baeumler, who was *Leiter der Hauptstelle Wissenschaft beim Beauftragten für die Überwachung der gesamten und weltanschaulichen Schulung und Erziehung der NSDAP* under Alfred Rosenberg. A careful study of his activities in this post shows that Baeumler did not always share the anti-intellectual opinions of the Party or support its policies;[23] Armin Möhler has justly remarked that he was "a writer of the first rank . . . who, despite his great services to the Party, always remained an outsider."[24] This intellectual ambivalence also appears when one considers not merely his writings such as *Gutachten* (expert opinions) within the Nazi movement, but also his original work on Nietzsche, Bachofen, and areas related to mythology, romanticism and the critique of modern civilization.[25] Nonetheless, it is one of his *Gutachten* that clearly enunciates the attainment of the irrational through the rational:

> At stake is nothing less than to create anew in the light of consciousness a form of existence that hitherto resided in the unconscious . . . to nurture the irrational with rational means . . . proceeding from the purest impulses of the race.[26]

The immediate context in which these words were written was the question of the position of the farmers in the Third Reich and their future status, a question discussed in a critical exposition of the anthroposophic teachings. The significance of these words went much deeper, however, for they reflected one of the basic principles of Nazism, both ideologically and politically.

Contemporary Insights

A number of contemporaries, although not many, recognized that the racial antisemitism of the Nazis was the central expression of this tension between rationality and transcended rationality. As early as 1927, after the Nazis had become a legitimate political party, Felix Goldmann, writing in the influential periodical *Der Morgen,* noted that: "Racial antisemitism then is rooted in the belief in the irrational."[27] Contrary to former times, as was pointed out by writers like Arnold Zweig as well as Goldmann, it was a feature of the political rise of Nazism with its anti-rationalism, mythological thought and fanaticism, and of the fading hopes of an era of liberalism and enlightenment, that "the magic word 'feeling' closes the gates [to reason] and exempts one from the necessity to prove and defend one's point of view."[28] There were those, Goldmann went on to assert, who flee "to the dense, primeval forest of the irrational where they find a refuge," so that in the attempt to combat this new antisemitism "we would be deluding ourselves to underestimate in any way the role of instinctive feeling." The Jews, and indeed the Western world, were finding themselves face to face with a new phenomenon, a new antisemitism with "its completely illogical arguments from the standpoint of the understanding, its altogether historically distorted judgments, its generalizations entirely impossible for thinking people."[29]

The same desperate understanding is sometimes found in personal correspondence such as a letter of July 1933:

> The present-day politicized racial antisemitism is the embodiment of myth . . . nothing is discussed . . . only felt . . . nothing is pondered critically, logically or reasonably . . . only inwardly perceived, surmised . . . we are apparently the last . . . of the age of the Enlightenment.[30]

When the Nazis seized power, Zionist spokesmen made a distinction between an antisemitism that could at least be explained by historical and rational motives, ones of an economic and social or even psychological nature and which could therefore be dealt with, and the new racial, irrational antisemitism that had now become dominant. The more the masses were influenced by these instinctive dark forces and the more that the latter were exploited by those in power, the less hope there was of solving the Jewish question in Europe:

> In the sphere of the irrational are no doubt to be found the roots of the other antisemitic attitude in which a metaphysical hatred that springs from the deep recesses of the soul appears as the primary element, a hatred that seeks to express itself in logical forms. . . . The irrational is governed by an inner logic of its own.[31]

A little later, in reaction to an important speech delivered on May 17, 1933 by Alfred Baeumler, the *Jüdische Rundschau* (July 7, 1933) emphasized the Zionist solution in a tone of despair:

> There is no point in advancing arguments that are not directed to the opponent's position; for the belief in the power of blood to determine our fate is so deeply rooted in National Socialism that neither references to patriotic sentiments nor cultural ties, and least of all to cultural achievements, can shake this foundation.[32]

Baeumler had plainly stated, the journal went on to say, that "the Jews . . . will never be able to share our destiny or have any part in determining it." In contradistinction to what the Jewish community had been accustomed to thinking ever since the era of the Enlightenment and Jewish emancipation, with its belief in rationalism and political liberalism, it was now explicitly stated that national identity depended "not on a mental attitude and its expression, but on the community of blood and nature."[33]

A similar note was struck by Hans Bach, this time in reaction to a speech that Hitler had delivered in Bad Reichenhall. In it he had proclaimed that one of the basic achievements of the National Socialist revolution was to make the racial problem, which was in reality the Jewish question, a central issue in the life of the new Reich. Bach's comment was:

> The questions of leadership . . . of authority . . . all go back to the same root of blood and peoplehood. . . . In the place of a political class of leaders formed from purely economic points of view . . . there must be erected a political leadership-elite based on race and blood.[34]

Such statements raise a question that has as yet not been adequately studied, namely, that of the reciprocal relations between the political views and conceptions that were prevalent in national and nationalistic circles in Europe, particularly in Germany, and views that were common in some circles of the Zionist movement. It was sometimes argued that various national movements, Jewish and European, had a number of characteristics in common that could make for better mutual understanding: romantic yearnings, a longing to return to the distant past, the search for a common origin as an important factor of national identity. Felix Goldmann, in the article for *Der Morgen* just mentioned, had criticized this tendency: "The national-Jewish ideology . . . has succumbed to the assimilation of general nationalism."[35]

On the other hand, the *Jüdische Rundschau* in its issue of August 4, 1933, devoted a special page entitled "Stimmen des Blutes" (Voices of Blood), to the dilemma facing Zionism as a result of the radicalization of the element of "blood" in German nationalism. The article inaugurated a series of discussions on the meaning of "blood" as a symbolic, historical, or sociological factor in Jewish nationalism, in nationalism in general and in German nationalism in particular. In the following issue it was suggested by Ignaz Zollschan, the author of *Das Rassenproblem unter besonderer Berücksichtigung der theoretischen Grundlage der jüdischen Rassenfrage* (Vienna, 1911), that the study of Jewish anthropology and of the racial character of the Jewish people should be developed accordingly.[36] However, a later issue of the journal resumed the discussion of "Nationalism in Europe" with a more critical attitude to the conception of nationality based on biological factors.[37]

The special institute for the study of the Jewish question *(Institut zum Studium der Judenfrage)* under the direction of Goebbels used these anthropological discussions for its own propagandistic purposes, as can be seen in a book published by the institute: *Die Juden in Deutschland* (4th ed., Munich, 1936). The book contained quotations (p. 14) from the 1911 edition of Buber's *Drei Reden über das Judentum,* in which "blood" had appeared as a biological factor of mystical and symbolic significance in Jewish nationalism and in determining the national identity of the Jew. Similarly, it cited (p. 409) a statement of Gustav Krojanker that had appeared in the *Jüdische Rundschau* in 1932, when the author, as a Zionist, had spoken of the inability of the Jews as a social group to assimilate into the German nation: "We really did not become integrated into the alien totality of the

Volk." Goebbels's publication summed up the essence of its arguments (p. 410) with another quotation from the words of Gustav Krojanker, according to which the Zionist point of view could contribute to "a deep understanding" of the German national movement and also to "the process and world of thought of National Socialism." But, the book commented (*ibid.*), this better understanding of German nationalism and even Nazism unfortunately came too late:

> These outspoken words of Krojanker, however, are too late. . . . Judgment has taken its course. . . . He who knows the history of Judaism in the last three thousand years will not be surprised at the delusion with which this people is always hastening to its obvious destruction. It is clearly a destiny that is insolubly related to its fate as a homeless people.[38]

Political Tactics and Political Faith

In a desperate attempt to win acceptance by the Nazis, Alfred Hirschberg, writing in the official organ of the Berlin congregation, urged Jews to demonstrate that Nazi aims did not require irrational faith in the power of race:

> The task of collective German Jewry is to convince the representatives of the State that race is not the prerequisite for creating a uniform national sentiment. . . . We must demonstrate that we as Jews possess those qualities that contribute to the common communal life, those that a National Socialist state demands of its members, namely, unconditional fidelity to its principles, acknowledgement of the *Führer*-principle, the subordination of the organization to the movement.[39]

Attempts such as these, however, were doomed to failure; for in the eyes of many of the Nazi leaders it was precisely the irrationalism of racial antisemitism that bore witness to the greatness of the Nazi revolution, an irrationalism that was formulated, among others, by Houston Stewart Chamberlain and Theodor Fritsch, and made respectable by men such as Ludwig Klages and by the mystical teachings of Stefan George and his circle, despite the sharp criticism directed against them.[40] Nevertheless, both the Nazi ideologists and the men of action agreed that the two aspects described above were both indispensable to the regime, namely, sober rationality, economic development, resolute action, perseverance and blind obedience on the one hand, and a vision, a mythical and even magical faith in the Reich and in the mission of the Aryan race on the other. Walter Gross, who was in charge of the Department for Racial Matters in the Nazi party, formulated this view in one of the departmental consultations as follows:

> Racial antisemitism is the consummation, and at the same time our most sacred symbol, of the far-reaching revolution brought about by National Socialism against rigid rationalism. . . . It leads us to the rebirth of our racial life-force, which has been drained of its strength by the abstract Jewish modes of thinking.[41]

The confrontation of these two opposing forces, rationality and trans-cended rationalism, was one of the central techniques of Hitler's practical policy. As early as the middle twenties, and even more openly after his seizure of power, Hitler was careful not to grant too much legitimacy to the prevailing romantic ideas that were opposed to what was called the "artificiality" of technical culture, the "shallow utilitarian rationalism" of the time, and that urged men to return to the primitive life of natural instincts and to the secret powers hidden in the blood and in the recesses of the folk-soul. These ideas were cultivated by the revolutionary conservatives, by the members of youth movements, and by the students who had joined the Nazi movement at the end of the twenties. At the same time, Hitler was astute enough to exploit these strong popular feelings among the people who looked forward with Messianic hope to a powerful leader who would introduce radical political policies. He was well aware of the need to sustain these anti-intellectual ideas, as well as the opposing personal and economic interests of the ambitious men around him, so that a not inconsiderable part of his political leadership was based on the maxim of "divide and rule."

On the one hand, Hitler adopted a skeptical attitude, being apprehensive or even contemptuous of many of his most devoted supporters, as well as of those within religious movements who supported Nazism and who regarded Hitler as both a political and a mythical leader.[42] Hitler himself feared the consequences of negative public opinion against such movements as the so-called *Heidenchristen* resulting from criticism by the Church within Ger-many and abroad. He therefore kept aloof from fanaticisms *(Schwärmereien)* and from the very beginning of his political career adopted a pragmatic policy. He thus avoided becoming too much involved with the various factions and rivalries within Protestantism and also with the Nazi supporters, the *Deutsche Christen*[43] who, despite all their loyalty to the Nazis and to Hitler, remained within the ecclesiastical framework and continued to cling to sources of authority more exalted than the *Führer* himself.

On the other hand, Hitler well knew that the youth and the broad masses, together with part of the leadership within the movement and the party, including some of his leading aides (like Heinrich Himmler) who were to be directly responsible for the Holocaust, insisted on the mystique of ritualistic forms, symbols, and rites, and on the power of historical consciousness to vindicate and glorify the rule of Nazism and its conquests.[44] Consequently, in his public appearances (especially after the year 1925), in his "May 1st speeches," and even when he addressed himself to the purely pragmatic needs of the wealthier classes and industrialists, he explicitly emphasized *both* of these aspects of his policy.[45] On the eve of his assumption to power, when Hitler asked the members of the *Industrieklub* in Düsseldorf for their unreserved support (January 27, 1932), he stressed the beneficial effects it would have on the German economy, insisting at the same time that the indispensable basis for a flourishing economy was the unquestioned loyalty of the masses and their deep faith in the future of the German Third Reich. In his own words: "the faith of millions of people in a better future, the mystical hope of a new Germany."[46]

At first sight, what we seem to have here is nothing more than the well-known phenomenon of an ideology in the service of socio-economic interests, the will to power, and the pragmatic or cynical justification of whatever means are employed in the attainment of these ends. It is plain that the policies of Nazism and of Hitler can to a certain extent be explained in this manner.[47] Nonetheless, a closer look into the careers of the Nazi leaders, their methods, and their psychological character,[48] reveals a much more complicated historical phenomonon. Together with political opportunism, yet often contrary to its implications, we find a conscious and sometimes even self-critical faith in Nazism as a power destined to rule Europe, a belief in racial laws and the Germanization of parts of Eastern Europe, the negation of rationalism and Western culture together with its Christian sources, and the annihilation of the Jew as the symbol and embodiment of all that. The entire framework bore a mythological character that was presented as a political program to be carried out by rational, technical means. The resulting ideology was expressed by a commander in the SS as follows: "The myth is a humanization of the divine. . . . The divine, however, has now become the final and unshakeable humanization of the Reich's mystery."[49] Hitler himself, even in the early years of the struggling movement, had defined the structure of Nazism in sacral-religious terms, as one in which faith *(Glauben)* preceded understanding *(Erkennen)*.[50]

We are thus faced with a historical phenomenon that combined political tactics with political faith, the two ingredients serving both as ends and as means; latent, unconscious motives in conjunction with clear aims, an idea and an ideology to justify it. Eric Voegelin was one of the first to recognize the historical significance of this phenomenon:

> The pragmatic trait of the wordly attitude of faith necessarily leads a man of this religious type to a knowledge of the psychological technique involved in the creation of myths, their value as propaganda and their social role, but does not permit this knowledge to disturb him in his faith.[51]

A systematic and critical insight into the source materials reveals that the structure of this political religion consisted of two basic forms: the secularization and politicization of theological roots on the one hand, and the sacralization of politics and its social functioning on the other. The investigation of this double process of transformation will be the subject of the remainder of this study.

From Theology to the Realm of Politics

A typical document illustrating this first direction in the process of structural transformation is a lecture by Hanns Johst, an SS *Brigadeführer* and president of the Reich Chamber of Writers, which was delivered to a group of Nazi leaders apparently a short time after the law *Zur Sicherung der Deutschen Evangelischen Kirche* of September 24, 1935 had been published. The original manuscript, found in the collection of documents that was placed at my disposal by the late historian Eleonore Sterling, does not include the references to the biblical sources. These references are here inserted in brackets together with some additional remarks in order to indicate those sections where theology has been explicitly and systematically transformed into political mythology:

> It had once pleased God to choose the race of Israel as a people unto Himself, and with this people He made a covenant. This, however, was preparatory, a portent of the new covenant that was to be ratified in Christ. "Behold the days come, saith the Lord, that I will make a new covenant. . . .I will put my law in their inward parts, and write it in their hearts" [Jer 31:31–34; He 8:8–12] Christ instituted this new covenant in his blood [1 Cor 11:25] by calling together a people consisting of Jew and gentile and making them one, not according to the flesh but in the Spirit [Eph 2:11–22]. The time has now come to complete this process of salvation by means of a **dialectical negation.** The blood is now our blood, pure and racial; the people, once of flesh and then born of both water and Spirit [Jn 3:5–6] is now the new Chosen Race, a royal priesthood to be called to rule over the earth. . . . You who in times of Jews and Christians were called to be a holy people and yet remained chained to your Old Testament impurity . . . are now no longer the people of God [1 Pet 2:9–10] but the Race.
>
> The Reich our life [instead of "Christ our life"—Col 3:4] and our blood and soil [instead of "creation itself"] will be delivered from bondage of corruption, that is, from its impurity, its Jewishness, into the glorious liberty of the children of our *Führer* [instead of "the children of God" as Rom 8:21]. We are the redemption of the world, sent forth into the world as the light of the world and the salt of the earth [Mt 5:13–16].
>
> The uniqueness of the Aryan race is a manifestation of the *Volk*-spirit. Since this spirit is from and for the *Volk* by virtue of its elitist essence, "it cannot be given to every man to profit" [1 Cor 12:7]. These charismatic gifts are uniquely Aryan. It is enough to look at the Jew and at his history of suffering, the Jew who is the very embodiment of moral decay and physical perversion, of spiritual petrification and aesthetic degeneration, in order to realize that only the counter-Jew, the anti-Jew, is the one on whom the charisma of world leadership, of life, power and destiny has been bestowed.[52]

Several Nazi leaders, some of whom were directly responsible for the Holocaust, principally Heinrich Himmler,[53] took part in this process of converting religion into a substitute religion *(Ersatzreligion)* by means of what structural analysis defines as the "reversal of meanings." In the Third Reich, as in the entire tradition of cultural pessimism *(Kulturpessimismus)* since the middle of the nineteenth century, concepts of religion were not simply invalidated; nor were their socio-institutional functions, those co-hesive factors that served to hold the social structure together and ensure its functioning. These concepts and their functions were rather retained by the

Nazis as a legitimate part of their racial theory. They merely deprived them of their original theological content and converted them into political weapons for combatting the ideals of Western civilization, its humanism and its religion, and their prototype in Judaism.

This was aptly formulated by Christian Stoll, a Lutheran theologian from Bavaria and one of the editors of the periodical *Bekennende Kirche,* when in 1934 he stated that the Nazis were using theological concepts for the sake of appearances. But no compromise was possible, Stoll insisted, between myth, especially as interpreted by Rosenberg, and revelation; it was the task of the Confessing Church to combat this system that was creating "a secular form . . . as the racial form of German Christianity."[54]

To see how Nazi ideology created its substitute religion, it is necessary to examine many sources, especially the materials collected and produced by a number of special institutes established under the Third Reich for the study of the Jewish question.[55] For instance, the communications of an institute for investigating "the Jewish influence on German ecclesiastical life" contain important information which has so far hardly been studied. At its opening session in May 1939 its chief, Oberregierungsrat Leffler, explained that:

> An emancipation from the enslavement and servitude of the German essence by Judaism as a result of the National-Socialist revolution must now be extended to the sphere of religious life, if the Jewish influence in Germany is to be completely broken.[56]

The original sources of these institutes are still scattered in a number of archives, collections and libraries, often in files not especially connected with the institutes, so that the material is only now becoming available.[57] A systematic study of these sources, however, already shows how Nazi ideology, with all its inner contradictions, made use of structural transformations in relations between theology and politics and between myth and politics. In particular, it shows how theological concepts of God and man were now used as anthropological and political concepts. God became man, although not in the theological New Testament sense of the incarnation of the word ("And the word was made flesh, and dwelt among us" Jn 1:14), nor in accordance with Paul's understanding of the incarnation of God in Christ (in whom "dwelleth all the fullness of the Godhead bodily" Col 2:9). In the new conception God becomes man in a political sense, as a member of the Aryan race whose highest representative on earth is the *Führer.* Communication with the *Führer* became communion. The transformation took place through public mass meetings staged and celebrated as sacred cults, as well as through education, indoctrination, and the inculcation of discipline.[58] All this was designed to achieve a personal identification with the *Führer* as the Father of the State, the Son of the Race, and the Spirit of the *Volk (Volksgeist).*[59]

This change in the essential meaning of the concepts of God and man was effected, from the standpoint of cognition, by converting the relative into the absolute and, from the standpoint of theology, by transferring the Pauline conception of "putting on" the new man that is about to rise (Eph 4:24; Col 3:10) from the level of metaphysics and eschatology to that of nationality and statehood. The radical change from the metaphysical to the physical realm expressed itself in the worship of life and power, and of the sun, mountains, rivers and forests and also (as the National-Socialist *Studentenbund* proclaimed in 1934, echoing an early nineteenth-century romantic sentiment) "Germanic soil . . . the promised land, the kingdom of priests and the holy *Volk.*" Nazi mythology exalted the old pagan Adam, "the primordially human in the primordial German" *(das Urmenschliche im Ur-Germanen),* as the Son of God into whom the German man had become transformed by "a new creation" (thus Wilhelm Stapel's exegesis of Gal 6:15 and 2 Cor 5:17). The Germans would be liberated, as Emanuel Hirsch and Hans Schomerus assured them, by overcoming death and the obsolete Law of the Old Testament, and by exalting the *Bios,* the sacralized vitality that resides in the *Volk,* in its blood and in its exclusive election.[60]

Similarly, the theological concepts of sin and redemption were transferred to a legal category of administrative regulations demanding outer conformity and inner obedience. In the traditional Pauline conception man's redemption, and hence his eschatological existence, depends on his faith (Rom 3:21–24). On the other hand, the concept of sin and redemption in the Nazi regime was in the hands of the State or the party, and it was used to convert man into a loyal subject whose allegiance is assured by instilling in him a constant fear of deviating in any way from the official ideology. The Christian belief that man could be saved through faith in the forgiveness of Jesus who died for his sins "so that the body of sin might be destroyed, that henceforth we should not serve sin" (Rom 6:6) was transferred from the theological to the secular, political plane. Even the comforting assurance of the believer that his sins will be forgiven, and that he will be found worthy to receive the purifying influences of grace, could now be gained only by his complete identification with the State, the party, and the superior Aryan race.

Protestant Transfigurations

The practice of transferring and transfiguring forms of theology was to be found not only among the ideologues of Nazi racism or, in a different way, among *Deutsche Christen*, as might be expected, but also among Protestant theologians who disagreed with Nazism and opposed the doctrine of race, and even among those who took part in the struggle against the anti-church policies of the Third Reich.[61]

One of the new arguments that arose in the days of the Third Reich, especially after the *Arierparagraph* of April–May 1933 (excluding "non-Aryans" from public service) came into force,[62] sought to compare the Jewish attitude to Christian salvation with that of Nazism. In a public answer to Alfred Rosenberg's book on "the myth of the twentieth century,"[63] a distinguished theologian of the Confessing Church, Walter Künneth, declared that Rosenberg had erred, among other things, in his interpretation of Paul's view of Israel's election by maintaining that it was based on blood and race (Rom 9:4f; 11:24f), whereas the truth was actually the reverse.[64] The election and salvation promised to Israel, according to Paul, were based not on race or biology or its peculiar status as a nation, "for the old things are passed away; behold, all things are become new" (2 Cor 5:17). Neither the Jews, in their obstinacy and unbelief, nor the Nazis would acknowledge this, Künneth claimed, but both continued to define the Jews as a people, nation or race. The Jews also remained obdurate in failing to acknowledge that their election is by

> grace and not by works (Rom 11:6). . . . This Pauline view of salvation excludes every form of Judaism. . . . A misunderstanding of this deep Pauline insight is possible only if election is taken to be a special privilege based on *Volk* and race, that is, salvation and revelation are recast in political and worldly terms.[65]

Hence, Künneth continued, neither the Jews nor the Nazis acknowledged the principle of "Israel according to the Spirit."[66] Neither believed that "Jews can be saved . . . only by conversion to Christ, by being incorporated into the new community of Christ. . . . The chosen people of God are, according to Paul, no longer the racial Jews." Neither the Jews nor the Nazis, therefore, believed that it is the holy spirit of God and not blood and race that determines who is to be God's chosen people. Künneth accordingly concluded that there was "hardly a more glaring antithesis to the political-*völkisch*, secular conception of election," which Jews and Nazis held in common, than the one believed by the true Christian:

> The situation here has thus been remarkably reversed. Paul does not make election dependent upon blood and race; his thinking here is Christian and not Jewish. Myth, on the other hand, bases everything on blood and race; its thinking is not Christian but runs parallel to Judaistic conceptions.[67]

As already remarked, Künneth's arguments were a response to Rosenberg's work on "the myth of the twentieth century," whose influence has recently been investigated. The widespread notion that this book of Rosenberg had no appreciable influence, because of the awkward and incomprehensible style in which it was written or because it was taken to represent Rosenberg's personal philosophical system and not the official views of the party, is a notion that needs to be reconsidered. The book seems to have been significant on two levels. The first was the popular level of the general public,[68] though it was apparently not the book's content as such that the public found to be important, since this content was abstruse and confusing, but rather the book became significant for parts of the population as a kind of sacred manual that replaced the Bible.[69] The second level on which the book had great importance was that of the regime, where it served a vital function as the focal point of an intense public debate that was carried on in hundreds of books, periodicals, pamphlets, articles, speeches, and sermons among Protestants, Catholics and Nazis. This debate enabled the churches to give expression to their opposition to various ideological aspects of Nazism and even to the latter's official ecclesiastical policies, but without any danger to the regime. It was another step in Hitler's policy of "divide and rule."

Similar thoughts to those of Künneth were expressed by the conservative Lutheran theologian, Rudolf Homann, in a work regarded as having complemented Künneth's reply to Rosenberg's "myth of the twentieth century" and which appeared after the publication of another polemical work by Rosenberg, *An die Dunkelmänner unserer Zeit*.[70] Homann also declared that the unwillingness on the part of the Church to separate itself from its biblical Jewish source was in no way to be regarded as a recognition of Judaism. Two manifestations, two meanings are attached to the concept Israel—"Israel as a *Volksreligion* on the one hand and as a prophetic religion on the other,"[71] two opposing forces that existed side by side until "the hero came" (Gen 49:10) and with his death on the cross resolved the contradiction in favor of the prophetic religion of Israel in the Spirit. Biblical tradition makes plain this contrast between an Israel that believes in grace and an Israel that pursues only glory and fame and whose religion has degenerated into "the religion of Baal."

Every principle of prophetic revelation, from its beginnings in the Old Testament until its consummation in the New Testament, is relentlessly opposed to that which the Jews and the Nazis now had in common, according to Homann, which was "the idolatrous cult of the forces of nature and of blood." Homann then went on to point out the similarities between the rulers of Israel in biblical days, such as Ahab and Jeroboam II, and the rulers of the Third Reich. In both cases we meet with "powerful and able rulers from a political and national point of view," rulers who established

> a natural religion based on race as the religion of the *Volk* and the State. . . . The Old Testament prophecy therefore serves as a great danger signal to warn us against all attempts, ancient and modern, to establish and support a religion based on the *Volk*.[72]

Similarly Adolf Schlatter, the influential theologian, openly declared that Judaism and Nazism had joined forces in their struggle against the Church, and especially against acknowledging Jesus as the Messiah. In his criticism of enthusiasts for the Aryan and Nordic races, Schlatter stated: "What is it they want, those who know nothing higher than their racial soul. . . . Their thinking is completely Jewish."[73]

A similar thesis was expressed by Eduard Putz in a public lecture delivered during a theological training course under the auspices of the Bavarian *Volksmission*, the purpose of which was to provide suitable material for clergymen, teachers and educators in their efforts to combat anti-Christian influences in the Third Reich.[74] The Jews, Putz told his audience, had stubbornly refused to accept the glad tidings of Christian salvation and retired to a national religion based on *völkisch*-racial religiosity:

> In the fullness of time, the struggle for the religion of revelation was consummated . . . in Jesus Christ . . . but the Pharisaic religion preferred the national God, and nailed Jesus to the cross. Jesus Christ is in the deepest sense the complete overcoming of Jewish-racial religiosity . . . and also he who overcame the *völkisch* religiosity of every people.[75]

Turning to the struggle waged by the Church against attempts to make National Socialism into a kind of secular and political religion, Putz declared that the biblical story of the burning bush must today be interpreted in the light of contemporary events: "In this blaze, all idolatrous attempts to establish a human *völkisch* religion must be recognized as impossible and sinful, and to be destroyed."[76] The attack that had been launched against the racialism of the Aryans and the *Heidenchristen* was thus at the same time directed to what was called the national religion of the *Judenvolk*. Furthermore:

> If the advocates of a *völkisch* religiosity reject the biblical God and the Savior Jesus Christ as the Son of God, then they are in rebellion against God even as were the Baal priests and the Pharisees. Then they are in the deepest sense neo-Jews, Judaists.

From now on, Putz concluded, the believing Christian must fight on two fronts, on the one hand against anti-Christian Nazis like Alfred Rosenberg, and on the other against the Jew who in his obduracy still clings to his tradition, for "apostolic Christianity is the complete overcoming and dissolution of Jewish religiosity."[77]

Catholic Viewpoints

There also prevailed within the Roman Catholic Church the traditional conception of Judaism as the religion of a people that had been promised salvation and to whom the Messiah had come (Rom 9:4; 1 Pet 1:10); but the reprobate Jews in their obstinancy had not acknowledged the truth of this redemption, and to this day did not believe that the coming of the Messiah fulfilled the prophecy of the Old Testament (Rom 10:4), thus resulting in the rejection of Israel.

Variants of this conception, however, did occur. In the internal struggle that took place among Catholics, especially during the late twenties and early thirties, over the question of whether the Reich as an actual political state was to be invested with biblical and messianic significance, Judaism was regarded from two opposite points of view. There were those who pointed to Judaism as the embodiment of a purely physical and secular tradition bereft of all spiritual values and unable by its own strength to free itself from "the powers of the flesh."[78] Others, like the church historian Erik Peterson, cited Judaism as a perfect illustration of a tradition that sanctifies the State and endows with theological authority a phenomenon that, properly speaking, is political and entirely removed from the theological realm. Both sides in their criticism connected Judaism with paganism, whose historical manifestations were reflected in the present: "Only on the soil of Judaism or paganism can there exist such a thing as political theology."[79]

Among Catholic spokesmen there were also those whose style of expression resembled more closely that of the antisemitism in the Third Reich; for example, the statement of the prelate Bernhard Bartmann:

> Christianity is not a "semitic embryo" that receives its life-force from its Jewish mother. Such a vital relationship never existed; and wherever it has lived in the Jewish imagination it appears just as fragile as the dry leather skins into which the Lord declined to pour his new wine.[80]

Similarly, P. Tharsicius Paffrath attempted to separate Judaism from Christianity by employing an emphasis on race. In order to have the Old Testament retain its validity for the Christian believer, Paffrath severed it from its source in the Jewish people:

> The religion of the Old Testament did not arise from and in accordance with the (Israelite—Jewish) natural, peculiar character. . . . It is something altogether unique, fundamentally independent of the peculiar racial character of Israel.[81]

There were prominent Catholic theologians, historians and educators who outspokenly deplored the racial doctrines and the efforts to create a kind of "neo-German religion" *(neugermanische Religion)*. At the same time, attempts were made to point out the reciprocal relations between the ancient German religion, with its primitive forms of worship, and historical Christianity in Germany.[82]

From the Political to the Sacred

The second direction, parallel and complimentary to the first, in the development of structures of political theology and myth, elevated the concept "political" to a supreme place in the Nazi scale of values and investing it with a sacral character. Already in the writings of some of the fathers of racial antisemitism in the last third of the nineteenth century, and especially after World War I, we find a nearly sacral character conferred upon concepts such as "political biology," "political anthropology," "political education," and thereafter also upon "the political man," "the political soldier," "political faith," "political psychology," or "political myth."[83]

One of the most instructive documents for the understanding of this development is a talk entitled "Die Autorität des Politischen" given by Max Wundt to the students in Berlin at the end of 1932 on the eve of the seizure of power by the Nazis. The following excerpt deserves special attention not only because of the importance of Max Wundt as an ideologist who had great influence on the younger generation, particularly in the days just before the

establishment of the Third Reich, but also because this speech was subsequently used in the preparation of antisemitic propaganda literature:

> The political purpose of the racial idea is to give the *völkisch* experience of
> unity the power of a political faith. . . . Only when we think and believe
> politically will the total absoluteness of the Reich idea . . . the all-embracing
> Germanization of the *Volk*-soul, become possible. The realm of the political is
> now sacred above all else, bringing us grace and liberation. . . . From now on,
> gentlemen, once and for all no more Jewish-Bolshevist Marxism, no levelling-
> down liberalism, no abstract conceptual rationalism; we must stamp out the
> Judaizing of the German soul . . . at stake from now on is the primary
> experience of the German that is sacred to us all, our recognition of the rebirth
> of Germany, the unshakeable faith in the liberating mission of the *Führer*. . . .
> The politically conscious National Socialist will free himself from paralyzing
> parliamentarianism by his total emotional commitment to the will of the
> *Führer*, of blood, of race. . . . To act politically means to sever the Reich once
> and for all from the corrosive processes of Jewish Social Democracy. . . . The
> Reich must be completely cleansed of party rule, of the rule of the unworthy
> rabble and of Jewish egalitarian tendencies. . . . Our political faith will bring to
> completion the secularization process of Revelation. . . . The equivalence God-
> man is from now on our new confession.[84]

The Example of Huber

Admittedly, this principle of the absolute elevation of the political plane took
different and even contradictory forms. There was, for instance, controversy
over what should be the authorized bearer of political power: the State (or the
Reich) or National Socialism as a movement or party. On the one hand, we
find a group of jurists and philosophers of law who insisted on preserving the
sovereignty of the State above the movement and the party, a view that was
advocated by Carl Schmitt, Ernst Forsthoff, Ernst Rudolf Huber, and in a
more extreme form by Wilhelm Merk.[85] These scholars were in favor of
curbing the power of the Nazi party and conserving the constitutional
character of the State and Reich. On the other hand, there were those who
fought for the supremacy of the Nazi movement and party above the State as
the embodiment of the highest political principle, among them some of the
leading Nazi figures, besides Hitler himself, including Heinrich Himmler,
Robert Ley, and intellectuals among the SS such as Prof. Reinhard Hohn. (It
seems that until the outbreak of World War II the party was unsuccessful in
obtaining all its demands; even during the war it did not succeed in becoming
the sole bearer of what was called "the totality of the political." However,
the controversy was largely limited to the question of identifying the bearer
and representative of the principle of the supremacy of the political plane.
The supremacy of the political, as an absolute value endowed with a sacral
authority, was itself hardly disputed.

This was particularly evident in the relatively moderate group of jurists
such as Huber. One of the principal aims of the political and constitutional

thought of Huber in the days of the Third Reich was to safeguard the supremacy of the State and within it "the principle of *völkish* wholeness." This was derived from the Hegelian idea of *organische Totalität* and then converted to the principle of *politische Totalität.*[86] Accordingly, Huber argued, the people will achieve full freedom only if it succeeds in integrating itself as a "unity and wholeness" (*Einheit* and *Ganzheit*), as an uncircumscribed and all-embracing *politisches Volk.*[87] This political totality or even this principle of a *totaler Staat* may become oppressive as, for example, dictatorships or totalitarian regimes if they remain only restricted to "the exclusivity and unconditionality of an external claim to power."[88] In order that this totality of the State should not acquire an oppressive character, Huber concluded, it is necessary for the people to reach a degree of maturity where "the principle of *volkisch* wholeness precludes the separation of the individual and the vital areas of his economic-cultural life from the *Volk.*"[89]

The political plane here acquires a supreme and absolute value, the purpose of which is to avoid a conflict of interests between the individual and the State or between the State and society, and thus to prevent the State from assuming an oppressive character. The political plane must therefore include

> all of life's processes and phenomena. . . . The principle of wholeness [*Ganzheit*] is not content with outer conformity and accommodation but demands . . . voluntary adjustment. There is no neutrality of individual areas of life over against the political *Volk.*[90]

This process of elevating the State above all areas of life without turning it into a coercive and dictatorial power is possible only if all the citizens belong to the same race. The race, however, is only the "natural basis of the *Volk,*"[91] and in order to rise from the level of a *natürliches Volk* to that of a *politisches Volk*[92] the people must reach a stage of self-consciousness and have a sense of its historical mission.[93] The power that enables a people to reach this stage, and hence its full freedom, is the *Führer.* The legal and moral basis of this leadership (*Führerrecht*)[94] becomes plain, according to Huber, when we compare it with parliamentarian democracy and liberalism. Parliamentarianism enslaves man to society by maintaining "a conflict of social interests" which makes it impossible for the will of the people to achieve full expression and complete freedom. The *Führerreich,* on the other hand, is a regime "in which the collective will of a genuine political unity is proclaimed. . . . The *Führer* is the bearer of the people's will."[95] Hence, "the *Führer* is not a 'deputy' who carries out the will of a superior. . . . His will reflects the will of the people. He transforms the pure feeling of the *Volk* into a conscious will."[96]

In contradistinction to Rousseau's principle of *volonté générale* which, according to Huber, did not completely liberate individuals or the various groups in society from their private interests, the *Führer* embodied the *Volkswille,* which is distinct from and superior to the sum of individual wills. Here again we have the concept of political totality as a free and not a coercive framework. Since the will of the *Führer* is itself rooted in a race that is common to all the citizens of the Reich, it is not the arbitrary will of a dictator and is not expressed in "external, compulsory regulations, but . . . in *Führungs*-regulations . . . in a freely undertaken accommodation."[97]

Huber's idea with respect to *politische Totalität* represented, as we have already noted, the views of the more moderate group among the jurists. On the other hand party leaders, such as Heinrich Himmler and through him the leadership of the SS, endowed Nazism as a party with sacral and mythical authority which then, through the party, also extended to the Reich, as indeed has been pointed out lately by scholars such as Josef Ackermann.

Sacralization through Language

One of the means used by the regime to endow the political plane with a sacral character was language.[98] The employment of language as one of the means to politicize life and endow the political realm with supreme sacral character was both spontaneous and at the same time a well-prepared, calculated plan. Sigrid Frind, in his important study of Nazi language, correctly observed that for language to be converted into an instrument in the service of the Nazi regime

> concepts that could be made into symbols, together with their ideational content and rich associations, were taken chiefly from three areas: 1) from the religious realm; 2) from the speech areas of *völkisch* circles with their archaic modes of expression and their Pan-Germanism; 3) from biological turns of speech, culminating in the "blood and soil" myth.[99]

By relying on these associative sources, Nazism developed a mechanism designed to increase the power of language to penetrate both the deep, sensitive layers of man's emotional life and his conscious and intellectual activities. The aim was defined by the psychologist Walter Poppelreuther as follows: "Language should give free, conscious expression to the primordial impulses of the German man, who is bound to a racial stock, and to the sound, vital impulses of his natural life, precisely by overcoming the counter-race."[100]

The material for instruction and propaganda put out by SS headquarters and by other governmental and party offices, through public speeches by some of the Nazi leaders and in parts of the press and literature, reveal a number of typical forms of articulation. At first sight it would seem as though the coarse and aggressive nature, rude insults, abusive language, and calculated campaigns of slander—as they constantly appeared in antisemitic newspapers, principally in the *Stürmer*—were the only characteristic traits of Nazi language. Certainly, in the speeches of Hitler, his ministers, and party leaders coarse language was not infrequently heard. But in the process of sacralizing the political sphere other patterns of speech emerged that were probably of no less influence.

An example is the constant repetition of the same words, concepts and motives, often in a tautological form and aiming at emotional intensification. Or again the use of terms selected because of their high affective charge, and calculated to recall to the mind of the listener or reader memories from the days of early childhood, or from the historical and even primordial past of the nation as reflected in its legends and folklore. Motives borrowed from nature or even from daily social life were converted into tangible, living entities in a form similar to animism: the light of the sun cheers us and the darkness frightens us; fire hail, hunger, lightning are menacing, but the spring with its sprouting buds and its blossoms awakens feelings of joy and confidence; the oak tree is a tangible symbol of stability and power, while the fields and plains serve as a spacious background for the *Volk*-soul. Recurring stereotypes intermingled with obscure, allusive generalities calculated to embellish otherwise commonplace ideas and to reduce the listener or reader to an emotional state which would hinder clear, logical thinking; pronunciamientos and dogmatic statements, abounding in superlatives, generated a temper of unreasoning loyalty.[101]

In this linguistic structure many words acquired new meanings. A word like *fanatisch* was used in a positive sense; *rücksichtslos* ("ruthless") and *brutal* appeared as terms of praise; *unverrückbar* ("immovable"), *restlos* ("to the last drop"), *radikal* ("extremist") indicated ideal qualities to be admired and emulated. Concepts taken from the sphere of theology, such as "salvation" *(Heil)*, "kingdom" *(Reich)*, " confessing," "resurrection," "faith" and "mission," underwent a process of politicization. Thus, the general framework of articulation became pervaded by meanings of a mythological nature. Myth was converted into reality, and reality took on a mythological form. The distant, primordial past was transformed into experience, into reality. Qualities attributed to legendary figures, idols, giants, or beasts were held up as models for the younger generation. Structures of magical function acquired political significance; intuition was put in the place of truth, while empirical, objective truths became illusions; contingencies and uncertainties took on a character of permanency, while the constant, invariable and permanent became relative, subject to the political authority of the *Führer* and his will.

As with most of the goals of Nazism, the attempt to mythologize and politicize language was only partially realized; it achieved considerable success, however, in respect of the Jewish question. Already on the very eve of the Nazi seizure of power at the end of 1932, the periodical *Der Jüdische Student* published a brilliant analysis of these semantic changes as they later manifested themselves in the thought and policies of the Third Reich. The analysis was written by Ephraim Szmulewicz of Breslau and entitled "Zum geistigen Gesicht des Nationalsozialismus." In it he pointed out that the most insidious result of Nazism was that it succeeded in substituting hatred for thought and thus encouraged the growth of irrationalism and anti-intellectualism:

The National-Socialist intellectuals knew ... how to devise a strictly anti-democratic *"Kulturtheorie"* according to which all democratic-liberal ideas appear alien and hostile to the arche-language [*Ursprache*] of Germanism. . . . The new intellectual order that is to be erected on the ruins of the democratic system of reason bears the closest relation to the elementary emotions of the life of the soul. The political emotions . . . are concentrated in the desire for power and in the feeling of hostility to everything outside its own group. . . . The National Socialist movement considers itself to be the apex of the pyramid of creation. . . . Political thinking is mythicized so as to remove it from the control of reason. . . . To be different means here, in mythological terms, to be inferior . . . the Jews [are] the natural point of attack . . . [the point at issue is the] "struggle of annihilation against Judah". . . . Above all else the *Führer*-elite is surrounded by a radiant divine aureole. . . . The political—its rule is boundless.[102]

A Closing Note

In 1943, at the height of the Holocaust, Alfred Baeumler pointed out that in Rosenberg's teachings, from the early days of Nazism, the Jew represented not only Judaism, but the forces against which Nazism was struggling—the legacy of monotheism, Western civilization, critical rationalism, and humanism. Therefore, Judaism is

... the demon who became visible and who is the primordial enemy of the German ... hence this is a fight for life or death, it is either us or him [the Jew] ... The nation demands the whole person and thus reaches into the religious domain.[103]

Indeed, on this point there seems to have been full agreement between the various conflicting trends within the Nazi leadership, including Hitler and Himmler. Moreover, this interpretation of anti-Judaism was perhaps one of the few consistencies in Nazi ideology and policy, from the early twenties up to 1945.

In this study we have seen that the Jewish question and its solution reflected a fundamental feature of Nazism, one that was structured in terms of a transfiguration of reversing meanings. Forms of thought, feeling, expression, and behavior rooted in historical tradition were now transferred to the political domain. Theology and religion were secularized while politics and the state became consecrated and served as a substitute religion.

This process of reversing meanings assumed the form of a political myth which then was to become a main instrument in the creation of a new image of man, a new society, and a new Reich. Political myth was intended to contribute to the crystalization of a new consensus, new conventions, and new taboos. It had to motivate the Aryan to internalize civic commitment and political discipline, so that in the future no police enforcement would be necessary. Political myth was meant to establish a system of values that would penetrate into the realm of personal and family life, into culture, education, art and economy. In the individual's daily life, political myth had to give relief from tension and fear, from uncertainty and frustration, from feelings of existential alienation and civic powerlessness. Political myth had to encourage a historical consciousness, an awareness of mission to what was called the political cosmos. Political myth was meant to bring home to the Aryan citizen that the Reich was founded on law and order and on normative standards, all of which were embodied in the *Führer*.

The framework in which political myth had to function was that of the race. The race, chosen and mighty, was to give the individual a sense of belonging to a higher, a transcended entity. This entity was above rational criticism or scientific verification. Race was seen, like the family, as an entity into which the person is born, to which he belongs by virtue of nature or fate. A man is one of the limbs of the organism called race, connected to it by blood and descent as a son, father, or mother might be. This blood pact between man and race, constitutionally affirmed in 1933, served as a cornerstone in Nazi anti-Jewish policy. The pact was considered stronger than any social contract or rational consensus; it was a "given" that could not be changed, and thus was expected to bring about stability, security, confidence and truth. He who did not belong to it was its enemy, since he was an alien body endangering the wholeness of the organo-sacralized organism.

In this political myth the word—spoken and written—became a source of inspiration and of hope. Less than its verbal content, it was the sacral form of the word which imposed normative authority. The word expressed by the *Führer*, or in his name, was interpreted in many forms on various hierarchical levels in the movement, Party and Reich: in the forms of law, decree, order or command, in those of reproof, chastisement, judgment or verdict, in those of anger or praise, of assessing reality or of revealing a vision. By virtue of the word, objective cognition was replaced with subjective faith and intuition, which then acquired the validity of objective truth.

In reality Nazism accomplished but few of its goals. But in one area, that of the Jewish question, political myth achieved its purpose to the full. Here the regime met the least opposition from those who in other matters were hardly in accord with Nazism be it intellectuals, the churches, or public opinion in the Reich or abroad. The Jew served as the focal point around which Nazism turned and on which the structural process of value-transformation and reversal of meanings took place. Among the values and meanings that were transformed, the symbol itself was turned into substance; consequently, the negation of Judaism had to be transformed into the annihilation of the Jew, this time not spiritually but rather physically, not symbolically but in substance.

Notes

List of Abbreviations:

BA   — Bundesarchiv, Koblenz, Germany.

CL   — Cisler Library, Wayne State University, Detroit (now in New York), USA.

IZG — Institut für Zeitgeschichte Archives (HW—"Hauptamt Wissenschaft"), Munich, Germany.

YIVO — YIVO Archives, New York, USA.

NFI—source materials pertaining to the "Institut zur Erforschung der Judenfrage" (HW—"Hauptamt Wissenschaft"), at YIVO archives.

1.   A. Hitler, *Mein Kampf* (76th ed., Munich, 1933), pp. 423–24. Compare *Völkischer Beobachter,* March 3, 1929: "Das nationalsozialistische Manifest zum Reichsparteitag," pp. 1ff.

2.   Quoted by Detlev Grieswelle, *Propaganda der Friedlosigkeit—Eine Studie zu Hitlers Rhetorik 1920–1933* (Stuttgart, 1972; henceforth cited: *Grieswelle*), pp. 59–60.

3.   *BA,* NS 19/14. The speech was given on September 24, 1943. See also Joseph Ackermann, *Heinrich Himmler als Ideologe* (Göttingen, 1970; henceforth cited: *Ackermann*), p. 171; compare our essay on Ackermann's work in *Freiburger Rundbrief* 27 (1975), 14–26.

4.   An instructive example of this may be found in the writings of Georg Schott, a student of Houston Stewart Chamberlain and one of Hitler's friends in the early days of the movement until he fell out of favor. See his *Das Volksbuch von Hitler* (1st ed., Munich, 1924; 4th ed. by the semi-official publishing house, Verlag Frz. Eher, Nachf., Munich, 1934); *Von Gott und der Welt* (Stuttgart, 1937), esp. pp. 219–22, also "Das 5. Buch Mosis in seiner kulturpolitischen Bedeutung," pp. 85ff. G. Schott in his speech at a mass convention of the Nazi movement as early as June 23, 1923 explained "in which respects the National Socialists do not wish to be Christians . . . if we understand Christianity as the continuation and consummation of a spiritual tendency . . . and this tendency can be no other than Judaism. . . . It is in great measure owing to this dogma . . . that misfortune has overtaken us today." See Jakob Nötges S. J., *Nationalsozialismus und Katholizismus* (Cologne, 1931), pp. 81–82.

5.   Among the first scientific studies of this subject was Fritz Nova, *The National Socialist Führerprinzip and its Background in German Thought* (Philadelphia, 1943), chs. 1–3, 5, 6.

6.   In recent years the term *politische Theologie* has been introduced into current socio-religious thought. See, for example, the periodical *Politische Theologie—Evangelische Kommentare* (1967 ff.).

7.   One of the many examples is the speech of Robert Ley of February 10, 1937 published in *Der Schulungsbrief der NSDAP,* no. 4, 1937. On the political use, or rather abuse, of terms rooted in religious tradition during the Nazi era, see Hans Buchheim, *Glaubenskrise im Dritten Reich—Drei Kapitel Nationalsozialistischer Religionspolitik* (Stuttgart, 1953; henceforth cited: *Glaubenskrise*), pp. 9–39. Also *Grieswelle,* esp. chs. 4, 10; see also: Gunda Schneider-Flume, *Die politische Theologie Emanuel Hirschs 1918–1933* (European University Papers, Series 13, vol. 5; Frankfurt, 1971).

8. Carl Schmitt, *Politische Theologie: Vier Kapitel zur Lehre von der Souveränität* (2nd ed., Munich, 1934), p. 49.

9. See Schwab's introduction to his translation of: Carl Schmitt, *The Concept of the Political* (New Brunswick, N.J., 1976), p. 14; also Schwab's major work on Schmitt: *The Challenge of the Exception—An Introduction to the Political Ideas of Carl Schmitt between 1921 and 1936* (Berlin, 1970; henceforth cited: *Schwab*), especially part II, pp. 101–50. A significant example of a Nazi critique of Schmitt's political thought and teachings, tracing them to his Catholic background, is the official and confidential publication: "Der Staatsrechtslehrer Prof. Dr. Carl Schmitt" in *M.W.L.*, January 8, 1937, pp. 1–15; *BA*, NSD 16/38. On the renewed controversy between Carl Schmitt and Erik Peterson, see Carl Schmitt, *Politische Theologie II—Die Legende von der Erledigung jeder politischen Theologie* (Berlin, 1970; henceforth cited: *Schmitt II*), parts II and III.

10. See Reinhard Bollmus, *Das Amt Rosenberg und seine Gegner, zum Machtkampf im nationalsozialistischen Herrschaftssystem* (Stuttgart, 1970), p. 10; also Peter Diehl-Thiele, *Partei und Staat im Dritten Reich—Untersuchungen zum Verhältnis von NSDAP und allgemeiner innerer Staatsverwaltung 1933–1945* (Munich, 1969; henceforth cited: *Diehl-Thiele*). The latter author describes Hitler's regime as a "permanent improvisation within the framework of a fundamental tactic of divide and rule," see p. IX and esp. pp. 184ff. Regarding the improvisations in Nazi policy toward the Jews, see Uwe Dietrich Adam, *Judenpolitik im Dritten Reich* (Tübinger Schriften zur Sozial- und Zeitgeschichte, no. 1; Düsseldorf, 1972).

11. See the discussion of the memorandum from Martin Bormann to the gauleiter in January 1941 ("National Socialism and Christianity are irreconcilable . . .") in J. S. Conway, *The Nazi Persecution of the Churches 1933–45* (London, 1968), p. 363; also Conway's lecture (manuscript) on "The Politics of Persecution—Antisemitism and Anti-Christianity in Nazi Ideology and Practice." In an earlier signed circular letter dated February 2, 1939, Bormann had called attention to the "Erlass des Reichs- und Preussischen Ministers des Innern vom 16 November 1936," according to which Christianity was not to be described as *gottgläubig,* for this term had now been applied to those sects that believed in the doctrine of race and had left the organized Church; see H. Hermelink, *Kirche im Kampf* (Tübingen, 1950), pp. 503–4. On the sects concerned, see *Die 'Dritte Konfession?' Materialsammlung über die nordischreligiösen Bewegungen* (Berlin, 1934), pp. 13–47 (a publication of the Evangelischer Presseverband für Deutschland).

12. One of the many popular expressions of this attitude was a song sung by the SA (see *CL*, C-13):

> Wir sind noch nicht zu Ende
> Solange noch die Pfaffen
> Von Beichtstuhl und Altar
> Die deutschen Seelen raffen
>
> . . .
>
> Solang die Christenlehre
> Der Norden Art verrät
> Solang wird deutsche Ehre
> Vom Judenthum geschmäht.

On some aspects of the historical background, see Uriel Tal, *Religious and Anti-Religious Roots of Modern Antisemitism* (Leo Baeck Memorial Lecture, no. 14; New York, 1971).

13. See correspondence and newspaper clippings in *BA*, NS. 8/99, NS. 8/500. Also *CL*, C-3 (3, 4, 5, 6, 7).

14. See Fritz Klein, "Zur Vorbereitung der faschistischen Diktatur durch die deutsche Grossbourgeoisie (1929–1932)," in Gotthard Jasper ed., *Von Weimar zu Hitler* (Cologne and Berlin, 1968), pp. 124–55. Also Reinhard Vogelsang, *Der Freundenkreis Himmler* (Göttingen, 1972) and Anson Rabinbach, *Beauty of Labor: The Aesthetics of Production in the Third Reich* (manuscript).

15. For some of the more systematic deliberations on behalf of the department *Hauptsamt Wissenschaft,* see *I.Z.G., H.W., Vortragsmanuskripte* of the year 1938, *Wissenschaft und Weltanschauung,* MA/607, pp. 55627–49; 55748-55; *Arbeitsethos und Wissenschaft, ibid.,* pp. 55650–58; *Weltanschauung, Wissenschaft und Wirtschaftswissenschaft, ibid.,* pp. 55659–71 (55672–734). For the term *Weltanschauung* see *I.Z.G., H.W.,* MA/255, pp. 201ff.: "Bedeutung des Wortes 'Weltanschauung' und Probleme seiner Übersetzung" (November 14, 1938).

16. See his correspondence with H. Kretschmer in February 1933, *BA,* NS. 8/22.

17. See Uriel Tal, *Christians and Jews in Germany—Religion, Politics and Ideology in the Second Reich 1870–1914* (Ithaca and London, 1975; henceforth cited: *U. Tal*), pp. 121ff., 223ff.

18. See Uriel Tal, "Young German Intellectuals on Romanticism and Judaism—Spiritual Turbulence in the Early 19th Century," in S. Lieberman and Arthur Hyman eds., *Salo W. Baron Jubilee Volume* (New York and Jerusalem, 1974), vol. II, pp. 919–38.

19. See Jenö Kurucz, *Struktur und Funktion der Intelligenz während der Weimarer Republik* (Sozialforschung und Sozialordnung, vol. 3; Cologne, 1967), pp. 146ff. Also, Kurt Sontheimer, *Antidemokratisches Denken in der Weimarer Republik—Die Politischen Ideen des Deutschen Nationalismus zwischen 1918 und 1933* (Munich, 1962; henceforth cited: *Sontheimer*), part I, "Politischer Irrationalismus," and ch. 8b, "Der Ruf nach dem Führer."

20. Werner Siebarth, *Hitlers Wollen—nach Kernsätzen aus seinen Schriften und Reden* (3rd ed., Munich, 1936), p. 132.

21. Karl Beyer, *Jüdischer Intellekt und deutscher Glaube* (Leipzig, 1933), p. VIII and Wilhelm Stapel, "Die deutsche Intelligenz heute," *Deutsches Volkstum,* June 1935, pp. 1–8. We also found instructive source materials from the Third Reich reviling the Jew as a symbol of intellectualism in the legacies of families who remained in Central Europe until the end of the war. These documents are now being prepared for publication, *SC.* B/4, 8, 9, 10.

22. "Die Geisteswende—Kulturverfall und seelische Wiedergeburt," *Mitteilungen des Kampfbundes für deutsche Kultur,* vol. 1, no. 1 (January 1929), pp. 1ff., 13ff. Alfred Rosenberg, "Weltanschauung und Wissenschaft," Reichstagung der Reichsstelle zur Förderung des deutschen Schrifttums, November 21, 1937, *BA,* 16/37 (pp. 11–13). See also the following important bibliographical lists: *Schriften zur seelischweltanschaulichen Ausrüstung,* Amt Weltanschauliche Information in der Dienststelle Alfred Rosenberg, *BA,* NSD 16/42. Eberhard Jäckel, *Hitlers Weltanschauung—A Blueprint for Power* (Middletown, Connecticut, 1972), chs. 1, 3, 5.

23. For example, his evaluation of the work of the historian Robert Holtzmann, *BA,* NS. 8/264 (pp. 86ff.).

24. Armin Möhler, *Die konservative Revolution in Deutschland 1918–1932: Grundriss ihrer Weltanschauung* (Stuttgart, 1950), p. 16.

25. Rich source material reflecting Baeumler's intellectual ambivalence is contained in the collection *Hauptamt Wissenschaft* of the YIVO Archives, New York.

26. *I.Z.M., H.W.,* MA/610, pp. 57711–23. Alfred Baeumler, *Gutachten* of December 13, 1940. See also Baeumler's lectures on "Philosophy of History" delivered in strict

confidence *(streng vertraulich)* as recorded by U. Goede, 1939, in YIVO 236, MK-3. The lectures are important for the study of both the ideational development of Nazism and the complex nature of Baeumler's intellectual activity within the party machinery.

27. Felix Goldmann, "Das Irrationale im Antisemitismus," *Der Morgen,* August 1927 (henceforth: *Goldmann*), p. 314.

28. *Goldmann,* p. 314.

29. *Goldmann,* p. 315.

30. This and similar expressions by several Jewish intellectuals, teachers and lawyers are preserved in the collection *S.C.* E/2, 8, 14, 15, 16, 22 (compare notes 17, 21 above). For the broader background of Jewish reactions prior to 1933, see Werner E. Mosse, "Der Niedergang der Weimarer Republik und die Juden," in W. E. Mosse and A. Paucker eds., *Entscheidungsjahr 1932–Zur Judenfrage in der Endphase der Weimarer Republik* (Tübingen, 1965), pp. 3–49; and Arnold Paucker, "Der jüdische Abwehrkampf," *ibid.,* pp. 405–99.

31. Ernst Hoffmann, "Der Antisemitismus und die Lösung der Judenfrage," *Jüdische Rundschau,* April 4, 1933; (henceforth cited: *Hoffmann*), p. 135. For the far-reaching political impact of the "irrational futuristic visions of the Third Reich," see K. D. Bracher, *Die Auflösung der Weimarer Republik—Eine Studie zum Problem des Machtverfalls in der Demokratie* (Institut für politische Wissenschaft, vol. 4; Stuttgart, 1957), p. 107.

32. *Jüdische Rundschau,* July 7, 1933, p. 305.

33. *Ibid.*

34. Hans Bach, "Die neue Ordnung," *Der Morgen,* August 1933, pp. 161–66.

35. *Goldmann,* p. 313.

36. *Jüdische Rundschau,* August 11, 1933, p. 413.

37. *Jüdische Rundschau,* May 29, 1934, p. 5.

38. For the polemics among the Jews regarding Krojanker's booklet *Zum Problem des neudeutschen Nationalismus,* see the reply by David Schlossberg in *Der jüdische Student,* vol. 29, no. 5 (June 1932), pp. 134–38, and Krojanker's remarks, "Die unangenehme Parallele," *ibid.,* pp. 138–39. The historical study of this complex problem is only of recent origin. See George L. Mosse, "The Influence of the Volkish Idea on German Jewry," in *Germans and Jews* (New York, 1971), pp. 77–115; also Kurt Loewenstein, "Die innerjüdische Reaktion auf die Krise der deutschen Demokratie," in *Entscheidungsjahr 1932,* pp. 349–403, (esp. pp. 378ff.). For an excellent background study see Jehuda Reinharz, *Fatherland or Promised Land—Dilemma of the German Jew, 1893–1914* (Ann Arbor, 1975), pp. 171ff. Abraham Margaliot, in "The Political Reaction of German-Jewish Organizations and Institutions to the Anti-Jewish Policy of the National Socialists 1932–1935 (in Hebrew, Ph.D. dissertation, Jerusalem, 1971), has made a major contribution to a more balanced and objective understanding of the controversy among political Zionists regarding a possible mutual understanding between the Nazi regime and German Jewry (see ch. 4 and p. 250). For further studies on the complex mythic forms of M. Buber's Zionism cf. Uriel Tal, "Mythos und Solidarität im zionistischen Denken und Wirken von Martin Buber"; *Toleranz Heute,* Institut Kirche und Judentum, No. 9, ed. by Peter von der Osten-Sacken, Berlin: 1979, pp. 116–126.

39. Alfred Hirschberg, "Wege zu Deutschtum und Judentum," *Gemeindeblatt der Jüdischen Gemeinde zu Berlin,* vol. 23, no. 4 (April 1933), p. 167.

40. *I.Z.G.,* M.A., 116/4; 116/5; 116/7. Compare *Guide to Captured German Documents,* no. 2, p. 65.

41. *S.C.* A/6a. Compare Walter Gross, "Aufgabe und Anspruch der nationalsozial-

istischen Rassengesetzgebung," Sonderheft, *N. S. Monatshefte,* series 64, 1935, 16 pp. At the same time, however, Walter Gross also warned against excessive irrationalism and anti-intellectualism; see his *Rassenpolitische Erziehung* (Schriften der deutschen Hochschule für Politik, no. 6; Paul Meier-Bonneckenstein ed., Berlin, 1934), pp. 1–31.

42. For original sources that are both critical and informative, see Carl Schweitzer, *Das religiöse Deutschland der Gegenwart,* vol. I (Berlin, 1928), pp. 32, 123–238, 273–95, 324–36, 365–95; P. Erhard Schlund OFM, *Modernes Gottesglauben—Das Suchen der Gegenwart nach Gott und Religion* (Regensburg, 1939), sections 5, 10, 12, 13, 14, 19, 24–41, 42–46. Among the original sources that were sympathetic to the ideas of a German pseudo-religion but, nevertheless, informative, see Hermann Mandel, *Deutsch-Theologie,* part III (Leipzig, 1934), pp. 1–109, and *Heerschau deutschen Glaubens und deutscher Frömmigkeit—Eine Führung durch das deutsch-religiöse Schrifttum* (Leipzig, 1933), pp. 3–21.

43. Kurt Meier, *Die Deutschen Christen—Ein Bild einer Bewegung im Kirchenkampf des Dritten Reiches* (Halle, 1964). Compare Carsten Nicolaisen, "Die Stellung der Deutschen Christen zum Alten Testament," in *Zur Geschichte des Kirchenkampfes* (Gesammelte Aufsätze), vol. II, pp. 197–200.

44. George L. Mosse, *The Nationalization of the Masses—Political Symbolism and Mass Movements* (New York, 1975; henceforth cited: *Nationalization*), chs. 1, 3, 6, 8, 9. See also *Ackermann,* parts II, III, IV, V.

45. Margarete Wedleff, "Zum Stil in Hitlers Maireden," *Muttersprache* 80 (1970), 109–27. For further documentation, see Werner Jochmann ed., *Im Kampf um die Macht: Hitlers Rede vor dem Hamburger "Nationalklub von 1919"* (Veröffentlichungen der Forschungsstelle für die Geschichte des N.S. in Hamburg, vol. 1; Frankurt am Main, 1960) and H. Phelps, "Hitler als Parteiredner im Jahre 1920," *Vierteljahrshefte für Zeitgeschichte* 11 (1963), pp. 274ff.

46. M. Domarus ed., *Hitler—Reden und Proklamationen 1932–1945,* vol. I (Munich, 1965), p. 71.

47. For the methodology of the interrelationship of socio-political motivations and ideology, see Hans Albert and Ernst Topitsch, *Werturteilstreit* (Darmstadt, 1971), part I, pp. 3–63, and part II, pp. 67–309. Also Janet Wolf, *Hermeneutic Philosophy* (London, 1975), chs. 2, 3, and 7.

48. See Saul Friedländer, *L'Antisémitisme nazi: Histoire d'une psychose collective* (Paris, 1971); also his *History and Psychoanalysis* (New York, 1978), esp. ch. 3. Among the Nazi leaders, Heinrich Himmler is of the utmost importance for our study; hence, in addition to the works already mentioned, the following are essential: Werner T. Angress and Bradley F. Smith, "Diaries of Heinrich Himmler's Early Years," *Journal of Modern History* 31 (1959), 206–24; Bradley F. Smith, *Heinrich Himmler—A Nazi in the Making 1900–1926* (Stanford, 1971); Peter Loewenberg, "The Unsuccessful Adolescence of Heinrich Himmler," *American Historical Review* 76 (1971), 612–41. For the psycho-historical background of Hitler, see R.G.L. Waite, "A Hitler's Guilt Feelings," *Journal of Interdisciplinary History* 1 (1971), 229–49, and Dietrich Orlow's critique on Walter C. Langer's *The Mind of Hitler* (London, 1973) in "The Significance of Time and Space in Psychohistory," *Journal of Interdisciplinary History* 5 (1974), 131–38.

49. *S. C.* A/24, d, e, f. For the fear of these circles on the part of the rulers of the Third Reich, and the regime's ideological surveillance of these circles, see *I.Z.G., H.W.,* MA-116/4; MA-116/5.

50. *Grieswelle,* p. 55.

51. Eric Voegelin, *Die politischen Religionen* (Stockholm, 1939), p. 54.

52. Uriel Tal, "Forms of Pseudo-Religion in the German 'Kulturbereich' Prior to the Holocaust," in *Immanuel* 3 (1973–1974), 68–73 (on p. 71, instead of "Alfred Baeumler" read "Hanns Johst"). Siegfrid Casper, editor of *Hanns Johst spricht zu Dir* (Berlin, 1942), wrote in his introduction: "Through his [Johst's] writings . . . the creaturely-organic 'things'—*Lebensraum,* homeland, *Volk,* fatherland, mother-tongue, political life-form—have become life's basis for us all, an evident and *weltanschauulich* possession" (pp. 7–8). Also by Hanns Johst: *Erkenntnis und Bekenntnis* (Georg von Kommerstadt ed., Munich, 1940) and *Ich Glaube— Bekenntnisse* (Munich, 1943). For the ideological background, as officially approved and proclaimed by the SS leadership, see the review of Friedrich Murawski's *Die politische Kirche und ihre biblischen "Urkunden"* (Leipzig, 1938), in *SS Leitheft,* vol. 4, no. 3, pp. 55–56. Compare *Nationalization,* p. 124.

53. See above, notes 3 and 48.

54. Christian Stoll, *Mythus? Offenbarung!* (Schriftenreihe Bekennende Kirche, no. 14; Munich, 1934), p. 18. Baumgärtner, *Weltanschauungskampf im Dritten Reich,* Mainz: 1977, pp. 206 ff.

55. The first important pioneering study of these institutes and allied scientific organizations was : Max Weinreich, *Hitler's Professors—The Part of Scholarship in Germany's Crime against the Jewish People* (New York, 1946), chs. 8, 9, 11 and 12. This subject is also treated in the comprehensive work by Helmut Heiber, *Walter Frank und sein "Reichsinstitut für Geschichte des neuen Deutschlands"* (Quellen und Darstellungen zur Zeitgeschichte, vol. 13; Stuttgart, 1966). Some of these institutes, especially the work of Wilhelm Grau, have been discussed in the above researches of U. D. Adam and R. Bollmus. For a systematic study of the series of publications (1936–1943) of the institute entitled *Forschungsabteilung für Judenfrage des neuen Deutschlands,* see Fritz Werner, "Das Judentumsbild der Spätjudentumsforschung im Dritten Reich—dargestellt anhand der 'Forschungen zur Judenfrage' Bände I-VIII," *Kairos* 8 (1971), 161–94.

56. *Verbandsmitteilungen—Institut zur Erforschung des jüdischen Einflusses auf das deutsche kirchliche Leben* (Eisenach), no. 1 (December 1939); see also no. 4 (September 1941).

57. Much information is to be found in the source collection, *Institut zur Erforschung der Judenfrage, N.F.*-1 (Rolls 1-13) at YIVO, New York, and in the *Himmler Files MK 193* (Reels 16-20), also at YIVO (copies from the Library of Congress Photoduplication Service, Washington, D.C.). Additional source material is located in the Rosenberg Archives at the *Budesarchiv-Koblenz,* such as BA NS. 8/237 (Archiv Forschungen zu Gunsten des Amts Juden- und Freimaurerfrage), NS. 8/239; NS. 8/264; N.S.D. 16/41. A comprehensive and annotated collection of these sources is now in preparation, and further on will be quoted under the heading I.J.Q. ("Institutes on the Jewish Question").

58. *Nationalization,* pp. 100ff.; pp. 207ff. See also Klaus Vondung, *Magie und Manipulation—Ideologischer Kult und politische Religion des National-Sozialismus* (Göttingen, 1971), pp. 159ff.

59. In addition to the obviously reversed meaning of the idea of the trinity, Nazism used the terms *Volksgeist* or *Volksseele* in various ways. This has its origins in the teachings of the earlier nationalists and antisemites; compare *U. Tal,* pp. 54–55, 105, 182. Hubert Kiesewetter traces these concepts to Hegelian influences in his *Von Hegel zu Hitler—Eine Analyse der Hegelschen Machtstaatsideologie und der politischen Wirkungsgeschichte des Rechtshegelianismus* (Hamburg, 1974), pp. 233ff. A different approach has been suggested by Wolfgang Tilgner in *Volksnomostheologie und Schöpfungsglaube—Ein Beitrag zur Geschichte des*

Kirchenkampfes (Arbeiten zur Geschichte des Kirchenkampfes, vol. 16; Göttingen, 1966; henceforth cited: *Volksnomostheologie*). Tilgner, referring to Wilhelm Stapel, points out that "the various *völkisch*, national and religious thoughts constitute . . . the basis for the coming *völkisch*-national movement in Germany, which will then have justified its pseudo-religious intentions also theologically in a 'theology of nationalism' " (p. 58).

60. *Volksnomostheologie,* pp. 88–157.

61. Joseph Ganger ed., *Gotthard Briefe—Chronik der Kirchenwirren* (3 vols., Elberfeld, 1934, 1935, 1936; henceforth cited: *Chronik*). Compare John S. Conway, "Der deutsche Kirchenkampf—Tendenzen und Probleme seiner Erforschung and Hand neuerer Literatur," *Vierteljahrshefte für Zeitgeschichte* 17 (1969), 423–49.

62. *Chronik,* vol. I, pp. 102, 104, 105; vol. II, p. 286; *Jüdische Rundschau,* November 7, 1933, p. 771 and November 17, 1933, p. 814; "Das Judenproblem und die Kirche," in Walter Künneth and Helmet Schreiner eds., *Die Nation vor Gott—Zur Botschaft der Kirche im Dritten Reich* (Berlin, 1934), pp. 117ff.; Kurt D. Schmidt ed., *Die Bekenntnisse und grundsätzlichen Äusserungen zur Kirchenfrage des Jahres 1933* (Göttingen, 1934), pp. 96, 134, 178, 189f. The exclusion of Christians of Jewish background from the Church aroused quite some opposition among theologians, such as at the Marburg theological faculty (September 20, 1933), at Erlangen (September 25, 1933), also among a group of twenty-two New Testament scholars who declared that the racist policy contradicted the faith in baptism, for indeed ". . . by one spirit are we all baptized into one body, whether we be Jews or gentiles . . ." (1 Cor 12:13; see also 7:20). In fact the struggle against the introduction of the *Arierparagraph* into the Church was one of the major concerns of the members and supporters of the *Pfarrernotbund* out of which later the Confessing Church emerged. See Carsten Nicolaisen ed., *Dokumente zur Kirchenpolitik des Dritten Reiches,* vol. I (Munich, 1971), pp. 35, 130–31. Also Heinrich Hermelink ed., *Kirche im Kampf—Dokumente* (Tübingen and Stuttgart, 1950), pp. 48–53.

63. Full title: *Protestantische Rompilger: Der Verrat an Luther und der Mythus des 20. Jahrhunderts* (5th ed., Munich, 1937).

64. W. Künneth, "Revolution in der Kirche?" in *Junge Kirche—Mitteilungsblatt der Jungreformatorischen Bewegung* (Berlin), June 21, 1933, pp. 1–3. See Carsten Nicolaisen ed., *Dokumente zur Kirchenpolitik des Dritten Reiches,* vol. II (Munich, 1975), p. 31.

65. Walther Künneth, *Antwort auf den Mythus* (3rd ed., Berlin, 1935), p. 90.

66. *Ibid.*

67. *Ibid.;* also Künneth's booklet *Evangelische Wahrheit—Ein Wort zu Alfred Rosenberg's Schrift "Protestantische Rompilger"* (Berlin, 1937).

68. Its reaction is attested by personal letters from different classes preserved in the Archiv Rosenberg, *BA*, NS. 8/14, NS. 8/99, NS. 8/163.

69. From a methodological point of view, we are here confronted with one of the most interesting questions in historiography, namely, the various ways in which a text can be influential although its importance resides not in its content but in its form, in the circumstances under which it is published, and the needs or even longings to which it gives expression.

70. Rudolf Homann, *Der Mythus und das Evangelium* (4th ed., Witten, 1936), p. 161. Homann, like other conservative Lutherans, believed that Nazism and racial doctrines, insofar as they were in opposition to conservative tradition, should be regarded as products of liberalism and the anti-religious attitudes of rationalism. Here also the Jews were blamed for the *Zersetzung*—the demoralization and disintegration.

71. *Ibid.,* p. 162.

72. *Ibid.*

73. Adolf Schlatter, *Wird der Jude über uns siegen?—Ein Wort für die Weihnachtzeit* (Freizeit-Blätter, no. 8; Delbert im Rheinland, 1935), p. 15.

74. Eduard Putz, *Völkische Religiösität und christlicher Gottesglaube* (Schriftenreihe Bekennende Kirch, no. 4; Th. Ellwein and Chr. Stoll eds., Munich, 1933), pp. 46ff.

75. *Ibid.*

76. *Ibid.*

77. *Ibid.*, p. 47. Another important example of rejecting the justification for Judaism's existence after the rise of Christianity, as seen from a critical point of view with respect to racial antisemitism, is Hugo Flemming, *Gottesvolk oder Satansvolk—Luther, die Juden und wir* (Schwerin in Mecklenburg, 1929), pp. 7–27, 48–55, 61–65, 79–81. For opposite points of view, such as that of Dietrich Bonhoeffer, see Jorgen Glenthoj, "Dietrich Bonhoeffers Kampf gegen den Arierparagraphen," *Kirche in der Zeit* 20 (1965), 439–44; also Ruth Zerner, "Dietrich Bonhoeffer and Jews: Thoughts and Actions, 1933–1945," *Jewish Social Studies* 37 (1975), 235–50.

78. See Hermann Greive, *Theologie und Ideologie; Katholizismus und Judentum in Deutschland und Österreich 1918–1935* (Heidelberg, 1969), p. 163 and the entire section "Von 1930–1935," pp. 127ff. Section 7, "Die Judenfrage im Widerstand gegen den Nationalsozialismus," pp. 190ff., is a significant contribution toward a more balanced understanding of the political and spiritual turmoil of those days. See also the analysis of the attitudes of Albert Mirgeler, Robert Grosche and others in Klaus Breuning, *Die Vision des Reiches— Deutscher Katholizismus zwischen Demokratie und Diktatur (1929–1934)* (Munich, 1969; henceforth cited: *Breuning*).

79. *Bruening,* p. 271; compare *Schmitt II,* pp. 94ff.

80. Bernhard Bartmann, *Der Glaubensgegensatz zwischen Judentum und Christentum* (Paderborn, 1938), pp. 77–78. The parable of the wine alludes to Mark 2:22.

81. P. Tharsicius Paffrath OFM, "Die alttestamentliche Religion und die semitischen Religionen," in P. Erhard Schulund OFM ed., *Theologische Gegenwartsfragen* (Regensburg, 1940), pp. 107ff.

82. For example, Dr. Hugo Dausend OFM, *Germanische Frömmigkeit in der kirchlichen Liturgie* (Wiesbaden, 1936), pp. 23–57, 90–127, 139–43, 145–50. See also D. Dr. Anton Stonner, *Die deutsche Volksseele im christlichdeutschen Volksgebrauch* (Munich, 1935), pp. 3–8, 165–213. One of the many examples critical of this subjection to the spirit of the times is Dr. Heinrich Helnigs's booklet *Die altgermanische Religion und der Christ unserer Zeit* (Schriftenreihe Der Christ in der Zeit, no. 11; Paderborn, 1935). Despite the outspoken words against the revival of the ancient Germanic myth as a kind of a new national religion *(neugermanische Religionsbildung),* there was no longer any reason for the continued existence of Judaism, and the only thing left for it was to adopt Christianity: "Only one people, the Jewish, can see religion" fulfilled in Christianity. Otherwise, if "the religion of the Old Testament" continues to reject Christianity as its own fulfillment, it cannot but forfeit the rationale for its very existence, pp. 31–32.

83. Ludwig Woltmann, *Politische Anthropologie* (1903), in *Woltmann's Werke,* vol. I (Leipzig, 1936); see also *Politisch-anthropologische Revue* (Leipzig), 1902–1922. Also Ernst Krieck, *Völkisch-politische Anthropologie* (Leipzig, 1936), part I, "Die Wirklichkeit," section 2, "Das völkischpolitische Bild vom Menschen," pp. 42–102. For Krieck's National-Socialist teachings and his controversial position in the party (especially in later years), see *I.Z.G.,*

H.W., MA/611, pp. 59052–139, 59144–201, 59286–404, 59469–543; regarding his polemics with Hartnacke, see pp. 59163–424. For an example of popularized teaching materials, see Dr. Hanjörg Männel, *Politische Fibel—Richtlinien für die politische-weltanschauliche Schulung* (5th ed., Leipzig, 1935).

84. *I.J.Q.*, section 4. For Max Wundt's impact on political thought and ideology prior to the seizure of power by the Nazis, see *Sontheimer*, pp. 36, 273. Compare Max Wundt, *Deutsche Weltanschauung—Grundzüge völkischen Denkens* (Munich, 1926), pp. 10ff., 28ff., 160ff.

85. *Diehl-Thiele*, pp. 5, 13; *Schwab*, part II, pp. 101ff.

86. Ernst Rudolf Huber, *Verfassungsrecht des Grossdeutschen Reiches* (2nd ed., published by the semi-official publishing house Hanseatische Verlags-Anstalt, Hamburg, 1939; henceforth cited: *Huber*), pp. 157–59. An example criticizing the concept "totalitarian" on the part of the Catholics is Dr. Desiderius Breitenstein OFM, *Geist oder Blut?* (Schriftenreihe Der Christ in der Zeit, no. 4; Paderborn, 1934), pp. 16ff.

87. *Huber*, p. 158.

88. *Ibid.*, p. 159.

89. *Ibid.*

90. *Ibid.* Heinrich Himmler, in his speech at the "Tagung der Dozentenbundsakademien" in Munich, June 1939, criticized the use of the term *Gleichschaltung*: "as the head of the German police he knows, more than anyone else, that a revolution is victorious only when it has succeeded in overcoming the enemy spiritually and in justifying its own power spiritually." *I.Z.G.*, MA/607, p. 55109 (the *Report* includes a remark according to which the leaders of the Nazi Faculty Members Associations wore SS uniforms).

91. *Huber*, p. 153.

92. *Ibid.*, p. 154.

93. *Ibid.*, p. 159. The idea of the historical mission of the Third Reich fulfilled an essential function in Nazi ideology and policy, on both popular and scholarly levels. See *SS. Leitheft*, June 3, 1937, p. 4. Also, Prof. Karl Reichard Ganzer, *Reich und Reichsfeinde* (2nd ed., Hamburg, 1943), vol. II, pp. 8–80.

94. *Huber*, p. 194.

95. *Ibid.*

96. *Ibid.*, p. 196.

97. *Ibid.*, pp. 198–99. Compare the indispensable contributions on this point, as well as to the entire phenomenon of the eschatological structure of politics, by Jacob L. Talmon, *The Origins of Totalitarian Democracy* (London, 1952) and *Political Messianism—The Romantic Phase* (London, 1960).

98. Werner Betz, "The National-Socialist Vocabulary," in *The Third Reich* (London, 1955), pp. 784–96; Victor Klemperer, *Die unbewältigte Sprache—Aus dem Notizbuch eines Philologen "LTI"* (3rd ed., Darmstadt, 1966); Cornelia Berning, *Vom "Abstammungsnachweis" zum Zuchtwart: Vokabular des National-Sozialismus* (intr. by Werner Betz, Berlin, 1964). Paradoxically, concepts such as "antisemitism" and "Third Reich" were so deeply rooted in the thought and speech patterns of the people that the instructions of the authorities not to use them, for reasons of foreign policy, were of no avail. On August 22, 1935 the Ministry of Propaganda asked the public to refrain from using the term *antisemitisch* out of consideration for the Arabs, and to use instead such terms as: *Judenfeindschaft, Judengegnerschaft, Antijudaismus.*

Similarly, in July 1939 and again in May 1943 the authorities attempted unsuccessfully to substitute for *Drittes Reich* the term *Deutsches Reich* and *Grossdeutsches Reich*; compare the first part of the study of R. Glunk mentioned below (note 100), pp. 64–69.

99.   Sigrid Frind, "Die Sprache als Propagandainstrument des National-sozialismus," *Muttersprache* 76 (1966), pp. 129ff.

100.   *I.J.Q.*, section 8. Compare Rolf Glunk, "Erfolg und Misserfolg der nationalso-zialistischen Sprachlenkung," *Zeitschrift für deutsche Sprache* 22 (1966), 56–73 and 146–54; 24 (1968), 72–90 and 112–19.

101.   As with the ideology and policies of the Nazis in general, so also in the development of the language different and even contradictory tendencies are to be found. An interesting example of this is provided by the instructions of the SS leadership to refrain from using those very expressions that it itself had cultivated and to observe "simplicity and clarity in the German written language . . . an unclear and bombastic style of writing is not in keeping with National-Socialist sensibilities. . . . Adjectives that are already superlatives . . . cannot be intensified further"; see *SS—Leitheft,* vol. 3 (1937), pp. 48–49. On the lack of unity in National-Socialist ideology, see Martin Broszat, "Die völkische Ideologie und der Nationalsozialismus," *Deutsche Rundschau* 84 (1958), 53–68.

102.   Ephraim Szmulewicz, "Zum geistigen Gesicht des Nationalsozialismus," in *Der Jüdische Student,* December 1932, pp. 308–11.

103.   Alfred Baeumler, *Alfred Rosenberg und der Mythus des 20 Jahrhunderts* (Munich, 1943), pp. 19ff.

II. WITNESSES AND CASE STUDIES

A First Attempt to Tell

ABBA KOVNER

At Number 6 Strashun Street

There, on the spot where our last barricade stood, in the yard of a ruin, among heaps of filth and scraps of paper, amid the rubble left behind by the life of the past—I actually found the manifesto.

After I had extracted the torn piece of paper from the pile and taken in the first faded, gray letters, I started trembling all over:

"Jews! Rise up in arms!"

"The German and Lithuanian butchers have reached the gates of the Ghetto. They are going to murder us. Very soon they will lead us out through the gates in groups. So hundreds were led out on Yom Kippur. So they led people out in the days of the white, yellow, and pink *Scheine.*[1] So they led out our brothers and sisters, fathers and mothers, our children. So tens of thousands were led out to death.

"But we will not go!

"We will not be led like sheep to the slaughter!

"Jews! Rise up in arms!

"Do not believe in misleading promises of the murderers. Do not believe the traitors. For those led out through the gates of the Ghetto there is only one destination: Ponar.[2] And Ponar means death.

"Jews! We have nothing to lose! Death will overtake us in any case. For who can still believe that he will live, when the murderer is systematically taking our lives? The hands of the hangmen will overtake everyone. Concealment and cowardice will not save our lives.

"Only by rising up in arms can we save our lives and our honor.

"Brothers! Better die fighting in the Ghetto than be led like sheep to Ponar!

"Let it be known: within the walls of the Ghetto there is an organized Jewish force which will rise up with weapon in hand.

"Join in the armed uprising!

"Don't hide away in the bunkers, for in the end you will fall like mice into the murderers' hands. Jews! Go out into the streets in your masses!

"If you have no arms, take hold of a pick, and if you have no pick, take hold of an iron bar, a stick.

"For our parents, for our murdered children, for Ponar, strike at the murderers—in every street, in every yard, in every room in the Ghetto and outside the Ghetto. Beat the dogs!

"Jews! We have nothing to lose. We can save our lives only by killing the murderers.

"Long live freedom! Long live the armed uprising! Death to the murderers!"

The manifesto was signed: "Command of the Jewish United Partisans Organization, FPO (Fareinikte Partizaner Organizatzie), in the Vilna Ghetto, September 1, 1943."

I read it and here, as before, my eyes are suffused with blood. Not because it is mine, the order is mine, the voice is my voice; and not because I've just this moment pulled my own life out of the ashes, but because I feel burning within me the petrified pain of those days, that dumb, strangled grief that no one, probably, can completely grasp or understand any more.

One by one the houses are being emptied of their Jews; soon all the streets will be empty. Old men with their bundles; weeping women (so many women). And we crouch on the roofs and walls embracing the cold iron of our weapons, a prayer on our lips that the butchers should come closer—so that all of us together can discharge, as we fire, our pain, our burning hate, our souls.

September 1943. I look up now at the strange whitewashed walls of the ruin rising amid the blackness of the surrounding desolation, and I feel that the sorrow still hangs over the walls.

Like torn and tattered cobwebs, the agony of the last fighters hovers over them.

In Number 16 Rudnitzka Street

At the gate of the Ghetto no trace of them remains. You face a wide open street. A street corner. At the bend of the street stands a tall church, the Church of All Saints, a dream for thousands of Jews. How many despairing glances clung to the spires of that church as the last hope of those nights. How much sweat and blood the Jews spilled during those days of the final liquidation to dig an underground tunnel that would lead them into the church on the other side. And when they did not succeed, they were taken out and shot. No doubt they forgot at the time that to the Church of All Saints, to the other world, it was only one step. Today you just put out your hand and touch it.

A man who has never been on the inside cannot understand it; his senses are incapable of grasping the meaning of the gate.

Again they stand beside it.

"Maurer is at the gate!" Maurer was the man in charge of Jewish affairs on behalf of the regional authorities, the master of the Ghetto. He would drive headlong in his cab into the Ghetto, jump off at the gate, and immediately start work. He would arrest a Jew who had smuggled potatoes into the Ghetto, notice that one point of his Yellow Star was not properly sewn on his back, crack the Jew's scull with his pistol and send him dripping with blood to the Lukishki jail. After such a visit, the Jewish representatives would collect valuable objects and send them to Maurer to redeem the Jews who had been thrown into jail. If Maurer's heart was softened, the Jews were saved, but sometimes Maurer appeared again next day at the gate, and this time a hundred Jews were dragged to their deaths. The Jews tried to get the better of him and fixed a secret electric bell push at the gates of the Ghetto to announce his coming. The Jew on guard would press the hidden button. One ring meant: Maurer is here; two—the Gestapo.

And when Weiss, the black-clad murderer from Ponar, would stroll into the Ghetto with his sadistic look, the Jewish guard would ring three times and everyone would disappear from the streets. Old people and children hid in their holes, for they were "illegal."

Only a dark dread hung over the streets.

Every morning the Jews would go to the window when they got up and, through the bedewed panes, look toward the gate: Life?

Twenty thousand Jews ran barefoot through the night to that gate: Death?

At the narrow wicket in the broad wooden door, thousands queued up day by day to be spat on. Brutal stormtroopers would examine them with their hands, compel women to lift up their dresses, feel all their limbs, order them to strip naked, look for potatoes between the women's breasts.

April 2, 1943 was a beautiful spring day. At the gate, a wonderful sight: a group of children was leaving the Ghetto for an excursion, with teachers and a doctor at their head.

A few days before, Maurer had expressed surprise as to why the children of the Jews sat pent up all the time between the walls of the Ghetto. Let the children have an excursion, Maurer pleaded. So the children went out into the forest, saw the trees, broke off branches.

Three days later, four thousand Jews from the provinces were brought to Vilna in eighty-three railway trucks and shot in Ponar. The Jews of Mikhailishok and Swienczany were told to appear with their bundles, as they were to be sent to Kovno. Documents, tickets were issued. Signs were fixed on the carriages: "To Kovno." The Polish drivers were given a route list for the Swienczany—Vilna—Kovno Line. At the Vilna station the train stopped. From the Vilna Ghetto 340 people laden with bundles were marched out and pushed into the train that was leaving in the evening for Kovno. In the morning, the Ghetto was horrorstruck. The eighty-three carriages, with the four thousand Jews in them, had been deceitfully sent off to Ponar. The carriages were surrounded by a cordon of troops and the people driven into the pits. Hundreds of Jews broke out of the sealed carriages and scattered in every direction. The soldiers opened fire on the fugitives, and afterwards six hundred were found shot on the fields and the railway track. At seven in the evening, fifteen fugitives from Ponar were back in the Ghetto; by nine in the evening there were over thirty. Among those saved was a child of two, who had run straight on without a stop. A Christian woman, who lived not far from that valley of slaughter, heard someone weeping all night. At dawn she went out of her cottage and followed the sound. There, among the heaps of corpses, she found the child.

At three o'clock, as if nothing had happened, Maurer went into his office. As if nothing had happened, he asked the dejected, half-dead Jewish representative "Was gibts Neues?"—that is: What's new today? And when Gens replied that no doubt he was aware of the news, Maurer replied calmly and coldly: "The Vilna Ghetto is safe . . ." Later, he paid a visit to the baths and went inside. There were women there at the time, but Maurer was not embarrassed. He looked at them and said: "The Jewish women are too fat." Next morning, a train of wagons came through the gate loaded with foodstuffs and clothes—the property of those that were killed. Maurer had sent gifts to the hungry Jews.

Suddenly a dreadful weeping burst from the synagogue. The pious had declared a special Yom Kippur and the rabbi recited psalms. The same evening, Baruch Goldstein smuggled a machine gun through the gate. Herschel Gordon hid the magazine in his trousers. This machine gun was not the first.

The Proclamation

It happened at the beginning of 1942. In those days, before the rivers of blood from the slaughter of the "yellowslip holders"[3] had dried up, a heroic enterprise was taking shape in one of the seven dreadful lanes: the first organization of partisans in the ghetto was established.

Although the first living witnesses had already reached the Ghetto from Ponar, people refused to believe that all those who had been dragged there had really been murdered. They pointed to "documents" brought to the headquarters of the Jewish militia which proved conclusively that there was a third ghetto; mothers assured each other that somewhere their children were alive. "My son is still young and very strong, he'll surely hold out." And the old woman of sixty-three from Number 3 Strashun Street used to swear to her neighbor: "As surely as I'll see my husband safe and sound again." Her husband, aged about seventy, had been dragged off on Yom Kippur.

Since the Jews of Vilna knew of no similar instance of appalling mass slaughter, and since they had heard of the existence of the Warsaw Ghetto with its half million Jews for the past three years, and the Bialystok Ghetto with its 40,000 Jews, those in Vilna, encompassed by a ring of fire, thought they were doomed to a life of suffering, trouble, and persecution. But that the slaughter of millions was a possibility—no; that was something the darkest imagination could not conceive, something no one wanted to believe.

And then there broke out, into the midst of the despair in the Ghetto, from some yet unknown corner, the cry: "We will not be led like sheep to the slaughter!"

This was a phrase of the proclamation we issued in the Vilna Ghetto at the beginning of January 1942, the first call to revolt.

Last survivors of families and towns, despairing and indifferent to suffering, the Jewish youth suddenly saw a goal, a sacred goal that lit up their almost extinct lives. A Promethean fire burst forth over the lanes of the Ghetto, befouled with ashes and blood: the call to revolt.

The house in Number 2 Strashun Street is in ruins. But I feel I can clearly see the dark hall of the soup kitchen in the yard of that house, those 150 pairs of tear-filled eyes in the darkness, when I read out the proclamation dated January 1, 1942:

"Jewish youth!

"Do not trust those who are trying to deceive you. Out of the 80,000 Jews in the 'Jerusalem of Lithuania'[4] only twenty thousand are left. Before our eyes they took away our parents, our brothers and sisters. Where are the hundreds of men who were conscripted for labor? Where are the naked women and the children who were taken away from us on that dreadful night? Where are the Jews who were deported on Yom Kippur?

"And where are our brethren in the second Ghetto?

"Of those taken out through the gates of the Ghetto not a single one has returned. All the roads of the Gestapo lead to Ponar. And Ponar means death.

"You who hesitate, cast aside all illusions. Your children, your wives and husbands are no longer alive.

"Ponar is not a concentration camp. They have all been shot there. Hitler plans to destroy all the Jews of Europe, and the Jews of Lithuania have been chosen as the first in line.

"We will not be led like sheep to the slaughter!

"True, we are weak and defenseless, but the only reply to the murderer is revolt!

"Brothers! Better to fall as free fighters than to live by the mercy of the murderers.

"Arise! Arise with your last breath!"

When I closed, the air was filled with the stifling silence of a graveyard. Then suddenly, a cry broke out, and a song:

"Never will we stretch out our necks to the slaughter . . ."

This was the birth of what was to become a fighting organization. On the night of January 23, representatives of various groups met after preliminary talks. The meeting took place at Number 6 Rudnitzka Street, in Glasman's little room with six people present: Haina Borevsky, Joseph Glasman, Itzik Wittenberg, Meir Frucht, Abba Kovner, and Nisel Reznik. We decided to organize an armed uprising in case of a general destruction of the Ghetto, to conduct sabotage activities in military installations, to contact the partisan movement, and to help in every way we could to strike at the enemy. Our organization would be called FPO (Fareinikte Partizaner Organizatzie). Members of the command would be: Itzik Wittenberg, Joseph Glasman, and Abba Kovner (Reznik and Chwoinik were co-opted). The first problem was how to get arms. This question gave us no rest from the moment the idea of organized resistance appeared. I remember that in a meeting with one of my friends, later to be one of the closest, he said to me: "You are proposing to establish a fighting organization. The idea is basically correct. But there's no such thing as a fighting unit without weapons. And it's out of the question to get arms in the Ghetto. Where can we get the first pistol?"

Next morning, however, we tenderly fondled the sanctified steel of our first pistol.

Arms

Baruch Goldstein was popular with all the workers of Borbishok. That day he came to work with his hand bandaged and his friends kept asking him how he was. During working hours, they had an unusual opportunity: a number of Christians came up to the fence with flour for sale. The Jewish workers hastily prepared sacks specially sewn for the purpose, bought the flour, and one by one stole off to pack it and hide it until the end of the day's work. Baruch was unable to buy flour because he was busy that day with an important task. In the German captain's anteroom there was a pistol lying on a high shelf. Baruch seized an opportunity, went in quickly, stuffed the pistol into his pocket, shut himself up in the lavatory, took off the bandage and put it on again over the pistol that was now tied to his hand. The sentry at the gate of Borbishok looked suspiciously at the eighty workers leaving the place, but the stormtroopers at the Ghetto gate searched the workers with greater thoroughness and brutality. As one of them touched Baruch he groaned pitifully and gripped his swollen hand.

In Number 7 Rudnitzka Street, the Jews breathed more freely and took out the eighty bags of flour from their trousers, but Baruch Goldstein brought into the Ghetto the first pistol.

No one who has never been in the Ghetto will understand the mass fear of collective responsibility. The week before, an entire camp of Jewish forced laborers had been sent to the Lukishki jail because one man had stolen salt from a truck.

This was a notice that was posted in the streets in those days, signed by "The Representative of the Ghetto":

"On Friday, April 30 this year, the workers Aaron Shulkin and his wife, of 11/21 Strashun Street, who work in the brick factory in Ponar Street, went out into the countryside to buy food. They were arrested and shot without enquiry.

"I hereby warn, that, in accordance with SD orders, no Jew must be found outside the area of the city. Any Jew found outside the city without a permit from the German authorities is liable to the death penalty."

Where was it possible to get weapons? How could they be brought into the Ghetto? Were we entitled to endanger the lives of the last few thousands of Jews in case arms were discovered in our possession? With full consciousness of the responsibility we were undertaking, our reply was: Yes. We can. We must.

It was decided to act with the utmost caution. Our work would be based on the strictest conspiratorial methods. On January 27, 1942, Baruch was given a further mission. At five in the afternoon, three comrades waited for him near the gate. At the entry, stormtroopers stood in line and meticulously examined everyone from head to foot. It was 5:15. The Borbishok group appeared in the distance—now they were at the entry. Baruch was the ninth in line. He was limping with his right foot (He was bringing something!). The tension among the waiting comrades grew from one moment to the next. A bad business. Baruch won't pass with such a "load." There was the sixth in line being examined. The seventh. Baruch stood there calmly, tall, dark, with deep-set eyes. He is considering everything that is liable to happen very soon. His mind is made up. If he is caught he will take all the responsibility. He has no ties with anyone. Baruch will suffer all the tortures in the world but he will not betray his comrades. At the gate, the eighth is being examined. Suddenly one of the three men waiting breaks out and runs like a madman toward the stormtroopers. It's Yashke Raff. The stormtrooper strikes him in the face and arrests him. Baruch exploits the opportunity and hurries through the open gate.

"Baruch—what?"

"Half a machine gun," he replies calmly. "Tomorrow it'll be the second half"—and goes on limping on his right foot.

The same day I brought the first hand grenades that I had been given by the Mother Superior of the Benedictine Convent.

In those days, the Jews would have destroyed us for fear of punishment if they had had any hint of these activities. They would have blessed us in their hearts, but they would not have hesitated to stone us. In those days it was out of the question for us, shut up in the Ghetto and exposed to all kinds of betrayal, to buy arms. So how could we get them?

During a short period, our fighters got machine guns, rifles, pistols, hand grenades, and ammunition from German stores, bunkers, and sealed trucks. It was a difficult and perilous task to bring the weapons into the beleaguered Ghetto. They were brought disassembled into parts and hidden in clothing, in the double bottom of a toolchest, a manure cart.

One morning, vehicular traffic was suddenly halted in Stefan Street opposite the Ghetto gates, not far from the German guard. A red sign in the street showed that the sewers were being repaired. Two young workers in overalls took off the cover and started work. As they were working they pushed two thick pipes into the space. The two sewerage workers were Kaplinsky, a platoon commander, and Matis Levin, who had succeeded in stealing the necessary plans and tools from the municipality and hidden rifles in the pipes. In the dead of night they went down, through the opening made for the purpose, into the sewer and the arms were brought in through the chilly tunnels for the fighters of the FPO.

After prolonged negotiations with the police on guard at the gate, we were allowed to bring in a little food for our hungry comrades. During the morning, a truck carrying Jewish workers drove up to the gates of the Ghetto. Two lads, innocently carrying two sacks on their backs, jumped off the truck.

Sacks of salt.

The policemen looked into the sacks—yes, it was salt.

In reality, however, these were two sacks of ammonite, which had been stolen by the Gordon brothers, who belonged to the FPO, from a German arms store in the Pioneer Park.

Josephus's Maccabees and the Dichtirov Machine Guns

If it was difficult to bring in weapons, it was no easier to camouflage them and keep them inside the Ghetto, in that appalling congestion, with dozens of eyes watching your every move, when you went out to the lavatory, when you got up and when you lay down. Surrounded as we were by police and detectives, we had to beware even of our best friends, who found it unthinkable that anyone in the Ghetto would risk his life to get arms. With great caution, we would move the weapons by day or night. Our arsenals were in the cellars, under the floor, behind the wall, or in hollow blocks of wood specially prepared for the purpose that lay about innocently in the kitchen. We had to shift our stores from place to place, to the soup kitchen in Number 2 Strashun Street, to the caves in Carmelite Street, to the cellars.

In the Dissemination of Jewish Culture Library, there was a secret hideaway in one of the rooms behind the book-lined walls. On the shelves stood the volumes of Josephus's *Jewish War* and behind them lay Dichtirov light machine guns. In the dead of night a shape would slip in, pull down the window blinds, and light a small lamp. A knock at the door. No reply. Then two and again one—the password of the FPO. One by one they all come in. With trembling hands they take down the Maccabean heroes from the dusty shelf and take out parts of weapons from their hiding place. The instructor explains how to use a machine gun. This is how you take it to pieces, this is how you reassemble it, this is how you load the magazine, this is how you aim. "Don't forget! A machine gun swallows bullets at top speed, and no doubt we won't have too much ammunition. So remember, every one of you, fire in *small* bursts and aim as accurately as you can. . ."

Number 2 Strashun Street, third story. You come into a tiny room. In a corner, on a stool, a pail of water. It has a double bottom, concealing two sparkling Parabellum pistols.

Many times have I gulped fresh water from this bucket.

Yearnings

Cut off as we were from the world, in the darkest days of the Ghetto regime, the political bulletin used to bring a little consolation to the young fighters. The command set up a secret radio in the Ghetto and issued a statement every day.

A sheaf of such statements that we found among the relics, lies before me now.

It was Winter 1942, a season of titantic struggles. The Red Army tanks were sweeping westward and, as youngsters in the corners of the Ghetto read the FPO bulletin with bated breath, hope broke through in the tormented hearts: perhaps, after all . . .

And even if *we* did not succeed, our struggle was sacred. And if we had to fall—let it be as free men with weapons in our hands.

On April 30, 1943, our radio caught the voice of the Polish announcer in the broadcasts of Swiet.

"The Warsaw Ghetto is going down in battle. We appeal to the whole world: the Warsaw Ghetto is going down in battle. For six weeks, thousands of Jews have been heroically fighting the German murderers. Old and young are fighting in the streets of the Warsaw Ghetto. The Germans are using tanks and heavy arms. House after house is falling. Planes are bombarding from above. The fighters are defending every house, every room. In another day or two, the Warsaw Ghetto wil go up in flames!"

We published this manifesto in a special communiqué to the fighters of the FPO. I added a note: *"Gloria Victis!"*

Deeply conscious of the goal of the fight, the organization of the FPO grew. The groups of three became groups of five. Every group of five was a fighting unit. Four fives constituted a platoon headed by a commander. A large number of platoons made up a battalion headed by a battalion commander who was a member of the general command. The organization had two battalions headed respectively by Josef Glasman and Abba Kovner. The organization was headed by a General Staff, and the chief commander was Itzik Wittenberg.

The general command organized platoons of bomb throwers, machine gunners, and grenade throwers; and a special platoon of instructors who trained the fighters in the use of their weapons.

Never have I seen such readiness for self-sacrifice as radiated from every fighting member of the FPO. It was a fighting organization in the full sense of the term.

In pain and yearning, we sang the song of daring and faith:

> This song was written in blood and lead;
> It was not the birdsong of the open land,
> But a people, amid the crashing walls,
> Sang it together, weapon in hand.

The police searched for our radio. They searched for arms. The Gestapo began to wonder: how did all the political news filter into the Ghetto? Stalin's Order of the Day was published in the bulletins and passed on by word of mouth. With infinite devotion and self-sacrifice, everything was kept absolutely secret, so that no one should know where it came from. With infinite love, the fighters kept all the secreta that had any connection with the sacred fight.

Borbishok

A broad field stretches beyond Ponar: Borbishok. Here there stood a large German factory for arms and ammunition. Here the fighters of the FPO, risking their lives and the lives of thousands of Jews, did their duty to the fighting organization at the orders of the general command, by destroying the enemy's property and getting arms for the Ghetto. Here the Gordon brothers, Tiktin, and Goldstein put out of order (by spoiling their locking mechanisms) 365 guns that were sent to the front.

It was Summer 1942. The Germans were in the midst of their second offensive. On a branch line of the Borbishok Station stood a train loaded with ammunition. On the open trucks stood, four by four, tanks that were to be sent to the Smolensk front. With the help of engineer Rattner, our fighters prepared six tiny incendiary mechanisms and secretly introduced them into the petrol tanks. As the train went on its way, a fire broke out and the tanks went up in flames.

Baruch Goldstein, who had brought the arms inside the Ghetto, continued to pass the German guard every day smuggling in disassembled rifles and machine guns. This modest, simple fighter destroyed 345 Zenith mechanisms and 90 machine guns that were to be sent to the front by taking out vital parts, despite the searching inspection of pyrotechnical inspector Mikolauskas.

Then there was the time when the Germans forced Jewish workers to blow up large stores of Soviet bombs no longer fit for use. Our men used to stick German ammunition under the bombs.

One day in Spring 1943, a German reserves soldier, who had recently arrived, picked up a G.B.W. hand grenade and, knowing nothing of the mechanism, pulled out the safety pin. Standing near him at the time was Rattner, who, seeing the German's bewilderment, shouted at him "Throw!"

and coolly pointed toward the ammunition store. There was a tremendous, reverberating boom. That day a million and a half rounds of German ammunition went up in smoke. The Gestapo surrounded the yard and arrested all the workers, but they were all set free after a thorough investigation. Only the German soldier remained under arrest. This was the first time German hands took revenge for wrongs to the Jews.

It was at this place that Tiktin died a heroic death. A number of trucks laden with ammunition and grenade bombs had reached the station platform. Zalman Tiktin knew how great the demand for them was in the Ghetto. In the arsenals of the FPO there were dozens of grenades without the fuses. Zalman did not delay long. He stole onto the platform. The truck was sealed and wrapped around with barbed wire. Zalman cut the wire, went into the truck, girded himself with machine gun ammunition belts, and filled his pockets with bombs and grenades. As he was trying to climb through the wire, Mikolauskas caught sight of him and fired after him. Tiktin was caught and assaulted by eleven Germans. "Who did you steal the arms for?" "For you!" Tiktin cried. "For the blood of my mother and my sisters!" He was arrested, and the German commander summoned by telephone.

The Jewish workers were assembled in the yard opposite. Fifteen armed Germans guarded Tiktin. Here the assembled Jews witnessed this sight: the door of the prison cell suddenly burst open and Tiktin charged through it straight at the Germans. The soldiers were confused for a moment. Opposite the spot the railway passed over a steep slope. Tiktin turned to the slope. He had to climb over a hill before he could reach the line, and here he was an excellent target for the soldiers. When the first soldier aimed with his rifle, Tiktin was only four meters away. He was wounded in the leg, but did not stop running. When the German soliders caught him, he was wounded in seven places: the legs, the stomach, the back. German officers gathered around and the commander came up. The Jewish workers took Tiktin out on a stretcher. He whispered: "Ich hob sei in der adomah!"—"To hell with them! Friends—revenge. . ." The Gestapo sent Tiktin to the hospital because they were very anxious to solve the riddle of the grenades, but Zalman died of his wounds. Before he died, he said to one of the interrogators: "You murderers! Your time will come!"

The fighters' organization held mourning parades in memory of the young hero and platoon 16, to which he had belonged, was named after him by order of the command.

The Cellar in Number 3 Carmelite Street

In Number 3 Carmelite Street there is an underground artifical cave that has been preserved intact. Here, under the ground, 300 Jews hid during the slaughter. There were mothers and infants among them. Here they would cook, eat, ease themselves, even give up the ghost. Here, into this cave, we would bring the machine guns by night and hide them in the earth, take them out to learn how to use them, and bury them again. Here we would practice with the new grenades prepared by platoon commander Kaplinsky; here we completed the preparation of the first land mine.

In June 1942, the command decided to carry out the first attack on the railway—an idea bordering on madness. It was before the partisan groups had started sabotage operations around Vilna. Could we, imprisoned in the Ghetto, without the slightest opportunity for free movement in the town, destroy a military train? We decided to try, but our hearts were gnawed by doubts. What if we did not succeed? If Jews were caught with a land mine, how many thousands would pay with their lives?

Vitka Kempner went out for a three-day reconnaissance trip. She dyed her hair, discarded the yellow patch, mingled with the crowd outside the gate, and turned toward the railway that ran in the direction of Vileika. At the same time, preparation of the mine was completed inside the cave. Without experience or tools, we prepared by ourselves a mechanical detonator, forged a firing pin. Zadok Gordon got some dynamite from a German bunker. I remember Izka at that time in the cave. He protested at my preparing the mine; he was afraid I might be killed. I had not known Izka Matzkevitch before then; the only tie between us was his membership of the FPO. "Stop it," cried Izka, "you mustn't."

On June 8, Vitka, Izka, and Moshe Braus left the cave in the Ghetto in order to blow up the first German train. In the moments of the most deadly danger, our hearts sang: "This is for Ponar." Next day, when I got the news, I forgot all the rules of conspiracy, ran like a madman into Glasman's room, fell on his neck and kissed him: "Josef—it's been blown up!"

On the night of July 24, the first group of our partisans who were to set out to the forests under the command of Josef Glasman met in the cave. Here I saw for the last time the Gordon brothers, Izka Matzkevitch, Rosa Shareshniosky, Hayim Spokoyni, Malka Hazan, Zindel and Rachel Borkiska. All of them stood there, ready and confident. Thirty kilometers from Vilna the group was ambushed by the enemy. This was their last journey. Next day, the Gestapo marched into the Ghetto and took out 32 families to Ponar. The Ghetto was shocked by the new slaughter. It was paying for the first organized attempt to break out to the forests.

The Picture

Among the scraps of paper I found Lisa's picture. Lisa did not succeed in getting to the forest. Her black eyes look straight ahead, as always, with their deep, kind look. Lisa Magon was a fighter in the FPO. When the Germans were beginning their slaughter of the Jews in the Oshmyany Ghetto, she was sent there by the command to warn the Jews. She was provided with a Polish passport and penetrated the Ghetto the same night. When she reached Oshmyany it was already surrounded, but she succeeded in getting inside at the risk of her life. She appealed to the Jews: "You are being led to your deaths. Don't trust them." Not all of them believed her, or even grasped the significance of what she was saying. Some of them asked: "Where shall we go?" "Wherever you can," Lisa replied. In the dead of that same night a few dozen Jews slipped away to the forests.

When she returned from Oshmyany, she was given other missions that she carried out. For the sake of her work she needed unchallengeable Aryan documents, so she went to the German police station. When she was taking the documents, one of the policemen recognized her as a Jewess and she was arrested. In the Gestapo, she was interrogated and tortured. All our efforts to save her were fruitless: we bribed the interrogating judge, but the documents had already been sent off to Kaiser, the Gestapo chief. Five days later, Kaiser's maid, who had also been bribed, reported that she had seen a cross, which meant a death sentence, on Lisa's documents. Through the intermediacy of a Pole, we tried to bribe the firing squad at Ponar. One of them even promised, in return for a handsome payment, not to shoot, but he had to take her to Ponar. "We'll shoot without aiming," he said. She would drop to the ground and in the evening she would be able to escape. We saw a ray of hope. But at the last moment, Weiss decided to be present at the execution. Lisa's doom was sealed.

On the 10th of March, about a week before she died, she wrote from the Lukishki jail:

> Abba, I know exactly what I have to expect, but it's hard to accept the idea that I'll be taken to Ponar. I am calm. Give my regards to every one. I press your hands. Be strong, Lisa.

Our comrades commemorated her by collecting 18,000 rubles and giving them to the command to buy a pistol in her name. On the thirtieth day after her death, Baruch Goldstein stole a machine gun from the Germans and brought it into the Ghetto. We called it after her, and in the last days of the Ghetto, during the uprising, when we broke through into the forest to continue our struggle for vengeance, the man who marched at the head, leading the advance, carried in his arms the machine gun named after Lisa.

The Sewer

The house at Number 31 Daiche Street is burned down. In a corner of the yard there used to be the workshop of the Ghetto. In the third dark room there was a secret opening through which we went down into the sewer that led us from the Ghetto to the forest. I am still at the entrance to the sewer. When I came down here two years ago with Shmuelke Kaplinsky to find a way to bring in arms into the Ghetto, it did not occur to me, as I stepped into the damp dark sewer, that in the course of time this would be our only way out.

We did not expect to see the picture that appeared before us in the last moments of the uprising when we went down into the sewer.

During my stay in the forest I saw many partisans' camps. Each had its beginnings: one had its roots in a prisoners' camp and another in a house that became foreign soil because of the enemy. The beginnings of our partisans' camp go back to a sewer.

We left behind us the mass grave of a whole people, shattered ruins with blood-spattered walls, and two years of struggle and battle.

Those who went down into the sewer did not feel that they were saved.

Whoever has not seen the line that plodded on beneath the surface will not grasp the significance of that nightmare procession, the grim, angry faces and the guns—like partly burned candles—in their hands.

There was nothing accidental about the deaths of Yankel Kaplan, Chwoinik and Ossia Bick. As they emerged from the sewer they came upon a German guard, opened fire and killed one German. They were caught and hanged together. The large group that passed through the sewer turned toward the dense Rudniki forests, where four battalions of Jewish partisans were organized and joined the other groups.

But the will to live, the hope for a *personal* yearning for happiness and a brighter tomorrow, remained buried for a long time—for some of us forever—in the sewer. Only one powerful desire flooded our hearts on the edge of the forest: revenge. We called ourselved "The Avengers." When I went with my comrades to set fire to the enemy's bridges or attack him almost empty-handed, I felt keenly that it was not I, the commander, who was leading them, but that they were advancing by the light of the funeral pyre.

I remember the first time I blew up a train. I went out with a small group, with Rachel Markevitch as our guest. It was New Year's Eve; we were bringing the Germans a festival gift. The train appeared on the raised railway; a line of large, heavy-laden trucks rolled on toward Vilna. My heart suddenly stopped beating for joy and fear. I pulled the string with all my strength, and in that moment, before the thunder of the explosion echoed through the air, and twenty-one trucks full of troops hurtled down into the abyss, I heard Rachel cry: "For Ponar!"

In the course of the struggle, during those cruel experiences, there were some who broke and collapsed, but there were others who were tempered like steel. Those who crossed the sewer remained fighters to the end.

The Battle Orders

It is beyond my powers today to tell the whole story of the FPO's struggle and its way in battle. The impression of those days is too powerful for me to be able to describe them.

How we asked for help from the political underground forces outside the Ghetto.

How the Polish organizations promised us arms and refused to give them.

How we contacted the central command itself—in Warsaw.

How we, the Ghetto Jews, issued as early as 1942 a manifesto to the Polish population calling on them to fight the invader.

How, in our quest for contacts, we met the representatives of the first partisans, emissaries of the Lithuanian command in Moscow, Margis and his colleagues.

How two of our women fighters, Sonia Madaiska and Cessia Rosenberg, were sent through the front lines to get to Moscow, to transmit important material on the activities of the FPO, so that these still unknown facts should be revealed to the world. How, without contacts, they reached Velikie Luki, were intercepted several times by the Gestapo and finally compelled to escape in order to return to the Vilna Ghetto, and Sonia finally shot near Polotzk.

How Itchele Kovalsky set up a secret printing press that published all the underground literature of Vilna.

How the two Silber sisters fell while they were bringing the call to uprising to all the Jewish localities in the occupied zone.

How Adek Boraks, Chaika Grossmann, Aryeh Vilner, Entin and Israel Kempner went out on our behalf to set up the FPO in Warsaw and Bialystok and ultimately became part of the leadership of the revolt there.

How, shut up in the Ghetto, we used to help the Soviet prisoners and the wives of the commanders at Sobotch.

How we set up, together with Vitas, a united partisans' organization of Poles, Lithuanians, and Jews, and even made contact with Jurgis and Markov, the leaders of the partisan movement in Belorussia and Lithuania.

How a large campaign was conducted to raise funds for buying arms. With what religious devotion the fighters gave up all their property, money, dresses, watches, wedding rings—last mementos of murdered wives and parents, recalling the ancient days in the wilderness when all the people gave up their jewels for the building of the Tabernacle.

And the dozens of acts of sabotage carried out by our fighters—in the military post offices, in the airfields, the fuel dumps, and so forth.

And the detailed reports of troop movements and the Gestapo documents we sent on to the partisans' command.

And the unity in battle between people of completely different education and political outlook.

And the unique way of life of the FPO fighters.

And the day of July 16, and the martyr's death of Wittenberg.

And how we organized and sent out units to the forest.

How we brought out arms, hidden in coffins, from the beleaguered Ghetto.

And the life and death of Sonia Madaiska. I see her weaknesses, her mistakes, and her acts of heroism—one of those remarkable women who sometimes find their way into revolutionary movements.

And the scores of our unknown fighters who gave their lives with utter dedication, those comrades who carried out with such simplicity every dangerous mission.

And those who offered themselves on July 16, of their own free will, to go to death in place of Wittenberg.

And those who went to their posts during the days of the revolt with grenades in their hands, clearly conscious that this was their last journey.

All of them were men and women with profound, heroic faith.

There lie before me a few pages containing the battle orders of the FPO. Here, in the ashes, amid the scraps of paper I found them.

The pages have been fully preserved. The three opening pages are in manuscript. And again I do not feel the presence of my own words, but I imagine I can hear how Sonia or Grisha read them out to their companies. What comes to me are the voices of those that have gone.

And what I find impossible to tell may be told by these lines, dated April 4, 1943:

Battle Orders of the FPO

1. General

1. The fight we are about to start will serve as a touchstone of the moral and physical qualities of the FPO fighter and his individual ability to hold out and endure.
2. We shall have to go into battle after severe nervous strain, in an atmosphere of panic, after serious blows which the FPO may suffer even before the battle starts.
3. The FPO fighter must not lose his *sang-froid* under the most difficult battle conditions, and he must never recoil from personal danger.
4. Every company commander and every fighter must prepare for battle by undergoing conditions as close as possible to the future reality of battle, so that he should not be stunned or overwhelmed, so that a man who has never fired in his life should not panic at the sound of his own shots.
5. This will be achieved by continual training and careful thought to describe to every individual every possible situation he may face in the moment of battle. . .

3. Automatic Mobilization

32. In case the command is put out of action for unforeseen reasons, the FPO organization must carry out automatic mobilization.
33. What is the situation which calls for automatic mobilization? If the Ghetto is suddenly endangered, if the population is gripped by panic, and that is accompanied by flight to places of concealment; that will be a "special situation."
34. In such a case, every FPO fighter must report to his post, ready for orders from the command, without waiting for a mobilization order. . .

4. Independent Action before Battle

42. If the command is arrested, the leadership of the FPO will be taken over by the deputy command, which will act according to prearranged orders. . .
50. The battle must continue whatever the number of fighters, irrespective of the quantity of ammunition in their possession. . .

57. In time of danger, every member of the FPO must give an example of courage and heroism, arousing the largest possible number of men, by deed and word, to fight.

58. If the command falls into the hands of the Gestapo and all attempts to save it fail to succeed, the struggle must continue and the FPO be led independently into battle. . .

SUPPLEMENT TO THE STANDING ORDERS

C. Should We Go Immediately to the Forests?

19. No. The desire to go to the forests immediately shows a lack of understanding of the FPO's ideas.

20. The idea of the Jewish United Partisans' Organization is national and social: to organize the struggle of the Jews and protect their lives and their honor.

22. *We shall go to the forests only as the result of battle.* After we carry out our mission, we shall take with us as large a number of Jews as possible and move to the forests, where we shall continue our struggle with the murderous occupant, as part of the general partisan movement.

The Cry of the Blood

I stand on the ruins of Number 12 Strashun Street, where the forward outpost of our resistance stood. Here fell the commander of the outpost, Ilya Schoenbaum. In this yard we hid arms for the first time. Here, amid the blood and the muck, young legends grew.

Jews who have remained alive go as pilgrims to Ponar today to fortify the vengeance in their hearts with the ashes of the bones.

I have not yet been on the hill of death. The most appalling thing in the Ghetto was not death. It was infinitely more terrible to be defiled to the depth of your soul every hour of the day for twenty-five months—and to wait. To look at the funeral pyre of the Jerusalem of Lithuania, to look at life by the mercy of the butcher. Number 12 Strashun Street was blown up by the Germans with dynamite. Nothing was left of the house but a pile of stones. Only one wall remained intact: the eastern wall of the old synagogue. And on the wall an ancient inscription:

"Lift up the miracle-banner for the ingathering of our exiles."

I mount to heap the ashes right up to the wall. On the wall I see a splash of blood. And the blood cries out to the heart of the nation:

Arise in action and be free!"

Notes

1. Slips of paper that supposedly gave their holders a lease on life.
2. Ponar—a wooded area near Vilna where the mass murder of Vilna Jewry took place.
3. See note 1 above.
4. Jewish Vilna was known as the "Jerusalem of Lithuania."

The House Committees
in the Warsaw Ghetto

Michel Mazor

The House Committees that were set up in all the houses of the Warsaw Ghetto constituted a very special social movement of the Jewish masses; the Committees mobilized thousands of voluntary social activists. As far as I know, there exists no monograph or systematic treatment of this subject, for the simple reason that the sources for such a study are lacking. They disappeared for the most part in the catastrophe together with the human animators of this movement. Of necessity, my account here will be of a fragmentary character; it is based solely on my experience and personal memories. Nonetheless, all the facts that I shall recount are significant, illustrating as they do the totality of the phenomena in question. My aim is to give, as far as possible, an adequate picture of the true nature and scale of this popular movement.

In order to see the true historical perspective, one must locate the House Committees in the general structure of social organizations in the Warsaw Ghetto that served as a framework for their activities. At the very beginning of the occupation, the Germans created an organ of social assistance for the whole population (including the Jews) entitled the "Central Council of Assistance" (with the initials RGO in Polish). The seat of its social activities was Cracow. Its funds were distributed amongst the various nationalities according to coefficients such that approximately 80 percent went to Poles, 15 percent to Ukrainians, and 5 percent to Jews. This disproportionate allocation evidently represented a prejudice against the Jews, and it is doubtful whether even the tiny proportion allotted to them was actually distributed.

At the local level, social assistance functioned separately for each nationality. For the Jews it was the Urban Committee of Assistance (KOM).

According to German plans, the KOM was to become the sole Jewish social organization, absorbing and replacing all the others. The latter were intended to lose their specific character and their autonomy, and to disappear by fusing with the KOM, a sole and controlled body. The great merit of the KOM, however, was that instead of profiting from its officially assigned monopoly, it restricted itself to distributing its funds amongst all the Jewish social institutions and to conducting relations with the Germans. Thus, the institutions retained their autonomy and could carry out their work.

This situation changed when the engineer Stanislaw Szereszewski was replaced by the lawyer Gustav Wielikowski. The necessity of fusing the various institutions in the KOM was presented to us as a categorical demand of the Germans, without our being able to know whether that was true. Equivocations on this matter continued until July 1942, when the mass exterminations got under way; so that during this whole period (in which the Ghetto formed a community of more than 400,000 persons) the social institutions retained their independence. This applies both to those institutions that had existed earlier (OSE, Centos) and to the principal organ of social assistance created at the beginning of the occupation as the "Jewish Society of Social Assistance" (ZTOS), later termed the "Jewish Social Assistance" (ZOS).

The latter institution offered services to the refugees, operated refugee centers, and concerned itself (at first) with the collection and distribution of clothes, but its primary task was the organization of the people's kitchens. In addition to its direct activity, the ZTOS became the center around which there were grouped, in the so-called "Public Sector," the vital forces of the Ghetto that mobilized the mass of society for rescue work—for offering help to the most destitute part of the population.

In the Public Sector itself one must distinguish between two branches. On the one hand, there was an official administrative apparatus, which from an organizational point of view formed a service of the ZTOS and was subordinate to it. It was headed by Dr. Emanuel Ringelblum, the prime animator of the whole movement. On the other hand, the Public Sector comprised thousands of charitable social workers who organized: 1) House Committees in all the houses; 2) various District Commissions, each overseeing the House Committees in some area, with which were associated groups of social workers, women's circles, etc.; 3) the Central Commission of the House Committees, which was set up at a later stage (the end of 1940) and acquired the role of "parliament" of the Public Sector.

At first Ringelblum intended to restrict the charitable social work to the level of the districts and to have it directed by his central apparatus. This attitude somewhat retarded the creation of the Central Commission. But once the latter was formed, Ringelblum was the first to appreciate its importance, and the collaboration between the Central Commission and the administrative apparatus of the Public Sector proceeded in a completely harmonious manner as part of the common effort to mobilize all available persons of good will. Gradually, the administrative apparatus took on the character of an "executive" of the Public Sector; Ringelblum used to say that he regarded himself as "prime minister" of the Public Sector, responsible to its parliament.

The Formation of the First House Committees

In a still rudimentary form, the House Committees began to take shape at the very beginning of the occupation. The new conditions of life, which transformed the Jews into pariahs, created a psychological climate that encouraged them to come together. During the long winter evenings Jews could communicate only with occupants of the same house, since the curfew began earlier for them than for the rest of the population: generally at nine o'clock, but sometimes even at seven o'clock. In addition, the danger threatening all Jews, the violence and pillage of which they were the victims, the sinister rumors about the fate awaiting them—all this stimulated amongst them the need for an exchange of thoughts and closer contact. As a result of this very natural need to unite and to alleviate the precarious situation of those Jews who had lost their work and income or who had been ruined by pillage— whose number constantly increased—the outlines of what turned into the House Committees of the Warsaw Ghetto began to become discernible.

The House Committees were emphatically a national institution of the Ghetto, an emanation from the masses. It would be a false interpretation of the historical truth to attribute their birth to any political party or particular person. Nonetheless, one must note the preponderant role of Ringelblum: having been the first to understand the importance of the House Committees, he was their prime animator, outlining the forms of their organization, and attracting the initially small number of groups of social workers—the pioneers of this great popular movement.

Up to October 1940, Jews were living in all parts of the city. The ZTOS was then organized in eight districts, of which five were located in areas where the Jewish population was very dense and later formed, in part, the site of the Ghetto. The sixth covered the right bank of the Vistula (the Praga suburb), while the seventh and eighth covered the southwest and most prosperous part of Warsaw. In each district there was a "Commission for the Instruction and Control of the House Committees" (the "District Commission").

I presided over the District Commission in the eighth district, and it is in this capacity that I am in a position to describe the sequence of events precisely. In that part of the city the Jewish population was less dense and the houses did not contain enough Jewish occupants to form House Committees in each of them. Consequently, we decided to organize in blocks of from three to ten houses, in conformity with the local conditions of each individual case.

The following method was applied in our work. The streets of the district were divided amongst members of the Commission, who visited the houses assigned to them, made the acquaintance of the occupants, and took note of the active elements capable of being utilized for social work. Employing this information, we then set about delimiting the blocks. Representatives of each were invited to a meeting in the district office to form the Committee of that block. Sometimes propaganda meetings were organized in the houses, to which all the Jewish occupants were brought. But the formation of the Committees took place only at the district meetings that were convened daily during the spring and summer of 1940, up to the month of September.

In that period, when the idea of House Committees was still vague for most of the Jews, it was impossible to proceed by election; membership in the Committees came about by the natural selection of the most active elements. All those daily meetings ended with the formation of Committees. I did not encounter a single case of refusal, but that did not mean all the Committees were effective. Some became energetically active, but a considerable number displayed inertia as a result of insufficient liaison between houses on the block. However, they all remained under our control even after they were formed. We made efforts to resuscitate the less effective ones by introducing new elements into them.

It is of interest to mention a stormy meeting during which there was formed the Committee of a block of buildings in Hoza Street. At that time the ZTOS was conducting a collection of clothes, and rumors circulated accusing certain collectors of abuses (replacing garments of good quality with other more worn ones). As the Jews were in general very sensitive to the failings of their social institutions, a violent speech was delivered, followed by a series of others that were even more vehement. The atmosphere was against any collaboration with an institution as incompetent as the ZTOS.

At that moment one could observe the correctness of our system, according to which it was charitable social workers who dealt with the formation of the Committees, not employees of the ZTOS. Such employees would have been obliged to defend their institution and this could only have aggravated the situation. I advocated a completely different point of view and told this agitated public that, although I had no information on the matter, I did not deny the possibility of abuses. But, I continued, if for that reason we all decided to return home without undertaking anything, the only outcome would be an increase in abuses, since the only means of combatting them was public control and such control could be attained only through influencing the ZTOS by our energetic work in the domain of social assistance. As a result a Committee was formed without a single voice in opposition and, as we were later able to observe, the Committee was very active.

In general, however, the movement was in an embryonic state during this period. It acquired definitive form and historical significance only within the walls of the Ghetto where, because of the density and cohesion of the population, Committees were formed in all houses and—in contrast with the first period—by way of election. In the work of the House Committees and the institutions that emerged from them, there participated masses of independent collaborators, who brought to their task the greatest enthusiasm and devotion, even though they sometimes realized the hopelessness of their attempts to solve the social problems in the condemned universe that was the Warsaw Ghetto.

One may affirm unhesitatingly that the social forces of these institutions represented the will and conscience of the Ghetto. Their activities were jointly conducted by persons from all backgrounds and all professions, and especially by members of all the political parties, who had sometimes lost contact with them in the Ghetto. All such people came to work in our institutions not as representatives of their respective parties, but in a spontaneous spirit of alleviating the sufferings of the destitute. The activity of these persons of different orientations, from Revisionists to Bundists, took place in an atmosphere of fraternal solidarity without conflicts deriving from opposed political opinions. Of course, the social workers sometimes had different ideas about one problem or another and there were often heated discussions at the meetings, but such discussions were never conducted along party lines.

It is important to emphasize that this movement arose and developed outside the parties. Such detachment from politics, almost unimaginable in contemporary society, especially among Jews, who tended to excess in this respect, represented a characteristic trait of the social institutions of the Ghetto up to July–August 1942. They were unique in kind with features determined by the exceptional circumstances out of which they were born.

The Reorganization inside the Ghetto

The aid provided when Jews were transferred to the Ghetto was the last manifestation of activity by the eighth district of the ZTOS, since no Jews remained in that part of the city. Those days had demonstrated the extent of Jewish misery: although this was the most well-off area of the city, great crowds had overwhelmed the district office with demands for subsidies, whether for the hire of a vehicle to transfer furniture or for a deposit on the miserable dwelling found in the Ghetto.

In accordance with the new circumstances, the ZTOS was radically reorganized. Our district and that of the Praga suburb were abolished. On the area corresponding approximately to the site of the Ghetto, there remained only five districts of the ZTOS, a new sixth district having been formed where the population was most dense and most indigent. It was in the latter district that I, together with all the members of the corresponding Commission of Instruction and Control, undertook the task of dealing with the House Committees.

Our District Commission acquired an office at 29a Nowolipki Street; it covered part of this street (between Karmelicka and Smocza Streets) together with parts of Dzielna, Pawia, Gesia, Smocza, and Mila Streets, but also Lubeckiego, Ostrowska, and Niska Streets—these three being peopled by Jews in direst straits. How can I convey the emotions that I feel when enumerating all these streets? During the two years or so spent in this district, we encountered the miserable life of the people who swarmed in these streets, sometimes driven to despair, sometimes grasping at the illusion of uncertain and improbable hope. All of this life, the thoughts and the emotions of these human beings, was eventually stamped out like vermin without a trace, as though it had never existed. Even the streets disappeared. Not one house remained standing, only piles of debris where there had once been a living community.

At the time when the Ghetto began its existence, we could not foresee this terrible apocalyptic annihilation. For us this area was full of living beings reduced to misery. They had to be helped to fight for the right to live, helped to maintain their faith in the future. There were more than 100,000 people and some 250 houses in the area, so we had to set up a corresponding number of House Committees. The district included a high percentage of newly arrived families lacking any source of income and not yet adjusted to the new conditions of life. The misery, the overcrowding, and the chaos were indescribable. And since the ZTOS could not gain control over the situation, the immediate aid given by the House Committees, directly from one individual to another, became all the more important.

Having begun to visit the inhabitants of these houses, we saw the "apartments" of the Ghetto with our own eyes. They were hovels, over-crowded in the extreme, real seats of hunger and sickness. The words of our comrades who reported to the District Commission about their visits were filled with despair; and it was with the vision of the city of death before us, that we made every effort to organize our work in this unleashed chaos of human misery. For those of us whose earlier work had been in the most well-off part of the city, the difference between the problems to be solved now and the previous conditions of work was striking. We were faced with the masses of destitute small businessmen, artisans and workers, socially disintegrated and morally disoriented.

As we soon observed, the multitude of the newly arrived had disorganized the activity of the previously created House Committees, which had to be reorganized if the new elements were to be integrated and involved in the work, which itself needed to be intensified. After considerable reflection, we decided that the only way was to reelect all the House Committees in the district afresh. But this plan required immense preliminary work: taking cognizance of the situation in each house, reaching agreement with the existing Committee, calling a general meeting of the occupants, and having all these activities guided by instructors.

The realization of this vast project surpassed the capabilities of our District Commission, which consisted of only seven or eight members. We therefore set about recruiting charitable auxiliary social workers, who soon amounted to forty persons, each taking charge of from five to seven houses.

After some time a number of them left us, some out of despair and others on account of their own terrible situation, but a group of about twenty persons remained at their posts up to the massive extermination of July–September 1942. New volunteers also took the place of those who left, so the activity of our auxiliaries covered the whole district and was pursued uninterruptedly.[1]

The working conditions of the auxiliary social workers were very hard, as the masses amongst whom they worked were in a state of disarray. Hunger, typhus, and dysentery cut down these individuals who were inspired with the desire of serving their even more destitute brethren. Particularly in such conditions a continual process of orientation and control was necessary to give their generous impulses the greatest effect. Meetings devoted to orientation and to elections took place on the spot, in each house, after the evening curfew. Consequently, the auxiliary social worker taking part in the meeting had to remain in the house until morning; mostly he spent the night sitting on a chair in the corner of an overcrowded room. Some of them contracted typhus, a number succumbed to this disease, and all the others—without an exception known to me—perished in the exterminations from 1942 on.

As the conditions of our work became more difficult and complicated, we closed ranks; our District Commission together with all our auxiliaries became a kind of fraternity. The intensity of the work, the gravity of the problems facing us, and the permanent contact with the masses gave a profound sense to our lives. Despite individual differences, distinct social backgrounds, and a variety of political points of view, we were united by the consciousness of highly tragic events and sought to face them without becoming dominated by paltry considerations. A spirit of implacable austerity, and yet one infused with comprehension and humanity, emanated from the members of our team.

I recall our regular meetings, in which reports were presented about the situation in the houses, current problems raised, policies of the ZTOS discussed, etc. All this took place in an atmosphere of austere sincerity and unvarnished truth. Our auxiliary social workers were in touch with the ocean of suffering that surrounded them and they did not mince words; their demands were often impossible to satisfy, their criticisms pitiless. In moments of unleashed anger, the person best suited to calming them was the secretary of our District Commission, Czeslawa Rajfeld-Pechnik. She was a woman of about thirty who through her sincerity, her goodness, and her devotion had the gift of moving the hearts of those around her. If a desperate crowd of refugees besieged the district office, she would mix with this louse-ridden multitude, taking children in her arms and finding a word of consolation for everyone. Our warnings had no effect upon her. She saw things more clearly than others and would answer: "In present conditions dying from typhus transmitted by a louse is not the worst of deaths."

Placed by the decision of fate at the head of this unique team, I have the duty, through the scattered memories that I have retained, to preserve my brave comrades from oblivion. Alas!—I have forgotten certain names and certain faces, my recollections of others return surrounded by haze, and there are few of whom my memory has preserved an exact picture.

One is Isaac Notes. All winter he lived with his sister in an unheated room whose door was staved in; they never undressed. Finally his sister contracted pneumonia and died. He, hungry and shabby, continued his untiring work amongst the poorest houses. Another is Frenkel, a costermonger 65 years of age. Neglecting his business, he devoted all his time to the houses entrusted to him. One day he fell ill and his aged wife came to see me and said: "I do a little trade, but my husband must work for those who are suffering; that is what one must do at present." Yet another is the Revisionist Kirszenberg, a young man full of vitality and optimism.

I also recall a trio of former Bundists. One was a young worker named Szwarcenberg, whose face was frank and smiling. In order to live he accepted the hardest physical labor, without interrupting for a moment his activity as an instructor in the houses of his sector. The second was Goldheimer, a man with thin features and sad eyes, radiating goodness. Before the war he had made a good living as a commercial representative. In the Ghetto his material situation was very precarious. He literally melted before our eyes, yet his whole attention was fixed on the suffering of others. The meetings between our District Commission and the auxiliaries took place every Saturday at the end of the morning. Goldheimer never missed them. I learned, however, that at that time of day he had the opportunity of eating his fill for once in the week, since on Saturdays he was invited to lunch at this friend's. My insistence that he should go there had no effect, and I was obliged to change the hour of our weekly meetings.

The third member of this group was Zanwel Dywan, a true representative of the "intelligentsia." For several successive years he had been the leader of the Bundist faction in the municipality of his birthplace, Plock. Later he lived for a long time in Britain, from where he had brought back a library of English classics. In the Ghetto he existed by giving English lessons, but the number of his pupils shrank and his situation became catastrophic. When one day I saw amongst the stock of a street vendor of secondhand books some volumes of Macaulay's *History of England* bearing Dywan's initials, I realized the degree of misery into which he had fallen. His sensitivity to human suffering and to injustice was extraordinary. In his reports on the misery and misfortunes that he had observed, his voice never betrayed anger, but was always imbued with a deep sadness.

As an exception, the auxiliary social workers of the sixth district acquired the right to have a representative on the Central Commission of the House Committees;[2] they sent Dywan. He was a man of such integrity that he was unable to adjust to the complicated machinery of the social institutions of the Ghetto. The idealism permeating his speeches was sometimes utopian, but his whole personality imparted such humanism that we called him "the conscience of the Central Commission."

In our organization there were people of all ages, all professions (from workers to intellectuals) and all political tendencies (from Revisionists to various kinds of socialists), who carried out their activity independent of their political convictions. If one considers that all these people were unpaid workers, many in tragic material situations, never eating their fill, the existence of this united and dynamic team can be likened to a miracle.

The House Committees and the ZTOS

In trying to portray these institutions, which in large measure sprang up out of the humanism and the solidarity of the masses, I can only trace the few elements that I remember. Additional information on these matters has not been found in the exhumed part of Ringelblum's archives, where it should have been. Already in the Ghetto we realized that the life we were leading and especially our social institutions would be of considerable interest to future generations. The archives accumulated by Ringelblum were to be the essential record, but we in the Public Sector sought to preserve traces of our work in reporting the activity of all these institutions.

Even for the smallest cell in the system—the individual House Committee—a unique form of report was devised that took note of all its activities: the collection and distribution of funds, as well as all other kinds of assistance. Numerous House Committees regularly edited minutes of their meetings. District Commissions prepared exact reports of all their meetings, copies of which were sent to the Centre of the ZTOS. As for the Central Commission of the House Committees, since questions of principle were debated there its minutes were real stenograms. The latter would be of inestimable value for understanding the life of the Ghetto; in their absence one can only attempt to bring out the essential features of these institutions.

The reorganized House Committees that emerged from the elections in each house gradually changed the form of their activities. According to the original conception, a House Committee was to be the local organ of the Center of the ZTOS and to follow its instructions. All funds were to be sent to the Center, which had the task of distributing them according to need. The system aimed at an equitable distribution of assistance, independent of whether this or that house had more or less rich or poor occupants. But it collapsed. As time went on and the extent of the misery increased, certain houses were populated by indigent persons alone, and even the houses that were considered well-off contained so many impoverished people that it was impossible to provide for their most essential needs.

Under such circumstances, it was difficult to ensure that funds were remitted to the central organ. Each Committee sought, by every means available, to render aid in the first place to the needy occupants of its own house. This form of activity stimulated the energy of the individual Committee, while giving it an immediate humanitarian character, since the direct aid from one person to another was a concrete phenomenon. Each donor could see with his own eyes the results of his good will. On the other hand, this autonomous activity of the House Committees demanded an increase in our function of orientation, instruction, and control. From the very first months of the Ghetto's existence, we had to recognize this evolution in the role of the House Committees as an accomplished fact. The Committees, which were originally supposed to be mere instruments of collection and distribution for the ZTOS, had turned into autonomous organs of local assistance.

The ZTOS limited itself to demanding a certain allotment of funds—a question that did not fall within the competence of the charitable social workers, but within that of the financial administrators of the Public Sector. The House Committees were always opposed to this view and generally remitted to the central purse only a minimal percentage of the sum collected. With this money the ZTOS had created a fund for individual aid, whose distribution was decided by the administrative apparatus of the Public Sector (in the person of Ringelblum) and by the Central Commission of the House Committees. The latter was represented at the relevant meetings by me personally or my nominee.

A tragic atmosphere dominated such meetings. We were overwhelmed by requests; each case testified to the most extreme misery, to the hopeless situation of the supplicants. We were powerless in the face of this ocean of human suffering. How should we proceed? By dividing the available money equally between all supplicants? The aid would have lost all meaning: it would not have been enough to buy a kilogram of bread. On the other hand, if we were to be selective how should we choose? How could we decide to give aid—even temporary aid—to one person and not to another? Forced by circumstances to make distinctions, we gave assistance either to persons of special value to the Jewish community or to specially urgent cases: to improve the diet of people who had been stricken severely by typhus. We were continually faced by a problem, which like all other vital problems of the Ghetto, could find no solution in this city of death.

In general, the individual aid rendered by the Center of the ZTOS was of limited importance; the main impact of the Public Sector came from the direct action of the House Committees, who jealously retained their autonomy. Their representatives were heard to say: "We are little Joint Distribution Committees, each house should have its little Joint." The Commissions of Instruction and Control in the various districts tended to give these little "Joints" the form of organized institutions and to apportion duties among their members. In each house a meeting would be convened for the election of a president, a secretary, and a treasurer; depending on the strength of the House Committee, members might also be given responsibilities for food, clothing, assistance to children, reporting procedures, supervision of refugee centers, etc.

Sometimes conflicts arose within House Committees, conflicts—especially in our own sixth district—that could become acute. To overcome them an arbitration tribunal was set up, which operated according to precise procedures. The subjects of the conflicts escape my memory. But I remember well the atmosphere that prevailed at sessions of the tribunal: the parties concerned would often arrive in a highly agitated state, but as the discussion proceeded and everyone expressed his grievances, the atmosphere would become calmer. Usually an accomodation would be reached without the tribunal needing to issue a decree.

The tribunal had, in addition to its immediate task, a moral and educative function that it shared with other organs of the Public Sector. These organs created the conditions that enabled people to work, and even to come into conflict with each other, in an atmosphere of mutual esteem while preserving the civilized forms. In this way people did not lose faith in themselves and had the feeling that human values remained intact, that the whole catastrophe was a temporary eclipse, and that one had only to wait for the dawn of the liberation.

The Role of the Central Commission

At the Central Commission of the House Committees, I made order reign and maintained strict rules of procedure with an insistence that bordered on pedantry. Meetings took place regularly every Tuesday at five o'clock in the afternoon; members prevented from coming had to supply an explanation. In general there were no absentees. Such details were perhaps trivial, but in the period of the Ghetto, when one had the impression that the world had gone mad and was rushing toward a precipice, such rules preserved the stability of moral values and gave us the feeling that our activity was not in vain.

In general, this approach was appreciated by many people involved in social work. But some elements in our social institutions, notably those who sought to pursue their activities without control, accused me of playing at British parliamentarianism. I replied that if, from a certain point of view, this was a game, I preferred it to the game of authoritarian totalitarianism.

The moral authority of the Central Commission was great and its influence extended beyond the sphere of the House Committees. As already mentioned, the Germans intended the KOM to become the sole organization of Jewish social assistance. But whenever this body wished to undertake some scheme requiring the participation of the masses, it could not do so without first seeking the approbation of our Central Commission. Otherwise, as the KOM knew, its intentions would be frustrated. Amongst other schemes thus affected was the project, proposed in Spring 1941, to "confiscate" the food cards of 30,000 well-off Jews and transfer the foodstuffs entitled by these cards to social assistance.

The implementation of this project would have required the participation of the House Committees. In April 1941 the KOM accordingly submitted the project to the Central Commission. After a thoroughgoing consideration of the proposal, the Commission rejected it with a resolution stating its motives. Among these was the danger of letting the Germans know that some Jews could do without food cards, since wherever the system of such cards was in operation it had a universal character entitling everyone without exception to certain quantities of foodstuffs.

On another occasion I, together with Alexandre Landau and the lawyer Szulman, as members of the Central Commission, took part in a meeting of the KOM that also included members of all the political parties and representatives of the *Judenrat.* The problem at issue was the arrest of 19 Jews (mostly adolescents) by the Germans outside the Ghetto. This was an offense punishable by death and the executions could take place at any moment. In these conditions the Gestapo had proposed a deal to the *Judenrat:* if 1,500 fur jackets were supplied for the German army, "the fate of the 19 condemned persons might be reviewed."

We were thus faced with a very painful case of conscience: should we maintain our principle of excluding all aid to the Germans and abandon 19 human beings to death, or should we save them by accepting the compromise? Diametrically opposed opinions were expressed at the meeting. Some insisted on refusing aid to the Germans and held that if the 19 were consequently executed they should be regarded as soldiers fallen at the front. Others supported the compromise, invoking humanitarian principles, the Bible, and the value placed by Judaism on the human person. As for the *Judenrat*, it wished not only to accede to the demand for fur jackets but also to collect the necessary funds by way of a large-scale appeal with the participation of the House Committees.

It was this specific proposal that explained our invitation to the meeting. We refused to agree to this plan, emphasizing the demoralizing effect that it would have. On the other hand, we held that it would be right to take advantage of the promise to spare 19 condemned persons in exchange for 1,500 fur jackets; the Germans could have demanded 5,000 and had already seized all our fur garments without giving anything in return. Only the funds should either be taken from the purse of the *Judenrat* or raised by a collection amongst a very restricted number of persons. The meeting terminated at this point, but we learned later that the 19 Jews had been set free.

Of course, we did not withold agreement to all proposals, but supported, for example, the "winter-help" scheme in 1941–42 (on the model of the German *Winterhilfe*). But we in the Central Commission posed exact conditions for gaining the participation of the House Committees.

The Central Commission of the House Committees turned into a kind of parliament of the Public Sector and its moral influence went beyond its formal responsibilities. The most active social workers were represented on it. At the same time, "parliamentarians" of the Central Commission had to continue their work in the districts, while workers there in turn took an active part in the work of the House Committees. In this way the very structure of our organization was such that those at the top of the pyramid—the Central

Commission—did not hold themselves aloof from and lose contact with the masses.

Activities of the House Committees

The House Committees were so deeply rooted in the life of the Ghetto that its existence is unimaginable without them. A whole folklore sprang up about them, a series of anecdotes underlying their role. All of those tales now escape my memory apart from one joke: that if a woman needed to explain a prolonged absence, she would claim to have been having a meeting with the secretary of the House Committee.

Were it possible to establish the statistics of what was achieved by the House Committees, the results would be impressive. Unfortunately, all such data vanished in the total destruction and there is no hope of reconstructing them. For the same reason, one cannot give an adequate account of the many activities and individual nature of the Committees, which differed considerably amongst themselves. I shall therefore simply describe, as an illustration, the activities of the House Committee at 32 Elektoralna Street, where I and my wife lived. This will give an idea of the Committees in the better-off houses.

In addition to the individual aid given to the indigent occupants of our house, the Committee supplied funds for the maintenance of the refugee center at 12 Elektoralna Street, which was patronized by two female members of the Committee. A collective kitchen was set up and functioned for some time; it distributed nourishing meals free to indigent occupants and at cost to the others. Occupants paid regular monthly contributions, while special collections were organized in urgent cases. For his part the president of the Committee, who was very well-off, gave generous aid to the needy. The Committee had a three-room office with the character of a club. Every evening groups of occupants would meet there, a buffet was available to them, and they could play cards at a number of tables. A certain percentage paid by the players went to the funds of the Committee, as did the proceeds of the buffet. Sometimes the Committee organized evening functions with invited guests from which the receipts were considerable.

In noting the undoubted efficacy of such activities, it must be said that a real enthusiasm—all the more touching for being displayed by people who were themselves in misery and exhausted—was shown in some houses of the poor. Occupants of these houses, rather than giving from their surplus, were sharing out their last resources. The solidarity shown by the occupants of some of the most indigent houses had a moving character. Unfortunately, the details of hundreds of cases illustrating this attitude escape my memory, obliging me to speak in generalities rather than concrete and convincing pictures.

I hope, nonetheless, to have given a fair idea of the true nature of this very special popular movement, together with the mentality of the great majority of those who participated in it. Of course, one should not imagine that every one of these people shone in immaculate whiteness against the dark background of their surroundings. The Public Sector was made up of human beings who lived, for the most part, in miserable conditions and were not free from weaknesses. Even if corruption did not exist, personal ambition sometimes made itself felt. The local interests of their own house or district sometimes hid from them the magnitude of the general situation. On certain issues it was necessary to struggle energetically against excessive regionalism of this kind.

Yet such details have little importance in comparison with the overall perspective, which reflected the comprehending, altruistic, and humanitarian spirit that reigned in the area of the Public Sector and gave birth to our unique institutions created in the equally unique conditions of the Warsaw Ghetto.

Notes

1.   In other districts the number of auxiliaries was smaller and organizationally they were part of the corresponding Commission of Instruction and Control.

2.   See note 1 above.

What Did They Know and When?*

RANDOLPH L. BRAHAM

In the agonizing debate over the activities of the leaders of the doomed wartime Jewish communities, the behavior of the Hungarian Jewish leadership has come under special scrutiny. Hungarian Jewry managed to survive largely unharmed until the second quarter of 1944, when many of the "secrets of Auschwitz" had already surfaced and the downfall of the Third Reich was generally considered inevitable. Yet when the mass deportations of Hungarian Jews began on May 15, 1944:

- The "provincial" Jews (those living outside Budapest) were destroyed at an unprecedented speed in the most ruthless deportation and massacre program of the war.
- These Jews behaved in a resigned and docile manner throughout the ghettoization, concentration, and deportation processes.
- The deportation of the Jews of Budapest, the last surviving community, was halted on July 7, 1944 by Admiral Miklós Horthy, the regent of Hungary, after he had been approached, *inter alia,* by the king of Sweden, the Vatican, and his own son, Miklós Horthy, Jr., who had been informed about the realities of Auschwitz by the national Hungarian Jewish leaders sometime in June.

These facts, which are generally recognized, give rise to a number of controversial and bewildering questions. What exactly did the national leaders of Hungarian Jewry in Budapest know about the extermination of the Jews in Nazi-occupied Europe and when did they acquire this knowledge? If they were aware of the Nazi program for the "Final Solution of the Jewish Question in Europe," why did they not inform the Jewish masses—or at least the leaders of the provincial Jewish communities—in time? Why did they fail

---

*This issue is discussed in greater detail in chapter 23 of the author's *The Politics of Genocide.* (New York: Columbia University Press, 1981).

to enlighten Hungarian public opinion and why did they not inform Horthy and the other governmental leaders of Hungary until the second half of June when the bulk of the provincial Jews had already been deported? These are the questions that arose most conspicuously in the postwar controversy over Rezső Kasztner (Rudolph Kastner).[1]

Currently available evidence indicates that many, if not all, of the national leaders of Hungarian Jewry were fully aware of the progress of the Final Solution in Nazi-occupied Europe well before the German occupation of Hungary. Although their information about the mass extermination of the Jews was perhaps not totally substantiated during the first two years of the war,[2] the hard-core evidence was fully at hand weeks before the beginning of the mass deportations from Hungary.

The sources of information of Jewish leaders were many and varied. They included:

- Newscasts by "enemy" radio stations including the BBC, the Voice of America, and "Kossuth Radio," the Hungarian-language transmissions from Moscow;
- "Illegal" contacts with Jewish organizations abroad, especially the Zionist and Orthodox units in Switzerland, Palestine, Istanbul, and Bratislava;
- Refugees and camp escapees from Poland, Slovakia, and elsewhere;
- Reports by Hungarian soldiers and officers;
- Contacts with German military, police, and intelligence officers, including those affiliated with the *Wehrmacht,* the SS, and the *Abwehr.*

The First Revelations about the Mass Murders

Although the details of the "Final Solution of the Jewish Question in Europe" were discussed only at the Wannsee Conference on January 20, 1942, the mass execution of Jews had begun soon after the invasion of the Soviet Union on June 22, 1941. Hundreds of thousands of Polish and Soviet Jews had been systematically rounded up and shot by the SS *Einsatzgruppen,* the mobile killing units that followed the Nazi armies, before the extermination camps were set up in Poland.[3] Among these were also the 14,000 to 16,000 "alien" Jews who had been deported from Hungary in August 1941. Their liquidation near Kamenets Podolsk was, in fact, the first five-figure massacre of the Holocaust period.[4]

In spite of the stringent security measures taken by the SS, the killings were too massive to be totally concealed either from the local population or from members of the Nazi satellite armies, including the Romanians and the Hungarians. Numerous Hungarian soldiers, appalled by the machine-gunning of innocent men, women, and children, expressed shock in letters to their families, giving detailed reports when home on furlough. Many of these accounts were brought to the attention of the Jewish leaders and some of them were even reported in the American press.[5] Such accounts were also fully corroborated by those escapees who managed to return to Hungary. One of the survivors by the name of Stern, accompanied by a delegation from the Magyar Izraeliták Pártfogó Irodája (Welfare Bureau of Hungarian Jews) led by György Polgár, gave details of the massacres at Kamenets Podolsk to Ferenc Keresztes-Fischer, the Minister of the Interior. The latter was visibly shocked and ordered a halt to all further deportations.[6]

The first public disclosure relating to the mass killings of Jews was made by Thomas Mann, the noted novelist, in his BBC broadcasts of December 1941 and January 1942.[7] Soon afterwards, Slovak escapees from camps in the area of Poland under the "General Government" (Generalgouvernement) confirmed that Jews were being massacred in them. The first of many transports of Slovakian Jews left from Poprad for Auschwitz on March 26, 1942; by the end of April a few escapees managed to return and provide the earliest evidence about the fate of the deportees. Their accounts were forwarded by the Ústredňa Židov (Central Jewish Office), the Nazi-established central "authority" representing the Jews of Slovakia, to Jewish organizations in Britain, Palestine, and Switzerland as well as to the leaders of the Slovakian state, including President Josef Tiso.

The Vatican was apparently also aware of the realities in Poland by this date. During the first wave of deportations from Slovakia, the Papal Nuncio in Bratislava, Mgr. Giuseppe Burzio, informed Tiso and his Prime Minister Vojtěch Tuka, that the Jews were being gassed and pleaded for the ending of the deportations. In response to this intervention, Tuka asked Dieter Wisliceny at the German legation, who had been organizing the deportations, for permission to send a Slovak delegation to inspect the situation of the deportees (June 1942). Wisliceny denied the "rumor" of the gassing, but adopted dilatory tactics concerning the request. At the same time he alerted Berlin and recommended that, in the interest of continued good German-Slovak relations, the deportations be halted. By that time about 55,000 Jews, or two-thirds of the Slovak Jewish community, had already been deported.[8]

In May 1942 the Jewish Socialist party of Poland, the "Bund," transmitted a detailed report to London informing the world that the Germans had "embarked on the physical extermination of the Jewish population on Polish soil." The report was broadcast over the BBC on June 2 and 26, 1942; details were also published by the *Daily Telegraph* on June 25 as well as by the Jewish press. However, the world at large remained complacent. Jewish leaders in the free world "made no visible attempt to put pressure on their governments for any active policy of rescue."[9]

Late in July 1942, representatives of some of the leading Jewish organizations in neutral Switzerland received firsthand information about the resolution of the Nazi hierarchy to bring about the physical liquidation of European Jewry in the course of the war. There has been, however, a certain lack of clarity as to how the information reached them.

According to Arthur D. Morse's account, Gerhart Riegner, the representative of the World Jewish Congress in Switzerland, was informed on August 1, 1942 by a leading German industrialist who had access to Hitler's headquarters, that the *Führer* had ordered the extermination of the Jews of

Europe. The informant had overheard a discussion of the order, which also stipulated the use of prussic acid, the lethal ingredient of the Zyklon B gas that was actually used in the extermination camps. By that time, presumably, Riegner was already aware of the Bund report and had information about the "resettlement" of 380,000 Jews in the Warsaw Ghetto, which had begun on July 22, and about the deportation of Jews from occupied Belgium, Holland and France.

Because of wartime censorship regulations, and in order to asure privacy, Riegner forwarded his report in the form of a telegram through the American Consulate in Geneva on August 8. Vice-Consul Howard Etling Jr. included a covering memorandum to the State Department in which he evaluated Riegner as "a serious and balanced individual," requesting that the message be delivered to Rabbi Stephen S. Wise, head of the World Jewish Congress. The telegram was at first suppressed by the State Department, but when it was discovered that the British Foreign Office had forwarded its copy to the London branch of the World Jewish Congress, Rabbi Wise was finally notified on August 28.

According to evidence now available, however, the real source of Riegner's information was a fiercely anti-Nazi officer, Lt. Col. Artur Sommer. A highly esteemed economist, Sommer had been attached early in the war to the Wehrmacht High Command. In this capacity, and as a member of a German economic delegation, he often visited Switzerland officially and ostensibly for the advancement of German economic interests. An anti-Nazi who opposed Hitler's war, Sommer reestablished and maintained discreet contact with Professor Edgar Salin of Basel University, his former teacher. Sommer became the conduit of invaluable information for the Allies. It was Sommer, for example, who tipped off Stalin some time in June 1941 about the Nazis' plan for the imminent attack on the Soviet Union.

Appalled by the Nazis' design to exterminate the Jews, Sommer revealed the information to Stalin with the following request that it be relayed to Churchill and Roosevelt:[10]

> In the East, camps are being prepared where all the Jews of Europe and a great part of the Russian prisoners of war will be exterminated by gas. Please relay this information immediately to Churchill and Roosevelt personally. If the BBC comes out every day with a warning against lighting the gas ovens, then perhaps they may not be put into operation, for the criminals are doing everything to prevent the German people from finding out what they are planning to do and will certainly carry out.

Salin passed on the information received from Sommer to another former student of his, Dr. Chaim Pozner, co-director of the Palestine Office in Switzerland. Pozner gave the information immediately to V. C. Farrell, head of the British Passport Control Office in Geneva, who also served as the center of British Intelligence in Switzerland. Concurrently, Dr. Pozner informed Dr. Benjamin Sagalowitz, director of the press bureau of the Union of Jewish Communities in Switzerland, who in turn alerted Riegner.[11]

In addition to the information received from Sagalowitz, Riegner continued to submit corroborative documentation concerning Hitler's resolution to "solve" the Jewish question. But this, like all subsequent communications by Riegner and others, remained for a long time unheeded.

In desperation (months after receiving Riegner's first information), Rabbi Wise contacted President Roosevelt on December 2, 1942 and again on December 8, when he also submitted a 20-page document titled *Blueprint for Extermination* in which he presented a country-by-country analysis of the extermination program. The Allies were reluctant to diminish their general war effort for any overt rescue scheme in behalf of the Jews, arguing that an Allied victory offered the only remedy for the Jews' plight. The Jewish leaders in the West, on the other hand, apparently feared that by pressing for direct action to rescue European Jewry their own patriotism might be impugned.

Having rejected suggestions for an overt and direct rescue operation as incompatible with their war aims, the Allies nevertheless agreed to issue a joint statement on December 17, 1942, in which they condemned the Nazi extermination of the Jews. The conspiracy of silence was at last broken. From then on, Allied broadcasts aimed at the world at large contained more specific information about Nazi exterminations of the Jews.

The Revelations by Polish and Slovak Refugees

The Hungarian Jewish leaders were particularly well placed to ascertain the veracity of the foreign radio broadcasts, since thousands of Jewish refugees had escaped into Hungary from Poland and Slovakia in the wake of anti-Jewish measures. Some had been smuggled into Hungary with the assistance of the Budapest Relief and Rescue Committee, which was organized by the Zionists, including Kasztner, Ottó Komoly, and Joel Brand.[12] The latter was in charge of the *Tiyul* section, dealing with underground "human smuggling" operations. One of the major functions of the Rescue Committee was to collect and transmit the personal accounts of the escapees to its Jewish Agency contacts in Istanbul and Switzerland. The Budapest office set up a regular underground intelligence unit, where escapees were closely questioned and details about the ghettoization, concentration, and extermination program in Poland and Slovakia carefully scrutinized and counterchecked. It has been claimed that hundreds of such accounts were thus authenticated in Budapest and forwarded to the Rescue Committee offices in Istanbul and Switzerland.[13]

Reports of this nature were also collected and forwarded to the Jewish Agency offices in Istanbul and Switzerland by Gisi Fleischmann of the Rescue Committee of Bratislava.[14] She also kept the Hungarian Jewish leaders, especially those associated with the Kasztner group, abreast of developments in Poland and Slovakia on a regular basis.[15] Moreover, members of the Bratislava and Budapest Rescue Committees exchanged visits periodically. In addition, the Orthodox leadership of Hungarian Jewry was also informed separately by Rabbi Michael Dov Weissmandel of the Bratislava Committee.

The Bratislava Rescue Committee, for example, reported to the Budapest Committee, some weeks before the beginning of the Hungarian deportations in May 1944, that a railways agreement had been signed between Hungary and Slovakia and that the SS were in the process of improving and renovating the gas chambers and crematoria in Auschwitz in anticipation of the imminent arrival of the Hungarian Jews.[16] The report even quoted the words of a *Scharführer* that the SS "will soon eat fine Hungarian salami."[17]

It was Gisi Fleischmann who had established contact with Wisliceny on May 7, 1943, for the negotiation of the so-called "Europa Plan" for rescuing the Jews of Europe.[18] She was then already reporting to Jewish Agency offices in Istanbul and Switzerland; for instance, on March 24, 1943 she had identified the three major centers where Jews were still in existence as Auschwitz, Birkenau, and Lublin, emphasizing that those still alive were basically healthy men and women able to work.[19] On May 9 she reported further that even those selected for work in the camps were liable to be murdered there. "As long as the individual continues to be capable of working he justifies his right to exist. Should he become weak, or prevented by illness from carrying out his work, he simply ceases to exist."[20]

On May 10 (a few days after her meeting with Wisliceny), Gisi Fleischmann communicated not only the conditions worked out by Wisliceny and his "superiors" for the effectuation of the "Europa Plan," but also further details about the annihilation of the Jews in Poland. She wrote, *inter alia:*

> We are under the spell of the *schlichim* [couriers], who brought us reports that make the blood run cold. Over one million *chaverim* [comrades] have already been resettled from *Ziwiah* [Poland], the location is unknown. Hundreds of thousands more lost their life due to starvation, disease and cold, and uncounted others, numbering many many tens of thousands, have fallen victim to violence. The reports state that the corpses are used as chemical raw materials. The reports also agree with the news of some *plitim* [refugees] who were fortunate enough to escape in the most daring ways. We have also received written reports to the same effect from the *schlichim.* Into a cattle wagon which would normally hold 40 are crammed 120 *chaverim.* There is a layer approximately 10 centimeters deep of unslaked lime on the floor, and since the people in the wagons must relieve themselves where they are standing, when the wastes touch the lime gases are formed which bring about an exceedingly high mortality rate. It is presumed that those who were resettled from *Ziwiah* are being taken beyond the Bug, but so far no sign of life has reached us from there.[21]

The communications by Gisi Fleischmann, like those of the Budapest Rescue Committee,[22] constitute some of the most convincing evidence that Jewish leaders in various parts of the world, including, of course, Hungary, were fully acquainted with the Nazi massacre program.

Among Jewish refugees in Hungary, some were partisans who had been captured, but had managed to escape, acquire Aryan papers, and live semi-legally in the country. One of these was Bruce B. Teicholz who, after capture north of Munkács, was brought to Hungary in March 1942. He managed to escape in Budapest and joined a Polish-Jewish underground organization under the code name "Glick." He was also registered with the Külfödieket Ellenőrző Országos Központi Hatoság (National Central Alien Control Office), the agency entrusted with jurisdiction over foreign nationals living in Hungary, as a Polish Christian under the name of Bronislaw Szczepipiorka. In this triple capacity Teicholz maintained close contact with the Polish refugee organizations in Hungary and abroad, with Dr. A. Silberschein of the World Jewish Congress in Geneva, with the official leaders of Hungarian Jewry, including Samu Stern and Fülöp (Philipp de) Freudiger, and with the members of the Budapest Rescue Committee, including Kasztner, Komoly and Brand.

Teicholz claims that sometime in April 1943 he had a meeting with the leaders of Hungarian Jewry, including Freudiger, Kasztner, Moshe (Miklós) Krausz of the Palestine Office, and Dr. József Pásztor of the Országos Magyar Zsidó Segitő Akció (National Hungarian Jewish Assistance Campaign), the major Jewish fund-raising organization. At this meeting he claims to have explained in detail the techniques employed by the Germans in pursuing the Final Solution in Poland. He further claims to have reviewed the techniques used to lull Jews into submission and cooperation in their own destruction, and warned the Hungarian Jewish leaders to take all necessary precautionary measures. These leaders "assured" Teicholz that what was happening in Poland could not possibly happen in Hungary.

Teicholz's account is also corroborated by that of Hermann Adler, the German-Jewish poet and author, who fled to Budapest in October 1943 after having spent the previous two years in the underground movement in the Vilna, Bialystok, and Warsaw Ghettos. As a member of the underground in Poland, Adler was also in touch with Anton Schmidt, the by now legendary German army sergeant, and a number of other Germans involved in the anti-Nazi resistance, among them Franz Fritsch. By the time of his arrival in Budapest, Adler was fully familiar with the extermination of the Jews at Treblinka and the realities of the Final Solution program in Poland as a whole. He revealed all he knew to Professor Valdemar Langlet, the representative of the Swedish Red Cross in Budapest, and to the leaders of Hungarian Jewry, including those associated with the Budapest Rescue Committee. These leaders, Adler claims, refused to believe his accounts about Treblinka. Kasztner, for example, wanted to know whether he (Adler) was in Treblinka personally and whether he was speaking from personal experience. "It wasn't easy to convince the Hungarian Jews," Adler complained.[23]

Acknowledgements by Jewish Leaders

Hungarian Jewish leaders have since admitted that they knew the facts about the camps, facts such as those revealed by Teicholz and Adler. Describing the circumstances under which he had emerged as head of the Jewish Council of Budapest, the agency entrusted with "power" over all of Hungarian Jewry, Samu Stern wrote:

> The good-will faking, hypocritical and treacherous debut of the Gestapo did not take me in, nor others, I suppose; I knew of what they had done in all German-occupied states of Europe. . . . I heard enough about the methods of the Gestapo's ill-famed Jewish department to know that they always shunned sensation, disliked creating panic and fear, worked noiselessly, coolly and in deepest secrecy, so that the listless, ignorant victims should be without an inkling of what was ahead of them even while the wagon was travelling with them toward death. I knew their habits, deeds and terrifying reputation, and yet I accepted the chairmanship of the Council. *And the others knew as much as I did when they entered the Council as members.*[24]

Kasztner was perhaps even better aware than Stern of the anti-Jewish measures throughout Europe, in view of his contacts with Jewish organizations abroad through various underground channels. In 1946 Kasztner issued a detailed report on the wartime activities of the Budapest Rescue Committee.[25] In it he provided both direct and indirect evidence that he and his colleagues on the Committee were fully aware of the anti-Jewish measures in Nazi-occupied Europe. While admitting this, however, he was basically silent about the failure to inform Hungarian Jewry, though all the more pugnacious and bitter over the passivity and complacency of the Jewish and non-Jewish leaders in the free world, who (he repeatedly insisted) had indeed been constantly supplied with ample information from Budapest.[26]

Appearing as a witness for the prosecution in the Veesenmayer Trial on March 19, 1948, Kasztner stated in answer to a question from Mr. Caming, one of the prosecutors: "We had, as early as 1942, a complete picture of what had been happening in the East with the Jews deported to Auschwitz and the other extermination camps."[27] Yet when he was asked by Dr. Doetzer, Veesenmayer's defense counsel, why Horthy had not been informed, Kasztner gave an evasive reply:

> We certainly should have tried this. We ought to have tried it, and we did, but you must visualize the situation in Hungary at the time immediately after the German occupation. It was a state of terror. Many of the friends and acquaintances through whom we could have informed Regent Horthy were already gone. Others were afraid to get in touch with us. It took quite some time before we had found the men and the opportunity to inform Horthy about it.[28]

While Kasztner was partially correct in depicting the situation *after* the German occupation, why were Horthy and other governmental leaders not informed *before* the occupation about what Kasztner's organization had known since 1942? This is particularly important in view of the power demonstrated by Horthy to halt the deportations in July 1944, allegedly after he had been enlightened about the exterminations.

During the trial of Malkiel Grünwald in 1954–1955 on a charge of having libelled Kasztner,[29] the latter testified:

> Toward the end of April 1944, the German military agents informed me that they had finally decided on the total deportation of Hungarian Jews. . . . An agreement was made between Hungary and Slovakia for the transfer of deportation trains from Hungary to Auschwitz.
>
> I also received information from Auschwitz that they were preparing there to receive the Hungarian Jews. . . . I was allowed by . . . Krumey to go to Kluj (Cluj, Kolozsvár) and contact . . . Wisliceny. This was approximately May 3, 1944. . . . A few days later I visited Wisliceny at his home in Budapest. He told me that it had finally been decided—total deportation.[30]

The visit of Kasztner to Kolozsvár, during the ghettoization of the Transylvanian Jews early in May 1944, has emerged as a major focus of the controversies surrounding the behavior of Jewish leaders during the Holocaust. Allegedly, Kasztner failed to inform the local Jewish Council and Rescue Committee leadership about the impending disaster. His closest friends there, including Hillel Danzig and Dezső (David) Hermann, denied having been told anything about Auschwitz. Danzig made his denial at the Grünwald trial,[31] and Hermann in a taped interview with this writer (October 8, 1972).[32] It should be mentioned, however, that Hansi Brand, the wife of Joel Brand and herself a leading member of the Budapest Rescue Committee, was especially bitter about such details of knowledge by witnesses at the Grünwald trial when she in turn gave a taped interview (October 10, 1972). She claimed that the Jewish leaders in Kolozsvár were well aware of the impending threat.[33]

According to some of the witnesses summoned in Grünwald's defense, among them Jacob Freifeld and Yechiel Shmueli of Kolozsvár, several of the local Zionist leaders inadvertently supported the rumor planted by the Nazis that the Jews were being transferred to Kenyérmező for labor[34] for the duration of the war.[35] Perhaps these leaders were as convinced about the genuineness of the plan as were most of the Jews deported from Northern Transylvania. But then the question is: why did they decide to abandon the flock during a time of great peril? Instead of going with the masses to Kenyérmező to provide continued leadership, most of them joined the group of 388 Jews taken to Budapest in accordance with the scheme agreed upon between Kasztner and the SS. From there they were removed on June 30, together with about 1,300 other "prominent Jews," to a special camp in Bergen Belsen and then eventually to Switzerland and freedom.[36]

Ernő Marton, the noted Zionist and former chief editor of the newspaper *Uj Kelet* ("New East"), escaped to Romania shortly after Kasztner's visit.[37] But the only "news" the Jewish masses received was that they would be transferred to work in Kenyérmező or some other area in Transdanubia.

There are in fact clear indications that these leaders were informed by Kasztner about certain realities of the deportation of which the masses were kept in the dark. In response to a question by Judge Halevi, Kasztner confirmed that in Kolozsvár he had given his father-in-law Fischer certain hints and that "he had to know that there was deportation and that extermination would follow." When asked why the Jews of Kolozsvár did not know about all that, he confessed that his colleagues in Kolozsvár, including his father-in-law, "did not do all in their power—did not do all that could have been done—all that they had to do."[38]

The Auschwitz Protocols

The revelations by five Jewish excapees from Auschwitz in April–May 1944, just as the deportation of Hungarian Jews was getting under way, dispersed any doubts about the realities of the Nazis' "solution" of the Jewish question. While many attempted to flee the camp to save their own lives, these five escaped with the aid of the resistance movement to inform the world and warn the Jewish communities, especially in Hungary, about the impending disaster.[39]

The first to escape (on April 5, 1944) was Siegfried Lederer, whose mission was to alert the Jews in the Theresienstadt Ghetto and the International Red Cross in Geneva.[40] But by far the most important from the point of view of Hungarian Jewry was the escape of Walter Rosenberg (Rudolf Vrba)[41] and Alfred Wetzler (Josef Lanik)[42] on April 7. Both had enjoyed relatively special positions in the camp, enabling them to move freely throughout Auschwitz and collect exact information about the incoming transports and about the selection and extermination of the victims. On April 25, four days after reaching safety on Slovakian soil, they were telling their story at the Žilina headquarters of the Jewish Council to Dr. Oscar (Yermiyahu) Neumann, Oskar (Karmil) Krasznyansky and others. The escapees were closely scrutinized, their stories counterchecked and verified. The following day, after they had been interrogated anew, Krasznyansky prepared with the assistance of the escapees a detailed report in German.[43]

The report contained a detailed description of the camp, extensive data on the gassings, and sketches of the building plans, which were prepared by a professional architect. Krasznyansky's introduction to the report included biographical notes on the escapees and vouched for the accuracy and authenticity of their account.[44] He also added a supplement in which he urged the Allies to destroy the crematoria and the railroad lines leading to Auschwitz.[45] The so-called "working group" of the Jewish Community of Slovakia (including Gisi Fleischmann, Neumann, Weissmandel and

Krasznyansky himself) decided to forward the report, *inter alia,* to the Jewish Agency unit in Istanbul, to Nathan Schwalb of the *chalutz* youth movement in Geneva, to the Papal Nuncio in Bratislava and to Kasztner.[46]

The accounts of Vrba and Wetzler were fully corroborated a few weeks later by Arnošt Rosin of Snina, Slovakia, and Czezlav Mordowicz of Mlawa, Poland, who escaped from Auschwitz on May 27 (i.e., shortly after the Hungarian deportations had begun). Their account, recorded by Krasznyansky during the first half of June 1944, provided data on the extermination of the Hungarian Jews up to the time of their flight.[47]

As to the exact date when the first set of Auschwitz Protocols (containing the testimony of Vrba and Lanik) were forwarded, the record is rather obscure. Vrba claims that he was assured by Krasznyansky and Neumann on April 26 that the report had already been sent to the Hungarians.[48] The memoirs of Neumann are vague about the dates,[49] but he has claimed that the Protocols were forwarded "shortly" after being typed.[50] Krasznyansky, on the other hand, claims that Kasztner, who visited Bratislava during those days, had read the original German text there and had him (Krasznyansky) translate the Protocols into Hungarian as well. He recalls that the Hungarian translation was forwarded to Budapest within two weeks.[51]

In his postwar report on the activities of the Rescue Committee of Budapest, Kasztner made absolutely no reference to the Auschwitz Protocols. They are also ignored by Samu Stern, who admits only to having received "in the middle of April" the news about a "railway conference" and the consequent allocation of "rolling stock for some unknown purpose."[52] Ernő Pető, one of the leading members of the Budapest Jewish Council, merely alludes to them in recounting how he tried sometime in June to contact Andor Jaross, the Minister of the Interior, and Secretaries of State László Baky and László Endre, "to inform them personally of the already known horrors of Auschwitz." Unable to see any of the three, he managed to reveal his knowledge about Auschwitz to Lajos Reményi-Schneller, the Minister of Finance, and to the Nunciature.[53] Freudiger was also silent about them in the "Report on Hungary," which he coauthored a few months after his arrival in Bucharest on August 10, 1944.[54] But later, in a taped interview with this author (October 10, 1972), Freudiger declared that he had received a copy of the Protocols from Weissmandel sometime between June 5 and 10, 1944.[55]

While Krasznyansky and Kulka claim that Kasztner had taken along a copy of the Protocols from Bratislava in April 1944,[56] it appears that the "official" leaders of Hungarian Jewry learned about their content from Freudiger's copy. At the time that Freudiger admits having received the Protocols, the de-Jewification experts were already completing the deportations from Zone II (Transylvania) and beginning the concentration of the Jews in Zone III (Northern Hungary). But while German and Hungarian Nazis were pressing on with their program, Jewish leaders handled the Protocols "confidentially" in order "not to create panic"[57] and wasted invaluable time on translating them. In mid-June, Rabbi Fábián Herskovits was busy translating the Protocols from German into Italian with the assistance of Dr. Sára Friedländer and Lea Komoly Fürst, Ottó Komoly's daughter, "in order to transmit a copy to the Nuncio and the Pope."[58]

Only in late June did the Hungarian Jewish leaders begin to distribute copies of the Protocols among influential governmental and church leaders of Hungary and friends abroad. A copy was handed over by Pető to Miklós Horthy, Jr. for transmission to his father. On June 19 Miklós (Moshe) Krausz of the Palestine Office submitted an abbreviated English version of the protocols, together with a report on the ghettoization, concentration, and deportation processes in Zones I–III, to Switzerland on June 19, 1944, via Florian Manoliu, a member of the Romanian Legation in Berne. Krausz's material was duplicated and disseminated in Switzerland through the efforts of George (Mandel) Mantello, a Jewish businessman from the Transylvanian city of Beszterce, who was then serving as the First Secretary of the General Consulate of El Salvador in Geneva.[59] The credence of the material was enhanced through its distribution under a cover letter dated July 4, 1944, over the signatures of Professor D. Karl Barth of Basel, Professor D. Emil Brunner of Zürich, Dr. W. A. Visser t'Hooft of Geneva, and Pastor Vogt of Zürich.[60]

The Vatican, which was by that time well acquainted with the Nazi extermination program,[61] received the copy of the Vrba-Lanik Protocols handed by the Bratislava Rescue Committee to Burzio late in April. However, the first overt reaction of the Vatican took place around June 20, presumably after it had also received the Rosin-Mordowicz Protocols. It was around this time that the Vatican's legate, a certain Monsignor Mario, arrived in Bratislava on a mission to interview the escapees from Auschwitz and double-check the veracity of their accounts. Krasznyansky consequently accompanied Vrba and Mordowicz to the Svätý Jur monastery near Bratislava, where they were interviewed in depth for five hours through the intermediary of a French interpreter.[62] Apparently the Papal legate was fully satisfied with the outcome of the interview, since the Pope addressed a personal plea to Horthy[63] on June 25, which was followed by the warning of President Roosevelt[64] on June 26, and by the intervention of King Gustav of Sweden[65] on June 30.

There is no doubt that these official, diplomatic interventions played an important (if not determining) role in Horthy's decision of July 7 to prohibit further deportations from Hungary. It is safe to assume, however, that had the first set of Protocols been publicized abroad and secretly distributed in Hungary almost immediately after their preparation, the deportations might have been interrupted significantly earlier. For although the BBC broadcast some sections from the Protocols, such broadcasts were construed by world public opinion basically as horror propaganda material. Had the Vatican and neutral countries, like Sweden and Switzerland, begun a vigorous press and radio campaign as soon as the Protocols were received from Bratislava, Horthy might have been induced to act earlier.

In fact, the Vatican and the neutrals were more concerned with maintaining strict neutrality than with publicizing their concern for the Jews of Hungary. The Swiss press began the campaign of attacking Hungary only during the second half of June, largely due to the initiatives taken by Mantello after he had received Krausz's material of June 19.[66] The Americans did not publicize the Protocols until November 1944, by which time the Nazis, faced with the advance of the Red Army, were already eager to demolish the extermination facilities and remove all traces of their crimes.[67]

Hungarian Governmental Awareness of the Catastrophe

Although the copy of the Protocols given by Pető to Miklós Horthy Jr. reached the Regent only in late June 1944,[68] there is ample evidence that he and many of the other leaders of Hungary were similarly well-acquainted with the Nazi anti-Jewish program long before the German occupation of the country. In April 1943, for example, during Horthy's first Schloss Klessheim meeting with Hitler, the latter recommended that Hungary should copy Poland, where "the Jews who did not want to work were simply shot." Ribbentrop added that the Jews "should either be killed or sent to concentration camps."[69] Upon his return to Hungary, Horthy drafted a letter defending himself and the Kállay Government against the reproach that Hungary had "failed to take as far-reaching an action in the extirpation of the Jews as Germany had taken or as would appear desirable in the other countries." This sentence, although not included in the final version of the letter (sent on May 7, 1943), clearly reveals that Horthy and the officials of the Ministry of Foreign Affairs who prepared the original draft had been informed about what was happening to the Jews of Germany.[70]

Döme Sztójay, Hungary's Minister in Berlin, who was to become Prime Minister after the German occupation, apparently knew about the Nazi design to "solve the Jewish question in a radical manner during the war" as early as 1942. He revealed his knowledge to György Ottlik, a member of the influential Foreign Affairs Committee of the Upper House of the Hungarian Parliament and the editor-in-chief of the German-language *Pester Lloyd* of Budapest, the semi-official organ of the Hungarian Government. Ottlik, who visited Germany in the course of his West European tour of August–September 1942, transmitted this information to the Hungarian Ministry of Foreign Affairs on October 10.[71] According to Dieter Wisliceny, "both Endre and Baky had been accurately informed as to what the deportations meant."[72] In his report of May 29, 1944, Lt.-Col. László Ferenczy, who had been in charge of the deportations, openly referred to Auschwitz as a place where the deported Jews were subjected to a process of "selection."[73]

The evidence now available indicates that even some of the anti-Nazi leaders in Hungary were acquainted with the Nazi extermination program. Kasztner claimed, though without providing sufficient evidence, that various leaders of the Social Democratic Party had been kept informed about the destruction of the European Jews and about the methods the Nazis had employed.[74] Angelo Rotta, the Apostolic Nuncio in Budapest, was also familiar with the realities of the deportations. In his letter of May 15, 1944, protesting the measures that the Hungarian Government was taking or planned to take against the Jews, the Nuncio remarked that "the whole world knows what the deportation means in practice."[75]

Questions and Arguments

The conclusion to be drawn from the foregoing is clear. Many of the Jewish and Christian leaders of the world, including of course the Hungarian ones, possessed well-substantiated knowledge about the extermination program since the spring of 1942 and irrefutable evidence since April 1944. Nonetheless, the deportations that began in Hungary on May 15 were not halted until July 7, when only the Jews of Budapest remained.

It is almost universally supposed that Horthy decided to halt the deportations in response to the interventions made by foreign state and church leaders, who were motivated to act, *inter alia*, by the Auschwitz Protocols. The interventions were presumably reinforced by Horthy's own reaction to the Protocols, which had been shown to him by his son during the second half of June. Yet these assumptions give rise to a number of bewildering questions. Why were the first Protocols not forwarded to those world leaders soon after their completion on April 26? Why were the provincial Hungarian Jewish leaders and masses not alerted to their content? What would have been the result of alerting them before the deportations began?

These questions are obviously controversial and require a careful differentiation among facts, claims, and presumptions. The established *facts* include the following:

- The escapees from Auschwitz told their story to the Jewish leaders of Slovakia on April 25 and 26, 1944.
- Freudiger admits to having received the Protocols between June 5–10.
- Kasztner admitted having known of the mass destruction of the Jews in Nazi-occupied Europe before the German occupation of Hungary.
- The Hungarian Jewish masses were not authoritatively informed about them.
- The deportation of the Jews from Carpatho-Ruthenia and Transylvania (Zones I and II) began on May 15 and was completed on June 7, and the deportation of the Jews of Northern Hungary (Zone III) did not begin until June 11.
- The Hungary Jewish leaders were still busy translating and duplicating the Protocols on June 14–16 and distributed them only later in June.
- The Hungary Jewish leaders completely ignored the Protocols in their postwar memoirs and statements.

Although the *claims* advanced in connection with the Protocols are both plausible and to a considerable extent convincing, there is no conclusive evidence to substantiate them. Among the claims are:

- The contention of Krasznyansky in 1964 that he had handed a copy of the first Protocols to Kasztner during the latter's visit to Bratislava late in April 1944;

- The claim of Neumann that these Protocols were sent to Hungary, Switzerland and the Vatican "shortly" after they had been completed;

- Vrba's claim that he was assured by Neumann and Krasznyansky on April 26 that the reports were already in the hands of Kasztner;

- The assertion by Munkácsi that the Protocols were handled in Hungary in a "confidential" manner in order "not to create panic" among the remaining Jews;

- The claim that Kasztner deliberately remained silent in accordance with an agreement with Eichmann under which he was allowed to save a few thousand "prominent" Jews, including his own family and friends.

It is safe to *presume* that Krasznyansky's contention about Kasztner's visit to Bratislava is correct. It is also safe to accept Krasznyansky's claim to have translated the first Protocols into Hungarian and forwarded them to Hungary "within two weeks," i.e., around May 10. Krasznyansky, after all, played a pivotal role in the preparation and distribution of the Protocols. Moveover, Kasztner was a frequent visitor in Bratislava, especially after he had established contact with the SS early in April. He must obviously have been eager to consult the leaders of the Bratislava Rescue Committee, who had considerable experience in dealing with Wisliceny and other members of the Eichmann *Sonderkommando.*

Accordingly, given the evidence that by the time of the German occupation of Hungary both Kasztner and the official leaders of Hungarian Jewry were aware of the Nazis' extermination program, how can one explain their silence? To take Kasztner first, a case against him (and indirectly against some of his closest associates in the provinces and in Budapest) was made after the war by both Jews and non-Jews using a variety of political-ideological, historical-moral, and judicial arguments.

In his postwar "memoirs" Eichmann, for example, argued that he and Kasztner, the two "idealists" who pursued different and conflicting objectives, reached a "gentlemen's agreement" whereby Kasztner allegedly offered to remain silent (and "help keep the Jews from resisting deportation and even keep order in the collection camps") for the opportunity to rescue 15,000 to 20,000 "biologically valuable" Jews. For Eichmann this was a good bargain, since he could disregard the escape of small groups of Jews.[76] His primary concern was the orderly deportation of nearly 800,000 Hungarian Jews without encountering another "Warsaw uprising."

The same conclusion was reached by a number of anti-Zionist or anti-Mapai Zionist figures, including Vrba and Ben Hecht. According to them, Kasztner and his friends (both in Hungary and elsewhere) constituted a group of quislings that sold out Hungarian Jewry to save themselves, their friends, and a few rich Jews. A somewhat similar line has been taken by Communist historians and propagandists. The anti-Jewish drive in the Soviet bloc, launched in September 1948 and presented as a campaign against "Zionism and cosmopolitanism," has sought to identify Zionism with Nazism. As part of this still continuing campaign, Kasztner's activities have been portrayed as an example of Zionism and Nazism finding a common interest in the destruction of vast numbers of innocent people.[77]

At the judicial level, by far the most damning conclusion concerning Kasztner was reached by Judge Benjamin Halevi at the original Grünwald Trial. In his verdict, Halevi asserted that Kasztner and his colleagues in Kolozsvár and Nagyvárad, whom the Jewish masses had trusted, allowed themselves to be used by the SS in their calculated plan to mislead the Jews by spreading the false information about Kenyérmező. They did everything in their power to soothe the Jews in the ghettos and prevent resistance; in return the Nazis allowed Kasztner to rescue close to 2,000 "prominent Jews."[78] A similar conclusion was reached by Judge Moshe Silberg of the Supreme Court of Israel in his minority opinion against the reversal of Judge Halevi's verdict.

As for the silence of the leaders of the Budapest Jewish Council, the interpretations offered after the war naturally also vary. Ilona Benoschofsky,[79] for example, argues that they perhaps thought that "since Hungarian Jewry cannot be saved, it is better that it does not know the fate awaiting it. And since the Germans threatened to execute those who speak of deportation, the Council did not assist in publicizing the real objective of the deportation, namely the gas chamber and the crematorium."[80] She adds that if the "Jewish Council thought that there was no way out for the masses, there was one for itself."[81]

Ironically, a related argument was advanced by Chaim Cohen, the then Attorney General of Israel, in defending Kasztner against the accusation of collaboration with the SS. He claimed that Kasztner, convinced that there was no hope for the Jews of Hungary, did not disclose the secret of the extermination in order not to frustrate the rescue of the few.[82] Judge Shlomo Chesin of the Supreme Court agreed with this line of reasoning, arguing that Kasztner "didn't warn Hungarian Jewry of the danger facing it because he didn't think it would be useful, and because he thought that any deeds resulting from information given them would damage more than help . . ."[83]

According to the arguments just mentioned, Kasztner followed in the footsteps of Rabbi Dr. Leo Baeck, the former Chairman of the Reich Association of the Jews in Germany. While in Theresienstadt, where he was deported from Berlin on January 27, 1943, Baeck was fully aware of the realities of the Nazi's extermination program. Nevertheless, as he later explained:

> . . . I finally decided that no one should know it. If the Council of Elders were informed, the whole camp would know within a few hours. Living in the expectation of death by gassing would only be the harder and this death was not certain at all: there was selection for slave labor; perhaps not all transports went to Auschwitz. So I came to the grave decision to tell no one.[84]

So much for some of the arguments for and against. All of them are beside the point in one respect. As indicated earlier they do not explain or justify the silence of Jewish leaders *before* the German occupation. However relevant they may be to the desperate situation of Hungarian Jewry *after* the occupations of March 1944, they are irrelevant to the earlier period.

Perhaps the biggest mistakes were made when Hungarian Jews were still relatively well-off, when precautionary measures might have minimized the catastrophe, if not totally averted it. Although the official Hungarian Jewish leadership and the leading Zionists were remarkably aware of Nazi anti-Jewish actions elsewhere, they failed to inform the masses authoritatively and to heed the advice of Polish and Slovak refugees to take precautionary measures. As good law-abiding citizens, the official Jewish leaders heeded the censorship regulations and avoided using their organs for such "propaganda" purposes. The sermons in the synagogues at best only alluded to the suffering of the Jews in Nazi-occupied countries in rather general terms.

As a result the Hungarian Jews, living so close to Auschwitz, had no sure knowledge about the gas chambers, or about the mass murders committed further afield by the SS *Einsatzgruppen.* They discounted what they heard about these horrors as rumors or anti-Nazi propaganda. It was thus even easier for the masses than their leaders to delude themselves about their relative safety. They rationalized their predicament by arguing that whatever was really happening to the Jews of Poland and elsewhere, such horrors could not possibly take place in Hungary, where the destiny of Jews and Christians had been intertwined for over a thousand years.

The sudden German occupation of Hungary found the Jews not only uninformed about the Nazis' Final Solution program, but also generally disunited. Little effort had been made to end the constant bickering within and between the three major official (Neolog, Orthodox, and Status Quo) communities and the semi-illegal Zionist organization. There were also conflicts between the assimilated-acculturated groups and the Zionists, between the rich and the poor, and between the larger and the semi-autonomous congregations. All this was compounded by the petty jealousy and personal animosity with which many leaders of these communities pursued parochial objectives.

Uninformed, unprepared, and disunited, the Jews were an easy prey for the SS and their Hungarian hirelings. They were isolated and demoralized at lightning speed. The SS acquired exclusive jurisdiction over the Jews during the early and crucial phase of the occupation.[85] The quisling Sztójay government eagerly embraced the anti-Jewish measures suggested by László Baky and László Endre, the two ultra-rightist Secretaries of State who colluded with the SS in planning and implementing the Final Solution in Hungary. The one stratum of Hungarian Christian society on which the official Jewish leaders depended for protection—the aristocratic and conservative leadership with which they had good contacts—was itself decimated in the early phase of the occupation.

Trapped and abandoned by their own government, both the traditional official Jewish leaders and the Zionist ones tried desperately to save what could still be saved under the given conditions. The former tried to win a "race with time" by relying on dilatory tactics and the rapid advance of the Red Army. They consequently continued to employ traditional legal methods, including the filing of appeals and petitions, which had proved highly effective during the preoccupation semiparliamentary era, but were totally inadequate under Nazi rule. The Zionists, while agreeing with the objectives, if not the tactics, of the traditional Jewish leaders, basically believed that only by direct dealing with the SS, the *real* holders of power in Hungary, could the maximum be achieved for Hungarian Jewry.

In retrospect, both approaches proved equally disastrous.[86] Defying reason and logic, the German and Hungarian Nazis, driven by ideological considerations and a venomous racial hatred, largely succeeded in achieving their objective. This was due not so much to the lack of Jewish resistance,[87] but to the wholehearted support from the Hungarian government and its instruments of power—the civil service, gendarmerie, and police—for implementing the Final Solution program. The success was also assisted by the absence of any meaningful resistance on the part of leftist and democratic forces and by the general passivity of the Christian population.

While the silence of the Hungarian Jewish leaders, like that of the rest of the world, very likely exacerbated the tragedy of Hungarian Jewry, one must bear in mind that responsibility lies first and foremost with the Germans. Dedicated as the Hungarian Nazis were to solving the Jewish question, and poisoned as the Hungarians were by decades of anti-Jewish propaganda, Hungarian Jewry would probably have survived the war relatively intact had the Germans not occupied the country.

Notes

1. Kasztner, as deputy chairman of the Hungarian Zionist Organization, was involved with Joel Brand in attempting to rescue Hungarian Jews through negotiations with the Germans (and especially Adolf Eichmann). He settled in Israel after the war. There he was accused in 1953 by Malkiel Grünwald of complicity in the destruction of Hungarian Jewry. A libel suit against Grünwald was decided in the latter's favor by a lower court in 1955 after a brilliant defense by his counsel Shmuel Tamir. In 1958 the Israeli Supreme Court reversed the decision—a year after Kasztner had been murdered in the street following the controversy surrounding the earlier trial.

2. Ernő Munkácsi, the executive secretary of the Jewish community of Pest, asserted that the Hungarian Jewish leaders were then "more or less aware of the fate of German Jewry and of the fact that the Jewish population in the Nazi-occupied countries were deported."

However, he continued, only "indefinite and nebulous news was spread about all these things." Ernő Munkácsi, *Hogyan történt?* ("How did it happen?"; Budapest, 1947), p. 11.

3. On the Wannsee Conference see Raul Hilberg, *The Destruction of the European Jews* (Chicago, 1961), pp. 264–66. On the "Killing Center Operations" see pp. 555–635; on the *Einsatzgruppen,* see pp. 242–56.

4. Randolph L. Braham, "The Kamenets Podolsk and Délvidék Massacres: Prelude to the Holocaust in Hungary," *Yad Vashem Studies* 9 (1973), 133–56.

5. Arthur D. Morse, *While Six Million Died* (New York, 1968), pp. 304–5. Kasztner admitted that the tragedy of the Jews in Nazi-occupied Eastern Europe could be followed clearly from Budapest and that by late Summer 1941 he and his colleagues had solid information about the mass executions in the Ukraine, the Baltic States, Bessarabia and Bukovina. Around the same time they were also informed through Hungarian agents about the use of gassing vans. See Ernest Landau ed., *Der Kastner-Bericht* (Munich, 1961), p. 37.

6. Randolph L. Braham, "The Kamacets Podolsk and Délvidék Massacres" *(op. cit.),* p. 142.

7. Henry L. Feingold, *The Politics of Rescue: The Roosevelt Administration and the Holocaust 1938–1945* (New Brunswick, N.J., 1970), p. 168.

8. Livia Rothkirchen, *Hurban yahadut Slovakia* (intn. in English, Jerusalem, 1961), pp. xxiii–xxiv (on the escapes from the first transports), xxxii; *Der Kastner-Bericht (op. cit.),* pp. 15–16. That the Vatican informed Tuka about the killing of the "resettled" Slovak Jews was also confirmed by Hans Gmelin, the former Counselor to the German Legation in Bratislava (NO-5921).

9. Yehuda Bauer, "When Did They Know?", *Midstream,* April 1968, pp. 51–58 (contains the text of the Bund report in Polish original and English translation).

10. For details on Sommer's background and revelations, see Edgar Salin, "Über Artur Sommer, den Menschen und List-Forscher," *Mitteilungen der List Gesellschaft* (Basel), November 30, 1967, pp. 81–90 (quotation from pp. 85–86).

11. Riegner stated that Sagalowitz was also his source in a letter to the editors of *Das Neue Israel* (Zurich) on Arthur D. Morse's *While Six Million Died (op. cit.,* note 5 above). See *Das Neue Israel,* November 1968, pp. 359–61. The role of Pozner is reviewed by Shlomo Derech in his introduction to the Hebrew version of Morse's work, *Ve-ha-olam shatak et nispu shishah milyonim* (Tel Aviv, 1972). Note that the way in which the British are said to have first received the information is also different than in Morse's account.

12. The Budapest Rescue Committee operated as a branch of the United Rescue Committee of the Jewish Agency in Jerusalem. For a critical review of its activities, see Aryeh Morgenstern, "Va'ad ha-hatzala ha-me'uhad she-le-yad ha-Sokhnut ha-Yehudit u-fe'ulotav," *Yalkut Moreshet* 13 (June 1971), pp. 60–103.

13. Alex Weissberg, *Advocate for the Dead: The Story of Joel Brand* (London, 1958), pp. 30–31. Kasztner reported that one of the primary functions of the Rescue Committee was to transmit abroad "reports about the mass murders in the East"; see *Der Kastner-Bericht (op. cit.),* p. 26. In a taped interview with this writer on October 10, 1972, Hansi Brand, who also played an important role in the Rescue Committee, asserted that the Committee had received information about gassings in Poland in 1942 and that Hermann Adler had informed it in 1943 about the building of crematoria. All this information, she claimed, was forwarded to the Jewish Agency unit in Istanbul.

14. On her see the WIZO booklet by Y. O. Neumann, *Gisi Fleischmann: The Story of a Heroic Woman* (Tel Aviv, 1970).

15.   Kasztner acknowledged that Gisi Fleischmann transmitted authenticated personal accounts about "the mass executions and gassings abroad"; see *Der Kastner-Bericht (op. cit.)*, p. 28, and also Livia Rothkirchen, *Hurban yahadut Slovakia (op. cit.)*, p. xxviii.

16.   It was Rabbi Weissmandel who had obtained information about the railways agreement and who had also sent a copy of the so-called Auschwitz Protocols (on which more below) to Fülöp (Philipp de) Freudiger. See Weissmandel's *Min ha-metzar* (New York, 1960) and also Livia Rothkirchen, *Hurban yahadut Slovakia (op. cit.)*, pp. xxvi and xli.

17.   *Der Kastner-Bericht (op. cit.)*, p. 82.

18.   On the "Europa Plan" see Livia Rotkirchen, *Hurban yahadut Slovakia (op. cit.); also* Yad Vashem file M-20/93. Wisliceny had "established his credentials" with the Jewish leaders by his role in halting the Slovakian deportations in Fall 1942.

19.   Yad Vashem File M-20/93 (which contains most of her reports and letters, written in German).

20.   *Ibid.*

21.   *Ibid.*

22.   See, for example, the reports dated "Budapest, August 23, 1943" and "September 1943" at Beit Lohamei Hagetaot, the Yitzhak Katsenelson Institute in Israel, under file nos. G1054/5, G1054/8 and G1054/3.

23.   The above information was supplied in personal communications to this author from Teicholz on June 28, 1971 and from Adler on February 10, 1975. On Anton Schmidt, the German army sergeant who cooperated with the Jewish underground in Vilna and Bialystok (providing its members especially with false documentation and transport facilities), until caught and executed by the Gestapo, see Gideon Hausner, *Justice in Jerusalem* (New York, 1966), p. 258.

24.   Samu Stern, "A Race with Time," in Randolph L. Braham ed., *Hungarian-Jewish Studies*, vol. III (New York, 1973), pp. 5–6. Italics added.

25.   *Der Kastner-Bericht (op. cit.)* is a published version of this report.

26.   *Der Kastner-Bericht (op. cit.)*, pp. 21, 26, 77 and *passim.*

27.   *Ministries Case,* Court 4, Case 11, session of March 19, 1948, transcript p. 3622.

28.   *Ibid.*, pp. 3651–3652.

29.   See note 1 above.

30.   Ben Hecht, *Perfidy* (New York, 1961), pp. 59–60. Hecht's version of Kasztner's testimony (and of the trial) is highly condensed. For Kasztner's complete testimony (in Hebrew) of February 18, 1954, see District Court, Jerusalem, *Criminal Case 124/53*, at the YIVO Institute for Jewish Research, New York, Film 221 M, Roll 2, p. 9.

31.   In his judgment acquitting Grünwald, Judge Halevi recalled Danzig's testimony that he had first learned about the realities of Auschwitz after he got to the "Columbus Camp" in Budapest, where the so-called Kasztner group was housed before its departure for Bergen Belsen on June 30, 1944. See *Psak din shel beit ha-mishpat ha-mehozi . . . neged Malkiel Grünwald . . .* (Tel Aviv, 1957), p. 16. Hecht's description of Danzig's testimony in *Perfidy (op. cit.)*, p. 108, is over-condensed.

32.   In the interview Hermann, who was secretary of the Kolozsvár Jewish Council, claimed that he did not meet with Kasztner during in latter's visit in May 1944 and did not know who had met him. Hermann denied any knowledge of the extermination, except the "horror stories" he had heard from the Polish and Slovak refugees; he was convinced, like most Jews, that the deportees were being taken for labor.

33. In her taped interview Hansi Brand stated that it was "inconceivable that [these individuals] did not know what the German occupation meant in March–April 1944." She further insisted that the leaders of Kolozsvár had been informed exactly about what was happening to the Jews in Poland even *before* Kasztner's visit in May 1944.

34. Kenyérmező was basically a fictitious geographic name like "Waldsee." During World War I, there was a military training camp near Esztergom that bore the name of Kenyérmező. The rumors about Kenyérmező and Transdanubia were also spread by the gendarmes just before the deportation.

35. Ben Hecht, *Perfidy (op. cit.)*, pp. 105–8.

36. For details see *Der Kastner-Bericht (op. cit.)*.

37. Compare Bela Vago, "Political and Diplomatic Activities for the Rescue of the Jews of Northern Transylvania," *Yad Vashem Studies* 6 (1967), 155–73.

38. Ben Hecht, *Perfidy (op. cit.)*, pp. 117–18.

39. According to Erich Kulka, 280 attempts at escape were noted during the existence of Auschwitz and about 80 prisoners actually succeeded in escaping. Erich Kulka, "Five Escapes from Auschwitz," in Yuri Suhl ed., *They Fought Back* (New York, 1967), p. 201.

40. *Ibid.*, pp. 196–205.

41. Rosenberg acquired false identification papers bearing the name of Rudolf Vrba, a name which he kept permanently. His own account appears in his *I Cannot Forgive* (New York, 1964), written in cooperation with Alan Bestic.

42. Wetzler, who was given the name Josef Lanik, published under the latter name *Oswiecim, hrobka štyroch milionov ludi* ("Auschwitz, tomb of four million people"; 2nd ed., Košice, 1946) and *Co Dante nevidel* ("What Dante did not see"; Bratislava, 1964).

42. Statement by Krasznyansky, Institute of Contemporary Jewry (Hebrew University), Oral History Division, Catalog no. 3, 1970, p. 120, no. 410 S.E. Protocol in Czech, pp. 10 and 13.

44. The Auschwitz Protocols may be found, *inter alia*, at the Yad Vashem Institute Archives in Jerusalem under no. M-20/149. For their Hungarian version see Munkácsi, *Hogyan történt? (op. cit.*, note 2 above), pp. 88–110.

45. Erich Kulka, "Five Escapes from Auschwitz" *(op. cit.)*, pp. 206–7.

46. Burzio, the Papal Nuncio, was expected to deliver it to the Vatican and Kasztner was expected to hand over copies to Admiral Horthy and the Prince Primate, Cardinal Jusztinián Serédi. The Protocols were translated into Yiddish by Rabbi Weissmandel.

47. For further details see Erich Kulka, "Five Escapes from Auschwitz" (*op. cit.*), pp. 207–11.

48. Rudolf Vrba and Alan Bestic, *I Cannot Forgive (op. cit.)*, p. 250.

49. Oscar Neumann, *Im Schatten des Todes* (Tel Aviv, 1956), pp. 178–82.

50. Personal communication to this author on November 19, 1972.

51. Personal communication to this author on February 7, 1973. In his interview in Jerusalem in 1964, Krasznyansky stated that "a copy of the Protocols was handed over to Dr. Kasztner," Institute of Contemporary Jewry, Oral History Division, catalog no. 3, 1970, p. 117, no. 398. Protocol in German, pp. 5–6.

52. *Hungarian-Jewish Studies*, vol. III (*op. cit.*, note 24 above), p. 14.

53. *Ibid.*, pp. 52 and 56.

54. *Ibid.*, pp. 74–142. In his epilogue of November 21, 1972 (pp. 143–46), however,

Freudiger claims that "by the time [they] learned the truth about Auschwitz, the first phase of the deportation, involving some 310,000 Jews, was already over." That phase, involving the Jews of Carpatho-Ruthenia and Transylvania, came to an end on June 7, 1944.

55.   The circumstances under which he received a copy of the Protocols are described in his *Five Months* (manuscript dated November 21, 1972), p. 19.

56.   Erich Kulka, "Auschwitz Condoned," *The Wiener Library Bulletin,* vol. 23, no. 1, New Series, no. 14 (Winter 1968), p. 3.

57.   Munkácsi, *Hogyan történt? (op. cit.),* p. 111.

58.   Taped interview with Fábián Herskovits (October 9, 1972), and personal communication by Lea Fürst (October 13, 1972). The Pope in fact knew German.

59.   Manoliu, who had good, and apparently lucrative, relations with Mantello, got in touch with Krausz in Budapest at the request of Mantello. The latter, in turn, was contacted for this purpose by Dr. Chaim Pozner, who as head of the Palestine Office of Geneva was Krausz's counterpart in Switzerland, and whose note Manoliu took along to Budapest as his "letter of accreditation." For the text of Krausz's letter and reports, see Yad Vashem Archives, M-20/95.

60.   *Ibid.,* M-20/47.

61.   Secret World War II documents published by the Vatican on April 4, 1973, prove that aides to Pope Pius XII (including the future Popes John XXIII and Paul VI), and presumably the Pope himself, already knew of the Nazi slaughter of Jews. See Paul Hofmann, "The Vatican Knew of Nazi Pogroms, Its Records Show," *New York Times,* April 5, 1973 and "Pius Knew in 1941 of Drive on Jews," *ibid.,* April 27, 1974. See further Saul Friedländer, *Pius XII and the Third Reich* (New York, 1966), esp. pp. 103 ff. and 236–38. Also Carlo Falconi, *The Silence of Pius XII* (Boston, 1970).

62.   Vrba allots only a few paragraphs to the Svätý Jur meeting and completely ignores the presence and role of Mordowicz: *I Cannot Forgive (op. cit.),* pp. 256–57. For Krasznyansky's version of the meeting, see Erich Kulka, "Five Escapes from Auschwitz" *(op. cit.),* p. 210.

63.   For the text of the Pope's note and Horthy's reply of July 1, 1944, see Lévai, *Szürke könyv magyar zsidok megmentéséről* ("Grey book on the rescuing of Hungarian Jews"; Budapest, 1946), p. 21.

64.   *Ibid.,* pp. 56–57.

65.   For the text of King Gustav V's telegram of June 30 and Horthy's reply of July 1, see *ibid.,* pp. 72–73.

66.   In a letter to Vrba, dated May 18, 1964, Mantello made the following comments on the reports he had received from Budapest: "These reports . . . were short and arrived in Switzerland rather late. . . . If we had received your complete report about six or seven weeks earlier, say about the same time that you had sent it to Budapest, perhaps we could have put a stop to the deportations, since we would have started a big press campaign in Switzerland and abroad." Erich Kulka, "Five Escapes from Auschwitz" *(op. cit.),* pp. 217–18.

67.   A brief, unofficial reference to the Protocols and their contents appeared in the *New York Times* ("Inquiry Confirms Nazi Death Camps") of July 3, 1944. Judging by Raphael Vago's research, the Protocols were also unnoticed or ignored by the Palestine press, including the Hebrew language press. See his "The Destruction of Hungarian Jewry as Reflected in the Palestine Press," *Hungarian-Jewish Studies,* vol. III *(op. cit.),* pp. 291–324. This although the Jewish Telegraphic Agency (under the dateline London, July 10, 1944) issued an account based on the Protocols, which were most probably supplied by Mantello.

68.   Horthy wrongly claims that the secret information about the extermination camps

reached him only in August. Admiral Nicholas Horthy, *Memoirs* (New York, 1957), p. 219.

69.   Randolph L. Braham, *The Destruction of Hungarian Jewry* (New York, 1963), vol. I, pp. 218 ff.

70.   M. Szinai and L. Szücs eds., *The Confidential Papers of Admiral Horthy* (Budapest, 1965), pp. 248–57.

71.   Randolph L. Braham, "The Holocaust in Hungary: An Historical Interpretation of the Role of the Hungarian Radical Right," *Societas,* vol. 2, no. 3 (Summer 1972), p. 202.

72.   *Der Kastner-Bericht (op. cit.),* p. 302.

73.   Israel Police, Bureau 06, doc. no. 1319.

74.   *Der Kastner-Bericht (op. cit.),* p. 49.

75.   Ilona Benoschofsky and Elek Karsai eds., *Vádirat a nácizmus ellen* ("Indictment of Nazism"; Budapest, 1958), vol. I, p. 317.

76.   "Eichmann Tells His Own Damning Story," *Life,* December 5, 1960, p. 146.

77.   For samples on this theme from a variety of Communist newspapers, consult *Jews in Eastern Europe,* a periodical newsletter edited by Emanuel Litvinoff and issued by European Jewish Publications of London.

78.   See *Psak din shel beit ha-mishpat ha-mehozi . . . (op. cit.),* pp. 22–24 ff. and 45. Also Ben Hecht, *Perfidy (op. cit.),* pp. 178–83.

79.   Miss Benoschofsky is known as the Director of the Jewish Museum of Budapest, as well as being a co-editor of the first two volumes of *Vádirat a nácizmus ellen* cited above (note 75).

80.   *Vádirat a nácizmus ellen (op. cit.),* vol. II, p. 44.

81.   In justification of this remark (*ibid.*, pp. 44–45), she argues that since the anti-Jewish measures of the Horthy era, including the major anti-Jewish laws, affected primarily the little Jews (the lower civil servants, small traders and artisans), the members of the Jewish Council, "who knew of these restrictive measures largely only by hearsay, obviously had hoped that they would be exempted this time as well."

82.   As quoted by Judge Moshe Silberg in Ben Hecht, *Perfidy (op. cit.),* p. 273. For the Hebrew original see *Arar Plili 232/55, berur shel ha-me'ar'er: Ha-yo'etz ha-mishpati la-memshala neged Malkiel Grünwald* (duplicated by the Students' Union of the Hebrew University, Jerusalem, 1957).

83.   Ben Hecht, *Perfidy (op. cit.),* p. 270; *Arar Plili 232/55 (op. cit.), pp. 174–97.*

84.   Eric H. Boehm ed., *We Survived: The Stories of Fourteen of the Hidden and the Hunted of Nazi Germany* (New Haven, 1949), p. 293. The matter is discussed further in Jacob Robinson's introduction to Isaiah Trunk, *Judenrat* (New York, 1972).

85.   *Inter alia,* through the Hitler-Horthy agreement of March 18, 1944; see my "The Holocaust in Hungary" (*op. cit.,* note 71 above).

86.   The leaders of the Jewish Council claim that their tactics saved the Jews of Budapest. The Zionists claim credit for having saved close to an additional 20,000 Jews—some 1,700 in the so-called Kasztner group and around 18,000 in Strasshof, Austria.

87.   By the time the Jews were placed in the ghettos, they were deprived of their dignity and property. It is likely that even if they had been told the truth they could not have organized any meaningful resistance in the absence of many of the able-bodied males in the labor companies. Moreover, the Jews were not psychologically prepared to accept the truth by that time.

Contrasting Jewish Leaderships in Wartime Hungary and Romania*

BELA VAGO

Passionate polemics about the role and capability of wartime Jewish leaderships, both in Hungary and in Romania, started during the war and preoccupied Jewish opinion in the early postwar years.

On March 11, 1947 the Hungarian Zionist Federation, hopelessly struggling for existence under the Communist-dominated regime, addressed a letter to Lajos Stöckler, then president of the Budapest Jewish Community and an early exponent of the Communist disruption of Jewish political life. The letter claimed that "the so-called confessional point of view exclusively prevailing in the Jewish life of the past system, and the readiness of the former Jewish leaders to comply with servility with the demands [of the authorities], largely contributed to the tragedy of Hungarian Jewry."[1] In his answer to the Zionist Federation, while condemning traditional Jewish leaders for their incompetence and sectarianism (and accounting for his own role in the wartime Jewish Council),[2] Stöckler implicitly denounced the Zionists themselves, suggesting that they cared only for their own people and were nowhere to be found when the Budapest Ghetto fought its struggle for life.[3]

At about the same time Ernő Munkácsi, legal adviser and later secretary general of the Pest Neolog Community (prior to the German occupation) and a senior official of the Jewish Council, started publishing his memoirs. In his

*I am greatly indebted to the following participants in the wartime events for their valuable information: Y. Artzi, J. Cohen, H. Danzig, the late P. de Freudiger, Dr. F. Herskovics, M. Iancu, T. Lavi, Dr. A. Safran and S. Springmann.

opinion, the official Jewish leadership had not been able to perform its task appropriately because it stood aloof from the masses; there was actually no Jewish leadership as such, capable of guiding the Jewish masses in those critical hours.[4] The venomous controversy over Rezső Kasztner's leading role in 1944 and his approach to rescue work is well-known. Less known, but not less passionate, is the controversy over the attitude and policy of the traditional leaders in the framework of the Budapest *Judenrat.*[5]

Somewhat similar controversies arose in Romania. The role of the old assimilationist leaders and the new men who emerged in the late thirties, mainly those who were active in the Centrala Evreilor din Romania (Center of the Jews in Romania) set up in 1942 under the Antonescu regime, has not ceased to preoccupy the politically involved survivors of the Holocaust. In the Romanian case, however, the attitude of Jewish survivors to their wartime leadership has been far less vehement than that of survivors of the Hungarian tragedy to their former leaders.

Insinuations and accusations, answered by apologetic rationalizations and whitewashing pleas, emerged from the complex and delicate problems of the Jewish leaderships in both countries during the Holocaust. Would the fate of Hungarian Jewry, for instance, have been different in 1944 under a purely Zionist leadership, as suggested in that letter of the Hungarian Zionist Federation? Would young, dynamic, and radical leaders have achieved more than the conservative, establishment-bound leadership? Was there any real alternative to the existing leadership groups in wartime Hungary?

There hardly seems to be an answer to these hypothetical questions. But a basic question inevitably arises when looking from Budapest to Bucharest. Why did Romanian Jewry, closely linked geographically and in many other ways to Hungarian Jewry, manage to escape a major tragedy even though both regimes shared an almost identical satellite status?

A comparative study of these two great Jewish communities indeed reveals similarities in their objective and subjective conditions that led to similar *general* developments. At the same time, it is striking that differences in their social, economic, and political life brought to the surface a type of leadership group in interwar Romania that was absent from the Hungarian Jewish scene. One cannot escape some features of the social and political profile of the Jewish leaders in Romania—including their militant Jewish nationalism—which had a favorable influence on the fate of the Jewish masses. Hungarian Jewry was handicapped by the lack of such characteristics among its leaders during the Holocaust.

Admittedly, nowhere in Europe did the Jewish leadership have a decisive or even an essential role in the outcome of the Holocaust. But within certain limits there was room for maneuver. The possibility of exploiting circumstances was not only a function of the attitude and the political character of local governments, or of their susceptibility to German pressure, but also of the ability of those who represented (or appeared to represent) local Jewry. Moreover, the fact that the persons who stood in the forefront of Jewish public life in the two countries during the Holocaust belonged to differing types was not accidental. In large measure, the primary characteristics of these types were the result of a long process of economic, political, and cultural development in the two Jewish communities.

Contrasts of Situation and Background

Already at the end of World War I, there were clear differences between Hungary and the new Greater Romania. The overwhelming majority of Hungarian Jews—including the religiously observant—were assimilated and organically integrated in the nation's economic, cultural, and intellectual life. Romania's Jewry achieved complete emancipation (officially) only in 1923; the assimilated stratum was rather small and the great majority of the Jews in the Old Kingdom, mainly in the rural areas of Moldavia, were remote from Romanian national life.

In the early interwar years, despite the anti-Jewish pogroms of the White Terror in Hungary (1919–1920) and the antisemitic "Christian course" of the Horthy regime, the Budapest Parliament included a number of politicians of Jewish origin who had started their careers in the prewar Greater Hungary,[6] while Romanian Jews took their first steps in the political arena only after 1919.[7] The Hungarian ruling class of a semi-feudal character was permeated by Jews, even by Jewish nobles. But the Romanian ruling circles, though more popular in their social structure and more democratic in their views, did not favor intermarriage and social intermingling with Jews; they included practically no Jews throughout the interwar period.

In spite of the "race-protecting" psychosis and the "Christian course" of interwar Hungary, Jewish leaders were unshaken in their loyalty to the Hungarian nation; that is, to the establishment consisting of aristocracy and gentry. They wanted only a restoration of the old coexistence of the prewar liberal era with the help of the conservative, Rightist ruling forces, rather than a revolt against existing conditions. They even desolidarized themselves from those world Jewish organizations that pressed at the League of Nations for abolition of the anti-Jewish *numerus clausus* law of 1920.[8] By contrast, in 1919 a delegation of Romanian Jewish leaders had appeared at the Paris peace conference to urge external pressure on the Bucharest government to grant emancipation and assure Jewish minority rights.[9] Romanian Jewry was striving for the status of a national minority, while Jewish leaders in Hungary, in consensus with the Jewish masses, opposed being treated as a separate national group, considering themselves a part of the Hungarian nation that differed only in religion from the rest.[10]

There were assimilated or assimilationist Jews in post-1919 Romania too, and they had their own country-wide non-political organization: the Union of Romanian Jews. It was, however, led by politically active persons, some of whom became members of Parliament in the 1920–1937 period by campaigning on Jewish platforms for specifically Jewish interests.[11] Such an organization did not emerge in Hungary. Eventually, a Jewish political party was set up in Romania in 1928, gathering the majority of the Jewish votes at two general elections (in 1932 and 1934). In Hungary the very idea of a Jewish political party would have been inconceivable.

Zionism was a mass movement in Greater Romania, mainly in the newly acquired provinces (Transylvania, Bessarabia, and Bukovina). In Hungary prior to the Holocaust, Zionism was weak and amateurishly organized with no effective influence on Jewish life.

Whereas Jewish members of the Hungarian Parliament never specifically represented the Jewish voters,[12] in interwar Romania, until the last days of parliamentary life (the end of 1937), Jewish deputies and senators were acting with a Jewish mandate on behalf of Jewish interests even when representing such parties as the Rightist and nationalist National Liberal Party.[13] This was reflected in a remarkable paradox. Hungarian politicians of Jewish origin, seeking to *safeguard* their earlier acquired rights, felt obliged to prove their loyalty to the Rightist, nationalist, and irredentist policy of Horthy's Hungary.[14] Nonetheless, a yawning gap separated the conservative, assimilationist, and establishment-loyal Hungarian Jewish leadership from the ruling political and administrative circles in Hungary. In Romania, on the other hand, the Jewish leaders had to put up a fight in order to *achieve* the most elementary civil rights, and to weaken the anti-Jewish trends among nationalist leaders, including those of the so-called liberals (the National Liberal party) and the democratic National Peasants party. Even so, the Romanian ruling circles, lacking gentry or aristocratic elements,[15] did not stand aloof from Jewish leading personalities—with the exception of extreme antisemitic elements—and were not opposed to political cooperation with them, though considering them Jews and not Romanians.[16]

When the first Nazi-type events struck Jewry in both countries at about the same time (the emergence of the antisemitic Goga-Cuza government in Romania in late 1937 and the First Jewish Law of 1938 in Hungary), the Jewish reaction was strikingly different. Hungarian Jews sought to avoid a confrontation with the regime, so as to avert more radical steps. On the contrary, Romanian Jewry was mobilized by its leaders on two fronts: they appealed to the democratic Western powers and the League of Nations, while also taking practical steps to weaken the economic position of the new government and undermine it.[17] Jewish leaders, assimilationists and Zionists alike, made common cause in opposing the Goga-Cuza regime.

After the collapse of Goga's administration and the installation of King Carol's dictatorship, when the Jewish party was disbanded along with all political parties (February 1938), its leaders joined Dr. W. Filderman, the leader of the so-called "Romanian Jews" (i.e., the assimilationists), in constituting a "Jewish Council" designed to represent the whole Jewish population.[18] There was permanent contact between the local Jewish leaders and the authorities of the royalist dictatorship (1938–1940),[19] but there is no evidence of such relations between Hungarian Jewish leaders and any official political factor during the administrations of Count P. Teleki, L. Bárdossy, or M. Kállay (1939–1944).

The short period between the Munich Conference and Summer 1941 brought essential changes in the numerical composition of the Jewish population in the two countries. Hungary acquired Southern Slovakia, Carpatho-Ruthenia, Northern Transylvania, and later the Yugoslav Bačka and Vojvodina with a total Jewish population of about 324,000. This brought the number of persons of the Jewish faith to around 800,000 in 1941. In the same period Romania's Jewish population of 800,000 dwindled to 442,000 after the loss of Bessarabia, Northern Bukovina, Northern Transylvania, and Southern Dobrudja in 1940.

No essential changes occurred among Romanian Jewish leaders, despite the loss of some 360,000 Jews, since many of those leaders were persons originating from the Old Kingdom.[20] Yet neither did the near doubling of Hungarian Jewry essentially affect the composition of the Budapest-based Jewish leadership, though leaders with a Jewish nationalist outlook from Southern Slovakia and mainly from Carpatho-Ruthenia had a certain impact on it by activating social welfare assistance and strengthening the Zionist movement. It was the young and dynamic, mostly labor-oriented Zionist leadership of Northern Transylvania[21] that brought a fresh invigorating element into Jewish public life; but they (like leaders from the former Czechoslovak areas) remained outside the official leadership in Budapest.

In 1941, when Hungary joined the anti-Soviet war, Jewish public life was still dominated by the three confessional organizations (Neolog, Orthodox, and Status Quo). Various social, welfare, and cultural organizations were actually controlled by the Neolog and (to a lesser extent) the Orthodox leadership.[22] The only extra-confessional organization with some weight in the early forties was the Zionist movement, although most of its Budapest leaders did not essentially differ in social background and status or general political views from the confessional leaders.

The community leaders, both Neolog and Orthodox, constituted a largely homogeneous body; they belonged mostly to the upper middle class and partly to the lower gentry or nobility. They were well-to-do, conservative-minded, and identified themselves with the irredentist nationalism of the Hungarian ruling classes.[23] Although various eminent personalities from the free professions, mainly lawyers, were prominent in Jewish public life, the Jewish leadership completely lacked leading intellectuals and first-class representatives of the arts. Young people were also conspicuously absent. High moral standards characterized the Jewish community leadership; those in its first ranks were supposed to behave like their upper-class counterparts in non-Jewish public life. But they lacked a democratic mandate from the rank and file and their mass support was usually more than questionable.

In social status Jewish leaders in Romania lagged far behind what was required in Hungary. They were mostly first-generation newcomers to public life and came from the lower middle class. Many were young men, chiefly lawyers, but also university graduates practising other free professions.[24] Besides the "national-minded" and the veteran Zionist leaders, even the assimilants and the so-called "Romanian Jews" were emphatically "Jewish" and sometimes (like Adolphe Stern, Horia Carp, and Dr. W. Filderman) militantly active in the Jewish political arena.

Whereas only a handful of Jewish parliamentarians in Hungary were ready to concern themselves with purely Jewish matters, all the Jewish members of the interwar Romanian Parliament, with the conspicuous exception of Hegedüs Nándor, a longtime speaker of the Hungarian party's parliamentary faction, embraced the Jewish cause irrespective of their party affiliation.[25] Zionism was less influential in the Old Kingdom than in the annexed provinces, but the Jewish party as a whole was led by Zionists, quite a few of them from Transylvania, Bukovina, and Bessarabia.[26] Many Jewish public figures in Romania, both "nationals" and assimilants, had consequently accumulated ample experience in political struggle when the time of trial came, while most of the Jewish leaders in Hungary in the early forties were lacking parliamentary or other political experience. Yet another difference between the two countries concerned the masses besides the leaders. World War II broke out in an atmosphere of tense awareness of danger among Jews in Romania, but there were no signs of a similar reaction in Hungary.

Wartime Romania

Romanian Jewry experienced the Nazi calamity long before the Hungarian Jews. King Carol's rule collapsed when Greater Romania disintegrated in July–September 1940;[27] the "National Legionnaire" regime of the Iron Guard and General (later Marshal) Ion Antonescu then disrupted Jewish life with terror and massacres.[28] When the abortive *coup* of the Iron Guard against Antonescu in January 1941 ended in utter failure,[29] Antonescu's military dictatorship curtailed the physical threat to the entire Jewish population. Nevertheless, Antonescu's own antisemitic administration jeopardized not only the continuation of Jewish life at a subsistence level, but soon (after Romania joined Hitler's anti-Soviet war in June 1941) even Jewish survival itself.[30]

Inevitably, the new conditions created by these two successive fascist-type dictatorships led to an alteration in the status, role, and composition of the Jewish leadership groups. During the four years of these dictatorships in Romania (1940–1944), new Jewish organizations and public figures emerged; a great diversity of new tactics were applied by both the old and the new leaders.

After the Legionnaire-Antonescu seizure of power, chaos reigned in Jewish matters. No explicit law governed the legal status of the Jewish organizations or the sphere of authority of their leaders.[31] The Jewish party had ceased to exist since February 1938, and Zionist activity was semi-legal. But the Federation of Jewish Communities continued to function, as the authorities did not much interfere with the activity of the welfare organizations. The dominant personality was Dr. W. Filderman, head both of the Federation of Jewish Communities and of the Union of Romanian Jews. His approach was authoritarian, concentrating all leadership activity in his own hands and demanding docile collaboration from his fellow leaders. An excellent orator, an experienced parliamentarian, and a successful lawyer, Filderman maintained good relations with a great number of politicians, among them I. Maniu and Dr. N. Lupu, the agrarian leaders, and C. Bratianu, leader of the disbanded National Liberal party.

Filderman had been a schoolmate of Marshal Ion Antonescu and he exploited this connection from the very first days of military dictatorship. Throughout those four years he pursued a form of classical *stadlanut* or intercession on behalf of fellow Jews. He obtained audiences with both Antonescus (Ion Antonescu and his deputy, Mihai Antonescu) and with quite a few ministers and other high-ranking officials and generals, bombarding them with memoranda, letters, and protest notes against anti-Jewish measures and suggesting possible solutions to the Jewish question. Filderman emerged as a "one-man institution," though not unchallenged by other leaders (mainly Zionists and Leftists). His courageous and incessant *stadlanut* was not void of tactical blunders that cost him a Communist-inspired slander campaign after the war and a brief period of arrest in Summer 1945 Owing to his pathetic declarations of loyalty to Marshal Antonescu, and to a disastrous and misinterpreted request to enroll Jews in the Romanian Army (i.e., in the fight against the Soviet Union),[32] he was accused by the Communists of Nazi collaboration, an accusation which in Hungary was not even levelled against leaders of the Jewish Council.[33]

During the first six months of dictatorship a small group of Zionist leaders, headed by L. A. Mizrahi and S. Singer (a former member of Parliament for the Jewish party), was also granted audiences on the highest governmental level. This group, known as the Mizrahi Action Committee, was trying to alleviate the anti-Jewish terror. Though no palpable results were achieved, it should be noted that the Antonescus and their entourage were ready to discuss Jewish matters with various Jewish mandataries. It seems that the new rulers did not care about the distinction between the assimilants (i.e., the "Romanian Jews" of Filderman and the Union of Romanian Jews), the Zionists, and the Jewish nationalist leaders of the former Jewish party.

In May 1941 Antonescu's government agreed to legalize the Zionist movement with a view to encouraging emigration. The reorganized Zionist Federation acquired a new leader, M. Benvenisti, a young, dynamic, and courageous lawyer, formerly head of the Jewish party's youth section. He and his close friends formed a more active and radical leadership that did not preclude recourse to illegal methods in aid-and-rescue work. The activity of this new Zionist leadership, and the expectation of many Jews that mass emigration to Palestine would shortly be possible, brought an upsurge in the Jewish nationalist camp during 1941 and 1942.[34]

A wave of anti-Jewish terror and deportations began when Romania joined the anti-Soviet war. The Iasi massacre in June 27–30, 1941, and the subsequent mass deportations to Transnistria from Bessarabia and Bukovina and even (for some categories of Jews) from Romania proper, threatened the whole of Romanian Jewry with the fate of the Polish Jews. The struggle against this terror was waged by various Jewish organizations on various levels. On the legal level Benvenisti's Zionists (virtually comprising every political shade) and Filderman's non-Zionist group grasped every feasible means,[35] even corrupting highly-placed officials, to prevent further deportations and massacres. At the same time, a new underground group emerged from the *chalutz* youth movement. Its hitherto unknown young leaders,[36] working mainly for the rescue of refugees from other countries (besides Romanian Jews threatened with deportation or arrest), accepted the authority of Benvenisti's Action Committee, so that during late 1941 the Jewish leadership concentrated around Benvenisti's and Filderman's groups. The latter acted officially under the aegis of the Federation of Jewish Communities, assisted by the younger officials of the Union of Romanian Jews, who were mostly graduates of law schools.[37]

A new chapter started in Antonescu's handling of the Jewish question with the drastic organizational measures taken toward the beginning of 1942. The Federation of Jewish Communities was disbanded, Filderman and other long-time leaders of the assimilationists (actually the traditional interwar leadership) forced to step down, and a Romanian version of the *Judenrat,* the Committee of the Centrala Evreilor din Romania (Center of the Jews in Romania, hereafter referred to as "the Center") set up in February 1942 by the Romanian authorities assisted by Nazi emissaries.[38] The Committee comprised seven sections (welfare assistance, emigration, press, education, etc.), headed by a president and a secretary general. It was supervised by Radu Lecca, as High Commissioner for Jewish Affairs, who evidently acted upon German instructions, at least during 1942, when Nazi influence was still strong. The composition of the Committee, unlike that of the Jewish Council in Budapest set up by the Germans in March 1944, was utterly unrepresentative. It was made up of second-rate public figures or unknown persons, who had never acted on any public scene.

The two key figures on the Committee were Dr. Nandor Gingold, the Secretary General, and A. Willman, the "ideologist" heading its press section. Gingold, a physician and convert to Catholicism, was in practice the head of the Committee, since its nominal Chairman (H. S. Streiman) played a secondary role. Gingold had been nominated by chance. His name may have been suggested to Lecca by Gustav Richter, in charge of Jewish problems at the Bucharest German legation, where Gingold was treating a German diplomat.

Willman was an obscure and controversial journalist who had published a few writings in the thirties about the need for mass emigration of the Jews, not particularly to Palestine. Emigration from Europe, possibly to Madagascar, was his only solution to the Jewish question. He was selected by the Germans because he held these "Territorialist" views. While there are no indications that Gingold had any German connections (apart from his diplomatic patient), Willman maintained secret contacts with the Nazis, bearing the marks of a collaborator or even of a Nazi agent. Most of the other members of the Committee were "technicians" in charge of various fields of activity, facilitating the implementation of instructions from the authorities.

The Committee of Dr. Gingold proved a failure even from the point of view of the Romanian government; the two Antonescus and other leading personalities continued to maintain working contacts with the *de facto* leaders of the Jews. During 1942 there were in fact three leaderships: the official Center, lacking mass support; the tolerated Benvenisti Zionist Action Committee, including some youth leaders who represented the *chalutz* movement; and finally the illegal but authoritative leadership group around Filderman. It should be added that unlike Hungary, where not one rabbi assumed a prominent role during the war years, in Romania Dr. A. Safran, the Chief Rabbi, was very active in rescue work, cooperating with different leadership groups and maintaining contacts with the heads of the churches, leaders of the underground opposition, and even the royal family.[39]

The first German plan of mass deportation from Romania, intended to start in Southern Transylvania and the Banat in mid-1942, prompted the appearance of Transylvanian Jewish leaders on the Bucharest scene. It was the interwar Banat branch of the strong Transylvanian Zionist leadership headed by K. Reiter, Dr. L. Ligeti, and V. Auscher. Like most of the interwar Transylvanian Zionist leaders, they were well-to-do middle-class centrist politicians, who took advantage of their connections with Romanian statesmen, especially the Maniu agrarians, and were supported by Benvenisti, whose leadership they acknowledged. They were helped also by Filderman and by A. L. Zissu, the lonely veteran Zionist, then acting alone behind the scenes and outside the Benvenisti group.

The small Reiter-Ligeti-Auscher group, not particularly eager for popular support among local Jewry (Ligeti was actually the Center's key figure in the Banat), enjoyed a virtual monopoly of leadership in Southern Transylvania and the Banat. It was the only provincial leadership group that maintained its own profile and relative independence from Bucharest, thus stressing the strong individual characteristics of Transylvanian Jewry, which never completely integrated into the Jewish masses of the Old Kingdom.

The vacillating Jewish policy of the Antonescu administration encouraged great mobility within the Jewish leadership. In August 1942 the authorities suspended the legality of the Zionist movement, thus leaving the Committee of the Center as the only legal Jewish forum. With both the Zionist Action Committee and Filderman's group working in semi-legal or even illegal conditions, a new non-legal supreme leading body, tacitly acknowledged by the authorities, emerged late in 1942. This non-official "Jewish Council" (anything but a Nazi-appointed *Judenrat*) was headed by Filderman and included the Chief Rabbi, Dr. A. Safran, and two non-Zionists (A. Schwefelberg and F. Froimescu, both lawyers). An additional group took shape toward the beginning of 1943 around A. L. Zissu, whose political views were close to Revisionist Zionism. Zissu was an outstanding intellectual, successful businessman, and authoritarian type of leader. He and his followers, mainly intellectuals, achieved importance and authority only in 1944. Their group, known as the "Zissu Clandestine Executive,"[40] concentrated on emigration and was strongly represented in the Romanian sections of the Jewish Agency and the World Jewish Congress, both working in semi-legal conditions.

It is amazing how tenaciously the Jewish leaders of various political affiliations clung to their illegal commitments despite the creation of the sole official leading body, the Committee of the Center. Their reluctance to quit the public scene inevitably led to arrests and deportations among them. In early 1943 Filderman was deported to Transnistria. Zissu was later imprisoned in Tîrgu-Jiu, while in January 1944 Benvenisti, Wilhelm Fischer (the head of the Romanian section of the World Jewish Congress), and some other Zionist leaders were arrested. It is worth emphasizing that both Filderman and Benvenisti rejected the Antonescu administration's offer of free exit from the country, refusing to leave their posts and their duties. The reaction of Hungarian and Transylvanian leaders to similar opportunities was entirely different, the sole exception being (to my knowledge) Kasztner.[41]

The deported or imprisoned Romanian Jewish leaders were in each case set free after a few weeks or months following mutual interventions by the various leadership groups. Their release, of course, was not mainly due to such interventions with the authorities. Rather the tolerant attitude of the authorities toward the illegally acting leaders stemmed from the tactical conception of the two Antonescus (mainly Mihai Antonescu), the influential General P. Vasiliu (Vice Minister of the Interior), and other leading personalities. Throughout the whole period they made a point of using those Jewish leaders who enjoyed mass backing to take maximum advantage of Jewish economic potential and industrial and technical know-how. In 1943, and mainly in 1944, Jewish leaders were also spared with a view to postwar perspectives, since most of Ion Antonescu's associates, including his deputy Mihai Antonescu, were convinced of the approaching Nazi defeat as early as the middle of 1943.[42]

Here it is relevant to emphasize once more the close contacts between several Jewish leaders (outside the Gingold Committee) and the leaders of the dissolved National Peasants party and National Liberal Party. Owing to the working relations of some opposition leaders with cabinet ministers, generals, and other high officials, and to the prestige enjoyed by I. Maniu and

C. Bratianu with the two Antonescus, their interventions certainly contributed to the relative freedom of action of Filderman, Benvenisti, Zissu, and other non-official Jewish leaders.[43]

Cooperation between leaders of the various Jewish groups, however, was far from ideal, confined as it was to occasional mutual assistance in cases of imminent personal danger, or joint intercessions with the ruling circles in critical hours. At other times the dissensions and the internal struggles among them, which frequently originated in personal motives (as in the case of Filderman and Zissu) rather than in politico-ideological disagreement, jeopardized the efficiency of the struggle for survival. Much controversy concerned the Center of the Jews in Romania. In an early phase of the Center's activity numerous Zionist leaders, both Leftists and Rightists, believed they should cooperate with the Committee of the Center with a view to controlling or at least influencing its activity. Thus, in 1942 Dr. T. Loewenstein (Lavi), active in the labor faction of the Zionist movement, was delegated by his friends to fulfill an important function in the Committee.[44]

Benvenisti and other Zionist leaders attended some of the meetings at Center headquarters. Filderman maintained working contacts with the Committee; and even the Communist underground was eager, it seems, to infiltrate its men onto the Committee. A group of Zionists headed by Zissu, however, vehemently opposed any cooperation with the Center and treated those who worked with it as collaborationists whatever their reasons. After the war, the Communists took the same attitude and condemned the Zionists who had joined the Center for tactical reasons or had maintained working contacts with it, despite evidence that they themselves had shared the view that joining the Center for tactical reasons could serve Jewish interests.

Another source of bitter controversy among the Zionist leaders was emigration to Palestine. The markedly conservative older leaders of the centrist group in the Zionist movement opposed the hazardous emigration, arguing that the risks were greater than facing the future in Romania. They were opposed by radicals, who gained the upper hand. Paradoxically the Communists, formally outside the Jewish national movement, but in close contact with Jewish bourgeois leaders during the war (and especially 1944), agreed with the conservatives, albeit for entirely different reasons; namely, that fostering emigration meant helping the fascist authorities to get rid of the Jewish population.

The ways and means of interceding with the authorities also caused bitter controversy. While Filderman embodied the policy of *stadlanut,* with many Zionist leaders pragmatically following suit, Zissu and his right-wing Zionist friends condemned any form of *stadlanut* and approved of contacts with the authorities only on a purely "political ground."[45] By this he meant the recognition by Antonescu of a quasi-official status for the Jewish leadership as a political body representing the vital interests of the whole Jewish population. Linked with this view was Zissu's demand for closer contact between the leadership and the masses, for consulting the Jewish population and informing it about developments of general interest.[46] As a matter of fact, Zissu himself had no mass backing; he was less linked to large sections of the Jewish population that Filderman or even other Zionist leaders like Benvenisti.

The feud between Filderman and Zissu was also a typical case of personal rivalry detrimental to the Jewish cause. In the first half of 1944, when they were the two main figures on the Jewish scene (with Zissu briefly representing the bulk of the Zionists after Benvenisti's arrest), a virtual schism occurred between the Zionist and non-Zionist leaders largely because of the personal animosity between the two rival leading personalities.

Late 1943 brought the first tangible results of the fight of Romanian Jewry for survival. Not only was mass deportation to Auschwitz or other death camps averted, but the deportations to Transnistria were actually reversed. The first deportees returned by the end of 1943, followed by others in early 1944. Those were the months when Mihai Antonescu was feverishly seeking a way out of the war; and when the anti-German opposition, with the tacit consent of both Antonescus, initiated peace feelers toward the Allies.[47] But those months also brought a new threat: the possible annihilation of the Transnistrian deportees by retreating German troops. The preoccupation of the Jewish leadership in Spring 1944 was thus twofold: to avoid a major catastrophe in Transnistria, and to hasten Romania's break with the Nazi coalition.

Both Filderman and Zissu joined the efforts to attain an armistice with the Allies. Zissu adroitly exploited the Nazi myth of an omnipotent "Jewish World Power" and hinted to Mihai Antonescu that the Jewish Agency and the World Jewish Congress might mediate between the Romanian government and the Allies.[48] Filderman gave letters of recommendation for Romanian emissaries to the Western Allies and did his best to facilitate the Romanian turnabout in the war.[49] On the internal front, quite a few Jewish leaders (even the arch anti-Communist Filderman) set about creating contacts with the anti-fascist underground, which included Communists along with Agrarians, Liberals, and Social Democrats.[50]

Months before the *coup* of August 23, 1944, Filderman and a number of Zionist leaders had been assisting in its clandestine organization and providing financial support.[51] Practically every shade of the broad Jewish political spectrum was represented in the internal and external preparations for the anti-Nazi—turn except the Center. These collaborationists were completely ignored by the authorities in Spring and Summer 1944; the regime considered them second-rate executors of its Jewish policy and worked exclusively with those leaders who had no legal capacity to act. When the August coup reversed Romania's position in the war, it was thus only natural that the latter personalities should emerge as the legal leaders of the liberated Jewish masses. Within a few days, legalization was granted to the Jewish party, the Union of Romanian Jews, and the whole Zionist arena, headed by Zissu, Filderman, and Benvenisti respectively.

Conspicuous all along was the obscurity of Leftist representatives in the Jewish leadership. Throughout 1940–1944 and even after August 1944, the political scene was dominated by bourgeois leaders representing centrist and more or less radical, but not Left-wing forces. Not one leading figure of the Zionist labor movement, or of the non-Zionist Left, emerged in the first ranks. While Benvenisti and his friends represented the younger interwar generation of Zionists, the *chalutz* youth movement, though working efficiently in the undergound, failed to produce any leading figures of national stature. The exclusively bourgeois and politically moderate Jewish leadership may be one reason why the Communists struck early at the Jewish establishment, depriving it retroactively of all its wartime merits, and already in Summer 1945 created the "Jewish Democratic Committee," a Communist front organization designed to integrate Jewish life rapidly into the Communist framework.

Wartime Hungary

Whereas from late 1937 the Jewish leaders in Romania were on the alert against the antisemitic regime, those in Hungary showed no awareness of impending danger even after Hungary entered the war on Hitler's side in July 1941. As time passed, and Hungarian Jewry was spared the catastrophes that struck the Jews of neighboring countries, its leaders—and the masses—nurtured illusions based on German military setbacks during 1943. Optimism was fostered by rumors about the impending turnabout being prepared by Prime Minister M. Kállay.

As already mentioned, the first war years brought little change in the official or nominal Jewish leadership in Hungary; it remained essentially apolitical, functioning mostly in confessional frameworks. Although younger Zionists from the newly acquired territories invigorated the Zionist movement, its conservative and static leadership was unaffected. The election of Ottó Komoly in 1942 as head of the Zionist Federation brought a gifted leader to the fore with fairly good connections in political circles, but failed to produce a radical change in Zionist politics or methods. Komoly himself stood aloof from radicalism and non-conventional forms of political struggle.

In 1942–1943 young Transylvanian Zionists, mostly from the Labor wing, together with a few left-wing Zionists from prewar Hungary, set out to form in Budapest a more popular, dynamic, and less establishment-bound alternative leadership to the existing one.[52] There was also an attempt to mobilize former Jewish parliamentary representatives of the interwar years to form a supreme political forum. Both initiatives failed to produce the desired result.[53] A marginal but typical phenomenon will illustrate the atmosphere of the negotiations: at a meeting with the former and the few still active Jewish parliamentarians, Manó Buchinger, a prominent Social

Democrat, was careful to address as "Your Highness" those participants whose status or function entitled them to this form of address.[54] Later, during the dramatic debates of the Jewish Council in the most critical days of 1944, Philipp de Freudiger similarly addressed the President of the Council, Samu Stern, as "Your Highness."[55]

When the Germans occupied Hungary in March 1944, they found in Budapest the Jewish leadership of the interwar period virtually intact. And when they ordered the creation of the Budapest Jewish Council, its members came almost exclusively from the confessional or Zionist interwar establishment.[56] The only political figure on the Council—and the only Zionist representative—was Nisson Kahan, an elderly conservative leader lacking in political ability, and even he left the Council after a short period of inactivity. It seems that the Germans did not bother to seek new figures for their purposes, as was the case in Romania. On the contrary, they insisted that Jewish Councils in the provinces should comprise the leaders of the local communities.

The Budapest Jewish Council was reorganized in July 1944, but even then the few additional names did not change the political or social character of this *Judenrat*. Admittedly, not all its members were passive executors of German or Hungarian orders; some sought to establish connections with prominent personalities and with anti-Nazi underground circles, and to assist the Zionist youth underground. They were hampered, however, by their lack of political experience, overcautious methods and the loose, non-political character of their connections with Hungarian personalities.

Unlike Romania, where the two Antonescus were not reluctant to grant audiences to Jewish leaders, even to ones without official status, in Hungary no leading personality was ready to meet officially any Jewish leader. Horthy agreed, perhaps twice, to receive Samu Stern in great secrecy at a time when the Jews from the provinces had already been deported.[57] Excepting Nicholas Horthy, Jr., not one of the anti-German politicians still at large met any Jewish leader during the Holocaust. Members of the *Judenrat* had no noteworthy connections with the anyhow feeble Hungarian resistance; their stature would anyway not have fitted in with such contacts. Workable contacts with the Hungarian opposition were also hard to develop because the German occupation of Hungary was immediately followed by the arrest, deportation, or even liquidation of most of the leading figures who opposed the Nazi alliance.

Besides the official Jewish leadership, a second one, the non-legal Zionist Relief and Rescue Committee of Budapest, emerged in January 1943 from the partisan rescue activity of a few Zionists, who had aided Slovak and Polish refugees and deportees from Hungary in 1941–1942. This second group differed in many respects from the legal and traditional leadership: in social background and status, in political views, and in age. Apart from A. Biss, who came to the fore rather late and by chance,[58] all of them had been active in the Zionist movement for years.[59] And apart from Ottó

Komoly, the head of the Committee, most were members of the labor wing of the movement. (Not that they were all socialists, but formally they belonged to one of the two socialist groups of the Zionist movement.) All belonged to lower social strata than the established leadership. Most were in their thirties or early forties, and some were already experienced in political struggle. Quite a few were fit for or even familiar with illegal methods of activity, including some who were engaged in illegal economic-financial transactions. At least four of them were Transylvanians including Rezső Kasztner. Conspicuously absent from their ranks were those Transylvanian Zionists who represented an upper-class type of leader; Dr. József Fischer, for example, and Dr. Tivadar Fischer, both former Jewish party members of the Romanian Parliament.

Most of the leading figures in the Relief and Rescue Committee were newcomers to the Jewish public arena, or at least unknown outside the narrow framework of their Zionist organization. Unlike members of the established leadership, however, those of the Rescue Committee were able to build a vast and intricate network of Hungarian and even German agents, officials and officers willing to help them—for money—in rescue work and maintaining contacts with the outside world. They succeeded in creating contacts in the Hungarian bourgeois and socialist anti-German underground, and were in permanent touch with some of the second-rank representatives of the regime, undersecretaries and members of Parliament who, in spite of their Rightist or even extreme-Right stand, turned their backs on their Nazi allies in the very last phase of the war.[60] They also made use of contacts with intelligence and gendarmerie officers.[61] Better known are the contacts of some five or six members of the Rescue Committee with various German organizations such as the SS and the Abwehr. As already remarked, the latter contacts are among the most controversial and most publicized chapters of the Holocaust.[62]

During 1942–1943 there also appeared a third leadership group, that of the *chalutz* movement. Although it could be considered the youth movement or later on even the military branch of the Zionist rescue group, in the last few months of the Jewish catastrophe it also acted independently, devising its own operations. The 12 to 15 prominent leaders were in their early twenties; several came from outside prewar Hungary, some not even speaking Hungarian.[63] They belonged to various political groups, the most active to the left-wing Hashomer Hatzair. After establishing contact with underground armed forces, they formed a nucleus of armed resistance besides pursuing conventional rescue work.

The triple leadership—the official established one, the Rescue Committee and the youth leaders—reflecting three different levels of social status, political views, and age, was a natural outcome of the circumstances in which the Jewish tragedy took place in Hungary. As often happens when the established social structure collapses owing to major political convulsions, new men ready to undertake unconventional tasks emerged in 1944. The

Jewish Council and the community leadership, with all its goodwill, was an anachronistic group of persons out of their depth in changed circumstances. The Rescue Committee rallied men who were more practical, closer to the masses than the established leaders, able to use unconventional methods, and more efficient in achieving limited goals. But some of them were men whose zeal outran their capacities.[64]

The third group, the Zionist youth, was the most effective and heroic. Its activity and influence, however, were limited by the narrow horizons of its leaders and their lack of political experience and political connections. The faulty cooperation between the first group and the second, and the personal rivalry and dissension within those groups, also impeded the rescue efforts. One notes the lack of confidence between Stern and Freudiger, the distrust between Freudiger and Kasztner, the controversial role of Béla Berend and the unaccountable rise of Lajos Stöckler in the reorganized Budapest *Judenrat,* the sectarian working methods of Stern, the authoritarian and haughty attitude of Kasztner, the rivalry between him and Brand, and the widespread disdain toward such "newcomers" as Brand and Biss.

The most respected and authoritative leader of the forties, Komoly, was not ready and presumably not even able to cope with the difficult task of both conducting negotiations with the Nazis and the Hungarian authorities and fostering underground resistance activity. The man who ventured to deal with the Nazis—thus overshadowing Komoly and dominating the scene during the most critical period of the Hungarian Jewish catastrophe—was Kasztner, who actually had no formal mandate apart from his task in the illegal Rescue Committee. Unlike Zissu, Benvenisti, and other Zionist leaders in Romania, most of the prominently active Hungarian Zionists were not recognized as "national" leaders by the Jewish masses.

Conclusions

The survival of most Romanian Jews cannot be attributed to the ability of their leaders. Nor can the destruction of most Hungarian Jews be attributed to the faults of those by whom they were led. But the significance of the role of these leaders cannot be denied. The Jewish leadership in Romania, including quite a few provincial figures, succeeded in diminishing the proportions of the catastrophe. And while there is no evidence that the absence of a more adequate leadership in Hungary, much less actual collaboration and treason, contributed to the overall dimensions of the tragedy, there is ample evidence—despite undeniable positive effects of the leaders' activities—of incompetence, hasty improvisation, lack of communication with the masses, and amateurish organization.

In both cases the reasons lay in the economic, social, political, and cultural development of the Jews from the late nineteenth century onwards. The characteristics of the leaderships were to a great extent determined by this development, together with the influence of the host-peoples and the specifically different conditions of the two countries during the late war years. It was not the leadership that shaped Jewish reality, but the reverse. We see in Romania the vitality of a less assimilated community that had long been harassed and imperilled. Under conditions of extreme danger, such a community and its leaders proved less vulnerable and more viable than their assimilated, self-confident, more established, more sophisticated and therefore less militant counterparts in Hungary.

Notes

1. *Uj Élet* (Budapest), March 20, 1947, p. 1.

2. Lajos Stöckler joined the reorganized Jewish Council following Szálasi's seizure of power (October 15, 1944). He was the deputy to the Council's President, Samu Stern.

3. Article in *Uj Élet,* April 17, 1947, p. 3.

4. Ernő Munkácsi, *Hogyan történt?* ("How did it happen?"; Budapest, 1947), pp. 10, 54–55.

5. See Y. Gutman and others eds., *Hanhagat yehudei Hungaria be-mivhan ha-sho'ah* (Jerusalem, 1976). About the Jewish Council see Randolph L. Braham, "The Role of the Jewish Council in Hungary: A Tentative Assessment," *Yad Vashem Studies* 10 (1974), 69–109, and his contribution to this volume (also concerning the case of Kasztner).

6. Among them were Vilmos Vázsonyi, Pál Sándor and Béla Fábian.

7. About Jews in the Romanian Parliament see my "The Jewish Vote in Romania between the Two World War," *Jewish Journal of Sociology* 14 (1972), 229–44.

8. See Thomas Spira, "Hungary's Numerus Clausus, the Jewish Minority and the League of Nations," *Ungarn-Jahrbuch* 4 (1973), 115–28.

9. The delegation (in which Dr. W. Filderman was prominent) was accused of treason by nationalist press and political circles in Romania.

10. The designation favored by most Hungarian Jews was: "Hungarians of the Israelite faith."

11. Prominent among the leaders of the Union of Romanian Jews were A. Stern, H. Carp, and Dr. W. Filderman, who competed for Jewish votes on different Romanian lists.

12. Jewish parliamentarians in Hungary were elected on bourgeois liberal, radical and social democratic lists.

13. Among the Jewish candidates and members of Parliament expected to assure Jewish votes for Romanian political parties were Aureliu Weiss (National Peasants party) and Mihail Szmuck (National Liberal party).

14. Among those political figures who identified themselves with the Hungarian *irredenta* were Dr. Géza Dési, Ernő Bródy, Béla Halmi, Ignác Hercz, and quite a few Transylvanian public figures such as Emil Veiszlovics, Benő Gombos, and Dr. Lipót Kecskeméti.

15. The Romanian *boiari* constituted the landowner class which, however, was not an equivalent of the hereditary nobility of a West or Central European type.

16.   Besides Marshal Averescu's Rightist party and the National Liberal party, even the extreme Rightist "Neo-Liberals" had Jewish followers, notably Lazar Halberthal, head of the Bucharest Jewish Community during the Holocaust.

17.   "Judah has vanquished" was Goga's reaction to his fall on February 10, 1938.

18.   The prominent members of the Council were Chief Rabbi Dr. Niemirover, Dr. W. Filderman and Dr. T. Fischer, formerly president of the Jewish party.

19.   See my "Ha-mediniyut ha-yehudit shel ha-diktaturah ha-malkhutit be-Romania (1938–1940)," *Zion* 29 (1964), 133–51.

20.   While most of the Zionist leaders came from the provinces acquired after World War I, leaders of the Union of Romanian Jews and the most influential Jewish public figures were based in Bucharest.

21.   Among them Dr. Ernő Marton, Dr. Rezső Kasztner, and Hillel Danzig.

22.   The OMZSA (welfare) distribution was controlled as follows: the Neolog communities 83 percent, the Orthodox 15 percent, the Status Quo 2 percent. See *OMZSA-Évkönyv* (Budapest, 1944), p. 206.

23.   Among them were Samu Stern, P. de Freudiger, Ernő Pető, Dr. György Polgár, Dr. Géza Ribáry, Dr. Géza Dési, Béla Alapi, Samu Kahan Frankl, Dr. Imre Reiner. About Jews in the Hungarian nobility and Jewish dignitaries see William O. McCagg, *Jewish Nobles and Geniuses in Modern Hungary* (New York, 1972). Stern and de Freudiger belonged to very wealthy families. But the most prominent Jewish industrialist and banker families (e.g., the Buday-Goldbergers, Baron Weiss, the Chorins) did not participate in the leadership, though helping with community activities (especially welfare).

24.   Among them S. Singer, M. Landau, M. Benvenisti, D. Rosenkrantz, Dr. C. Iancu, M. Moscovici, J. Cohen, L. A. Mizrahi, M. Weissman.

25.   See my "Jewish Vote in Romania" (*op. cit.*, note 7 above).

26.   Among them Dr. J. Fischer, Dr. T. Fischer, E. Marton, Dr. M. Ebner, M. Landau, Dr. R. Kasztner.

27.   Following the Soviet ultimatum of June 1940, Romania ceded Bessarabia and Northern Bukovina to the Soviet Union. The Second Vienna Diktat (August 30, 1940) deprived Romania of Northern Transylvania, which was annexed by Hungary. In September 1940 Romania ceded Southern Dobrudja to Bulgaria.

28.   About the antisemitic terror of the "National Legionnaire" regime, see M. Carp, *Cartea neagră* ("The black book"; Bucharest, 1946), vol. I.

29.   The armed rebellion of the Iron Guard led by H. Sima collapsed because Antonescu enjoyed massive army support and eventually Hitler's too.

30.   Besides Carp, *op. cit.,* vast documentary material has been published in *Pinkas ha-kehiiot: Romania* (Jerusalem, 1969).

31.   The Centrul National de Românizare (National Center of Romanization) was set up in May 1941 with a view to expropriating Jewish property; no clear-cut legislation was enacted against the Jews before the end of 1941.

32.   See the accusation of I. Chișinevschi (a member of the Politbureau of the Romanian Communist party) against Filderman and the fascimile reproduction of the incriminatory letter in *Scânteia* (Bucharest), October 19, 1945.

33.   The one member of the Jewish Council accused of Nazi collaboration was Rabbi Béla Berend, but even he was acquitted by a Budapest court.

34. The only exhaustive work about Romanian Jewry during the Holocaust that stresses Zionist activity is T. Lavi's *Yahadut Romania ba-ma' vak al hatzalatah* (Jerusalem, 1965).

35. An authoritative but not comprehensive survey of Zionist activity during 1942–1944 is M. Benvenisti's *Sionismul in vremea prigoanei* ("Zionism in the days of persecution"; Bucharest, 1944).

36. Of the few writings about the youth movement in the Zionist underground, the most informative is Y. Artzi's "The Underground Activity of the *Halutz* Movements in Romania during World War II" in *Yad Vashem Bulletin* 29 (July 1962). See also the Artzi Files, Historical Documentation Center, University of Haifa (hereafter: Documentation Center, Haifa University).

37. The Filderman Archives at Yad Vashem (Jerusalem) contain vast documentary material about Filderman's and his group's activity. See mainly the protocols signed by D. Rozenkranz.

38. About the Center the only extensive work is my "The Ambiguity of Collaborationism: The Center of the Jews in Romania," in Y. Gutman and C. J. Haft eds., *Patterns of Jewish Leadership in Nazi Europe 1933–1945* (Jerusalem, 1979).

39. See the Safran Files (Documentation Center, Haifa University).

40. See note 35 above. Further details about the "Zissu Executive" are provided by Jean Cohen, one of Zissu's collaborators, in *Adevărul* (Tel Aviv), October 17, 1958.

41. Among those who took advantage of the opportunity to leave Hungary were P. de Freudiger, Dr. M. Weinberger, and Dr. E. Marton.

42. Secret contacts with the Allies were established through Berne, Madrid, Lisbon and Stockholm by Mihai Antonescu or by his diplomats during 1943.

43. Among the vast amount of documentary evidence see the Filderman Archives, P.6–91, pp. 645–50; P.6–106, pp. 608–9; and Filderman's declaration (Bucharest, September 12, 1944), P.6–27, pp. 80–81.

44. See Benvenisti, *op, cit.;* also the pertinent chapter in the Lavi Files (Documentation Center, Haifa University).

45. Jean Cohen, *op. cit.*

46. *Ibid.*

47. In Spring 1944, contacts between the Romanian anti-Nazi opposition and the Allies entered a decisive phase; the key figures, Minister A. Cretzianu (in Ankara) and Prince Ştirbey (in Cairo), acted with Mihai Antonescu's tacit agreement. In the meantime Romanian diplomats in Stockholm established direct contacts with the Soviets at Mihai Antonescu's explicit instruction.

48. About the reasons for a change in the policy of the Antonescu regime toward the Jews, see T. Lavi, "Background to the Rescue of Romanian Jewry during the Period of the Holocaust," in Bela Vago and George E. Mosse eds., *Jews and Non-Jews in Eastern Europe 1918–1945* (New York, Toronto and Jerusalem, 1974), pp. 177–86. About Zissu's activity see "Raportul prezentat de A. L. Zissu la Conferinţa Organizaţiei Sioniste, April 28–30, 1946," in *Mântuirea* (Bucharest), May 6, 1946 and Beno Baruch's article in *Renaşterea Noastră* (Tel Aviv), November 26, 1953.

49. Filderman Archives, P.6–91, p. 493; P.6–95, pp. 326 ff.; P.6–27, pp. 81–81; and Filderman's relevant declaration (Paris, June 2, 1954), P.6–109, pp. 215–16.

50. *Ibid.,* P.6–106, pp. 608–9. See also the pertinent sections of the Mella Iancu Files (Documentation Center, Haifa University, R/2/d/2).

51.   *Ibid.,* recorded statement by Mella Iancu (Tel Aviv, April 9, 1977).

52.   *Ibid.*, recorded statement by Hillel Danzig (Tel Aviv, January 2, 1975).

53.   *Ibid.* See also the copy of a memorandum sent by H. Danzig to the Central Committee of the Hungarian Social Democrat party (March 18, 1946) in the Dr. E. Marton Archives (Yad Vashem), JM/2625/5.

54.   See note 52 above.

55.   Freudiger's recorded statement (Haifa, December 29, 1974) in the Freudiger Files (Documentation Center, Haifa University).

56.   See Braham, *op. cit.* in *Yad Vashem Studies* 10 (note 5 above).

57.   About the activity and the attitude of some of the leaders of the Jewish Council, as related by themselves, see Randolph H. Braham, ed., *Hungarian-Jewish Studies,* vol. III (New York, 1973), pp. 1–150.

58.   See Andre Biss, *A Million Jews to Save* (London, 1973).

59.   Among them Shmuel Springmann, Kasztner and Joel Brand.

60.   E.g., Miklós Mester, an undersecretary in the Sztójay and Lakatos cabinets, and Tibor Kóródy, a member of parliament representing the Imrédy party.

61.   Among them Lt. Colonel Ferenczy and Captain Lullay.

62.   Details about some intelligence aspects of the activity of the Rescue Committee are given in my "Budapest Jewry in the Summer of 1944—Ottó Komoly's Diaries," *Yad Vashem Studies* 8 (1970), 81–106, and "The Intelligence Aspects of the Joel Brand Mission," *Yad Vashem Studies* 10 (1974), 111–28.

63.   See Yosef Schaeffer, "Hanhagat ha-mahteret ha-halutzit be-Hungaria," in *Hanhagat yehudei Hungaria* (*op. cit.,* note 5 above), pp. 135–49. Among those who came from Slovakia or from Poland were R. Friedl (Ben Shalom), Peretz Revesz and Zvi Goldfarb.

64.   Excepting Komoly and Kasztner, everyone on the rescue scene lacked the political and formal education required for acceptance as negotiating partners by the Hungarian establishment or by the gentry-bourgeois anti-Nazi opposition.

III. THE *JUDENRAT* AND THE JEWISH RESPONSE

The Ghetto as a Form of Government: An Analysis of Isaiah Trunk's *Judenrat*

RAUL HILBERG

In 1972, more than a quarter century after the end of the Holocaust, Isaiah Trunk published his pathbreaking book, *Judenrat,* the first major attempt to portray systematically the institutions and conditions of Jewish life in the ghettos of Nazi Eastern Europe.[1] It is a big volume, some 700 pages long, but it is also, despite its size, an understated work; for Trunk is one of those uncommon authors who promise less than they deliver. His preface deals with limits and limitations, giving an outline of Nazi administration in the East and a recital of sources at his disposal. The introduction, which was written not by Trunk but by Jacob Robinson, is partly philosophical, partly polemic, and in no event foreshadows the dimensions of the contents. The substantive account is presented by Trunk in ordinary matter-of-fact language without buildup or climax. As he traverses his terrain, from schools to synagogues, from labor to deportations, his tone remains constant. In this evenness, Trunk has managed to submerge everything: his range, his depth, and his findings.

The title of the book is *Judenrat,* meaning the "Jewish Council" or rather hundreds of them in various Eastern European ghettos. Trunk wanted to "achieve an objective history of the Councils," and thereby "find the key to internal Jewish history under Nazi rule."[2] But his book is not merely a depiction of that key; it deals with the whole house, for it is a full-scale political, economic, and social history of the ghetto as such. The various headings of chapters and subchapters indicate the scope of the discussion, which comprises a whole gamut of topics: organizational developments in the ghetto bureaucracy, commissions and police; the problem areas of finances, taxes, production and purchases; and programs involving bathhouses, kitchens, welfare or medical aid.

There is a similar richness of documentation. Although Trunk calls special attention in the preface to a survey that netted replies from 927 respondents concerning 740 former Council members and 112 ghetto police, the questionnaire material constitutes only about 5 percent of the 2,000 citations in the notes, which are filled with references to orders issued by German supervisory agencies, reports of Jewish Councils to the Germans, minutes of Council meetings, newspapers, diaries, memoirs, and memorial books. Text *and* sources reveal the extent of Trunk's effort, while intricate facts on every page reflect the author's long preoccupation with numerous aspects of ghetto life.[3]

Trunk cautions against over-generalization. At the outset he stresses the importance of local conditions and the individuality of leaders in the Jewish communities.[4] Yet he does not present the Warsaw Ghetto in one chapter, Lodz in another, and additional ghettos down the line. The fragmentary nature of the source material would not have allowed for an approach of that kind. Instead, he addresses himself to the essence of the ghettos; that is, the mode of their operations with regard to such all-pervasive problems as crowding, hunger, or the demands of the Germans; and he does so implicitly by using almost any item of information about a particular ghetto as illustrative of the situation in all of them. In this manner, he builds a mosaic that is generalization *par excellence.*

More than that, his whole book is a demonstration (rather than the mere assertion) that, notwithstanding the different internal structures of the Jewish communities or the diversity of personalities in the Jewish Councils, the story of all ghettos must be read as one history. Jewish perceptions and reactions were remarkably similar across the occupied territories, despite the relative isolation of the communities and their Councils from each other. In the final analysis, the variation among ghettos is not as crucial as their commonality, nor is it primarily the classification of ghettos in terms of demographic or economic factors that counts, but the singularity of meaning in the very phrase "Jewish ghetto" as compared with everything else that has transpired in recent times throughout the world.

If Trunk had done no more than organize a compendium of facts in subject-matter categories, he would have furnished us with significant additions to our knowledge; but beyond any compilation he also set forth a series of propositions about the nature of the ghettos and the Councils governing them. One cannot find these propositions in some final chapter; Trunk eschews discoveries and there is no recapitulation at the end. His summation is confined to five pages and there he considers solely an issue raised by Jacob Robinson in the introduction: the question of the Councils' "collaboration" with the Germans. Thus, an entire set of observations and conclusions is left buried in the text, some in lengthy passages, others in single sentences, still others in recurring themes and characterizations. For a review of *Judenrat,* nothing is more important than a consolidation of these points in analytic form. Here they are, under four headings, partly condensed from his account, partly developed from it, but mainly rooted in his evidence.[5]

The Ghetto as a Political Entity

The principal characteristic of the ghetto was the segregation of its inhabitants from the surrounding population. The Jewish ghetto was a closed-off society, its gates permanently shut to free traffic, so much so that Trunk labels as relatively "open" those of the ghetto communities (in smaller cities) that dispatched labor columns daily to projects outside the ghetto limits.[6] This is not to imply the total absence of contacts with Germans or Poles. There were electrical, telephone, gas and water connections, removals of human waste, exports of manufactured goods, imports of coal, food or raw materials, mail and parcel shipments through ghetto post offices, loans from banks, payments of rents, etc. In examining these links one must, however, always differentiate between institutional transactions that had to be maintained if the ghetto was to function and private bonds, across the boundaries, that could no longer be tolerated because they were incompatible with the function of the ghetto.

Even the official correspondence of Jewish ghetto authorities with neighboring German or Polish agencies or firms was largely severed, and the flow of orders and reports confined as much as possible, though never completely, to a channel running from the German supervisors to the Jewish Council. The horizontal relationships that are built into so much of modern life were consequently replaced by an almost all-embracing vertical regime, sometimes complex as in the cases of Warsaw and Lodz, often simple as in outlying localities, but always standardized in a dictatorial manner.[7]

The hierarchical system of German supervision was designed for the purpose of absolutism. German orders were unqualified and Council members were required to carry them out promptly and fully. Trunk underscores the fact that the members of the Councils were not Nazi sympathizers: that although some were ambitious and many deluded, they were not, and could not be regarded as a German institution.[8] They were, in short, Jews and they could not fail to perceive the fate of Jewry as their fate as well.[9] All the more bitter then was their task of receiving and implementing German decrees. Yet the directives of the Germans were only half of their problem. Less stark, but equally burdensome, was the necessity of asking for authorization to carry out every function of government, including duties expected of them. The Councils had to obtain clearance for a variety of revenue measures; they had to "borrow" Jewish funds previously sequestered or confiscated under occupation ordinances; they even had to request permission to post German orders.

If the Councils were thus rendered totally subordinate and dependent in their relations with the Germans, a corresponding status was fashioned for the Jewish population subjected to Council rule. German sentiment in this matter was expressed unambiguously by one official when he asserted: "It lies in the interest of the difficult administration of the Jewish district that the authority of the Jewish Council be upheld and strengthened under all circumstances."[10]

Jewish executives, like the Germans in charge, could make use of coercion and take advantage of helplessness. Compliance and acquiescence were ensured by the Jewish police, which had the power to make arrests and guard prisoners.[11] Relief could be dispensed in that the Councils controlled food and space: German shipments of flour, sugar, or coal were doled out under conditions of constantly increasing privation.[12]

Throughout the system power was exercised in levels of dominance, and each level was reinforced in every way. An illustration of such reinforcement was the principle of limiting correspondence and conversations to immediate superiors and inferiors. The Jewish Council could make appeals only to the German supervisory authorities in its locality; it could conceivably urge the city commander or ghetto commissioner to submit a plea to higher officials,[13] but it could not carry messages directly to regional governors or their staffs. The ghetto inhabitants, in turn, might stand in line to see the "Elder" of the Council, but they had no ordinary access to German agencies. In fact, there is reason to suppose that the Councils acquired a stake in establishing themselves as the sole representatives of the Jewish population vis-à-vis German officialdom. They certainly felt themselves empowered to govern the Jews and, in some ghettos, announced that persons who had failed to pay taxes or report for labor would be handed over to a German organ because of their recalcitrance.[14] For Jewish bureaucrats, no less than German, there was no substitute for authority.

The physical and administrative constrictions of Jewry reduced its space and narrowed its horizon, but at the same time intensified its organizational activity. While the Germans outside became invisible,[15] the Jewish community machinery within evolved into the government of a captive city-state. Trunk explains the transformation as clearly stemming from two causes: one was the need to supply those regular municipal and economic services from which the community was now cut off and without which it could not have survived; the other was the burden thrust upon the Councils by the Germans, who used them to fulfill German needs.[16] The multiplication of tasks inherent in this dual evolution, coupled with continuing unemployment and periodic fears of disaster, led also to swollen ghetto bureaucracies that were filled with minor functionaries and clerks, both paid and unpaid. In ghettos featuring public enterprise (particularly Lodz and Vilna), the Council payrolls at the beginning of 1942 encompassed as much as a fifth of the employable population.[17]

Although ghetto office personnel often did very little, some officials wielded power—at times almost undisturbed power—in specialized spheres of jurisdiction. One area in particular lent itself to what Trunk calls, albeit between quotation marks, ghetto self-government. This island of Jewish freedom was located in the courts, where disputes between Jewish litigants were settled by Jewish judges without German interference.[18]

The ghettos were consequently political entities with governmental attributes much larger and fuller than the social, cultural, or religious functions carried out by the prewar communities. Soon, however, Jewish Councils everywhere came face to face with the basic paradox inherent in their role as preservers of Jewish life in a framework of German destruction. They could not serve the Jews indefinitely while simultaneously obeying the Germans. A good deal of what Trunk calls the "strategy and tactics" of the Councils[19] involved their futile attempt to resolve this contradiction. The Jewish leadership was completely non-provocative: it did not fight the Germans, it seldom fought the orders, but in its distress it made numerous offerings. From time to time the Councils offered words, money, labor, and finally lives.

Appeals were probably the most frequently used device. They were often generated by upheaval, especially at the beginning of the German occupation during the formation of ghettos and at the onset of deportations; but the content of the appeals was broad-ranging. The Councils asked for permission to turn on the lights after 8 p.m. (Lublin), for reductions of confiscations (Bialystok), or for the return of hostages (Warsaw). "Seldom did Jewish petitions have any success," states Trunk; yet one has the feeling from such documents as the Czerniakow diary that an occasional or partial German concession, even if only for the mitigation or postponement of some harsh measure, fueled the pleadings time and again. They remained, throughout, the strategy of first resort.

Trunk devotes considerable space to bribes, which he believes to have been widespread, but which obviously could have been used only under special conditions. They must have been more successful than intercessions, but the objects attained by bribery are likely to have been limited and the results short-lived. Typical were payments to effect the transfer of a particularly troublesome official or policeman, the ransom of young girls from forced prostitution (a practice which under German "race-pollution" law was in any case prohibited), or the tender of money to avert "resettlement."

Most extensive is Trunk's discussion of the "rescue-through-work" strategy[20] that reflected German dependence on products of Jewish manufacture, especially war material, but also simple things such as brushes, which in labor-hungry Axis Europe could not be turned out in quantity with ease. In Lodz, Vilna, and Czestochowa, such dependence led to the construction by the Councils themselves of fairly large-scale industries. The factories bought time for tens of thousands, but the Jews were playing a determined game in which the outcome was always under German control.[21]

Mass deportations forced the Jews to the extreme ends in the spectrum of alternatives. There was no longer any middle ground between open opposition and total compliance: the Jewish communities were bound to choose the one or the other. Trunk gives some examples of Councils with a "positive attitude" toward resistance. However, most manifestations of that inclination turn out to have been actions of individual Council members in aiding escapes or establishing contacts with partisans.[22] The predominant pattern was the active implementation of German directives.

Thus, the Councils themselves organized confiscations and forced labor. In most ghettos, they themselves delivered the victims for the death transports. Of course, the Germans would frequently ask for only a certain number of deportees. It was such requests that ignited internal Jewish arguments to the effect that if 1,000 Jews were given up, 10,000 would be saved, but if none were sacrificed, all would be lost. In delivering a part of the community, the Councils could also choose the less worthy.[23] Trunk quotes Zalman Shazar, the President of Israel, as having pointed out in 1964 that the negative selections in the ghettos had been preceded by similar behavior in Tsarist times, when the Jewish community leaders were forced to designate youngsters for 25 years of service in the Russian imperial army. Then, too, Jewish leaders chose the simpletons.[24]

Because of its compliance strategy, the *Judenrat* could be a dangerous organization precisely when it functioned most smoothly. Impersonality, as in the recruitment of the strong and the weak or the healthy and the sick for heavy labor, could become brutality. Order, as shown in Lodz where smuggling was curbed, could intensify deprivation. Efficiency, in the collection of taxes or furs, could bring about more suffering. Thus, many of the virtues of Jewish ghetto government became vices; responsibility was turned into unresponsiveness and salvage into loss.

The Ghetto as a Socio-Economic Organization

The Jewish ghettos mark an interim phase between prewar freedom and wartime annihilation. These last moments of organized existence in the Jewish community were endured in a vise of progressively diminished space and gradually increasing hunger. If social and economic policies in normal societies can have long-range effects on large groups of people seeking comforts, security, or some pleasure in life, the internal measures and practices of ghetto Councils were bound to have an immediate and massive impact on a population hovering between survival and death.

We may safely assume that many times the meager resources at the disposal of the Councils were strained for the benefit of the community. There were occupational training programs, workshops, rationing systems, housing authorities, hospitals, ambulances, and other services in a large number of ghettos. Their very existence demonstrates what Jewish bureaucrats and technocrats could accomplish even under these conditions. At the same time, Trunk leaves little doubt that the ghettos as a whole were no triumphs of social equality and economic justice. The ghetto was the scene of all forms of corruption including bribery, favoritism, and nepotism. Moreover, in the critical areas of labor, food, and taxes, prevailing regulations were particularly harsh for the most destitute families.

Instances of dishonesty are difficult to document, but Trunk cites relevant testimony of survivors from several ghettos. Council members accepted personal bribes for exemptions from labor duty (Zamosc) and deportation (Horodenka and other ghettos).[25] Bribes were said to have been taken for appointments to the ghetto police (Warsaw, etc.).[26] Patronage in the award of jobs to inexperienced applicants, sometimes resulting in the employment of entire families, was apparently widespread in Warsaw, Lodz, Bialystok, Lublin, and elsewhere.[27] Friendships were also important in the soup kitchens of Lodz, where the chairman, Rumkowski, is reported to have issued supplementary food ration stamps "at whim," favoring particularly Orthodox groups and rabbis.[28]

While abuses for private ends may be regarded as transgressions of individuals, a regime of exploitation through official routines can only be described as systemic. The difference is important; for the concealed bribes and favors were intrinsically unjustifiable, whereas the open decrees and decisions, which so often took advantage of the most helpless portion of the population, were defended by Jewish Councils as the best they could do under the circumstances. Nowhere is this posture more clearly expressed than in the pronouncements, correspondence, and diary of Adam Czerniakow, Chairman of the Jewish Council in the laissez-faire ghetto of Warsaw. During the early days, Czerniakow excused the well-to-do from forced labor for a fee to finance the compensation of poor families whose men were digging ditches for the Germans.[29] Later, as he struggled with the Council's unbalanced budget, he proposed as his principal revenue source a monthly tax on bread.[30] Still later, when the Council was threatened with declining German food shipments, cash reserves were created as a precautionary measure by increasing the surcharges on the bread and sugar rations.[31]

One of the effects of ghetto class structure was the emergence of what Trunk calls a "food pyramid." Quite simply, the social ladder became more and more conspicuous in the number of calories consumed. Thus, a survey in the Warsaw Ghetto during December 1941 revealed that Council employees were receiving 1,665 calories, artisans 1,407, shopworkers 1,225, and the "general" population 1,125.[32] A similar picture of relative starvation may be observed in the Lodz Ghetto, where differential rationing, by type of employment, was official policy.[33] This is how status became instrumental in the prolongation of basic survival. Czerniakow himself made the point obliquely at the end of 1941 when he observed that the intelligentsia were dying now.[34]

In retrospect, the tiers of privilege in ghetto society should not surprise us that much. Ghetto life rewarded special talents such as smuggling or wheeling and dealing. It accommodated the more usual skills of the doctors and artisans, or of people who could speak German. The ghetto protected its rabbis as well, for the Jews clung to the past and also approached their most extraordinary problems with all traditional means. Finally, the Jewish bureaucrat who ran the ghetto during its formation and who presided at its dissolution was granted his temporary reprieve. In the vast majority of instances, however, the last occurrence of even the most shielded existence was violent death.

The Ghetto as a Mirage

Adam Czerniakow was the sort of man who did not want to draw a salary so long as there was not enough money to pay his staff.[35] In the midst of starvation, he shunned elaborate meals, eating soup for lunch in his office.[36] During a contraction of the ghetto boundaries, he refused a German offer that would have allowed him to keep his apartment on a street from which the Jews were being expelled.[37] In July 1942, when he realized that the Jews were going to be deported *en masse*, he took his own life. Yet in February 1942, just about six months before that fateful day, Czerniakow had decided to have stained glass windows installed in the Council chambers.[38] Czerniakow, as well as most of the other Jewish leaders, acted on the premise that there was a future. From the outset, Council members at their desks and crowds in the streets bore their crushing burdens as temporary inflictions to be suffered until liberation. To the end, Jewish hospitals tried to heal the sick, schools continued to train the young, and kitchens fed the starving. There was no alternative.

Many ghetto activities, especially in education and culture, bordered on illusionary behavior—the Vilna Ghetto, for example, established a music school in the summer of 1942.[39] Readers in the Warsaw Ghetto fantasized in the pages of Tolstoy's *War and Peace* that a German collapse was imminent.[40] In the upper echelons of ghetto leadership, a kind of unreality surfaced in "power struggles" in and around the Council headquarters.

Jurisdictional questions were a major preoccupation of the ghetto managers. One of these contests was waged between the Councils and a centralized Jewish Welfare Service (JSS), which reported to the German Population and Welfare Division of the Generalgouvernement in Krakow and which maintained local committees in the ghettos.[41] A complex federal structure with built-in frictions evolved in the Warsaw Ghetto, where more than a thousand "House Committees" began to perform all sorts of voluntary and assigned functions, including the provision of shelter for refugees, the staging of one-act plays, emergency assistance, reports of illnesses, and collections of taxes.[42] In the same ghetto, the Council was challenged by an organization known as the "Control Office for Combatting the Black Market and Profiteering in the Jewish District" under Abraham Gancwajch. Czerniakow won that battle when the Gancwajch apparatus was dissolved, with provision for the incorporation of its members into the regular Jewish "order service" (police).[43] Again, the following story, told by Czerniakow in his diary, illustrates the manner and extent to which administrators in the Warsaw Ghetto were absorbed by problems of entitlement. A Provisioning Authority had been formed as a quasi-independent agency in Summer 1941 to deal with the approaching food crisis. In the Council's own labor department, an official wanted the local German labor office to approve applicants for positions in the Authority. Incensed, Czerniakow wrote on February 15, 1942: "This clearly amounts to undermining the authority of the Council and diminishing its prerogatives. According to the [Council's] legal department, there is no basis for this position in law."[44]

Ghetto government at times became a distorted facsimile of a viable political system. The politics in the administrative processes of the ghettos may strike us as a caricature, because so many of the functionaries had come to think of life in the German enclosure as a stabilized condition of existence; they claimed not only some of the food, space, or medical services for themselves and their families, they fought also for a share of power in this "weird, crippled structure." Yes, even in this run-down machine, which could no longer cope with its narrowest tasks, they wanted a piece of the action.

Trunk speaks at some length of "The German Policy of Fraud and Deceit."[45] The Germans, he says, kept the Jews in the dark about their intentions. Indeed, the German perpetrators did not install a warning system in the ghetto. They did not practice chivalry toward their victims. On the other hand, the Jewish leaders did not attempt to acquire information about the Germans systematically and they did not come to grips with disturbing news in time.

At the start, the Polish Jews viewed ghettoization as the culmination of German plans. They failed to think in terms of a further, more drastic stage in the destruction process. The diary of Adam Czerniakow, leader of the largest ghetto in Europe, is the most detailed record of that characteristic train of thought in the face of peril.

Anyone with a deep interest in the Warsaw Ghetto might well approach the diary with the direct question: what *were* Czerniakow's predictions? What were his plans? What did he think the Germans would do eventually and what did he see as his alternatives? Nothing, almost nothing of this kind will be found in these notes. Czerniakow does not make forecasts. He does not draw up options. He does not refer to the Germans as foes. From October 1941 to Spring 1942 he expresses himself only in subdued tones, very briefly in passing, about ominous reports. As early as October 4, 1941, he quotes an ambiguous and enigmatic statement of a German official: "Bischof disclosed yesterday that Warsaw is merely a temporary haven for the Jews."[46] The entry for October 27 states: "Alarming rumors about the fate of the Jews in Warsaw next spring." On January 17, he asks whether Lithuanian guards were coming. More rumors on February 16. Disturbing news reached him on March 18 from Lvov (30,000 resettled) and from Mielec and Lublin. As of April 1, he hears that 90 percent of the Jews of

Lublin were to leave their ghetto within the next few days. All this was written in entries of a sentence or two, in the middle of paragraphs containing other sentences on other subjects.

Czerniakow viewed himself as having taken over an impossible task to be pursued from morning to night against increasingly unfavorable odds. He lived through daily nightmares of blocked funds, labor columns, apartment allocations, bricks for the wall, furs for the Germans, soup for the poor. There was hardly anything that could be put off—everything was urgent. This is why, when the Germans accepted his revenue statute imposing a tax on bread, he felt that he had accomplished something and that he could face the next day. This is also why a modest collection of money for children was entered as a notable success. And this is the reason that in February 1942, when most of the Warsaw Ghetto had not yet starved to death, he could feel a sense of vindication. He and hundreds more on Jewish Councils all over Eastern Europe, had fallen into a cadence that did not allow for prolonged reflection about the real meaning of the ghettos in the Nazi scheme of things. In fact, any German laxity or inefficiency only served to reinforce the pace and intensify the activities of the Jewish officials who worked in tandem with their German supervisors, reporting to them, seeking clarifications, and requesting authorizations. Thus, administrative-economic dependence increasingly became psychological as well. It was a trap into which the Jewish leadership slipped and from which it could not extricate itself.

On July 20, 1942, the deportations in Warsaw were imminent. Trunk cites an excerpt from Czerniakow's diary describing that day.[47] At this moment of panic in the Warsaw Ghetto, Czerniakow went from Gestapo man to Gestapo man in desperation to ask whether the rumors of a "resettlement" were true. The Germans assured him that they did not know anything and that the reports were all nonsense *(Quatsch und Unsinn)*. The passage is a fairly good example of how crude the Germans could be in their policy of "fraud and deceit." One has the feeling that their simple denials were almost lame. Not so simple are Czerniakow's frantic requests for reassurances. He was not a naive man. At the beginning of the paragraph, he himself states that he left the office of the Gestapo man Mende "unconvinced," and later in the day he was to ask for permission to transmit German denials to the Jewish population. The Germans could see no harm in that and, by evening, in Commissioner Auerswald's office, promised an "investigation" of the rumors. Three days after that meeting, all the camouflage was gone and Czerniakow killed himself with poison. We do not know how long he had kept that pill in his drawer.

The Jewish communities were lulled by the continuation of sheer routines, including the endless rebuilding of walls and fences, the periodic exactions, confiscations, and arrests, and even the desultory firing by German guards into the ghettos. Yet, they did not lack indices of danger. The whole economic system of the ghettos was not geared to long-term survival. There was large-scale, chronic unemployment and, as Trunk points out in one of his important findings, a finite supply of personal belongings was mobilized to supplement the insufficiency of production in an effort to pay for legally and illegally imported food.[48] The clock was running down, and soon there were signs of massive German violence. As German armies crossed the Bug and San rivers in June 1941 to assault the USSR, mobile units of the SS and Police began to kill Jews by the hundreds of thousands in Eastern Poland, the Baltic states, Belorussia, and the Ukraine. By the Spring of 1942, deportations to death camps commenced in the heart of Poland. The deported Jews were not heard from again.

In the remnant ghettos of 1943, the issue of life and death could no longer be avoided. The alternatives were brought forth and discussed: one could plan escape, prepare resistance, or redouble efforts to produce goods for the Germans. Even in this drastic situation, there was a tendency to veer away from methodical dispersal or organized battle; for while it was not feasible for the entire population to participate in acts of defiance, it was possible for everyone to suffer the consequences.[49]

This is how the doctrine of "rescue through work" became paramount from Upper Silesia to Vilna. It was, in more ways than one, the strategy of least resistance, and it was founded on the assumption that Germans were rational and would not obliterate a work force that was engaged in so much war production for them. The thought was, of course, a misconception. The Jews had once placed their trust in rules and regulations for protection against the ravages of totalitarianism; now they clung to contracts and deliveries for safety from destruction. Thus, the Jews in Czestochowa were bewildered by the report that in the Warsaw Ghetto workers had been dragged from their shops.[50] Still, the rationale of work salvation was not dispelled. If the unskilled were lost, it was hoped that the skilled would remain; and when some of those were removed, it was reasoned that the raids would occur only once in a while. In this manner, Jewry sacrificed more and more for less and less until it was annihilated.

The Ghetto as a Self-Destructive Machine

We have seen now that the Jewish ghetto was a provider of administrative services, a social and economic laboratory, and a state of mind. It was also a form of organized self-destruction.

Once more, it should be emphasized that the Jewish Councils were *not* the willful accomplices of the Germans. Within the German superstructure, however, they were its indispensable operatives. Even when their activities were benign, as in the case of housing refugees or promoting sanitary conditions, they could contribute to the overall purposes and ultimate goals of their German supervisors. The very institution of an orderly ghetto was, after all, an essential link in the chain of destructive steps. In building this order and preserving it, the Councils could not help serving their enemy.

We know, of course, that the Germans expected much more than general government from their Jewish deputies. It was German policy to transfer to Jewish middlemen a large part of the physical and psychological burdens of destroying millions of men, women, and children. One aspect of that assignment was financial, another entailed selection, and the third enforcement; we shall examine these in turn.

The destruction of Jewry generated administrative costs and, throughout Europe, German agencies attempted to obtain some of the necessary resources from the Jews themselves. So far as possible, the destruction process was to be self-financing. In Poland, too, an effort was made to balance the books without drawing from the budget of the German Reich. Trunk cites the fact that the German administration of the Lodz Ghetto (the *Gettoverwaltung*) covered expenses by taxing deliveries to the Ghetto.[51] In Warsaw there was wall-building. The Jewish engineer Marek Lichtenbojm (who was to succeed Czerniakow as chairman of the Council) and a large crew of Jewish laborers were engaged at the site, and financial responsibility for the wall was passed to the Jewish community.[52]

Indirectly, the Warsaw Jews may have subsidized Treblinka. From a letter written to the Warsaw Ghetto Commissioner Auerswald by the first Treblinka commander Dr. Eberl, it appears that the Commissioner was to supply various materials to the camp where shortly afterwards the ghetto inhabitants were to be gassed.[53] (This is not to say that the Jewish leadership was able to decipher the nature of Treblinka while it was under construction.)[54] There may also have been remote funding of death transports from Jewish sources. We know, for example, that the German railways in Lodz billed the Gestapo in the city for the one-way fares. The Gestapo passed the bill to the Lodz *Gettoverwaltung* for payment.[55] We can only surmise how it was ultimately paid.

First the Jewish Councils handed over money; then they delivered human beings." Let us remember, though, that the process of selecting victims began with the social structuring of the ghetto population. We have seen that from the moment of their incarceration, the Jews were discernably divided according to their advantages and privileges in life. To be sure, few individuals had any inkling then that these stratifications would acquire a special meaning during the "Final Solution." However, growing suspicions and forebodings had the effect of accentuating the differentiations. Everyone was now concerned with his position all of the time, and soon the passes and identification cards made out by the Councils became more varied and colorful.[56] The papers spelled out a rank order of protection and, by the same token, vulnerability. Ultimately, separation was bound to be selection *per se,* since in the course of a roundup quotas were often filled with readily available old people, hospitalized patients, or children.[57] In the final analysis, the Councils only had to save some to doom all the others.

Jewry became at least passively a participant in its own undoing, by thus underwriting German operations through financial mechanisms and involvements, and arraying its own people on an axis defining degrees of safety or danger. But Jews were engaged also in a more active and virulent mode of self-destruction when their police were employed in the enforcement of German designs. Trunk devotes an entire chapter to the "order service."[58] Much attention has always been riveted on the Jewish police, because of the role that these semi-uniformed auxiliaries of annihilation performed in the pivotal occurrences of 1941 and 1942.

The "order service" exercised all the expected functions of a regular police department such as traffic control and the pursuit of petty thieves. Furthermore, it carried out tasks that were normal only in an abnormal society, from the collection of ghetto taxes, to the enforcement of compulsory labor, to the seizure of families for deportation, including the penetration of their hiding places. In some of the large ghettos the organization of the Jewish police revealed distinctly German features (particularly a division into ordinary and security police components), but even more visible was the adoption of German methods such as the arrest of parents whose sons did not report for labor duty,[59] or the sealing of houses in which individual tenants had not paid taxes.[60] The Jewish police arrested people in the middle of the night and beat up smugglers or reluctant volunteers for death transports. They ate well and frequently filled their pockets with the bribes and ransom payments of frightened fellow-Jews. So many were the instances of sheer brutality and corruption that Trunk patiently recites case after case of exceptions.

Yet the very composition of the "order service" deepens the paradox of Jews acting against Jew. Whereas some of the recruits may well have been drawn from the underworld (and Ringelblum complains that also a hundred baptized Jews were serving in ranking positions of the Warsaw Ghetto force),[61] some were included for their prior military experience, a large number were fairly well educated, and many were idealistic.[62] Here then was a concentration of healthy young men, uniquely capable of conducting intelligence operations or psychological warfare against the Germans, or of aiding in escapes or even engaging in physical resistance. On isolated occasions, Jewish police may have done just that, but most of the time they were the most conspicuous Jewish instrument in the German destructive machine.

Ringelblum wrote in his notes on February 19, 1941, that the Jewish population had an understanding of the difficulties of being a Jewish policeman. It was hard for Jews to take a *Jewish* policeman seriously and often, in those days, the "order service" would refrain from ordering people around and "discuss" things with them instead. At one point it was therefore said: "You would have minded a Polish policeman, so why don't you mind a Jewish one!"[63] However, this very trust in the Jewish police was to result in one of the greatest moral disappointments of the Holocaust, an experience from which Jewry has not recovered to this day. Irving Louis Horowitz, in reviewing Trunk's *Judenrat,* concludes: "Jewish policemen of Lodz, Vilna, and Warsaw were, after all, still policemen."[64]

The Jewish ghetto has just been opened and we see it now with all of its institutions and processes. This is Trunk's lasting achievement. On the other hand, the moral questions raised over so many years have not been closed; they have only become more complicated. We know that the ghetto leaders themselves were fully aware of their dilemma, that for some it was always on their minds. A small, sensitive book by Leonard Tushnet has illuminated the lives of just three of them: Rumkowski of Lodz, Czerniakow of Warsaw, and Gens of Vilna.[65] They were different men in background and ideas, but in the end all three declined to save themselves after they had failed to save their people.

Notes

1.   Isaiah Trunk, *Judenrat: The Jewish Councils in Eastern Europe under Nazi Occupation* (New York: Macmillan, 1972 and Scarborogh, 1977). Subsequent page references, where not otherwise specified, are to Trunk's book.

2.   P. xviii.

3.   Trunk does concentrate his attention on ghettos that were located within the prewar boundaries of Poland and Lithuania. There are a few details about Riga in Latvia and Minsk in White Russia, but the ghettos farther east as well as the Jewish communities under Romanian administration between the Dniester and the Bug are almost entirely, if understandably, omitted.

4.   Pp. xvii, xviii.

5.   To allow for deeper treatment of some of the problems, illustrations in this discussion will be drawn mainly from the Warsaw Ghetto.

6.   P. 104.

7.   Trunk discusses at some length intra-German rivalries for control of the ghettos (pp. 264–76). The police in particular wanted power over the Jews. See, for example, the letter by the SS and Police Leader in Warsaw (Wigand), November 11, 1941, claiming jurisdiction of his "protective police" (Schupo) over the Warsaw Ghetto's "order service." Yad Vashem microfilm JM 1112 (YIVO microfilm MKY 76).

8.   Pp. 572–74.

9.   In statistical terms, membership in Jewish Councils was in fact hazardous. Trunk reports on the basis of his questionnaires that the incidence of violent death among Council members in the period *before* the deportations was somewhat high. In his group of 720, about one in four was killed in the ghettos, most were deported, and one in nine survived (pp. 326–28). However, the 99 councils covered in his survey must cumulatively have contained several times as many members as the number of recollected names. If the forgotten members died in the gas chambers, the ratios would be less striking.

10.   Mohns (Deputy Chief of the Resettlement Division in the office of the Governor of the Warsaw District) to Leist (Plenipotentiary of the Governor for the City of Warsaw), January 11, 1941, Yad Vashem microfilm JM 1113 (YIVO microfilm MKY 77).

11.   Trunk, pp. 82–83.

12. P. 99.

13. For an example of such a request, see the diary of Adam Czerniakow, Chairman of the Jewish Council in the Warsaw Ghetto, entry for January 7, 1942, in *The Warsaw Diary of Adam Czerniakow*, eds. Raul Hilberg, Stanislaw Staron and Josef Kermisz. (New York: Stein and Day, 1979), pp. 312–13 (hereafter cited as *Diary of Czerniakow*).

14. See Trunk on Lublin, Bedzin, Zamosc, Vilna, p. 484.

15. See Trunk, pp. 528–29, on the psychological implications of this shift.

16. P. 44.

17. Pp. 50–51. Also Trunk's "The Organizational Structure of the Jewish Councils in Eastern Europe," *Yad Vashem Studies* 7 (1968), 147–64.

18. Pp. 180–81, 185. Other areas of autonomy were Saturday as a day of rest and the use of Hebrew or Yiddish in schools, etc. (pp. 189, 196–215).

19. Pp. 390–95.

20. Pp. 400–420.

21. Trunk indulges in the thought that if, in August 1944, the Red Army had not stopped about 75 miles outside Lodz, some 70,000 Jews in its ghetto might have been saved (p. 413). The same speculation is offered by Robinson in his introduction (p. xxix) and was reiterated on another occasion by Yehuda Bauer (Holocaust Conference at the Hebrew College, Boston, 1973). The question, however, is counterfactual. Red Army offenses, though broad, were conducted for limited territorial gain to allow for resupply and regroupment. The halting of the Russian drive so many miles from Lodz was in no sense an "accident." The chance event would have been its opposite—a rapid German collapse.

22. In the Minsk Ghetto, the entire Jewish Council appears to have favored a liaison with partisans (p. 466). Also of interest are the Councils in Bialystok and Vilna, which had "ambiguous" attitudes (pp. 467–71).

23. See Trunk on the Lodz resettlement commission (p. 52).

24. Pp. 435–36.

25. Pp. 385–87.

26. *Ibid.*

27. P. 354.

28. P. 385.

29. Czerniakow to the Plenipotentiary of the Warsaw District for the City of Warsaw, May 21, 1940: Yad Vashem microfilm JM 1113 (YIVO Institute microfilm MKY 77). The Warsaw District Chief was Gouverneur Fischer, his City Plenipotentiary Leist. For examples of similar labor recruitment in other ghettos, see Trunk, pp. 379–80.

30. Czerniakow to the Warsaw District Chief/Resettlement Division/Exchange, January 8, 1941: JM 1113. (Schön was in charge of the Resettlement Division.) Krakow also instituted a head tax (Trunk, p. 381). Levies on earnings were considered problematical, because in ghettos like Warsaw smuggling accounted for considerable income.

31. Proclamation of the Warsaw Ghetto Provisioning Authority, signed by Czerniakow, August 31, 1941; *Diary of Czerniakow*, pp. 273–74. On February 2, 1942, Czerniakow noted in his diary that the reserve had made possible free distributions of bread and sugar.

32. Trunk, pp. 356, 382. For a detailed discussion of the medical aspects of food deprivation in the Warsaw Ghetto, see Leonard Tushnet, *The Uses of Adversity* (New York, 1966). See also Trunk, pp. 146–48.

33. Trunk, p. 383. In several ghettos (Kutno, Kolomea, Chelm, etc.) the social pyramid was particularly visible in housing (pp. 374–77).

34. *Diary of Czerniakow,*, entry for December 4, 1941, p. 305.

35. Entry for May 24, 1941.

36. Entry for June 23, 1941.

37. Entry for October 6, 1941.

38. Entries for February 4 and 10, 1942.

39. P. 227.

40. Emmanual Ringelblum, *Notes from the Warsaw Ghetto* (New York, 1958), p. 300.

41. Pp. 332–42.

42. Pp. 343–45. Czerniakow diary, entries for June 27 and December 3, 1941, pp. 252–53, 304–5. Trunk mentions House Committees also in Bialystok (pp. 515–16).

43. Pp. 505, 644. The text of the agreement between the council and the "Control Office," dated August 5, 1941, appears in the *Diary of Czerniakow,* pp. 265–67.

44. *Diary of Czerniakow,* pp. 325–26.

45. Pp. 413–36.

46. The remark is cited in another connection by Trunk, p. 292.

47. P. 414.

48. Pp. 101–2.

49. See pp. 451–74.

50. P. 404.

51. Pp. 282–83. See also requisitions of furnishings, etc., pp. 66–67, 296. Also *Diary of Czerniakow,* entries for July 22 and November 28, 1941, pp. 260 and 302.

52. Documents in Yad Vashem microfilm JM 1112 (YIVO film MKY 76). Czerniakow letter of January 8, 1941. Czerniakow diary, entries for July 5 and December 30, 1941. In Warsaw, Lodz and Kovno, the councils had to build bridges to connect ghetto sections divided by Aryan streets (Trunk, p. 110).

53. Eberl to Auerswald, June 26, 1942. Facsimile in Jüdisches Historisches Institut Warschau, *Faschismus-Getto-Massenmord* (2nd ed., Berlin, 1961), p. 304.

54. While Czerniakow became aware of "resettlement" and was told about Treblinka, he did not connect the two. On January 17, 1942, he asked whether Lithuanian guards were coming and was assured that the rumor was false. That same day, he talked to Auerswald who informed him of a conversation with Generalgouverneur Frank as a result of which Jewish prisoners held in Warsaw's Pawiak prison would, if fit for labor, be sent to Treblinka to work. Two days thereafter, Czerniakow noted that Auerswald was going to Berlin. In this entry, Czerniakow also expressed fear of mass resettlement. (In fact, a conference of bureaucrats on the "Final Solution" was held in Berlin on January 20, 1942. Trunk comments on Auerswald's deception on pp. 295–96.) On February 19, 1942, Czerniakow complained that German prosecutors had failed to produce the appropriate papers for the "release" of prisoners at Treblinka. A day later, the prisoners left. On March 10, he recorded the departure of five Jewish clerks to the camp, and in April some 160 young German Jews, recently arrived from the Reich, were sent there. *Diary of Czerniakow,* pp. 316–17, 323–24, 333, 344.

55. Both items of correspondence, dated May 19 and 27, 1942, on a single sheet of paper. Facsimile, *Getto-Faschismus-Massenmord (op. cit.),* p. 214.

56. Trunk, pp. 175–77. The crass illustration is Vilna.

57. Pp. 507–8, 514.

58. Pp. 475–527; also passages in other chapters.

59. Bedzin, Sosnowiec, Zawiercie, Bialystok (p. 584). In Warsaw, members of House Committees were taken hostage if a tenant did not present himself for labor. Ringelblum, *Notes* (*op. cit.*, note 40 above), p. 176.

60. Czerniakow, Radom, etc. (Trunk, p. 483).

61. Ringelblum, *Notes*, p. 138.

62. Trunk, pp. 489–98. Interesting is the finding that Jewish militants (Betar, etc.) were well represented in the police.

63. Ringelblum, *Notes*, pp. 125–26.

64. Horowitz, *Israeli Ecstasies/Jewish Agonies* (New York, 1974), p. 197.

65. Tushnet, *The Pavement of Hell* (New York, 1972).

Jewish Leadership Reactions to Nazi Policies

YEHUDA BAUER

This article is devoted to a historical analysis of a number of problems connected with the Jewish reaction to Nazi policies and, more specifically, with the behavior of certain types of Jewish leadership groups. Three main issues will be discussed. First, the extent to which the available evidence permits the making of generalizations about the reactions of *Judenräte* to the different stages of Nazi genocide policy toward the Jew. Second, the extent of the division, or as some would have it, the abyss, within the Jewish leadership between the *Judenräte* and those preparing for armed struggle. And third, the policies of the *Judenräte,* or other leadership groups, and whether they were based on self-delusion or on a realistic assessment of power relations prevailing under Nazi rule.

No pretense will be made of analyzing these problems with tools other than historical ones, though neither will the legitimacy of sociological or power-structure analyses be denied or diminished. It is explicitly assumed that the analysis offered here is partial and not all-embracing.

The leadership groups involved were of various kinds. On the one hand, there were the so-called *Judenräte* (some of them went under different names) or "Jewish Councils"; that is, groups of Jews nominated or accepted by the Nazis as leaders of their respective communities. Their task—at least in Nazi eyes—was to execute or transmit Nazi commands, regulations, or wishes to the Jews while looking after Jewish communal matters, in that framework, as best they could. On the other hand, there was a range of "alternative" leadership groups engaged in various kinds of resistance to Nazi intentions. No unanimous definition of "resistance" exists, so I shall understand it broadly as all active and conscious organized action against Nazi commands, policies, or wishes, by whatever means: social organization, morale-building operations, underground political work, active unarmed resistance or, finally, armed resistance.[1] Thus, in addition to those preparing for armed struggle, we shall have to take account of numerous organizations "intermediate" between them and the *Judenräte*. Even the latter were fairly often involved in resistance of one kind or another.

The Problem of Generalization

The study of the Jewish Councils has been significantly advanced by Isaiah Trunk's great work entitled *Judenrat*.[2] However, the thematic analysis of Trunk's volume, while offering a great deal of information, does not greatly help to answer the first of our questions, that concerning the possibility of generalizing about the Councils. It is difficult to separate a discussion of *Judenräte* in Eastern Europe from a discussion of *Judenräte* elsewhere in Europe; but Trunk limited himself, presumably because of the vast quantity of material, to Poland and the Baltic countries. More important, his analysis is "horizontal"; that is, it takes a given theme such as health or social welfare, and illustrates it by citing indifferently the approaches of various Councils in that specific respect. This leaves unanswered the crucial question of what *overall* policy, if any, was pursued by any given *Judenrat*. A policy of social aid, coupled with the defense of individual Jews and a determined refusal to hand over any Jews to the Nazis (as in Siauliai), has very different implications from a policy of social aid exercised by a *Judenrat* that cooperated fully with the Nazi police organs (as in Lublin). Furthermore, policies of *Judenräte* that were established long before the phase of mass murder was reached—as in the parts of Poland under the Generalgouvernement, or in Germany and the Protektorat area of Czechoslovakia—may well have differed from policies of *Judenräte* that were immediately faced with the destruction process, as in Eastern Poland or the Baltic countries.

Taken alone, these considerations point to some of the difficulties regarding generalization that Trunk himself emphasizes in his introduction. Yet even in the very careful and measured "Conclusions" offered toward the end of his work, there are constant references to "the Councils" in general, and an attempt to explain why "the Councils" cooperated with the Germans. Cooperation is carefully differentiated from collaboration, which seems not to have been prevalent among *Judenräte* at all, after which Trunk generalizes about "co-operation" by Councils in the areas he examined.

Hilberg presented a much more simplified picture:

> Much has been said and much has been written about the *Judenräte*, the informers, the Jewish police, the Kapos—in short, all those persons who deliberately and as a matter of policy co-operated with the Germans. But these collaborators do not interest us so much as the masses of Jews who reacted to every German order by complying with it automatically.[3]

Presumably *all* Jewish Councils are here grouped together with informers, *all* Jewish police and Kapos as deliberate and willful collaborators. Reitlinger was more circumspect, differentiating between different *Judenräte*. But he, too, approvingly quoted the Bulletin of the Warsaw Jewish Historical Institut of 1949, which promised to investigate the dealings of *Judenrat* members with the Nazis, apparently in a spirit of vengeance. He comments:

> In the course of time the Jewish Councils became absorbed in the task of placating the Germans.[4]

A careful examination of the evidence now available suggests a different conclusion. For instance, Trunk mentions that the Jewish Council in Minsk—the fourth largest ghetto in Europe (after Warsaw, Lodz and Lvov)—"was, in fact, an important base of the partisan movement." He details in what ways the Council's first chairman, Mishkin, and the chiefs of the various departments "also cooperated with the resistance." Jaffe, Mishkin's successor, continued his predecessor's policies. "Several hundred" Minsk Jews, Trunk thinks, joined the partisans as a result.[5] A doctoral student of mine, who is trying to examine the Jewish partisan movement in Belorussia, believes the true figure to be nearer ten thousand.[6]

Trunk also mentions "Council members" actively participating in resistance,[7] though so far as Lachwa, Zdieciol, Tuczyn, and Marcinkance (four of his examples) are concerned, the resistance was initiated by the whole Council and not just by individual members. Quite a number of other *Judenräte* could be added to the list. In Rohatyn there took place on May 15, 1943 a meeting between the *Judenrat* and the Jewish police at which a decision was made to buy arms and send armed groups into the forests.[8] The Kovno *Judenrat* actively supplied the local resistance movement with money for arms and facilitated their exit into the forests, which in their case were a long distance away from the town (there, too, by the way, the main center of the resistance was in the local police force).[9] The Slovak *Judenrat* (the Ustredna Zidov or "Central Jewish Office") not only tried to save Jews by negotiating with the Nazis, but managed to supply the resistance group in the Novaky camp with some arms. Through one of its spokesmen, Rabbi Weissmandel, it also transmitted to the outside world the demand to bomb the approaches to Auschwitz.[10] Members of the Belgian Jewish Council belonged to the Comité de Défense des Juifs, the underground Jewish group whose task it was not only to save Jews but to direct Jewish men and women to the Belgian resistance movement.[11] More instances could be quoted from Belorussia and the Lublin district in Poland.

Besides such cases of involvement in armed resistance, there were *Judenräte* that took part in active unarmed opposition. This seems to have been quite common, for instance, in the West Ukrainian (Eastern Galician) area, where lack of forests and the absence of an anti-Nazi gentile population during the phases of destruction precluded armed resistance. An example is Kosow, where on Passover 1942 *all* the Jews hid in cellars or fled, obviously with the full support of the Jewish Council. Only four Council members

decided to remain and face the German wrath, apparently hoping that their
sacrifice would save the rest. When the telephone rang, one of the four
wavered. The other three then told him to hide, and remained to meet the
Germans.[12]

When the *Judenrat* of Wladzimierz was told to supply a list for deportations, its chairman Weiler replied: "Ja nie jestem Bogiem in nie będę
ludzi sądzit kto ma żyć, a kto nie" ("I am not God and I will not sit in
judgment on people to determine who should live and who should not").[13]
The case of Czerniakow in Warsaw, who committed suicide rather than hand
over lists to the Germans and participate in the deportation of fellow-Jews, is
not unique. Similar acts were committed by Moshe Krasnostawsky in Koryc,
Szmuel Werbalja in Kamen Koszyrski, Benjamin Landberg in Kremenica,
and others.[14]

Such cases of refusal to act in accordance with German wishes could be
multiplied. Unfortunately, a relevant detailed examination of *Judenräte* in
different parts of Europe, or even Eastern Europe, has not been made to date.
The only work on these lines is Aharon Weiss's examination of Eastern
Galicia.

Weiss's Analyses

Aharon Weiss, a researcher at the Institute of Contemporary Jewry in
Jerusalem, has, in fact, made two pertinent analyses based on the testimony
of survivors. They seem to corroborate fully, and to supplement, the survey
of eyewitness accounts that Trunk gives in an appendix to his book. The first
analysis was his work on the ghettos in Eastern Galicia, the main findings of
which were published as long ago as 1969, followed by a fuller version in
1972.[15] His other analysis formed part of his doctoral thesis on the Jewish
police *(Ordnungsdienst).*[16]

The work on Eastern Galicia dealt with 73 ghettos in the area. To arrive at
reasonably accurate findings, only those cases were chosen for detailed
examination where the author could find a relatively large number of
testimonies. Weiss employed a total of over 500 testimonies—many of them
written down immediately after the war—including those published in
Yiskor-Bicher (memorial volumes) concerning the individual communities.
An examination of these 73 ghettos was made for the period during which, in
each of them, the *first* Jewish Council functioned, and which we shall call the
"first period" of the ghetto in question.

Weiss began by seeking to determine the background of the heads of these
"first-period" Councils. For 44 of them a biographical sketch was available
from the testimonies or other sources; and—corroborating Trunk—it was
found that, despite the destruction of the Jewish communal system during the
period of Soviet rule in the area (1939–1941), 32 belonged to what can
legitimately be called the previous Jewish communal leadership. Ten had
been heads of their community prior to 1939, two were former members of

community councils, two had been village heads, twelve were described as having been the acknowledged leaders of their communities before the war, three were heads of the local Zionist organization, one was the town rabbi, and two were the heads of the local *Tarbut* high schools.

Then Weiss examined the evaluation of Council heads as expressed in the testimonies. Of the total of 73 heads of *Judenräte*, 44 (not entirely identical with the 44 mentioned above) were described by the witnesses *unequivocally* (i.e., by at least two witnesses without any contradictory testimony) as having refused to transgress what Weiss in his methodological analysis called "the limit"—that is, the handing over, or participation in handing over, of members of their communities to the Nazis for a known or unknown fate. Eight refused point blank and were killed; five committed suicide in the manner of Czerniakow; eight were murdered because they refused to obey German orders even before "the limit" was reached; four resigned because they refused to carry out the orders; two stood at the head of armed rebellions; two attempted to organize armed resistance but failed; two fled but were found and murdered; one fled, hid, and survived. Apart from these 44, the heads of 12 more Councils were described unanimously by survivors as having attempted to save their communities, but as the details were vague and the descriptions open to doubt, they were not added to the 44.

Basically the same method of research was followed in Weiss's second analysis, which concerned 160 ghettos in the Generalgouvernement and Upper Silesia.[17] Once again, Weiss began by seeking to determine the backgrounds of the various Council heads. This time, a biographical sketch was available for 279 heads from all "periods," of which 128 belonged to the "first period," including the 44 of Weiss's earlier analysis for which biographical details had been available. Of that 128, it was found that 88 had belonged to the previous Jewish communal leadership. Outside of Eastern Galicia, conquered by the Nazis in 1941, *Judenräte* had of course been in existence since late 1939 (sometimes, as in Lublin, they were officially nominated as late as January 1940, but were actually in existence before then); yet in most cases the "first period" extended to the major wave of mass murders in 1942. In other words, the "first period" generally comprised most of the lifetime of the ghetto (with many exceptions—such as Piotrkow Tribunalski, where a "resistant" Council was removed in Summer 1941).[18]

Weiss, as in his previous analysis, then examined the Jewish testimony regarding the Council heads. He could find unequivocal statements about 146 of them during the "first period." Of these, 45 were defined by survivors as "good" because of their refusal to obey German orders concerning economic measures or, more often, because of their evasion of such orders, or public warning of impending German "actions." Twenty-six more were removed by the Germans because they did not obey certain German orders; 18 at least refused, in the last stages, to hand over Jews and were murdered; 11 resigned because they refused to carry out German orders. Five committed suicide for the same reason, and two acted in unison with resistance groups. Thus, 107 out of the 146 Council heads in question did not go beyond "the limit" defined by Weiss. Only 21 were defined as men who faithfully complied with German orders and commands.

Two observations are in order. First, that the picture changes radically with the "second period" of the *Judenräte*—in most cases after the first and major wave of destruction. Of the 101 "second-period" Council heads examined by Weiss in which the prewar Jewish leadership was less strongly represented, 31 did not go beyond "the limit," but 61 did, and opinions diverged as to the rest. Then by the sheer mass murder of the Jewish population, the removal of groups of experienced and responsible leadership, and the imposition of agents and stooges, was the desired effect at last obtained, and even then a substantial proportion of "second-period" Councils did not fulfill German expectations.

Second, it must be remembered that just as German documentation, on which historians prior to Trunk relied almost exclusively, was apt to be one-sided and misleading, so Jewish sources must be examined critically, as Trunk does to some extent in his appendix. The recorded opinions of survivors may reflect their personal biases, while the mere fact that, for instance, a Council head was ultimately murdered may imply little about his previous behavior. Yet concerning the politics of *Judenräte*, the testimony of the Germans is more suspect than that of Jewish survivors. To be successful in, say, a policy of evasion, the *Judenrat* might need to create in German minds the impression that their orders were being fulfilled, and that would be reflected in the German sources, if any. A unanimous opinion of a fair number of Jewish witnesses, on the other hand, who knew much better what their *Judenrat* was up to, carries considerably more weight.

The Variety of Council Responses

Although Weiss tried to categorize at least the Polish *Judenräte*, it is doubtful whether even that is possible unless one keeps the categorization very flexible indeed. Admittedly, some Councils were—as we have seen—clearly resistant while others equally clearly fitted the derogatory descriptions of Hilberg and Reitlinger. A case of the latter kind is Lublin, where the *Judenrat* minutes have survived and were published by Nachman Blumenthal.[19] This particular *Judenrat* obeyed every order to the letter, and its attempts to aid the Jewish community showed no particular resourcefulness. A more detailed analysis of the documents, however, reveals points unnoticed by Blumenthal. Thus, for instance, the absence of a ghetto until a very late stage (April 1941) prevented the utilization of local resources for education and social work; the *Judenrat* was super-democratic, including members of all the political parties from the Agudah to the Bund, and took decisions by majority votes; it was basically a group of old-time politicians desperately trying to find some legal basis in the Nazi system that would regularize its position. It was also absolutely unaware of Nazi intentions: as late as May 9, 1942, after the mass deportation, Dr. Alten, now the Council head in the truncated community at Maiden Tatarski, wondered why the Germans did not tell him the addresses of the deported Jews (they were murdered at Belzec), because he wanted to send them packages (underground Jewish papers in Warsaw had already published the truth in mid-April). Similar or roughly parallel behavior of *Judenräte* can be quoted for a number of other places: the Netherlands, where the *Joodse Raad* was a rubber stamp of German commands or Vienna, for instance, where the *Kultusgemeinde* fulfilled a parallel function; or Cracow. Each of these was, as Blumenthal aptly subtitled his edition of the Lublin minutes, a *Judenrat* "without direction" (*ratlos* as the German expression has it).

Yet the main variety of responses lay in the middle between determined resistance and helpless compliance. Almost every *Judenrat* in this "middle" group had certain specific characteristics such that it cannot easily be put into a hard and fast category. There were Councils that concentrated on escape. A number of these appear in Weiss's study on Eastern Galicia; similarly, the Union Générale des Israélites de France maintained contact with the French underground, did not submit lists to the Germans, and provided a legal cover for the vast smuggling and escape operation. In the case of Hungary, the *Judenrat* in Budapest, while extremely compliant in everything else, knowingly allowed Zionist youth movements to operate from its offices and send emissaries to the provinces, to warn the Jews and tell then to hide or escape (they were not believed, but that is another story).[20]

In this "middle" group, the *Judenräte* that have become most controversial were those engaged in what might best be termed a policy of salvation through slavery."[21] One must be careful to include in this group *only* those Councils that pursued this policy consciously, actively, and with the full knowledge, at least in the later stages of the war, that the Germans were out to murder all the Jews. The policy was based on the assumption that slave-owners do not usually murder their own slaves, for reasons of economy and utility. Some of the outstanding proponents of this policy were the Jewish Councils of Lodz, Bialystok, Vilna, Siauliai, and Slovakia. From the foregoing it is clear that not *all,* but only *some* Councils followed this policy. It was also obviously not a concerted policy; each *Judenrat* arrived at its conclusions by itself, though there were some contacts between, for instance, Vilna, Siauliai, and Bialystok, or between Poland and Slovakia.

As Trunk points out,[22] Rumkowski's autocratic policies in Lodz, whatever else may be said about them, maintained the Lodz Ghetto in existence until July 1944 as the only remaining ghetto within the prewar boundaries of Poland. Had the Russian army not stopped its advance in that month, but done precisely what it did in January 1945 when it resumed its advance and captured Lodz in three days, the Lodz Ghetto would have stood a fair chance of surviving with tens of thousands of Jews. Would we not then have faced the dilemma of weighing Rumkowski's handing over—knowingly—Jewish children to the ovens of Auschwitz as against the results of his policy of "salvation through slavery"?[23]

I need not recount further the case of Lodz, because Isaiah Trunk has dealt with it fully and has shown that for economic reasons the Germans indeed delayed destroying the Lodz Ghetto. In the meantime, a whole literature has sprung up showing quite clearly, to my mind, that as the war continued economic considerations came to be more and more important in German policy, including policy toward the Jews. Hitler himself gave his assent to the postponement of murder actions; there is evidence for two such occasions.[24] Himmler's policies became two-faced as well. Ultimately, of course, the Jews would have to "disappear" *(verschwinden)*, in accordance with the *Führer's* wishes, but in the meantime economic considerations would have to be taken into account. During the final stages of the preparations for the destruction of the Warsaw Ghetto, in March–April 1943, Odilo Globocnik himself, responsible now for the success of the SS-firm Osti, tried to use the German entrepreneur Toebbens to persuade Jewish workers to go to the camps of Poniatowo and Trawniki where he expected to use them for production, at least temporarily. Elsewhere Jews did survive in Nazi enterprises because of economic considerations. This can be clearly shown in Czestochowa, where several thousand Jewish workers survived the war in the so-called Hasag complex of factories. It also appears that out of 30,000 Jews of Radom some 4,700 survived the war—one of the highest survival rates in Poland.[25] This was due partly to the *Judenrat's* policy of efficient bribery and mutual help, which is praised by the survivors, but also to the fact that the Jews of Radom were employed in important economic enterprises such as the labor camp of Szkolna and the arms factory in Radom.

Two more cases worth mentioning are Siauliai and Bialystok. The Siauliai *Judenrat* enjoyed the full support and confidence of the Jewish population, especially after the incident of August 29, 1942, when the Nazis demanded the handing over of a group of Jews, presumably for deportation, and the *Judenrat* offered itself instead. A shoe factory in the Siauliai Ghetto, and the fact that local labor was insufficient to build an airfield and provide necessary supplies of peat, are quite clearly what made the Nazis decide not to murder the 4,800 inhabitants.[26] Although the Germans eventually managed to deport the inhabitants (except for those who escaped) to Germany just before the Soviets arrived, a relatively high proportion of them survived. By Summer 1944, when their deportation took place, chances of survival in the death camps had increased (mass gassings in Auschwitz stopped in the Autumn). The same is true of the Kovno Ghetto.

Turning now to Bialystok, as long ago as 1953 Artur Eisenbach published an article (in the Yiddish *Bletter far Geshichte*) showing that the policies of *Judenrat* chairman Ephraim Barash had some real basis.[27] Barash is an interesting case for two reasons. First, because his worst enemies never accused him of ill will, rapaciousness, egotism, or any of the other failings attributed to some other Council heads. Second, we know through the evidence of both Mordechai Tenenbaum[28] and of Chaika Grossman[29] that Barash was well aware of the mass murders, that he knew about Treblinka; indeed, he even said so openly at some of the meetings of the *Judenrat* (or "public" meetings in the Council building) published by Blumenthal.[30] It is, then, beyond any doubt that Barash made a calculated attempt to exploit the differences between the various components of the Nazi regime, in order to keep his community alive until the Russians came. Eisenbach, in his work, has shown that the Jewish initiative, in this case, did in fact influence German policy. When a decision to destroy the Bialystok Ghetto was taken in October 1942, some of the German officials met in Königsberg and appealed the decision. As a result, a partial deportation was decided upon, and the local representative of the German Security Police declared to his Nazi colleagues that the Ghetto would probably be kept in existence until the end of the war because of its economic importance.[31]

Long ago Hannah Arendt warned against the misconception of viewing the two obvious examples of totalitarian regimes—the Nazi and the Soviet— as having successfully established truly totalitarian societies.[32] As far as the Nazi regime goes, it surely has been established by now that it was rent with disagreements, frictions, and enmities, and that the different fiefs established by major Nazi figures were in a state of constant mutual warfare. This fact is usually brushed aside in discussions of the mass murder of the Jews because this was, it is said, one of the few items on which there was no disagreement. The plan supposedly went to its execution with the different groups working in smooth harmony. This simply is not so. Consider Heydrich's order of September 21, 1939: Jews from the newly incorporated territories were now to be driven out and *Judenräte* established everywhere. Yet the Zaglebie and Lodz Ghettos existed till 1943 and 1944, while the *Judenräte* were set up at any time up to late in January 1940. Ghettos were also supposed to be established immediately. In fact, some were set up as late as April 1941; in Zaglebie, as late as 1943. Conflicting policies regarding Jews can be discerned at most stages—of course, within the framework of a consensus that, finally, Jews had to "disappear." The policy of "salvation through slavery" was designed, in the case of Barash quite consciously and explicitly, to evade mass destruction by exploiting those conflicts.

It is interesting to note a minor case where this policy actually met with reasonably full success. In the town of Tluste with 2,000 Jewish inhabitants a German firm worked some neighboring farms in the hope of producing plants that would aid in manufacturing a rubber substitute. This was apparently considered vitally important even by the SS, and in June 1943 close to 1,000 Jews were transferred there. Conditions were relatively reasonable. When the Russians arrived early in 1944, most of these Jews were found alive and saved.[33]

Thus, a detailed examination of the evidence tends to show that the policies of the *Judenräte*, and especially of those that tried to save their communities by labor, cannot be brushed aside as either unrealistic or traitorous. Each case, moreover, must be seen against its local background. For these reasons, generalizations regarding *Judenrat* policies are usually inaccurate and misleading. Council members reacted to the completely unknown and unimaginable with a wide range of responses, from complete passivity and frightened compliance, through a dogged pursuit of policies of salvation that had some basis in the realities of the situation, to acts of defiance, resistance or self-destruction that demonstrated a refusal to betray the trust put in them. This conclusion completely contradicts the outlook of some of our greatest and best historians who, from a moral premise of hatred of Nazism and shock at the policies of genocide, arrive at conclusions that ignore the Jewish and other non-German evidence. Indeed, if (as they say) Jewish leadership reactions were marked by compliance alone, how do they explain the phenomenon, mentioned by them with great approval and enthusiasm, of the rise of a supposedly completely different Jewish community in Israel distinguished by its militancy? If such a community had arisen from a European background of moral impotence and sheepish passivity, we would be faced with an inexplicable enigma.

There is another conclusion to be drawn from the above. Discussions of the *Judenräte* are too often taken out of the changing contexts of time and space. For instance, it must be emphasized that the Germans themselves took the Nisko and Madagascar plans quite seriously, and the actual decision to mass-murder the Jews of Europe (as opposed to forcing them to go elsewhere) cannot be ascribed to a date before early 1941.[34] If the Germans themselves did not know what would happen to the Jews until then, is it so difficult to see that the Jews could have had no clear idea either? Moreover, in the East the Jews were surrounded by peoples who, with relatively few—though very honorable—exceptions, wavered between open enmity and hostile neutrality toward their Jewish neighbors. Often with no access to arms, and with no open partisan warfare against the Nazis on any large scale before 1943 (by which time the Jews could no longer escape because most of them were dead), the choices were grim. A facile anachronistic demand that the leadership should have known, and if so, should have resisted, is no help to true historical analysis. Trunk, in his book, seems to be aware of these points, and implies as much in his careful and measured way; perhaps they ought to have been stated more explicitly.

Alternative Leadership Groups

Generally, one reads about "resistance groups," where they existed, as the only alternatives to the *Judenräte*. This is inaccurate, if by "resistance" only *armed* resistance—or preparation for armed struggle—is meant. Yet even if my own very wide definition of "resistance" (offered at the beginning of this paper) be disputed, armed resistance itself was more widespread than is often supposed.

As I have indicated elsewhere,[35] armed resistance in the East, which can be measured reasonably accurately, was most marked in those areas where forests, or a combination of forests and friendly partisans, made survival through fighting possible. It is my estimate, based on research done in Jerusalem under my direction, that there were probably anywhere between twenty and thirty thousand armed Jewish partisan fighters in the forests of Eastern Poland, Belorussia, the Ukraine, and Lithuania, including some wholly Jewish units. Additional tens of thousands tried to reach the forests, but failed to obtain arms and were murdered—mostly by the local population or through help given by the latter to the Germans. This has been documented in detail for the Lublin area,[36] where some 40,000 Jews tried to flee into the forests.

Similar acts of resistance occurred elsewhere. Probably over 2,000 Jews (out of the less than 20,000 still alive) participated in partisan activities in Slovakia in 1944–1945. Several thousand fought in the ranks of Tito's forces. And while the facts regarding Jewish participation in the French Maquis (and town guerrilla activities) remain to be fully ascertained, here too there were specifically Jewish units—as for instance the Jewish battle groups of the Main-d'Oeuvre Immigrée or the Organisation Juive de Combat—and their acts of armed resistance influenced the postwar policies of what was left of compact Jewish communities. They assumed, contrary to most historical analyses up till now, a mass character relative to the size of the Jewish population still in existence in 1943–1944.

The extent of resistance groups that aimed at obtaining arms in ghettos, or—in the West—amongst the general and Jewish population, was quite considerable. We have documentation on well over *forty* such ghettos in the East alone. In some of the major ghettos—Warsaw, Vilna, Kovno, Bialystok, Cracow, Czestochowa, Bendin—the Jewish resistance groups were part of an overall organization, and contact was maintained among them despite the complete isolation of the ghettos (an isolation facilitated by the hostility of the non-German gentile population). The organization begun in Vilna under the name FPO (Fareinikte Partizaner Organizatzie) became the ZOB (Zydowska Organizacja Bojowa) and transferred instructions, and even arms, from ghetto to ghetto.

The FPO-ZOB did claim, at a certain point, to be an alternative to the *Judenrat* leadership. In Warsaw the claim was substantiated, and the great Warsaw Ghetto rebellion resulted. Yet the opposition between the two leaderships was not always so clearcut. In some ghettos, such as Minsk, Lachwa, and Tuczyn, the *Judenräte* were either part of the armed resistance or acted in complete agreement with it. In other places the *Judenräte* lost their influence to the armed resistance, as in the last stages of the Nieswiez Ghetto,[37] or cooperated with it. The same variety applies to Western Europe.

The dividing line between the *Judenrat* and resistance organizations becomes further blurred in the case of *non-armed* resistance, which was of course much more widespread. In this area there often arose leadership groups "intermediate" between the Councils and those preparing for armed struggle. Consider, as typical examples, an organization like the Oeuvre de Secours aux Enfants (OSE) in France, which managed to hide and, together with other like groups, save 7,000 Jewish children,[38] or the organization comprising one thousand House Committees in the Warsaw Ghetto.[39] There can hardly be any doubt that these groups had a wide appeal, and they had very ambivalent relationships with their respective *Judenräte*; yet one cannot talk of a clear-cut line of division or opposition. Although these "intermediate" organizations were often centers of a ferment of opposition to the *Judenräte*, they did not, unlike many armed resistance groups, claim leadership of the community.

Not everywhere were there organizations "intermediate" between the *Judenrat* and the armed resistance. When there occurred both a "good" *Judenrat* enjoying the support of the ghetto, and also an armed resistance group or groups that opposed the *Judenrat* line, we find that there was no room for a third party. This was the case, for instance, in Bialystok where the *Judenrat* did not support the resistance wholeheartedly, although remaining in constant touch with it and giving it partial support; and in Kovno where the *Judenrat,* and especially its head, Dr. Elkes, gave full support to the resistance groups. But already in Vilna the situation was different. Here what were nominally certain departments of the Jewish Council were not only in close contact with the resistance but actually participated in it (e.g., Abrasha Chwoinik). The YIVO center in Vilna, composed of some forty members, of whom six were FPO fighters, was another such "intermediate" group, which became very important both in the cultural life of the Vilna Ghetto and in the preparation for armed struggle.[40]

"Intermediate" groups also arose in the West. There was the unsuccessful attempt of the "Coordinatie Commissie" of Judge Visser in Holland, which refused to have truck with the Germans, tried to organize Dutch Jewry in opposition to the *Judenrat,* but failed in the winter of 1941–42 to do so. One can add to the list parts of the Zionist movement in Holland. In France, besides the OSE already mentioned, the "Consistoire" was another "intermediate" group. The list is fairly long.

It was also rather leadership groups of the "intermediate" type that became involved, as the war went on, in negotiations with the Nazis for a large-scale rescue of European Jewry. Such, at first, was the character of the so-called "working group" in Slovakia,[41] whose members, began to examine the possibility of bribing the Nazis on a vast scale during the deportations of March–September 1942. Dieter Wisliceny, the Jewish expert at the German legation in Bratislava, promised them a stoppage of the local deportations, and in late 1942 and early 1943 began negotiations regarding the release of

European Jewry, outside prewar Germany and Poland, from the destruction process.

It seems fairly obvious that these negotiations were in reality held with the full support of Himmler. They were continued in 1944 by the Kasztner-Komoly group in Budapest and resulted in the mission of Joel Brand and Bandi Gross to Istanbul in May 1944. They were then transferred to the Swiss-German border, where they continued between Saly Mayer and Kurt Becher from August 1944 to February 1945. A detailed analysis of the material concerning this last phase has led me to conclude that Himmler was searching for a way to negotiate with the West.[42] This search began, moreover, probably before Stalingrad, and may have been a continuation of the prewar SS policy of getting rid of the Jews in return for certain economic and political advantages—a policy that was explicitly rearticulated in 1940 when it served as a justification of the Madagascar plan, this time by the German Foreign Office.[43]

Ultimately, I believe that the Swiss negotiations did lead to some saving of Jewish lives, specifically in Budapest, but possibly also in some of the concentration camps in the closing stages of the war. They may have been one of the factors that made Himmler stop the gassing operations at Auschwitz in October 1944. It was the distinct feeling of the Jewish negotiators involved that there was a real possibility of saving Jews in this way. Rabbi Weissmandel of the Slovak group argued that the way of a political-financial bribe held out the prospect of rescuing a community, whereas armed resistance might mean the heroism of a few young men and women, but the quick mass murder of all their relatives; what did the resistance fighters offer to their mothers, fathers, and children?

The leadership groups that engaged in this policy were of quite different kinds in Slovakia and in Hungary. The Slovak "working group" represented all Jewish factions from the Zionists to the ultra-Orthodox; leadership lay with Gizi Fleischmann, head of the local WIZO and representative of the JDC ("Joint"), and with Rabbi Michael Dov-Ber Weissmandel, son-in-law of Rabbi Ungar of Nitra, representative of the ultra-Orthodox segment of the Jewish population. In Hungary, on the other hand, the Kasztner-Komoly Rescue Committee really represented a tiny minority group: not only did it not represent the non-Zionists, who were the vast majority of Hungarian Jewry, but it did not even represent most Zionist factions. It was limited to the Labor Zionists, while even the Zionist youth movements, whose rescue actions probably saved thousands of Budapest Jews through the mass falsification of identity papers, were only loosely connected with the committee. Yet it is quite clear today that these "intermediate" groups—the Rescue Committee and the youth movements—represented Hungarian Jewry in its darkest hour much more than did the *Judenrat.* It is my contention that the Rescue Committee had a fairly clear concept not only of the real situation, but also of policies that it thought might lead to rescue. It is not our task here to examine in detail whether such policies had a real chance of success, but it is necessary to emphasize that they had at least a basis in real differences of approach between different Nazi power factors.

Resistance by the Councils

Besides the armed groups and the "intermediate" organizations, numerous Jewish Councils were themselves involved in resistance. To begin with, there were two kinds of situations in which even normal communal activities conducted by the *Judenrat* could be regarded as active, if unarmed, moral resistance. First, there were many cases in which such "normal" activities became very "abnormal" because they were undertaken contrary to German wishes, with all the possible consequences that such a situation could entail. The educational activities in Warsaw, for instance, until September 1941—and, for the high schools, after that date as well—fall into this category.

Second, in the conditions of the desperate struggle for life, the maintenance of cultural activities was a tremendously important antidote to Nazi oppression. Where such activity was consciously conducted in order to combat demoralization, it must be counted as a certain type of resistance. One could, of course, ask whether the Germans consciously subjected the Jews to indignities to prepare them for the ultimate murder. They may not have had such an intention at all, simply because for them Jews were subhumans, and subhumans had no right to be treated with any kind of dignity. On the other hand, Jews were the Nazi substitute for the devil, and as such had to be destroyed. Not being human in either interpretation, the question of dignity might not seem to arise.

We do not yet have, I think, sufficient material to say whether or not there was a German intent to destroy the Jews morally, as a matter of policy. Yet the answer to that question is really of secondary importance. The point is that the Jews *thought* that that was the German intention, and in many cases acted to fight this supposed policy. In that lay their resistance: "We are humans," they implied, "and that is the greatest and most important act of resistance we can offer to your policies."

Besides such moral resistance, we have already indicated that there was no universal chasm between even the armed resistance and the *Judenrat.* In Bialystok—to take one specific illustration—there were constant meetings between the Council head Barash and the heads of two armed resistance groups: Chaika Grossman and Mordechai Tenenbaum. The two groups had different policies. Grossman's group, comprising Hashomer Hatzair and certain Communists, had decided that it would come out into the open and fight, whether it had already obtained arms or not, whenever the Germans began an "action." The group under Tenenbaum, comprising the Dror, Hanoar Hatzioni, and Betar youth movements, had decided not to fight until it had arms.[44] In Bialystok it was very difficult to get arms contrary to the situation in Vilna, for instance, where Jewish workers slaved in German arms stores and factories.

A significant incident occurred early in February 1943. Barash informed Tenenbaum that the Germans would take out 6,300 Jews and murder them, but that he had reliable information that the others would not be molested. Tenenbaum let himself be convinced. On February 4 he met with his group: "I tell the meeting that if the 'action' is of that size—we do not react. We are sacrificing 6,300 Jews so as to save the other 35,000 Jews. The situation on the [Russian] front is such that a radical change may occur any day. But if they enlarge the 'action,' the group will fight."[45] Let it be said that the Germans murdered not 6,300 as "promised," but some 12,000. Tenenbaum still did not act, nor did he even inform the Grossman group. Most of the latter went out and fought—without arms—and called upon the population to resist. But later, in August 1943, Tenenbaum led an armed rebellion in Bialystok.

Tenenbaum's argument, as an advocate of armed resistance, was thus close to that of many *Judenräte*. He, too, was willing to sacrifice a part in the hope of saving the rest. He, like Barash, was hoping for a Russian-induced miracle. In addition, he wanted to convince the entire ghetto population that resistance was the only way, but he thought that without arms this could not be done. As it happened, the February "action" was met with mass unarmed resistance by the population, at least partly due to the example set by members of the Grossman group, whereas the August uprising failed to move a cowed and terrorized population.[46]

Generally, the claim of the armed resistance groups to leadership had to be substantiated and proved. When they found that the ghetto stood against them, the Vilna FPO sacrificed their commander, Wittenberg, rather than fight the ghetto. In order to substantiate and prove their claim, they had to contend with the same objective factors as the *Judenrat*. One of these was collective responsibility. In his contribution to this volume, Abba Kovner tells of the pangs of conscience felt by the FPO when they decided to send out Vitka Kempner to be the first to blow up a German train in Lithuania. There was no doubt that if the Germans discovered that the act had been committed by Jews, the whole ghetto would suffer. Yet the act was done. In some other known cases, resistance groups refrained from actions that might endanger the whole population. It must be remembered that there was a vast difference between the Jewish and the non-Jewish fighter in this, as in so many other respects: a non-Jewish fighter, if caught, might involve his immediate family or, in the East, sometimes part of a village. A Jew might well bring about the destruction of a whole large community.

There was, then, not a universal clear-cut opposition between all armed resistance groups and all *Judenräte*. There were two lines of approach that were sometimes contradictory, but sometimes complementary, and occasionally identical.

Mass Responses

False appreciations of the role of Jewish leadership groups can also arise from fallacies about the mass behavior of the communities that they led. I refer specifically to the way in which writings on the Holocaust, including some of the best ones, raised the misconceived issue of how the Jews came to be led "like sheep to the slaughter."

To begin with, no differentiation is made between mass responses up to the actual murder and responses at the time of the murder itself. As to the latter, no attempt is made to compare the behavior of Jewish victims with that of non-Jews in similar circumstances. I do not know of any evidence of physical resistance at the actual *execution* of French Maquisards caught by the Nazis; nor have I heard of any resistance, except in very few cases (just as there are a few cases among Jews as well), by Soviet prisoners of war murdered by the million in Nazi camps; nor have I heard that at Lidice in Czechoslovakia or Oradour in France—where whole villages were massacred—there was mass resistance. When the Polish population of Warsaw was deported from the city after the failure of the Polish rebellion there, and rumors spread that the Nazis were going to do to them what had been done to the Jews, the reaction was despair and fear, but no resistance whatsoever. No attempt has yet been made to examine this problem, which is clearly not a specifically "Jewish" one, in the light of psychological or socio-psychological research.

What is more important than the examination of the old question of "like sheep to the slaughter" is the problem of the mass reactions of Jews to the successive stages of Nazi persecution. Detailed research on this question is necessary, and some of it has already been concluded, or is in the last stages of formulation.[47] While no final statements can or should be made at this stage, intermediate results seem to indicate that the facile assumption of passivity of the majority of the population will have to be critically re-examined. This of course stands to reason: if we find, as we do, that leadership groups reacted differently at different times and in different places, it would be rash to assume that the reaction of the Jewish masses was all of one kind.

Conclusions

It is now clear that the story of the complete passivity or, in another version, the collapse and compliance of Jewish leadership in Europe during the Holocaust, is based on inaccurate and misleading factual foundations. Rather, as we have seen, the responses were variegated even among the Nazi-nominated or Nazi-approved Jewish Councils; the range of armed resistance, and of active unarmed resistance, was much wider than assumed until recently; there was no absolute opposition between all resistance groups and all *Judenräte*; there were leadership groups with policies that were attuned to the realities of the situation, even if these latter groups sometimes stood somewhere "intermediate" between the Councils and the armed resistance. In other words, a fairly wide range of policies were adopted and actively pursued by the various Jewish leadership groups, policies generally aimed at rescuing Jewish communities or parts of them. Of the whole Jewish leadership, only certain *Judenräte*—together with large sections of the Jewish police in the Eastern European ghettos—fit the descriptions of utter passivity or abject compliance.

The implications of these conclusions are far-reaching. On the most general plane, they indicate that the massive terror of the Nazi machine failed to destroy independent Jewish communal activity and to discourage Jewish attempts to save significant sections of the community. This might well cause us to pause and ask what the limits are of the efficacy of a terror regime even such as that of the Nazis. For we are considering the reactions to that terror by a hated minority, surrounded—in Eastern Europe—by hostile populations with no autonomous political unit to look to for help, largely without arms or access to them, treated with indifference by the world outside the realm of Nazidom. Viewed in this light, the Jewish reactions raise questions that are almost the opposite of those customary in most discussions until now. What made it possible for Jewish groups to grasp realities that had been deemed unimaginable and impossible? How did they organize, and on what principles? What is the historical background to this kind of active response? How do the reactions of post-Holocaust Jews relate to these responses? Is there indeed a complete break between the Diaspora, as evidenced by the life and death of European Jewry, and the reactions of present-day Jews, in Israel and abroad?[48]

Last, but not least: we live in a world where Holocausts are, unfortunately, possible. The Jews are likely victims, but not the only possible ones. The reaction of the Jewish leadership, if not that of the Jewish masses as well, points to the general conclusion that oppression, even frightful oppression, does not necessarily entail paralysis.

Notes

1. Definitions of what constitutes resistance in the specific circumstances of Nazi Europe are, of course, extremely problematical. In *The Shadow War: Resistance in Europe 1939–1945* (London, 1972), p. 247, Henri Michel says, in contrasting resistance with defeatism, that "acceptance of defeat whilst still capable of fighting was to lose one's self-respect; self-respect dictated that one should not yield to the blandishments of collaboration." Yet it is difficult to analyse Jewish resistance in such categories—the Nazis did not use any "blandishments of

collaboration" on the Jews. The Jewish case, therefore, seems to be *sui generis* and to demand a different kind of definition or description. See, for instance, Leni Yahil, "Jewish Resistance—An Examination of Active and Passive Forms of Jewish Survival in the Holocaust Period," in the volume prepared by Meir Grubsztein and Moshe M. Kohn, *Jewish Resistance During the Holocaust* (Jerusalem, 1971), pp. 35–46. Is it really accurate in this context to talk of "passive" resistance when what is really meant is very active, unarmed manifestations? Raul Hilberg, in his monumental *The Destruction of the European Jews* (2nd. ed., Chicago, 1967), states categorically (p. 14), and wrongly, that Jews during their Diaspora history did not resist (physically, one assumes). When he uses the term "resistance," he seems to limit himself, generally or totally, to armed resistance alone.

2.   Isaiah Trunk, *Judenrat: The Jewish Councils in Eastern Europe under Nazi Occupation* (New York, 1972).

3.   Raul Hilberg, *The Destruction of the European Jews (op. cit.)*, p. 666.

4.   Gerald Reitlinger, *The Final Solution* (2nd ed., London, 1968), p. 68.

5.   Trunk, *op. cit.*, p. 466.

6.   Shalom Cholawski, to whom I am grateful for this information. A detailed card index of partisans in the area is now being compiled.

7.   Trunk, *op. cit.*, pp. 471 ff.

8.   Aharon Weiss, "Le-darkam shel ha-judenratim bi-drom-mizrakh Polin," *Yalkut Moreshet* 15 (October 1972), 59–122.

9.   Zvie Bar-On and Dov Levin, *Toldoteha shel mahteret* (Jerusalem, 1962), pp. 74, 191, 224, 233–34, 352–55, 359.

10.   Livia Rotkirchen, *Hurban yahadut Slovakia* (Jerusalem, 1961), p. 239; see also the two group interviews which the late Shaul Esh and myself arranged with surviving members of the Slovak *Judenrat* and the Jewish resistance leaders, Oral Documentation Center (ODC), Institute of Contemporary Jewry, Jerusalem, OHD 8 (48), pp. 35, 45–47.

11.   Israel Schirman, *La Politique allemande à l'égard des juifs en Belgique, 1940–1944* (M.A. dissertation, Université Libre de Bruxelles, 1970–71).

12.   Weiss, *op. cit* (note 8 above), p. 98.

13.   *Ibid.*, p. 97.

14.   *Ibid.*, pp. 98–99.

15.   Weiss, *op. cit.*, and "Le-ha'arakhatam shel ha-judenratim," *Yalkut Moreshet* 11 (November 1969), 108–12.

16.   Aharon Weiss, *Ha-mishtarah ha-yehudit ba-Generalgouvernement u-vi-Shlezia ha-Ilit bi-tkufat ha-sho'ah* (Ph.D. dissertation, Jerusalem, 1974).

17.   *Ibid.*, esp. pp. 27–28, 35.

18.   Methodologically speaking, therefore, one might criticize an analysis that includes Eastern Galicia and the rest of the Generalgouvernement in one set of figures.

19.   Nachman Blumenthal, *Te'udot mi-Ghetto Lublin* (Jerusalem, 1967).

20.   Yosef Schaeffer, "Hanhagat ha-mahteret ha-halutzit be-Hungaria," in Y. Gutman and others eds., *Hanhagat yehudei Hungaria be-mivhan ha-sho'ah* (Jerusalem, 1976). See also my interview with Philipp de Freudiger (December 30, 1974), ODC, Institute of Contemporary Jewry.

21.   Trunk (*op. cit.*, pp. 400–413) calls this the "rescue-through-work" strategy.

22.   *Op. cit.*, p. 413.

23. A similar argument is offered by Jacob Robinson in *And the Crooked Shall Be Made Straight* (New York, 1965), p. 178 and p. 332, note 129, where he adds the case of the Kovno Ghetto inmates who "could all have been rescued if the tempo and direction of the Soviet offensive had continued as it had begun." My own statement of the argument in an address given in Boston, which Raul Hilberg cites in his contribution to this volume, was in fact an almost exact quotation from Trunk's book.

24. In the latter part of 1942, Hitler gave his consent to the employment of Jews in a conference with Speer and others. See Arthur Eisenbach, *Hitlerowska polityka eksterminacji zydow* (Warsaw, 1953), pp. 248 ff. In June 1944, he agreed to the employment of 100,000 Hungarian Jews in the Reich, which, of course, had been made practically *judenrein* after February 1943. See Speer's letter of September 4, 1944 in *Nazi Conspiracy and Aggression* (Washington, 1946), vol. VIII, p. 189.

25. This emerges from a collection of documents by Tuvia Friedmann of Haifa.

26. Sima Itzikas, *Ghetto Shavli* (M.A. dissertation, Jerusalem, 1975), pp. 27and 41, records the incident of August 29, 1942. For the problem of Jewish labor as a reason not to destroy the Jewish population, see the letter of H. Gewecke on September 3, 1941, Yad Vashem 366/PS and Itzikas, *op. cit.*, p. 163.

27. See Eisenbach, *op. cit.,* (note 24 above), pp. 456 ff.

28. Mordechai Tenenbaum-Tamaroff, *Dapim min ha-delekah* (Ein Harod, 1948).

29. Chaika Grossman, *Anshei ha-mahteret* (Tel Aviv, 1965).

30. Nachman Blumenthal, *Darko shel judenrat* (Jerusalem, 1962).

31. Eisenbach, *loc. cit.* (note 27 above).

32. Hannah Arendt, *The Origins of Totalitarianism* (2nd ed., New York, 1958).

33. Weiss, "Le-darkam shel ha-judenratim" (*op. cit.,* note 8 above), p. 76.

34. The date of the oral order from Hitler to Himmler is placed between the beginning of 1941 and the latter part of March by Helmut Krausnick in his detailed discussion in Hans Buchheim and others, *Anatomie des SS-Staates* (Olten and Freiburg, 1965), pp. 360–61. Uwe Dietrich Adam's recent attempt, in his *Judenpolitik im Dritten Reich* (Düsseldorf, 1972), pp. 301–16, to put off the decision until later is not very convincing.

35. Yehuda Bauer, *They Chose Life* (pamphlet of the American Jewish Committee, 1973).

36. See Shmuel Krakowski, *Lehimah yehudit be-Polin neged ha-natzim 1942–1944* (Tel Aviv, 1977).

37. See Shalom Cholawski, *Ir ve-ya'ar be-matzor* (Tel Aviv, 1973).

38. Nili Patkin, *Hatzalat yeladim be-Tzarfat* (M.A. dissertation, Jerusalem, 1974).

39. See Michel Mazor's contribution to this volume.

40. R. Korczak, *Lehavot ba-efer* (Tel Aviv, 1965), pp. 160–61.

41. Only in December 1943 did the "working group" become identical with the Slovak *Judenrat.*

42. Yehuda Bauer, "Onkel Saly—Die Verhandlung zwischen dem 'Joint' und der SS in der Schweiz," *Vierteljahreshefte für Zeitgeschichte* 25 (1977), 188–219.

43. Memorandum by Rademacher, March 7, 1940, NG-2586(B).

44. Until late in the war there had also been a third group, a separate Communist faction led by Yudita Nowogrodzka. Their policy was to send groups into the forests some 80 kilometers away to fight there, even though the few partisans in the forests before Summer 1943 were hostile to the Jews.

45.   Tenenbaum, *op. cit.*, pp. 67–68.

46.   Grossman, *op. cit.*, pp. 205 ff.

47.   E.g., a monograph on Danzig (Eliahu Stern); an examination of western Belorussian ghettos (Shalom Cholawski); Yisrael Gutmann *The Jews of Warsaw, 1939–1943* (Jerusalem, 1977); a monograph on the Plaszow camp (Shalmi Bar-mor); an investigation on Polish-Jewish relations (Shmuel Krakowski and Yisrael Gutmann).

48.   The stereotyped picture of an almost universally passive Jewish community and leadership is a product not only of certain historical writings, but also of the reactions of many Holocaust survivors to their experiences. In the testimony of these survivors, however, one frequently finds that although "the *Judenräte*" in general are believed to have been traitors, "my" or "our" *Judenrat* was an exception to that rule.

Resistance to the Holocaust: Reflections on the Idea and the Act

GEORGE M. KREN AND LEON RAPPOPORT

If one views the destruction of the European Jews as a unitary event without focusing on particulars, the perception gained is suffused with a feeling of mystery. The feeling is understandable: it is a basic human reaction to that which cannot be comprehended according to familiar standards of meaning. The extraordinary killings are thus frequently described in a language of mystery (including the term "the Holocaust" itself) and treated as such in Israel today, where monuments and museums variously convey it as a massive, dark horror, almost impossible to verbalize and then only in a whisper.

Among the elements contributing to this mystery, one that has remained especially obscure is the extent to which Jews forcibly resisted their destruction. Such resistance has remained a mystery even for those personally involved in it, as well as for the scholars and writers who have come later seeking explanations.

At least one fundamental part of the problem has to do with conceptual ambiguities surrounding the very idea of resistance, which has never been given a clear historical, psychological, and political meaning. Contemporary usage of the term was disseminated during World War II as part of a moralistic propaganda campaign (resistance "good," collaboration "bad") denying the legitimacy of Nazi authority in conquered territories. It follows that any study of resistance, Jewish or otherwise, may easily become an exercise in immediate political expediency or in word magic, unless analysis begins with a firm construal of what resistance means.

Accordingly, while this paper is ultimately concerned with Jewish resistance to the Holocaust, it begins with a broad theoretical discussion. Resistance is first considered in the context of struggles against political authority systems so as to develop a general definition of authentic resistance. Psychological dimensions of struggles against powerful authorities are next examined as part of the process of transformation "from victim to resister." The remainder of the paper is then devoted to working out the latent conceptual implications of diverse Jewish attempts forcibly to resist destruction. It should be clear, therefore, that this paper does not purport to offer an encyclopedia of Jewish resistance. Although our work touches on a wide spectrum of specific actions and is informed throughout by intensive study of the available evidence, it deals mainly with ideas and situations in order to articulate the *epistemology* of Jewish resistance rather than to demonstrate its reality or debate its feasibility.

The Idea of Resistance

In general there is no single convenient framework for discussing either the idea or the act of resistance except when it is considered in the context of revolution. Yet resistance is not revolution and need not invariably be intended to bring about revolution. Many forceful acts against a prevailing authority or power are aimed merely at self-preservation or reform. Revolutions, moreover, are overt affairs involving public statements of purpose, shadow governments, flags, and other symbols, whereas resistance may be covert and disorganized.

Nor should resistance be classified under dissent. Both terms connote opposition to authority, but dissent is better taken to mean opposition that is *tolerated* by authority. For heuristic purposes, it is appropriate even to suggest a bipolar scale for describing the quality of opposition to existing authority, with dissent as the least intense endpoint, revolution as the most intense endpoint, and resistance somewhere in between.

On such a scale or continuum of opposition, dissent includes all legal and mildly illegal expressions of disagreement or protest. Those who dissent may well risk various forms of punishment, officially or unofficially sanctioned by authority, but both the risk and the punishment are small. This assertion may seem absurd in view of examples that might be cited to demonstrate the contrary; yet insofar as dissent *does* carry the risk of severe punishment— exile, imprisonment, death—it becomes resistance. In many practical situations, therefore, it must be recognized that acts of opposition can be classified only *post hoc,* by the quality of the reaction that they provoke.

Most actions against the Vietnam War in the United States were clearly matters of dissent because they were either entirely legal (e.g., signing petitions), or only mildly illegal (parading without a permit). But such acts as refusal to serve when drafted or destruction of government records were acts of resistance—given the severe penalties involved. The point is that meaningful distinctions between dissent and resistance can be made only in situations where significant opposition is essentially legal. *Where there is no scope for dissent, all opposition is resistance.*

Apart from the reactions of those in power, another reason for separating dissent from resistance is a difference of purpose. If opposition is simply aimed at a change in policy (e.g., "stop the bombing"), and the legitimate right of authority to carry out its chosen policy is not challenged, then it is in the "loyal opposition" tradition of dissent. But if this dissent is ineffective, or repressed without being crushed, it may grow into an attack on the legitimacy of authority and thus be transformed into resistance. Opposition challenging the intrinsic right of authority to select and implement policy (e.g., "no taxation without representation") is the nucleus of resistance.

Here again the events of recent years provide numerous examples. The Black Panther organization signified the emergence of resistance from dissent concerning racism; draft board raids and Weatherman bombings of public buildings signified the emergence of resistance from dissent concerning the Vietnam War. Neither of these efforts was able to survive the harsh reactions of authority, and their failure demonstrates the difficulty of resistance in a society that allows substantial opposition in the form of dissent. Indeed, everything known about modern resistance movements shows that no amount of passion, charismatic leadership, or ideological agitation can sustain active resistance when the premise of resistance can be expressed legally and with at least the apparent prospect of some change. Such considerations, it is true, reflect only surface contingencies influencing the emergence of resistance. To go deeper, it is necessary to analyse resistance at its own level, beginning with the socio-political factors involved.

Defining Authentic Resistance

From the family to the tribe, and then to the modern industrial state, all organized human groups are characterized by some form of socio-political authority system. The system will inevitably include two essential components: values defining right and wrong behavior, and social processes enforcing these values through institutions such as those of the law and religion.

Obedience to the authority system is typically rooted in tradition as a historical norm, which, through the workings of institutions, is acted out in the immediate present as a socio-political norm. Furthermore, as Freudian theory takes great pains to explain, obedience to authority is most basically an individual psychological norm understandable as a dynamic aspect of personality (the superego), which provokes guilt feelings in the individual who may think of going against the system. Authority systems, therefore, are not easily challenged in a significant way because they are so deeply woven into the socio-psychological fabric of life. How then is one to understand serious forms of resistance?

Briefly, all paths of analysis lead to only one major premise: resistance requires an *existential leap,* a going beyond the complex of existing obedience norms. To resist authority, no matter how oppressive and corrupt it may be, is to leap over the boundary of conventional experience. And to do so is to defy the conservative, stabilizing forces that regularize social life and provide the basis for feelings of security within the social group.

Physical risk apart, one characteristic of every act of resistance is an opposition between its short-term and long-term psychological effects. The short-term effect is an immediate release of the emotional tension that has led to the act of resistance. In this respect, and for the purpose of formal analysis only, the sense of liberation (catharsis) felt by an adolescent in going against his parents is fundamentally the same as that felt by an adult taking action against a political authority system.

The longer-term psychological effect of resistance, however, is to generate new forms of tension. Significant acts of resistance carry the actors beyond the frontiers of shared behavior norms. And once they have breached them, important standards of behavior can no longer be taken for granted. Questions of trust, therefore, become paramount issues, constantly being raised, debated, and reevaluated. No hero or leader of today can rest easy, for he may well emerge as the traitor of tomorrow. Over and above physical risk, these longer-term effects constitute the true peril constraining resistance. Acts of serious disobedience open a Pandora's box of anarchy. Obedience norms are terribly strong because they keep the lid down on the chaos and distrust that Freud so brilliantly observed to be the concomitants of unleashed instinct.

It is striking, nonetheless, that despite the strong forces combining to maintain obedience, much of Western history is nothing if not a record of disobedience—of violent resistance and revolution impelled by the promise of significant change. The record consists of revolutions aimed either at the overthrow of authority systems *per se,* or, in the case of nonrevolutionary resistance, of demands for fundamental change in the obedience norms supporting an authority system. And the demand for such change has, of course, frequently turned into an attempt to bring the system down.

Very broadly, therefore, the idea of resistance constitutes both an abstract and a literal paradox. Little wonder that it has occupied a central position in the works of modern existentialist, Marxist, and psychoanalytic thinkers; for even when the paradox is described as an ultimate unknowable of "human nature," it remains a notable challenge to all serious social philosophies. Dealing with either the impulse toward resistance or the act itself, contemporary philosophical discussions have been influenced by, and have in turn exerted influence upon, the whole spectrum of social science besides those aspects of religion and law that are not social science. The result of all this, when confusion is set aside, would seem to be three separate, but related, criteria for evaluating the effectiveness of resistance. However different their particular views of society may be, serious writers from Mao to Marcuse to Arendt tend to agree that efforts at resistance depend upon the following three considerations.

First, the *probability of success*: how likely is it that resistance will succeed in achieving its purpose? Judgments here require analysis of the relative strength and weakness of both the established authority and the resistance. To be effective, the resistance must be concerned with plausible goals and offer a practical route toward their attainment.

Second, the *intensity of oppression*: how severe is the pain or suffering imposed by the established authority? Those physical and psychological perils of resistance discussed earlier will hardly be risked by rational men unless obedience to the status quo is accompanied by significant awareness of oppression. In situations where oppression is only latent, or else present but not experienced as such by its victims, some form of consciousness-raising is needed before effective resistance can be set in motion.

And third, the presence of an *alternative authority system*: to what extent is resistance supported or justified by values and norms contradicting those of the authority system in force? In common revolutionary parlance, this question is ordinarily understood to involve the ideological basis for denying the legitimacy of established authority. It is *not* ordinarily understood that the ideological basis for resistance is itself a real or nascent authority system, though no resistance can be genuine if it is not guided by alternative values and norms.

None of the criteria listed above is completely free of ambiguity. Each could indeed be treated as a proposition to be elaborated on and discussed. But that is more properly the business of scholars of revolution; our own aim is to emphasize that—residual ambiguities notwithstanding—the effectiveness of resistance can be evaluated in terms of rational and relatively straightforward standards, which form a heuristic "resistance equation." Thus, effective resistance would be a function of (1) the probability of success, (2) the intensity of oppression, and (3) the presence of an alternative authority system.

In many respects, this formulation can serve as the basic model of effective resistance. Much of the confusion in literature on the nature of revolutions derives from concentrating too exclusively upon particular factors in the equation. Marcuse has been roundly criticized, for example, because his work stimulates awareness of oppression, and indicates a Marxist-Freudian basis for alternative authority systems, without offering programmatic statements on how change can best be accomplished. He is, therefore, seemingly unconcerned with what we have called the probability of success.

Similarly, writers such as Che Guevara and Régis Debray, who focus upon organizational matters tied to the probability of success, are often criticized for neglecting alternative authority systems and the awareness of oppression, a judgment reinforced by the circumstances of Guevara's death. As for Camus, his classic work *Resistance, Rebellion, and Death* (New York, 1961) was devoted almost exclusively to the problem of oppression, and how it can reach sufficient intensity to generate resistance. His existentialist outlook apparently distracted him from concern with either the probability of success or alternative authority systems. The latter, indeed, is almost ignored, entering only when Camus naively pleads for "justice" as the alternative to oppression.

Beyond clarifying general discussions of resistance, the heuristic equation offered above has value, too, as a tool of historical analysis. For even a brief review of celebrated World War II resistance movements suggests that they could not have been sustained without the alternative authority system and probability of success provided by the Allied powers. In France, Greece, Yugoslavia, Italy, and Norway, for example, the intensity of German oppression varied immensely, but resistance increased in direct response to Allied support.

A somewhat contrary situation may be seen in the anti-colonial movements following World War II. In Algeria, Vietnam, Indonesia, and other places, resistance proceeded with relatively little outside support, depending mainly upon the recalcitrance and venial clumsiness of colonial reaction to the growing sense of oppression among native populations. Although resistance based primarily on the oppression factor can be as potent and as genuine as any other kind, it is the most difficult to maintain. So long as a powerful, established authority is determined to impose its will, and is not seriously distracted by other internal or external conditions, resistance tends to have a low probability of success.[1]

Useful as it is for discussing the socio-political logic of resistance, however, our three-factor equation omits an essential psychological element: the individual will to resist. Like so many other formulations based on a logical positivist, "scientific" mode of analysis, it serves well enough as a tool for reductionistic description, but offers little insight into the dynamics of personal causality. How is it possible for individuals to make the existential leap over the boundaries of established obedience norms? And what aspects of their experience can move oppressed persons to active resistance in the face of utterly hopeless odds? Questions of this kind cannot be addressed through formal-objective analysis. Instead, they require a more subjective, phenomenological approach.

From Victim to Resister

The transition from victim to resister is never accomplished without the reality or threat of violence. Frantz Fanon developed the psychological aspects of this thesis in relation to the struggles of colonial populations to achieve independence, but it fits virtually every serious effort at resistance.[2] Writing from a dual perspective—his professional background in psychiatry and his experience of the Algerian revolt against France—Fanon identified the existential moment of resistance as occurring when the victim is able to *act with the same violence* as his oppressor. Such violence is the means whereby persons oppressed to the point of internalizing a subservient, inferior self-image discard their role as victims. The direct action against their oppressors is a therapy enabling them to gain a new consciousness of self.

Tied as it is to the horrors most of us associate with violence, this view of resistance is at first very difficult to accept. Violence as a necessary component of revolt? Yes. But violence as a therapy? Bizarre! And yet the evidence supporting it is too strong to be ignored. Consider the testimony of Zivia Lubetkin describing one of the first acts of resistance against the Germans in the Warsaw Ghetto during January 1943. Hiding with a group of forty young people resolved to fight back with a few smuggled revolvers, she tells of the successful ambush and pursuit of a German search party:

> We were overjoyed; all the suffering seemed worthwhile. With our own eyes we had seen scared Germans, we had seen them turn to run; and we had pursued them. German soldiers who thought they were conquerors of the world were being chased by Jewish boys . . .[3]

Later that same day, while hiding in another building, Lubetkin saw German parties, previously confident and bold, moving cautiously and fearfully through the ghetto. Her reaction perfectly exemplified the psychological generalizations developed by Fanon some twenty years later:

> Our spirits rose. No more did we feel the worry, the anguish of the days that had gone before. We felt redeemed—we felt our lives were again useful. What we were doing would be recompense for the murders, and our own deaths, which seemed inevitable, would not be in vain—would make sense. Beyond that, a spark of hope remained: perhaps we might live.[4]

This type of statement appears over and over again in the writings of victims who were finally able to resist. Their reflections invariably convey a sense of intense euphoria at the discovery that their oppressors were human, after all, and vulnerable. Take, for example, the testimony of a Jewish partisan operating in Russia. During his first combat action, he was at the same time frightened and elated:

> But our joy was greater than our fear. For the first time we had fought the German soldiers face to face! We had proved that it was possible to do so and that it was possible to kill them.[5]

Even in less extreme circumstances than those created by the Nazis, one can find examples of such euphoria. It appears in such diverse sources as Norman Mailer's self-reported feelings while taking part in an anti-war march described in *The Armies of the Night* (New York, 1968), in the correspondence of the Berrigan group as they planned war-resistance activities, and even in the remark attributed to an American B-52 pilot who refused to fly missions in Indochina: "This is the first time in my life that I have been able to feel really happy and good, because I have made the right decision."[6]

In a more general psychological context, the euphoria characterizing the transition from victim to resister might seem of dubious importance. Why should any special meaning be attributed to the elation of resisters when others, including oppressors, have also reported euphoric "highs" following successful combat? Even civilians who have had a close brush with accidental death may feel elated at finding themselves alive. What is so special about resistance euphoria?

The answer is that, unlike most soldiers or accident victims, the resister is usually someone who has deliberately chosen to step beyond the boundaries of everyday life as defined by prevailing authority systems. By making the decision to resist—the "existential leap" as we have earlier described it—the resister not only accepts physical risk, but places himself in a very new psychological situation. Consequently, the general meaning of resistance euphoria cannot be equated with the emotions accompanying a straight-forward experience of severe risk or danger. To oppose oneself to a powerful, deadly authority system is not the same as making a parachute jump or volunteering for a dangerous military mission, for in these latter situations the individual does not necessarily undergo profound psychological change. His conception of himself and those around him may change *quantitatively* as a result of daring action—enhanced ego strength might follow from demon-strated bravery—but this is not the same as the *qualitative* changes that follow from resistance.

The euphoria characterizing serious resistance signals the experience of a new world-view. Once engaged, action against that which has been avoided, feared, and repressed works a sudden and deeply pervasive change on the individual. This is the therapeutic effect that Fanon observed in his dis-cussion of anti-colonial revolts. The release of pent-up energy allows the victim to feel himself suddenly different: healed of the internal conflicts that had troubled him, and relieved of the burden of tension and guilt that had accumulated in consequence of his status as a victim. In more general terms, the resister is one who has "taken arms against a sea of troubles" and ended them even at the cost of his own life.

Yet, like Hamlet's decision to oppose his stepfather, the individual's decision to resist does not come easily. In Europe under the Nazis and in many other situations as well, the mass of common people seem to be reluctant to risk forceful resistance so long as they are allowed to maintain themselves in minimally bearable conditions. As we have noted elsewhere, justification for such reluctance can be found in appeals to religious values, traditional norms, and the brutal considerations of *Realpolitik*: to resist might be to provoke repression worse than the one at hand.[7]

No responsible person can simply ignore such appeals. This point was made by respected members of every community of Jews in Europe. In the Warsaw Ghetto during 1941–1943, for example, the question of resistance was steadily debated by various leaders prior to the eventual revolt. As described by Izhak Zuckerman, a well-known Jewish historian argued that ". . . if we declared war we would only destroy that which it was possible to save." Another position repeated by a religious spokesman was simply: "The

Lord giveth and the Lord taketh away . . . we could not raise a hand against the Germans, and so bring about the murder of hundreds of thousands of Jews." Still others believed that no action should be taken except in collaboration with the Polish underground organization: "Let us fight when the Poles fight."[8]

After some unsuccessful attempts, several of the more militant groups, mainly Zionist youth and those with Communist connections, formed a united front in the Warsaw Ghetto and began to train for revolt toward the end of 1942 while accumulating smuggled and homemade weapons. But no decision was made as to tactics or timing. When the Nazis brought up forces to undertake a partial liquidation of the Ghetto in January 1943, the various combat groups were thus taken by surprise. They began to fight on their own initiative with little or no coordination in a series of sporadic actions against German patrols.

These unexpected firefights surprised the Germans. A final decision was taken to liquidate the Warsaw Ghetto, but before the Germans were ready several weeks elapsed, during which the Ghetto fighters prepared for the final battle that was to begin in April. Along with other surviving participants, Zuckerman stated later that if the combat groups had not spontaneously fought back in January, the revolt might never have occurred because the resistance leaders were still undecided about detailed plans of action.

One can see from all the available documents on the Warsaw Ghetto revolt how difficult it is to organize serious resistance so long as some hope of survival remains. One can see this, too, from documents on many other Jewish ghettos throughout Europe. But inasmuch as people in most of them later gained reasonably sure knowledge of the extermination program, the question arises: what prevents open resistance once it is clear that there is no substantial basis to hope for survival? Logically, nothing; psychologically, a great deal.

During the earlier period of Nazi domination, despite numerous arbitrary killings, the policy publicly announced and believed by Jews and their German overseers alike, was that if ghetto inhabitants followed orders and engaged productively in work enterprises contributing to the German war effort, they would in effect be "earning their keep" and thus be safe. Even when news of systematic killings leaked out, people in the ghettos were encouraged by their Nazi supervisors to believe that their particular community or work group would be spared so long as it was productive—a rationalization that was only abandoned in the very last extreme moments when it was contradicted by events making effective resistance all but impossible. Moreover, since the habit of defensive rationalization seems hard to break, there were many who boarded the trains for Treblinka believing the Nazi cover story of transportation to a new work project.

In the town of Grodno, for example, an eyewitness account states that when the deportation operation began, a few small groups of Jews tried to escape to the forest, but the majority were passive:

Everybody now knew that everyone taken out of the Ghetto was being shipped to Treblinka. Many rebelled. "We shall not go! Let them rather shoot us here on the spot!"

But their words fell on deaf ears. All of them went. They hoped that some miracle would occur on the train. They waited to be saved by a miracle—and they went to their death.[9]

A more complex but fundamentally similar pattern occurred in the Bialystok Ghetto. Here a resistance group prepared to make a last ditch fight against deportation with the understanding that none of the ghetto inhabitants would go voluntarily to the deportation assembly area. When the appointed time arrived, however, most of the people went quietly, ignoring the pleas of the young resistance fighters.

Our messengers were speeding to every corner of the Ghetto, explaining, trying to persuade.

"Jews, don't go of your own will. This is not an evacuation to Lublin. Every time they take anyone from the Ghetto it means death. Don't go! Hide yourself! Fight with everything that comes to hand."

Our colleagues turned from one group of Jews to another, exhorting, berating. But the wave was streaming into the streets, which were filled constantly with Jews . . .

Reflecting further on what she had seen, the writer quoted above was able to pinpoint the essential rationale of those who went to their deaths without struggling:

A family marched along in the sun. It was easier to die among many than to fight and suffer alone. As it looked, it was easier to die soon than to live a long, tortured life. Truly, living in a hole, in a cave, under a wall, in colonization sewers, in pits and cellars—*this was perhaps a curse to be weighed against a quick death that redeemed* [italics added].[10]

This is the quintessential psychological and socio-political dilemma facing those who consider resistance: when the promise of survival seems strong, resistance will appear to be folly—a threat to the object it aims to preserve. And when there is little or no hope of survival, resistance would appear to be absurd—a guarantee only of further misery in addition to death.[11]

Survival Is Not Enough

The transition from victim to resister does not grow primarily out of the desire to survive. Except in special cases, the hope of preserving one's own life stands as the least important personal factor in resistance efforts. More frequently than not, and despite popular views to the contrary, action against powerful authorities is undertaken on exactly opposite grounds. The first order of business for those planning acts of revolt usually involves the renunciation of personal concerns, including their own individual survival. Such total commitment to resistance action is not accomplished easily and is virtually never shared by large numbers of people. Yet the history of this century provides a very long list of relevant examples. From *fin-de-siècle* Russian nihilists to present-day Palestinian factions or the Irish Republican Army, one can find dramatic evidence of total commitment. Often revealing themselves only through terrorist acts, and dismissed as fanatics or psychopaths, such persons form the leading, visible edge of ideologically inspired resistance action.

This is not to say that resistance efforts can or should be defined by their most extreme manifestations, yet it cannot be denied that the extremes shed light on the process that nurtured them. Psychologically, the extraordinary acts of terrorists suggest the extraordinary motivating force of the ideological goals to which they are usually attached. Viewed in the broader context of contemporary history, moreover, there can be little doubt that the chief inspiration for all serious resistance movements is not survival but some value system. This may be rooted either in a fully articulated world-view such as Marxism or Catholicism, or it may involve only a simple belief in certain humanitarian norms; but whatever its roots, it must generate ideas powerful enough to overwhelm the desire for personal survival. In this connection, a good deal of relevant evidence suggests that the abstract values inspiring resistance may gradually come to dominate the individual and literally compel dangerous action despite contrary fears or rationalizations. The resistance ideation can take on a life of its own, and its logic may assimilate other factors in the person's life to such a degree that living *per se* becomes meaningless unless the logic is acted out. In more precise psychological terms, it may be said that the person's ego or self-image becomes so enmeshed with the values at issue that nothing but direct action can maintain his self-esteem.

Many examples of this process are described in Heimler's collection of essays on resistance. Sometimes the decision to act is sudden, as in the case of a journalist in Nazi-occupied Hungary who put up posters saying "National Socialism is Death":

> The idea occurred to him while he was shaving one morning. He stood in front of the mirror, he said, and suddenly saw his face in a way in which he had never seen it before. He said it was the face of a traitor. The face asked him, "What are you going to do about the injustice that is on its way?" By the time he had finished shaving he was ready with the answer. When everyone had gone home that night he used his own paper's presses to print the posters and then went out and put them up himself.[12]

At another extreme are those for whom resistance is a style of life be-beginning in childhood. Heimler describes his own life in these terms, explaining that as the son of a dedicated socialist who was also a religious Jew and, therefore, twice damned in the atmosphere of interwar Hungary, he was aware of oppression and determined to fight against it even as a young boy.

Small as I was I determined never to give in, never to go under, and I decided that one day when I grew bigger I would stand up against oppression of any kind.[13]

A very powerful example of how resistance may develop in persons who are not themselves direct targets of oppression occurred in Munich around 1943. Here a small group of students acting entirely on their own initiative produced and circulated leaflets attacking the Nazis. Known as the White Rose, the group was led by a twenty-four-year-old medical student named Hans Scholl. He had once idolized Hitler and played a prominent role in the local Hitler Youth. Yet as he grew into a sensitive teenager who loved poetry and the woodland rambling that had been a part of the earlier, anti-establishment German Youth Movement, brutal demands for conformity left him disillusioned. In this, Scholl was not different from many others of his background. What distinguished him was a particular set of circumstances allowing him to work out his ideas and emotions to a degree that led inevitably to action.

Briefly, these circumstances included a family that shared his feelings (his father saw Hitler as an anti-Christ), a small circle of student friends who were profoundly disturbed by their growing realization of what was happening in Germany, and direct experience with the war and the extermination program gained during a period of front line service in Russia as a medical aid man. It was in this general context that Scholl moved from confused doubt to conviction and to a belief in the criminality of the Nazi government as an evil force destroying the German people.

It followed that an honest man had no recourse except to struggle against the criminal regime. Discussions in a group that included his younger sister Sophie, a fifty-year-old professor of philosophy named Kurt Huber, and three fellow students, strengthened Scholl's beliefs. The group agreed that resistance was a duty they could not ignore: "We must do it for the sake of life itself—no one can absolve us of this responsibility."[14] A few months later, after distributing four different sets of leaflets calling upon Germans to understand their position under the Nazis and to engage in whatever forms of resistance might be possible, the group was caught by the Gestapo. They were beheaded for high treason in 1943.

The Scholl group exemplifies resistance in its purest form, originating as a matter of conscience, then dominating the individual's ego until action becomes imperative, a duty that cannot be ignored.[15] Here too, one may see how conscience or moral thought translates into ideology in the sense that it generates a rationale providing guidelines for action. Scholl's ideology was based on his belief in the innate integrity and continuity of the German people. He felt that leaflets protesting Nazi crimes would encourage resistance by demonstrating that it was possible to protest, thereby awakening people to their responsibilities. If the Nazi terror was so severe as to preclude open resistance, there still remained various forms of passive sabotage. And failing all else, if he and his colleagues were killed they would at least have shown to future generations that the German people were not entirely without honor.

Such material might appear irrelevant to the Jews. Their peril was so concrete that resistance would seem to have required no justification in conscience or ideology. But events show the contrary.

Jewish Resistance Ideology in the Ghettos

It is sometimes held that specifically Jewish resistance only occurred in Eastern Europe, most particularly in Poland and the Soviet Union. While Jews were active in resistance groups elsewhere, they participated, it is claimed, in a non-sectarian, nationalist fashion, much as any other citizen.[16] Evidence shows, however, that Jews in the West often conducted resistance in a deliberately obscure fashion. In France, for example, the Jewish poet David Knout organized a fighting group supported with Zionist funds. Consisting mainly of young people recruited from the prewar Jewish Scout organization, this underground group eventually fought with other French Maquisards in the South, but its Jewish identity was not widely known. The Jewish scouts themselves operated a clandestine escape and evasion network under the pretense of working with the German-sponsored French Jewish Council. According to Poliakov, these scouts helped to rescue more than 4,000 persons from deportation. Poliakov also makes the point that Jews played a disproportionately large role in French national resistance organizations, often assuming gentile names in order to avoid reprisals against their families.[17]

Qualitatively similar material can be found describing Jewish resistance in Italy, Holland, and other occupied countries: Greece, for instance, which had Jewish escape and fighting groups.[18] Indeed, close study of national resistance movements in Western Europe suggests that Jews often constituted a kind of underground within the underground. And for this reason, perhaps, their activities have not received much attention.[19]

On the other hand, it remains quite true that Eastern Europe was the preeminent arena for *visible* Jewish resistance. Here most Jews were cut off from native populations because of traditional antisemitism and Nazi ghetto regulations. Consequently, they could not follow the classic model of resistance based on popular nationalistic feelings. What is more, there was no significant external support:

> As far as the Allies were concerned, they refused to aid the Jews as such; they would give assistance to Poles or Frenchmen, but not to some mythical Jewish nation; they missed many opportunities of saving groups of Jews from genocide.[20]

Added to these conditions of isolation, which were in themselves an immense barrier to organizing resistance, the Jewish population was also divided by religious and political differences. The conservative, semi-mystical religious sects withdrew into themselves to await a heavenly judgment, while the assimilationist groups of petit bourgeois were inclined toward accommodation, if not outright collaboration. Zionists remained the largest organized portion of the Jewish population, but they were divided among themselves into at least four competing factions.

On the political Right, the Zionist-Revisionist party were anti-labor nationalists. They favored immediate mass migration to Palestine and military action to establish the Jewish national homeland. Moderates were represented by the General Zionist party, which included a liberal element opposed to more conservative, business-oriented members. The Left-wing Zionists were arrayed in several parties and youth groups that sorted themselves out according to whether they favored moderate or extreme forms of socialism. Finally, there was also the Mizrachi party composed of those who hoped for a Jewish homeland that would be organized entirely on the basis of religious law.[21]

Divided among themselves, isolated from the surrounding population, and unrecognized by the Allied powers, the Polish Jews were in the worst possible position to generate serious resistance, and for almost two years there was very little. Conditions were much the same in the occupied territories of the Soviet Union. But here many Jews of military age were already serving as soldiers, while many others, confronted by Nazi murder squads, made their way to regular partisan units. Here they fought explicitly as Jews; for instance, in its statistical breakdowns of partisan units the Soviet command listed Russians, Belorussians, Jews, Ukrainians, etc., separately, though serving in the same unit. Only in a few places, however, where peasant antisemitism was so severe as to prevent their joining general partisan groups, did Jews fight in *wholly* Jewish units.[22] This leads us to consider Poland as the most important case of specifically Jewish resistance and to concentrate on resistance in and around the Polish ghettos.[23]

By 1941, most of the remaining Polish Jews were concentrated in urban ghettos such as those in Warsaw, Vilna, Bialystok, Cracow, and Lodz. They were administered by miniature Jewish bureaucracies set up by the Nazis. Known as *Judenräte* or Jewish Community Councils, they were charged with overseeing daily life in the ghettos: housing arrangements, sanitation, and order. For this last purpose, *Judenrat* administrators were allowed to maintain their own police force, which became notorious as adjuncts of the Nazi control apparatus in many places.

Even Zionists and representatives of the socialist Jewish Bund participated in a considerable number of *Judenräte*. The Councils included sincere assimilationists, some who ultimately took a stand against the Nazis, others who believed in following the tradition of survival through cooperation, and still others who were simply opportunists. While one can distinguish between the attitudes of the Councils (the majority of whose chairmen refused to hand over Jews for killing), and those of the Jewish police (which generally collaborated more willingly), it can be argued that every action of this Jewish "self-government" ultimately facilitated the Nazi murder program.

Although the Zionist, socialist and Communist groups were later to initiate open resistance, until mid-1941 their activities were limited to propaganda and self-help projects designed to make ghetto life more bearable. Their most significant public action involved the circulation of illegal newspapers attacking the more blatant forms of collaboration and corruption of one *Judenrat* or another. Under the surface, however, these groups were preoccupied with organizational problems. Many of their older, better-known leaders had fled or gone into hiding immediately following the Nazi occupation. Younger people were moved up to replace them; and while this forcible change to a more youthful leadership was to be an important contributing factor in the later development of open resistance, initially it created a good deal of confusion. Organization was also hampered by poor communication between groups isolated in different ghettos. The Nazis prohibited free travel, and it took some time before a covert messenger system could be arranged. For obvious reasons, this system always remained relatively slow and unreliable.

First reports of mass killings started to circulate in Warsaw and other ghettos during Summer 1941. Most Jews, including the *Judenrat* authorities, dismissed these reports as rumors or exaggerations of isolated incidents. Systematic murder was unprecedented, unthinkable, and, therefore, unbelievable. But the underground Zionist and Left-wing political groups took the reports seriously enough to start further investigations; as additional information was gathered by trusted party members, it was established that large numbers of Jews were indeed being sent to killing centers under the pretense of relocation. In February 1942 a comprehensive summary of the evidence given to underground political groups in Warsaw showed that approximately half the prewar Jewish population in the eastern part of Poland had already been killed. Leaders of these groups were no longer in doubt about the killings. A few may have clung to the hope that only "unproductive" elements in the population were to be eliminated, but most realized they were facing extermination and reacted in accordance with the ideological character of their groups and the conditions in their particular ghetto.

The pioneer youth components of the Left-wing and Right-wing Zionist organizations formed themselves into combat groups and began accumulating weapons. This was a natural outgrowth of their activist (and in some cases paramilitary) orientation toward the problem of resettlement in Palestine, only now the focus of struggle shifted from emigration to defense. The decision to fight was clearly in line with prior ideology. Nevertheless, the strategy to be followed posed a hard dilemma. Should the fighting youth act primarily to save themselves, or should they try to protect the remaining mass of Jews? The first alternative would involve a retreat to forest hideouts where partisan activity would be aimed at self-preservation and maintenance of the Zionist movement. The second alternative seemed virtually suicidal, since it would require direct attack on Nazi forces deployed against the ghettos. Yet the emotional impact of the Nazi killing operations was so intense that most of the young people could not tolerate the idea of letting it go unopposed.[24]

What emerged from this dilemma was a complex situation that varied from one ghetto to another. In Warsaw, debates among the leaders of different factions continued until events reached the point (in Autumn 1942) at which only a last-ditch fight in the Ghetto was feasible. In Bialystok, a compromise was adopted whereby some joined partisan units in the forest, and others remained in the city to fight deportation. Not until 1943 did all factions agree to form an anti-Nazi coalition. Unified in a central command structure, and given some aid by Soviet partisan units, the Bialystok Ghetto fighters then held off German forces for over a week in August 1943, and after the Ghetto was burned out some managed to escape.

With only 15,000 Jews, the Cracow Ghetto was too small to sustain a sizable resistance force, but for this reason unity among the underground groups came easily. The Zionists and Communists pooled their resources and supported effective urban guerrilla units early on. These units operated against the Germans for almost two years, and small bands remained active even after the Ghetto was substantially wiped out in March 1943.

The Vilna Ghetto held 60,000 Jews and here the Zionist, Communist, and Bundist groups banded together for armed resistance early in 1942; the Vilna combat units were relatively well armed. When Nazi forces moved in to eliminate the Ghetto in September 1943, there was an attempt at a general uprising, but the Ghetto population did not support the rebels. After some fighting the mass of the Jewish population was deported, though hundreds were able to get away.[25]

In Lodz, German domination was particularly severe and the *Judenrat* cooperated very closely with their masters. These conditions prevented the formation of sizable resistance organizations, but small bands of Zionist youth conducted sabotage operations. There were also strikes by Jewish workers in the German war factories. Deportations could not be resisted with force, however, because of the strong German presence and the danger of betrayal by collaborators.

The ideological basis for resistance is very clear in all the cases noted above. It was founded on militant movements for Zionism, socialism, or Communism—movements that had always provided their members with a strong historical sense of struggle and an identification with group goals rather than individual satisfaction. Politically there were great differences between them, but they were quite similar in terms of the psychological orientation. And beyond their similar commitment to social values offering a direct foundation for resistance ideology, these movements also shared much practical experience with underground organizational techniques.[26]

Resistance in the Camps

Resistance fighting was not limited to the ghettos. There were major rebellions in the death camps at Sobibor, Treblinka, and Auschwitz, and a number of small-scale fighting escapes from slave labor units. On the surface, these actions differ sharply from the ghetto fighting because they may seem little more than last-minute attempts to avoid death. Yet here again, the available evidence shows that personal survival was not the major factor underlying the rebellions. Indeed, most of the prisoners involved were so deeply immersed in a world of death that life had lost its conventional meaning.

Aside from occasional escapes attempted during transportation or on casual labor parties, resistance in the camps was the work of "old" prisoners, those who had kept themselves alive under the most extreme conditions. The typical adaptation made by these men left them toughened to the point of indifference and seemingly contemptuous regard for the anguish surrounding them. It is impossible to exaggerate the psychological gulf separating old and new prisoners.[27] The general attitude of the former was described by Primo Levi, who survived 18 months in Auschwitz:

> In history and in life one sometimes seems to glimpse a ferocious law which states: "To he that has, will be given; to he that has not, will be taken away." In the *Lager,* where man is alone and where the struggle for life is reduced to its primordial mechanism, this unjust law is openly in force, is recognized by all. With the adaptable, the strong and astute individuals, even the leaders willingly keep contact. . . . But with the mussulmans, the men in decay, it is not even worth speaking, because one knows already that they will complain and will speak about what they used to eat at home. . . . And in any case, one knows that they are only here on a visit, that in a few weeks nothing will remain of them but a handful of ashes in some nearby field and a crossed out number on a register.[28]

Resistance by new prisoners was all but impossible. They arrived in the camps exhausted and bewildered by their strange new surroundings. If they were not killed within the first few hours they were placed in work groups among old prisoners indifferent to their distress. Suicide was not infrequent; and if there was any thought of attacking a guard or attempting escape, it was brutally discouraged by the constant reminder of extreme torture awaiting those who did not remain totally subservient. Old prisoners, for their part, were generally convinced that resistance was futile. Even if a revolt might allow some to escape, where would they go? In the absence of connections on the outside, the most immediate prospect was quick recapture and slow death by torture.

Overt resistance was consequently rare. Yet in the three major instances where it occurred, old prisoners were responsible. Their familiarity with camp routines, personnel, and subtle weaknesses in the control system provided the basis for effective planning. More important were the personal qualities of guile, toughness, and vicious determination that had developed in the course of their struggle to stay alive. While it is true that no formal ideological elements underlay any of the major rebellions, it is also true that in each case they were organized and carried out by men who had been transformed by their camp experience, thereby acquiring a drastically different set of norms and values.

Devoid for the most part of any commitment to ordinary ideological values, old prisoners had nevertheless become converts to conspiracy and deception in order to live. In this sense, they were revolutionized psychologically and prepared for violent action because of their experience rather than allegiance to abstract ideals. Almost by definition, no one could become an old prisoner without acquiring a value system emphasizing desperate struggle against an incredible environment.[29] When on certain occasions, therefore, groups of old prisoners learned that no such struggle could prevent death any longer, that they were all destined to be killed once their work assignments were completed, rebellion became the only alternative.

At Treblinka the rebellion in August 1943 occurred for precisely this reason. Maintained as a permanent slave labor force, several hundred Jews selected from among arriving trainloads had spent many months servicing the machinery of death. Gossip picked up from the guards, together with a new work pattern designed to destroy all evidence of the camp's existence, made it plain that sooner or later Treblinka was to be closed down and that they themselves would also be eliminated. A coordinated plan was developed to attack individual officers and guard posts with homemade weapons. After a core group of prisoners began the revolt, others joined in and succeeded in forcing several openings in the perimeter of the camp. Enough guards remained in action, however, to shoot down the majority of escaping prisoners. Of the 150 to 200 who got out of the camp, only twelve ultimately survived.[30]

The Sobibor extermination camp had a work force of approximately 600 prisoners, including a sizable number who had been captured while serving in the Soviet army. In concert with Polish Jews imprisoned for a much longer period, the Russian Jewish soldiers organized an uprising essentially similar to the one at Treblinka. Using hatchets and knives fashioned from their work tools, they killed several guards, took their guns, and used them to attack the main gate. According to the testimony of the Soviet Jewish leader of the rebellion, the breakout itself was a success, but many of the prisoners were killed by mines and gunfire as they ran across an open area to reach shelter in a nearby forest. Here the various Russian, Polish, and West European Jews split into small groups, some heading east toward Russia while others moved toward more familiar areas of Poland. Although no exact count has been made of the number of survivors, it is estimated that at least 60 men and women were able to link up with a Soviet partisan group.[31]

The third major revolt occurred at Auschwitz on October 6, 1944. It was the work of Jews assigned to the crematorium, some of whom had been active in the Greek resistance prior to being deported, including three former officers of the Greek army. Others were Slovak and Polish Jews, and there were some Soviet POWs. All the crematoria workers knew they were doomed because it was common knowledge that these prisoners were periodically killed as a matter of SS policy. In order to slow down the mass killing, the group resolved to blow up the body-disposal ovens. Acting with remarkable skill, they accumulated guns and dynamite and were able to destroy one of the four ovens. Others working at the crematorium joined the action, but the response of the SS was very swift: within two hours the rebellion was crushed and all were killed except for a few wounded who were later hanged in front of the other prisoners.[32]

Unlike the major prisoner risings that have become known through survivor statements or Nazi records, smaller scale rebellions have remained relatively obscure. Judging from accounts that have gradually emerged during recent years, these incidents of resistance were probably more frequent than has generally been known. In the Auschwitz complex, for example, Sim Kessel mentions a prisoner who dragged an SS guard with him as he leaped to his death in a mine shaft. Kessel himself, with four Polish prisoners, succeeded in escaping several miles away from Auschwitz before being recaptured.[33] Similar resistance actions, sometimes by a group of a hundred or more prisoners, occurred in the slave labor and extermination camps throughout Eastern Europe.[34] Yet there is no way of knowing how many further cases of resistance have gone unrecorded, either because there were no survivors or because the few who lived were unable to speak. Nazi reports of Jewish resistance are sometimes unreliable, and many of the lower echelon records were lost or destroyed.

Taken together, all of the material available on resistance in the ghettos and camps reveals an impressive struggle against hopeless odds. To fight back under such conditions, however, was not simply a matter of personal courage or desperation. Ghetto fighters were sustained by formal ideological commitments, while those who revolted in the camps were moved by an informal but powerful existential ideology. This latter was by no means an automatic response to the threat of death. Prisoners in the camps could organize resistance only when they had passed beyond the normal boundaries of confusion and despair.

Where a strong, in-group discipline based on shared political convictions or bitter camp experience was lacking, there was chaos, fear, and resignation, rather than resistance. Kessel, for example, says that he might have escaped by breaking through the floor of the boxcar carrying him to Auschwitz but for the outcry of others in the car who were afraid they would be punished if he tried. He also described the hopeless atmosphere prevailing in a French camp holding Jews awaiting shipment to Auschwitz:

> Among this wretched mass of humanity, twenty jammed into a room, were individuals from every social level—millionaire bankers to penniless bums. All

of them knew that, barring a miraculous change in the war situation, eventually and inevitably they were going to find themselves naked together awaiting death. . . . One might have thought that they would pool their resources, at least within the realm of possibility, to try to form a united front against their common misfortune. This never happened, or practically never. A few sensible people tried to preach wisdom, but they were preaching in the desert . . .

That famous racial solidarity so denounced by Nazi theoreticians as a peril to the world proved to be pure legend. It was every man for himself.[35]

Indeed, with the exception of those strongly committed to a militant ideology, Jews in Nazi-dominated Europe were hardly capable of acting contrary to the *sauve qui peut* principle. Raised in a subculture emphasizing individual achievement and primary responsibility to the family, and living in societies that permitted them few alternatives aside from competitive business enterprise, their immediate response to threat was to act in terms of this principle. In most instances, it led only to fruitless internal bickering and petty self-seeking behavior that hindered the organization of resistance activity.

Collaboration

Outright Jewish collaboration was rare, partly because fanatic SS enforcement of the extreme Nazi racial policies made it impossible. Yet no discussion of resistance can be complete without some mention of this other side of the coin.

Collaboration with the Nazis went on throughout Europe for one or more of the following three reasons: because of genuine belief in National Socialist ideals, cynical opportunism aimed at personal aggrandizement, or the conviction that compromise with existing power was the only feasible course of action. The first reason requires little elaboration. Every European state, including the Allies fighting against Germany, had native fascist and neo-fascist elements sympathetic to Hitler. As the Nazis gained control over one country after another, local sympathizers such as Vidkun Quisling (Norway), Anton Pavelic (Yugoslavia), and Leon Degrelle (Belgium) quickly sought positions of power. These collaborators, and many like them, typically saw themselves as patriots who would save their countrymen from the corruption and inefficiency of democratic government. Needless to say, there could be no Jews in this category.[36]

It was, however, possible for Jews to engage in various forms of self-seeking collaboration. Every internment camp and killing center, for example, had its share of prisoners who betrayed others to gain some small advantage. And some of those who managed to gain positions of power as work-gang leaders or barrack chiefs were known to beat and torture in much the same fashion as non-Jews. But opportunistic collaboration was most serious in the ghettos where many stories have been told of persons who attempted to profit from business deals with the Germans or by serving as informers.

One of the more extreme cases of collaboration centered on the activities of a rather mysterious character named Avraham Gancwajch. Known as a journalist (in Lodz) and sometime Zionist, he appeared in the Warsaw Ghetto as director of a group called the "committee of artists and professionals." It was soon apparent that the committee funneled information directly to the German authorities. Some of the Jewish agents for the committee operated openly with police powers, and because they worked from a house located at number 13 Leszno Street, they became known in the ghetto as the "thirteeners."[37]

While Gancwajch is the only known case of this kind, many ghetto *Judenräte* were notorious for corrupt practices and *de facto* collaboration. Officials were regularly accused of favoritism and bribe-taking in the underground press. It is clear, moreover, that some *Judenrat* officials believed that by working for the Nazis they could insure their own safety regardless of what happened to others. The Jewish police were the most obvious symbols and instruments of collaboration. Given full authority by the Germans, clothed in special uniforms, and provided with liberal food allowances along with opportunities to profit from black market enterprises, these policemen represented the most visible form of opportunistic collaboration.[38] In some ghettos the police operated virtually as a law unto itself, ignoring or bypassing directives from the *Judenrat* officials whom it was supposed to serve. So long as the police obeyed German orders to round up stated numbers and categories of other Jews for deportation, and continued to enforce other regulations, it was given a free hand.

Probably the most significant fact about the Jewish police is the way it was gradually transformed from indirect into direct servants of SS policies. Beginning with conventional duties such as enforcement of rationing, housing, and sanitation regulations, the police were later used to assemble people for deportation. This was usually rationalized by *Judenrat* authorities with the argument that if they refused, the Germans would do it themselves in a far more brutal fashion. When deportation became known as a euphemism for extermination, some of the *Judenrat* leaders and policemen resigned or began to work with resistance groups, but others continued to follow German orders, claiming that by this means they could help save a larger number of people. A tragic illustration of the justification offered for such action appears in the diary of Zelig Kalmanovitch, who recorded his experience in the Vilna area:

> Our policemen were sent there with passes to be distributed among the remaining workers, and to turn over the rest of the people, "the superfluous," to the hands of the authorities to do with them what is customary these days. The young took upon themselves this difficult task. They donned their official caps, with the "Star of David" upon them, went there and did what they were supposed to do. The result was that more than 400 people perished: the aged, the infirm, the sick, and retarded children. Thus 1,500 women and children were saved. Had outsiders, God forbid, carried out this action, 2,000 people would have perished.

The commandant [of the Jewish police] said: "To be sure, our hands are stained with the blood of our brethren, but we had to take upon ourselves this dreadful task. We are clean before the bar of history."[39]

The situation in Vilna was not exceptional: the Jewish police in other Polish ghettos performed similar service. To judge from the Kalmanovitch diary, collaboration in Vilna descended to its lowest point when the Jewish police arrested young people accumulating weapons for resistance. Writing in July 1943, Kalmanovitch saw the resisters not as heroes, but as extremists who were endangering what was left of the Jewish community.

It cannot be that our extremists believe in the possibility of victory. . . . Then why make a useless uprising? The strength of the prisoner lies only in his continued existence . . .

In reality, when these people speak of the so-called "honor" which they defend they bring disgrace upon the tens of thousands that perished. These martyrs are in truth no less worthy than those who took to the sword. . . . Only cowards and confused people can think of bringing in arms here.[40]

Kalmanovitch himself believed that the only appropriate course of action was some form of compromise: by playing for time and yielding to German demands when necessary, the Jews might outlast the oppression or at least minimize its brutality. This compromise seemed plausible enough in view of the overwhelming German power and was especially appealing to Jews with strong religious convictions. Unfortunately, as the war dragged on and killings increased, reluctant compromise became little more than a euphemism for reluctant collaboration.

Prominent Jews who accepted positions in the German-sponsored *Judenräte* found themselves being used more and more openly as tools of the SS. By aiding in the registration and concentration of their people, they smoothed the way for deportation; by promulgating benign Nazi cover stories for deportation and denying warnings distributed by underground groups, they made deportation operations more efficient; and by harassing those who called for resistance, they hindered development of any counteraction. During his trial in Israel, Adolf Eichmann testified that the Jewish Councils were so effective in these respects that German personnel could be released for other service.

Some of the *Judenrat* officials realized what was happening in time to resign or ally themselves with resistance groups. Others made direct protests to the Germans and were simply killed or deported. In many cases, however, those who were appointed to the Jewish Councils stayed on, often accused of using their positions to save themselves, but always maintaining that their actions were designed to save as many as could be saved. Under some conditions, of course, such rationalizations could not be maintained. In one dramatic instance, Adam Czerniakow, chairman of the Warsaw *Judenrat,* committed suicide in July 1942 after the first massive deportation of ghetto inhabitants began. Following his death, the *Judenrat* remained operating (ineffectively) under the direction of the deputy chairman, though some of its members worked together with the Jewish underground.

Collaboration originating from well-intentioned beliefs in compromise was not limited to Poland. The Jewish Council appointed by the Germans in Holland also aided in the process of registration, concentration, and deportation. At Westerbork, where a large camp served as the waystation to Auschwitz, the Jewish police are described by Jacob Presser as having hardly differed from their SS masters. Labeled by more than one camp prisoner as a Jewish SS, they not only imposed a harsh order in the camp, but occasionally helped Dutch Nazis and SS in rounding up other Jews. The two presidents of the Jewish Council in Holland, Asscher and Cohen, went along with German orders and used their influence to protect "important" (that is, well-off) members of the Jewish community. Both men were investigated by secular authorities and a Jewish "court of honor" after the war because of the many accusations of collaboration made against them. In defense, Cohen cited the usual rationale that matters would have been worse if they had not worked with the Germans, and he compared himself with a general who is forced to sacrifice a company in order to save a division. Even during the war, such statements were heard so often that they became the substance of a joke circulating among Dutch Jews in 1942:

> Asscher and Cohen are the only Jews left, and the Germans demand the deportation of one of them. Says Cohen to Asscher: "It had better be you Abraham—lest worse befall the rest of us."[41]

It should be noted, however, that not all of the Jewish Councils were so invariably collaborationist as those mentioned above. Among the counter examples, a major one occurred in France when, working through the Vichy government, the Germans created a Jewish Council called the UGIF (Union Générale des Israélites de France). This organization actively opposed and subverted German policies to such an extent that several Jewish officials, including both of its presidents, were sent to Auschwitz. Along with several other more significant factors, the conduct of the UGIF helps to explain why approximately 70 percent of the French Jews were able to survive the war.[42]

Romance and Reality

Resistance to Nazi oppression was enshrined early in the war as a romantic ideal by Allied propaganda. The victorious Allies and liberated peoples have all of them, intellectuals and laymen alike, found their martyrs and given them the special status of cultural heroes—mythic figures embodying the best qualities of their compatriots. This celebration of resistance is one of the few simplistic certainties of an earlier generation that has so far remained safe from the critical analyses of revisionist historians, for it is difficult to deny that the anti-Nazi struggle pitted the forces of light against darkness.

Yet the realities of resistance in general, and Jewish resistance in particular, were as far from the romantic ideal as any fresh battlefield is from the memorials later erected upon it. Resistance is in no sense a categorical imperative arising spontaneously in heroic victims facing oppression. On the contrary, all of the available evidence shows that resistance emerges slowly in a gradual process that depends more on situational factors than on unique personal qualities. The relevant evidence on this point is so strong, in fact, as to suggest that no claim of spontaneous resistance should ever be accepted at face value.

It is virtually axiomatic that among the victims of powerful oppressive forces both psychological and physical divisions will arise; otherwise they would not be victims. Hemmed in by the various situational constraints defining their condition, they are for the most part incapable of struggling against it. And the pathways awaiting those few who *are* capable of struggle are always ambiguous: although their struggle may ultimately lead to heroic resistance, it may also lead to collaboration. The cruel dilemmas of survival do not present themselves with moral signposts indicating whether victims may fight against their condition best through forceful action, compromise, or a mixture of both.

Psychologically, compromise is always the most appealing, because it promises to bring relief from oppression with a minimum of risk. Among people facing great force, it is extremely powerful, especially at the popular mass level. As we have seen, apart from scattered perceptions of compromise as a way station on the road to collaboration (a judgment that was easily discredited as adventurist, and which seemed compelling only after the fact), the only factor standing against compromise was ideology combined with organization. Ideological considerations set the boundary conditions for survival, the limits beyond which survival lost its meaning.

In much of Nazi-occupied Europe, however, and certainly among most of the Jews, initially there was no substantial organized, ideological opposition to compromise. Moreover, many of those who staked their lives and honor on the possibilities of compromise acted with the same integrity and courage as those who are today honored in resistance memorials. At the level of practical politics, there is no sure logic by which resistance can be set against compromise and the attendant dangers of collaboration because these are not mutually exclusive categories of action. They stand instead as intervals on a continuum describing the struggle for survival against oppression. This is not to say, of course, that all distinctions are meaningless. Those who could pass by the logical attractions of compromise in their existential leap toward resistance rightly deserve admiration. But to assume that such categories of action can be clearly perceived as a moral dichotomy during times of historical upheaval and extraordinary oppression, is to expect more than the unaided human psyche can provide.

The situation of the Jews is terribly clear in this respect.[43] We have seen that while their resistance was slow to develop, and might indeed be judged as being too little too late, they were perfectly able to fight in the ghettos, the forests, and the camps. What they lacked was neither skill nor courage, but effective consensus and morally authoritative leadership to issue the call to arms. Unlike the other oppressed peoples of Europe, the Jews had no government in exile, no encouragement from the Allied powers, and no strong nationalist tradition to serve as the basis for a coherent resistance program. It is impossible to conclude whether or not a more extensive, forceful Jewish resistance movement could have disrupted the Holocaust machinery or saved many more lives. Our own retrospective view is biased toward a fighting resistance. Yet perhaps the ultimate words on this subject were written by Emmanuel Ringelblum as he lay hidden in a basement after the Warsaw Ghetto had been destroyed:

> A paradoxical situation arose. The older generation, with half a lifetime behind it, spoke, thought and concerned itself about surviving the war, dreamt about life. The youth—the best, the most beautiful, the finest that the Jewish people possessed—spoke and thought only about an honorable death. They did not think about surviving the war. They did not procure Aryan papers for themselves. They had no dwellings on the other side. Their only concern was to discover the most dignified and honorable death, befitting an ancient people with a history stretching back over several thousand years.[44]

Notes

1. Jewish resistance was a near-perfect example of this situation, because it developed in desperate response to the Nazi mass-murder program. The extraordinary oppression factor was unsupported, however, by any significant possibility of success or alternative authority system offering substantial material or moral support. As will be shown later in this paper, success could be conceived only in terms of delaying SS operations and demonstrating to the world that Jews could fight. A further impediment to Jewish resistance was the absence of any unitary alternative authority system. The mixed ideals of various fighting groups in Eastern Europe ranged from personal revenge to Left- and Right-wing Zionism and socialism. Many West European Jews apparently fought out of a simple nationalistic loyalty to their home country. Consequently, apart from shared horror at Nazi oppression, there was no single ideology or affirmative goal orientation to provide a cohesive force for the disparate Jewish resistance groups.

2. Frantz Fanon, *The Wretched of the Earth* (New York, 1965).

3. Zivia Lubetkin, in Meyer Barkai ed., *The Fighting Ghettos* (Philadelphia and New York, 1962), p. 35.

4. *Ibid.,* p. 36.

5. *Ibid.,* p. 175.

6. *Time,* January 22, 1973, p. 21.

7. George M. Kren and Leon Rappoport, "Victims: The Fallacy of Innocence," *Societas* 4 (1974), 111–29.

8. Zuckerman was in the Jewish Young Pioneers (the *chalutz* movement), and was deputy to M. Anielewicz, commander of the rebellion. The above quotes appear in Barkai, *op. cit.,* pp. 22–24.

9. Zippora Birman, in Barkai, *op. cit.,* p. 108.

10. Chaika Grossman, in Barkai, *op. cit.,* pp. 116–17.

11. Another example is what took place in the Vilna Ghetto: the United Partisan Organization (FPO) had prepared a rebellion, but in early September 1943, when the Germans made an offer of life in Estonian work camps, the population streamed out of the Ghetto at their bidding, leaving the fighters alone among empty houses. See R. Korczak, *Lehavot ba-efer* (Tel Aviv, 1965), pp. 190–202.

12. E. Heimler ed., *Resistance against Tyranny* (London, 1966), p. xi.

13. *Ibid.,* p. 152.

14. Gertrude Scholl, *Students against Tyranny* (Middletown, 1965), p. 37.

15. In pre-Freudian language, one might have described this phenomenon in terms of simple self-respect. Today, Freudians could argue that since Scholl and his friends saw resistance as a "duty" or obligation, their behavior should be understood as resulting from a superego rather than an ego process. But close study of the Scholl group suggests that they were consciously committed to resistance in a fully rational fashion. Their long planning sessions, careful preparation and distribution of leaflets, as well as their conduct following arrest, all offer evidence of serious ego functioning rather than reflexive working out of guilt feelings usually associated with superego processes. They were, moreover, guilty of nothing.

16. "... the question remains whether this *action* by Jews within the resistance can properly be called Jewish resistance. It would seem that in Western Europe there was no such thing; ... the majority of Jews were completely assimilated and had no desire to be any different from their fellow-countrymen; many were no longer practising Jews. In the Resistance, therefore, the behaviour of the Jews in no way differed from that of other Frenchmen, Belgians or Dutchmen." *The Shadow War: Resistance in Europe 1939–1945,* H. Michel (London, 1972), p. 179.

17. Leon Poliakov, "Jewish Resistance in France," *YIVO Annual of Jewish Social Science* 8 (1954), 252–63.

18. Isaac Kabeli, "The Resistance of the Greek Jews," *ibid.,* pp. 281–88.

19. This conclusion is supported with the evidence presented in Lucien Steinberg, *Not As a Lamb* (Farnborough, 1974) and in Yuri Suhl ed., *They Fought Back* (New York, 1968). Suhl, in particular, maintains that Jewish resistance throughout Europe has thus far been drastically underestimated by Holocaust scholars because relevant documents and testimony have been slow to emerge and remain quite scattered. The second edition ("with corrections") of Steinberg's book was published as *The Jews against Hitler* (London, 1978).

20. H. Michel, *The Shadow War (op. cit.),* p. 180. See also Reuben Ainsztein (*Wiener Library Bulletin*, nos. 1 and 2, 1958), who concludes that the Polish government in exile followed a policy that explicitly ruled out military action to aid the Jews. However, Ainsztein's major work, *Jewish Resistance in Nazi-Occupied Eastern Europe* (London, 1974), has been subjected to some severe criticism.

21. For more details, see Alfred Katz, *Poland's Ghettos at War* (New York, 1970).

22. An example of all this is given in Suhl, *They Fought Back (op. cit.),* pp. 189–91: in

August 1942 the 2,000 Jews living in the small Belorussian town of Lachwa attacked an SS squad attempting to round them up for killing. Using hand weapons they broke through the SS cordon. Approximately 600 reached shelter in the forests, but many of these were killed by antisemitic peasants and native police acting as SS auxiliaries. Some 120 of the Lachwa survivors are stated to have eventually managed to join the partisans. Many similar cases in Western Belorussia, the Minsk area and the Ukraine are documented in Shalom Cholawsky ed., *Sefer ha-partizanim ha-yehudim* (Tel Aviv, 1959), vol. I.

23.   There were some 28 Jewish partisan units in central Poland alone. On the other hand, Jews also participated in the general resistance—about a thousand of them in the *Polish* Warsaw uprising of 1944. See now Shmuel Krakowski, *Lehimah yehudit be-Polin neged ha-natzim 1942–1944* (Tel Aviv, 1977).

24.   The story of 24-year-old Mordechai Anielewicz, who became commander of the Jewish Fighting Organization (ZOB) in Warsaw, exemplified this cruel dilemma. A leader of the Left-wing Zionist youth (Hashomer Hatzair), he became committed to armed resistance only in 1942, when it became plain that a fighting death to preserve the honor of and provide a heritage for the Jewish people was all that remained as an alternative to the extermination camps. "The young but quickly maturing Mordechai understood that at present there was but one question: What kind of death would the Polish Jews select for themselves . . . The moment Mordechai decided on struggle, no other questions existed for him." E. Ringelblum in Suhl, *op. cit.,* p. 112.

25.   Armed resistance attempts were also made at Czestochowa, a major Polish industrial center, at Bedzin, at Tarnow and in other places.

26.   These conclusions concern Polish Jews in the heart of German-controlled territory. In Western Belorussia, on the other hand, where the number of Jewish resisters is measured in tens of thousands, commitment to a militant ideology was not a determining factor. Here the nearness of the forests and the existence of Soviet partisans provided both a sufficient alternative authority system and a reasonable probability of success.

27.   An example comes from Elie Wiesel's *Night* (New York, 1960), p. 40. When the boy Elie reached Auschwitz with his father and others, they were accosted by an old prisoner as they waited for selection:

"What have you come here for, you sons of bitches? What are you doing here, eh?"

Someone dared to answer him. . . .

"You shut your trap, you filthy swine. . . . You'd have done better to have hanged yourselves where you were than to come here. Didn't you know what was in store for you at Auschwitz?"

. . . . His tone of voice became increasingly brutal.

"Do you see that chimney over there? See it? Do you see those flames? (Yes, we did see the flames.) Over there—that's where you're going to be taken. That's your grave, over there. Haven't you realized it yet? You dumb bastards, don't you understand anything? You're going to be burned. Frizzled away. Turned into ashes."

Later, Wiesel himself began to be transformed. When his father contracted dysentery he could do little except watch him sink slowly toward death. When his father finally died, Wiesel's sorrow was mixed with a feeling of relief, for a great burden to his own survival had been removed.

28.   Primo Levi, *Survival in Auschwitz* (London, 1961), pp. 80–81. A survivor from Treblinka expressed similar views while being interviewed by Gitta Sereny in connection with her book about Franz Stangl, *Into That Darkness* (New York, 1974). "Did we become hardened, callous to the suffering, the horror around us? . . . One did, I think, develop a kind of dullness, a

numbness where the daily nightmarish events became a kind of routine, and only special horrors aroused us, reminded us of normal feelings . . ." (p. 192). And he indicated how national differences influenced this process: "The (Eastern) Polish Jews; they were people from a different world. They were filthy. It was impossible to feel any compassion, any solidarity with them" (p. 198).

29.   The extraordinary transformation experienced by old prisoners is illustrated by the statement given to Gitta Sereny (*op. cit.*, pp. 212–13) by a Treblinka survivor. After first explaining that the Jewish workers lived on the supplies stripped from incoming transports, he described what happened when for a time the trainloads of victims ceased arriving:

> Things went from bad to worse that month of March. . . . There were no transports—in February just a few, remnants from here and there, then a few hundred gypsies—*they* were really poor; they brought nothing. In the storehouses everything had been packed up and shipped—we had never before seen all the space because it had always been so full. . . . You can't imagine what we felt when there was nothing there. You see, the *things* were our justification for being alive. If there were no *things* to administer, why would they let us stay alive? On top of that we were, for the first time, hungry. . . .
>
> It was just about when we had reached the lowest ebb in our morale that, one day towards the end of March, Kurt Franz walked into our barracks, a wide grin on his face. 'As of tomorrow,' he said, 'transports will be rolling in again.' And do you know what we did? We shouted 'Hurrah, hurrah.' It seems impossible now. Every time I think of it I die a small death; but it's the truth. That is what we did; that is where we had got to. And sure enough, the next morning they arrived. We had spent all of the preceding evening in an excited, expectant mood; it meant life—you see, don't you?—safety and life. The fact that it was their death, whoever they were, which meant our life, was no longer relevant . . .

30.   Raul Hilberg, *The Destruction of the European Jews* (Chicago, 1961), p. 586.

31.   See Alexander Pechersky, "Revolt in Sobibor," in Suhl, *op. cit.,* (note 19 above), pp. 33–79.

32.   Shmuel Krakowski, *op. cit.* (note 23 above); Isaac Kabeli, *op. cit.* (note 18 above).

33.   Sim Kessel, *Hanged at Auschwitz* (New York, 1972).

34.   For instance, those recorded in Meyer Barkai, *op. cit.* (note 3 above), and in Leon Wells, *The Janowska Road* (New York, 1963).

35.   Sim Kessel, *op. cit.,* pp. 43–44.

36.   For more detailed discussion, see David Littlejohn, *The Patriotic Traitors* (London, 1972).

37.   The "thirteeners" are discussed in detail (with documentary material) by A. Rozenberg, "Dos draytsentl," *Bletter far Geshichte* 5 (1952), 116–48.

38.   See Isaiah Trunk, *Judenrat* (New York, 1972) for details.

39.   Zelig Kalmanovitch, "A Diary of the Nazi Ghetto in Vilna," *YIVO Annual of Jewish Social Science* 8 (1953), p. 31.

40.   *Ibid.,* pp. 65–67.

41.   Jacob Presser, *The Destruction of the Dutch Jews* (New York, 1969), p. 276.

42.   See Lucien Steinberg, *op. cit.* (note 19 above), pp. 106–11; Leon Poliakov, *op. cit.* (note 17 above). A similar situation obtained in Belgium.

43.   In his memorial to the young leader of the Warsaw Ghetto fighters, Emmanuel Ringelblum spoke to the very point under discussion here:

Mordechai and his fellows of the young generation knew too little about the history of freedom or they would have known that in such stormy times one had to give less consideration to the resolutions of committees and administrations and depend more on oneself, and one's own healthy instincts. . . . That truth was understood by the youth only when it was too late, when the majority of Warsaw Jews were already in Treblinka.

In Suhl, *op. cit.* (note 19 above), p. 114.

    44. *Ibid.*, p. 113.

Discussion: The *Judenrat*
and the Jewish Response

Opening Statement by **HENRY L. FEINGOLD:** More than a decade and a half has passed since Hannah Arendt, in the *Eichmann in Jerusalem* (New York, 1963), labeled the actions of the Jewish leadership and communal organizations during the Holocaust as "the darkest chapter of Jewish history." Arendt argued that without those leaders, whom she described as collaborators almost without exception, far fewer Jews would have died. Her indictment raised a storm of protest in the Jewish community. Almost to a man, Jewish spokesmen rejected Arendt's contention. Jacob Robinson, in *And the Crooked Shall Be Made Straight* (New York, 1965), wrote a virtual line by line refutation of Arendt's narrative.

Yet her picture of millions of Jews going passively to their deaths, betrayed by their leaders, continued to lacerate the fragile Jewish self-image that had sought to reconstitute itself after the Holocaust. Despite the slaughter of a third of their brethren in the catastrophe, the rise of the State of Israel had helped Jews to live, if not with ease then with determination, in the post-Holocaust world. Moreover, the government of West Germany had acknowledged the guilt of the German people and was at least making a monetary restoration. Now they were being told that it need not have happened the way it did. Things would have been less difficult had they had better leaders, had they shown more courage. The bitter accusation regarding Jewish leadership, especially its Zionist component, had devastating implications, since it was that leadership, or its direct heirs, that was still making the community's decisions.

There was an element of futility in the debate over Arendt's book. Neither she nor her respondents had much concrete knowledge about the role of the Jewish Councils or *Judenräte* that the Nazis had everywhere created as representatives of the captive Jewish communities. It was only Isaiah Trunk who first provided a fragment of the missing evidence in *Judenrat* (New York, 1972), an exhaustive study of the Jewish Councils in a certain area of Eastern Europe.

In the mass of data that he compiled, one can find confirmation and negation for every contention regarding Jewish behavior under stress. We learn that for every seeming act of knavery and cowardice there was an exception, while even outstanding acts of courage can now be questioned as to their wisdom and price. Moreover, the behavior of Jews under Nazi hegemony was by no means uniform, but depended greatly on time, place, personality, and frequently sheer caprice. Given this glimpse into the extraordinary complexity of human reactions to those extreme conditions, no judgments should be passed lightly and no generalization *ex post facto* can fully encompass the reality.

It is difficult to define the nature of the Jewish Councils and their place in history. Were they examples of Jewish self-governance following the precedent of the *kahal* (Jewish communal representation) of former times, as Trunk maintains, or were they merely Nazi-controlled administrative instruments designed as preconditions for the Final Solution? The evidence indicates that they were both. The paradox inherent in the Jewish condition under the Nazi heel was that the same organization could serve both life and death. It required organization to keep Jews alive during the ghettoization period and subsequently it required organization to dispatch them to their death. In practice both functions existed side by side in the communal organization. And ultimately they merged when many Council leaders became convinced that the death of some would assure the life of others.

Amidst the appalling conditions of the ghetto, with starvation, congestion, epidemics, and separation trauma all purposefully created by Nazi policy to wear down the Jewish population, there developed a remarkable continuance of Jewish community life. The dependent part of the Jewish population, the orphans, the aged and the sick, were nurtured. For a time the traditional service agencies represented by the JSS (Jewish Social Welfare) and JDC (Joint Distribution Committee) continued to function in the ghetto. A lively cultural, educational, and economic life also characterized the initial phase of ghettoization. In the midst of their struggle for existence, Jews organized schools, vocational retraining, choirs, theaters, lectures, gardening clubs, orchestras, libraries, museums, factories, and even the manufacture of much needed pharmaceuticals. Jewish genius lay in that impulse toward community. The community dissolution suggested by Arendt was not remotely possible.

The persistence of such civic virtues explains why it was so difficult for Jews to understand that their normal attitude toward community and society had to be reversed. Their strength became a lethal weakness. They sought violinists for the orchestra and teachers for the children rather than machine-gunners and sappers. The former prospered in the Jewish community, the latter were nonexistent. As the screws of the Final Solution tightened, Jews understood only vaguely that the same administrative apparatus that had nurtured them could also be used to organize them for death. Indeed the aging, the dependent, the sick, and the starving, those who had first claim on community concern, were the first to be sent to die. Time transformed the function of the Jewish Council from the life-supporting one that Jews automatically assigned to it, to the death-dealing one that the Nazi authorities intended.

In the end it was those who actually had power, the Nazi authorities, who determined the role of the Jewish Councils. Indeed, it is only by ignoring this crucial question of power that Trunk was able to reach his one major conclusion: that the Jewish Councils created by the Nazis are examples of Jewish governance rather than some "unique and queer" episode, that they enter the mainstream of Jewish history through the *kahal* or local communal agency by which Jews governed themselves in the sixteenth, seventeenth, and eighteenth centuries in Russia and Poland.

In recruiting poor Jewish youth for military service, it is argued, the *kahal* (*kehillah* in Poland) had set a precedent for consigning Jews to death, at least in a symbolic sense, since the brutalization and frequent baptism involved in army service were considered to be a form of death by the community. Jewish leaders withheld the *gute kep,* the smart ones who would be an asset to the community. The merchants and the wealthy were able to gain exemption. Though the kahal did not deliver up life itself, the selection from the poor and powerless was not unlike that of the Councils during the Holocaust. It was a matter of degree rather than of kind, Trunk maintained.

But there is a qualitative difference between the *kahals* and the Jewish Councils. The latter exercised far greater power over their subjects than the former and they exercised it precisely because they ruled by proxy. While in the early stages of ghettoization they were able to alleviate the drastic conditions imposed by the Nazi overlords, it became apparent when the critical "resettlement" period arrived that they were merely instruments in Nazi hands. Power, the defining element in any government equation, was not ultimately theirs at all. The parallel drawn with the role of the *kahals* in Tsarist Russia is inadequate because it disregards those modern techniques of governing that allow the state to absorb virtually all the power in society, techniques that were not yet available to the Tsarist regime.

In assigning Jewish Council leaders a role for which the necessary power did not exist in the captive Jewish community, Trunk appears to fall into the same pit as did Arendt. The Nazis, it should be recalled, turned on the Jews of Eastern Europe with a special vengeance. The situation they created for Jews in the ghettos and camps most closely approximated the classic totalitarian condition of complete powerlessness of the governed confronted by complete power of the governors. In such circumstances it seems perverse to talk of Jewish governance, especially when a theoretical framework concerning the role of power in the government equation is omitted. What it does do is extend the idea of betrayal and collaboration back into Jewish history and diminish the horrendous particularity of the Holocaust.

Arendt's model of a passive Jewish community led like sheep to the slaughter by a defective Jewish leadership turns out, on close examination, to be a caricature. Take first the Council membership. The Councils were established by an administrative order of October 12, 1939 that gave the German Security Police power to select and replace the members of the Council at will. While some 43 percent of members had been active in prewar community life, according to Trunk the majority were chosen with "arbitrary recklessness" by the Nazi taskmasters. Frequently nothing more than a knowledge of German was sufficient, or newcomers forcibly transported from some distant point were selected.

Within the Council the reaction to crisis was far from uniform. Some members "assimilated the morals of the oppressors," especially after the first "resettlement" actions when the struggle for survival became even more pronounced. But there were instances of courage and self-sacrifice, too. Some Council leaders refused to carry out Nazi orders and were either shot by the Nazis or voluntarily joined the "resettlement" transports to the death camps. Nor did membership in the Council give a much better opportunity to survive. Only 12 percent lived out the Holocaust. And four of the most powerful Council leaders, Mordecai Chaim Rumkowski (Lodz), Roman Merin (Eastern Upper Silesia), Jacob Gens (Vilna), and Ephraim Barash (Bialystok) were killed by the Nazis. They ruled supreme in the ghettos but, like all Jews, were powerless in relation to their Nazi tormentors.

Arendt's model does not give a just picture of the Jewish communities. It understates, as already noted, both their social activities and the desperate conditions that prevailed. We should also recall that the population, especially of the larger ghettos, was highly disparate. Only for the Nazis was a Jew simply a Jew. Class, regional, religious, and political differences among Jews were accentuated by the crisis. The ghetto population was swollen by refugees from Central Europe whose cultural style and reaction to the crisis varied markedly from their Eastern European brethren. Frequently stemming from the German *Kulturgebiet,* these refugees tended to be highly legalistic, trusting in government and therefore more easily taken in by Nazi fraud; they were readier, for instance, to report to collection points and believe what the Nazis told them about their destination. They thought that fate would differentiate them from the Jews of the East while the latter had little love to spare for them, convinced, as they were, that their own had been "resettled" to make room for these "aliens." There were also baptized Jews in certain ghettos who were Jews only according to Nazi racial laws and neither thought of themselves, nor were thought of by Jews, as affiliated with Judaism. In a sense these were the most tragic victims of all, since they belonged nowhere, having been rejected both by the non-Jewish community to which they had sought to belong and by the Jewish one which they had left.

It was also difficult to grasp that the Nazis intended to liquidate *all* the Jews. There was daily evidence that utilitarian, commercial, and venial considerations motivated even the most fanatical Nazis. So if Jews could prove useful to the Nazi war effort and profitable to local Nazis, surely these would not choose to kill the goose that laid the golden egg. Most Councils therefore attempted the strategies of "rescue through work" and "rescue through bribery." They linked their plans for survival to the only reality they knew, that of petty capitalism. Had there been an element of bookkeeping rationale in Nazi plans for the Jews, the Councils might have had some success. But the totally irrational nature of Nazi thinking on the Jewish question made the Council's strategems for survival a death sentence for their subjects. The point is that it was a failure of mind, not a murder conspiracy.

The hope that some might be saved proved to be the strongest obstacle to armed resistance. Shaped by a pre-Nazi mentality, Council leaders and their ghetto subjects naturally assumed that strategies of survival other than resistance would save more lives. Even today their logic is difficult to refute. The slightest hint of resistance, even the shirking of compulsory labor, produced draconic reprisals against innocent ghetto inhabitants. The Council leaders opposed resistance not only because of the predictable toll it would take in lives, but also because they felt it would interfere with what they thought were "more practical" strategies.

Resistance often did not ultimately save many lives when it did occur. When the Lachwa Ghetto, under Council leadership, attempted mass flight to the surrounding forest, only 600 of the ghetto's 2,000 inmates escaped, and only 100 to 120 survived the war. In the case of the Warsaw Ghetto uprising, it was intended less as a strategy of survival than a way of redeeming Jewish honor. It was led by young, highly politicized elements who were concerned about such things. Most significantly, it occurred when much of the dependent civilian population of the ghetto had already been "resettled."

Still, today the question of resistance is raised over and over again, especially by young people. Why did they go "like sheep to the slaughter" rather than leaving us with a heroic model with which we could live? Before he was himself consumed by the flames, Emmanuel Ringelblum, chronicler of the Warsaw Ghetto, posed the same agonized question: "One of the problems of great import," he wrote, "is the passivity of the Jewish masses, dying without a whimper. Why are they so quiet? Why are the fathers, mothers and all the children dying without protest?"

To what extent can we answer Ringelblum's question, we who can experience their agony only vicariously? What do we know? At one point, certainly, we know that they wanted desperately to live. They dared hope that some might be spared and, failing this, that their lives might be extended for a few hours or days. "A shu gelebt is oichet gelebt" (to have lived an hour is also to have lived) became the conventional wisdom. Each extra day among the living was a separate victory. They did not lightly abandon their notion of a future because to do so would be taking the first small steps away from life. Real resistance could not develop until all hope was abandoned. It was part of the diabolical cleverness of the Nazi overlords that they developed all kinds of subterfuges to keep a glimmer of hope alive.

What we see is the behavior of a people who at first would not comprehend their fate and used every alternative, including the sacrifice of life, to keep death from their door. Only when every avenue had been exhausted did they withdraw into passivity and prepare themselves for death. Such withdrawal was not unlike that of a person with a terminal illness who at the irreversible stage withdraws from life.

The simple model of governance behind the Arendt indictment needs a more rigorous examination. We need to know the extent to which the policy of the Jewish Councils represented a consensus within the Jewish community rather than, as Arendt suggests, a decision imposed by an all-powerful corrupt Jewish leadership. Unfortunately, Trunk offers relatively little data on this crucial question. There are certain clues, however, which point to a measure of consensus in many cases. For example, relatively few of the respondents to Trunk's questionnaire, all of whom were survivors, condemned the policy of *their own* Council outright. One may also ask whether the remarkable economic and cultural activity in the early stages of the ghettos could have been achieved with a recalcitrant citizenry. Jews were inclined to accomodation because they thought it offered a better chance of survival. After the first taste of Nazi occupation policy, when Jews became aware of the dangers of living among hostile people, relatively few chose the option of trying to "pass" on the outside. Despite the rapid decline of their fortunes in the ghettos, the only alternatives seemed less hopeful.

Once the first small steps toward a policy of accommodation were taken, imperceptibly new steps were exacted by the Nazi authorities: compulsory labor, limited egress from the ghetto, statistical tabulations, and endless lists. Finally the surrender of life for "resettlement," which almost everyone soon knew was death. Why did the Council leaders not stop here? The decision was not taken easily, but often after many hours of debate. Yet in the end most Councils, viewing themselves as captains on a sinking ship with a limited number of lifeboats, decided to try to influence the selection rather than allowing the Nazis to do it themselves. In so doing they eschewed the well-known ruling of Maimonides, that all should face death rather than surrender even one Jew to be killed. They followed instead the advice of Rabbi Avraham Duber Shapiro, an elder of the Kaunus (Kovno) Ghetto, who shortly before a resettlement action in 1941, advised the Council leaders that "if a Jewish community (may God help it) has been condemned to physical destruction, and there are means of rescuing part of it, the leaders of the community should have the courage to assume the responsibility to act and rescue what is possible." Was this the choice of an opportunistic and short-sighted leadership willing to condemn Jews to death so that they themselves might live, as Arendt implies?

Of course, opportunism was not absent among functionaries and leaders especially in certain Councils. It was even more conspicuous among the ghetto police, many of whom were not above extorting money from those who wanted to avoid resettlement transports. Opportunism and corruption came to the fore wherever the Nazis held sway, among both the Jews and other subject peoples. But this was not the reason for following the path of Rabbi Shapiro rather than Maimonides.

Consider how many decisions taken during the Holocaust implied some choice between life and death. John J. McCloy decided not to bomb the death camps and the rail lines leading to them. Certain children in France were selected to be spirited across the Pyrenees while others were not. Certain Jews were given Palestine certificates while others were not. A ransom proposal to save Hungarian Jewry was rejected. As we draw closer to the inferno, the existence of these agonizing choices becomes even more apparent. Those who chose to resist in the Lachwa and Warsaw Ghettos could avoid the death of innocents no more than the leaders of the Councils, since resistance involved not only retribution but also conflict against a heavily armed and vengeful enemy whose victory was a foregone conclusion.

Once one realizes that *all* Jews were condemned to die, not by the cowardice of Jewish or even the indifference of Allied leaders, but by a demented Nazi leadership, there is no avoiding the life-and-death choices that had to be made. In that context the auxiliary decisions by Jewish leaders were intended to save some of the doomed. Rather than leave the selections to blind fate, they tried to influence them, usually without much more success. The charge by Arendt was callous and obscene, but not because it could not be made to fit the facts. In a superficial sense what she observed is not false, just as it is not false to say that a surgeon cripples his patient when he amputates a limb trapped in the wreck of a vehicle. By ripping the actions of Jewish leaders out of a context in which *all* Jews were condemned to death, her account transformed the victims into their own murderers.

Even when Arendt's charge is considered in its simplest terms, that fewer Jews would have died had there been no Jewish leadership, it does not stand up. The *Einsatzgruppen,* those special SS killer units that operated behind the German lines in Russia, slaughtered a million and a half Jews in relatively short order. Yet in these areas the Jewish leadership and community infrastructure had been eliminated by the Soviet regime for at least a generation. The labor roundups in the ghetto furnish another example. When they were conducted directly by the SS they were much crueler and more costly in lives, so much so, that Jewish leaders were compelled to organize their own compulsory labor system in order to avoid the gratuitous violence that accompanied SS actions.

Something perverse occurs when victims, and to some extent witnesses, are singled out for a large share of the responsibility as they have been by Hannah Arendt and Arthur Morse. There is, of course, an element of truth in all such accusations—Jewish leaders were guilty, the Pope was guilty, and Roosevelt was guilty. Eventually we are all guilty. It is a very distinctive aspect of the Holocaust that no one who was touched by it can ever again be innocent. It makes everything gruesome. Though in the face of such an enormous catastrophe enough could never have been done, the witness is nevertheless upbraided for not doing enough. The case of the victim is a special one. We are disturbed because he did not give us evidence of that kernel of courage whereby we could redeem *our* fallen image of man and of ourselves. So we rummage through the evidence and, behold, the witnesses find that actually the victims were guilty. We are off the hook. They were responsible for their own fate and they are not here to deny it. There is only one problem. When all are guilty—none are guilty. So here there appears another perverse feature of Arendt's charge against Jewish leadership and organization: it lacks particularity. In order to make sense of it, she must tell us how Jewish leaders were even more guilty than others touched by the Holocaust. A careful reading of Trunk's book tells us that they were not.

Isaiah Trunk's *Judenrat* is a well organized compilation of data, a good example of what an assiduous researcher can do. In the area of Holocaust research there is still a great need to unearth the facts and in that sense it is an important work. All the same, it lacks life and vision, and it does so because Trunk felt that the nature of the material and the diverse socio-psychological background of the individuals forbade generalization. Except for a brief moment in the last chapter, he resisted the temptation to break this self-imposed rule. His book is thus a compendium of data about the Jewish Councils; a somewhat quixotic book, especially in relation to that of Arendt, which undoubtedly motivated its being undertaken. After years of painstaking research and much thinking on the question of Jewish governance during the Holocaust, Trunk made only several minor judgments. Arendt, on the other hand, with almost no basic research available, made major judgments on the subject. The one ventured too little, the other too much. The ideal situation would have been to let an Arendt loose on Trunk's data.

Trunk's hesitancy was due partly to his method of research on the subject. Once he had decided to use what he calls the "inductive" method, Trunk avoided secondary works available in the field of government and totalitarianism. It not only led him into a rather naive error regarding the problems of power and governance, but gives his work an unwarranted *de novo* flavor. There are many secondary works, such as Karl Dietrich Bracher's *The German Dictatorship* (New York, 1970) and some of the superb works now available on the SS and other administrative agencies involved with the Final Solution, on whose shoulders Trunk might have stood. Stanley Hoffmann's concept of *collaboration d'état*—see his *In Search of France* (Cambridge, Mass., 1963)—is applied, if somewhat mechanically, by Trunk; it is nevertheless an indication of how the data might have been brought to life.

Paradoxically Trunk, who did not dare assign meaning to his data, had far less hesitation about the kinds of evidence he used. A questionnaire, a specimen of which the reader is never shown, was used to elicit information from select survivors. The testimony of survivors may have a bias, since they are bound to view rescue strategies in a certain light though other factors may account for their survival. They may be alive today because they were more ruthless, for example, or perhaps more fortunate, than others. But the mere fact of their survival predisposes them to view the whole notion of rescue more favorably. At the same time, those who might present countervailing evidence are not alive to make their case. Trunk, it is true, took great care in how he used the evidence elicited. But the statistical data are of questionable validity. One wonders at such daring with respect to evidence and such timidity with regard to synthesis.

But what Trunk set out to do, he did well. Indeed he came close to asking nothing of the victims except that they render their story. That is a refreshing change after the polemics about opportunistic leadership on the one hand, and heroes and martyrs on the other.

RAUL HILBERG: I am myself a political scientist. Here I represent that particular profession and that particular approach to the study of the mass destruction of the Jews. Years ago I began my study of the way in which the Germans organized the task of destroying Jewry throughout Europe. The clue to understanding what transpired was to be sought, I thought, in the first instance by close examination of the German machinery of destruction and the acts that emanated from it in all strata of the German bureaucracy. If we were to examine what happened to the Jews without an adequate knowledge of *who* it was and *what* it was that hit them, we would be talking in a void, we would not know what had actually transpired. As a matter of fact, words like "Holocaust" tend to obscure the fact that what transpired was a series of acts, acts by the thousands, measures, laws, which came out of a modern technological bureaucracy.

At the time I was writing, however, I was also aware of a particular differentiation in approaching this subject owing to the sources then at hand. The Germans had left a great many documents, which, of course, were found after the war and gathered up for war-crimes trials and archives. What was available from the Jews, on the other hand, was in the main their biographical accounts, their memoirs, and their recollections. So there was a great discrepancy between these two kinds of source materials and between the resulting kinds of histories: the history of the Germans and the history of the Jews, one emanating from documents, the other from personal recollections. The documents were relatively brief, though their implications were often sweeping. The personal recollections of the Jews were long, but they dealt with isolated detail.

It was not until I visited Jerusalem for a somewhat lengthy stay in 1968, in the archives of Yad Vashem, that I became aware of something I should have known or predicted all along, but which I simply could not grasp until I saw it physically. Namely, the records of the Jewish bureaucracies—of the Jewish Councils and their departments—in Jerusalem, whether on microfilm or in the original, now still fragmented, still very partial, but already amounting to hundreds of thousands or millions of documents. From this I had my first inkling of the fact that not only was German destructive activity bureaucratic, but so also was Jewish dying. That there was a Jewish history which was not merely personal but also organizational, having to do not only with the way people felt, with their attitudes and reactions individual by individual, but also a very voluminous, complex and difficult subject matter, namely, the organization of Jewish life under the Nazis during the thirties and early forties.

It was some years after this first experience that I received a letter from an editor of the Macmillan Publishing Company. "Would you," asked the letter, "like to do a book? Anything. How about ghettos?" And I immediately replied that I knew of a person who had labored all his life on that very subject and that his name was Isaiah Trunk. I had not actually read his manuscript, although I had seen portions of it published in various places such as *Yad Vashem Studies.* And thus there came into print the first pathbreaking major study of Jewish ghetto life: Trunk's book entitled *Judenrat.* Here was for the first time a really comprehensive work, even though limited to Eastern Europe, and one that was written, may I say, with extreme modesty. Although the title seems to promise only an examination of the personnel of the Jewish Councils, in point of fact the book is much more. It is one of those rare works, which instead of promising more than it delivers, delivers more than it actually promised.

It is a study of the entire domain and its various aspects, socio-economic, political, legal, cultural, and religious. It is some 700 pages long and contains approximately 2,000 footnotes taken for the first time in a major way from documentation, whether reports of Jewish Councils or minutes of Council meetings or whatever fragmentary data there may have been from departments within the various Councils, or some critically important diary such as that of Adam Czerniakow of the Warsaw Ghetto. There are also, of course, German documents and personal recollections, and finally a survey in which survivors were asked to give their recollections of Council members: what they did, how they acted, and what happened.

I find it rather important that the book is organized not under chapter headings such as "Warsaw Ghetto," "Lodz Ghetto," etc., and that it is not an enumeration of the various ghettos of Eastern Europe, but rather that it is a book in which each chapter takes up some basic aspect of ghetto life and examines the way that aspect was manifested in all of the ghettos. Such organization is of the utmost importance because it demonstrates once and for all not only the feasibility, but in my view, the *inevitability* of looking at the ghetto structure as a whole. Admittedly, the ghettos were isolated with relatively little communication among them. Admittedly, too, there were profound demographic, economic, and social differences between Western and Eastern Poland and between small and large ghettos in each of these regions. Yet all these differences are submerged in the totality of the one and overwhelming concept of the ghetto as a particular kind—a particular form— of Jewish government. And rightly so. For while we may make distinctions among the various ghettos and the various experiences, the distinctions do not have much meaning unless they are anchored within a single phenomenon, unless they represent positions on a scale measuring whatever there is to be measured. Before, in other words, we try to separate one instance from another, let us recognize the totality to begin with.

Trunk has done just that. But he came to his conclusions very tentatively, very modestly, and he divided them up amongst the various chapters, sometimes even in very brief passages and sentences rather than, as one might have expected in a work of that magnitude, in a vast concluding chapter. It is as if he did not wish to come to conclusions. All the more so, the conclusions that emerge from his manuscript and his facts are compelling because he did not necessarily welcome them.

As it was the purpose of my paper to extract those conclusions from his book, I need not recapitulate them here. Nor will I now go into the inevitable question about resistance. I will say but one thing on that subject and that is that there is a tendency to investigate resistance and resistance strategy as if individual Jews made their own decisions. Somewhere to find a gun, or somehow to escape, or in some way to take some action against the German occupation forces. But just as the destructive activity of the Germans was not merely or even primarily the activities of individuals, just as one can see how the destruction was bureaucratic and organized, so we must also look at resistance in a somewhat broader perspective. It is not an individual or even a bunch of individuals that will resist, but an organization.

So if you ask where the resistance was, why there was or was not resistance, you inevitably ask questions about Jewish social organization, about Jewish traditions, about the political climate—to borrow a phrase from my own discipline—within the ghetto communities. Why was there apparently no intelligence service, pure and simple? Why did perhaps no one think of that? Why, when the ghetto walls were closing around Warsaw or the fences around some other ghettos, were there hardly any weapons inside? It is not a question of how difficult it was to procure them; it was that in the Jewish community there were hardly any to begin with, even before the formation of the ghettos and before the German occupation itself.

In short, the question is not why particular acts took place at a particular moment, but why many preceding acts had taken place in a particular way. The Jews were prepared for pogroms, for sporadic acts of violence against them. But they were not prepared for the death blow from the nation of Goethe and Schiller that struck them in 1942 and 1943. And this is the crux of the matter.

Let me add in conclusion that the whole subject of Jewish life under the Nazis in the terminal hours of its existence is really just now surfacing as a field for study. Perhaps it was inevitable that the gathering of documents, which took a whole generation, should have made us wait until now before asking more detailed questions. Should we ask them? This I need not answer. Safe to say that the victims—and that is what I call them, rather than heroes or martyrs—were all human beings. And because they were all human beings they displayed all the contradictions and all the faults and drawbacks that human beings have as well as all the strengths. It is not serving the cause of memory to leave out one half of their personalities, their failures as it were, their quandaries, their uncertainties. Yes, even their great anxieties and paralysis. It does not serve them well, and it does not serve us well, because they are we and we are they.

YEHUDA BAUER: I think that our great problem, when dealing with the life of Jews under Nazi rule, is that of discerning the kind of reaction that prevailed amongst Jews, as individuals and as communities, to a totally unprecedented and absolutely unexpected development. This immediately raises the problem of predictability—could they have foreseen what was coming? Here I, too, am of the opinion that they could not possibly have known.

Of course there were anxieties, there were fears. People went around with poison in their pockets and purses years before 1942. But their knowledge of what was happening around them was qualified in two significant respects. There was, first, the feeling that this could not possibly be true—even after receiving knowledge which an outsider, living after the event, might consider incontrovertible. For it was a unique situation, in the sense that that had not happened before, and the adjustment to such knowledge would have taken longer than the Jews had time.

The second qualification is that certain groups of Jewish people in certain places were more apt to receive such knowledge and understand it, internalize it, than were others. Those that were less interwoven with the life of their surroundings, Jewish or otherwise, such as the youth movements— Zionist, Communist or Bundist—and other individuals or groups who had torn themselves consciously apart from their communities prior to receiving the knowledge, were more apt to understand it and internalize it. Even for them the time was extremely short and limited because Jewish groups and organizations, the *Judenräte* and the people, knew only in part that they were living within a system of Nazi bureaucracy that had decided on their destruction. The part that was known was that they were living in what the Nazis intended to be a self-destructive organization.

There is another major problem: the common misunderstanding and failure of historians to appreciate the quality of what I term unarmed resistance amongst the Jewish population. The case of the stained-glass windows in Czerniakow's office is a good example because they were not put up for any other purpose than to provide work for somebody who would otherwise have perished of starvation, and to express a morale-building reaction to what was happening all around. It is the same with the over one thousand House Committees in the Warsaw Ghetto. Ineffective in preventing destruction, certainly. But very often effective in providing a moral answer to a situation in which the human being was deprived of his humanity.

The same energies that Jews expressed in certain areas of Europe in armed resistance, which was much, much broader in scope than is normally realized, went in other areas—where arms simply were not readily available—into other forms of activity. The fact that the Nazi domination in these areas was complete is just one half of the story. The other half is that which says what the human being under such domination did in order to preserve certain elements, at least, of his dignity.

A relevant point is that the Nazi bureaucracy itself cannot (to my mind) be understood as a successful totalitarian regime, in the sense that successful totalitarianism would imply the complete domination of a clear-minded bureaucracy over all aspects of life. In fact, the Nazi bureaucracy was split and divided on a large number of issues. It was composed of conflicting factions. The realism of some of the *Judenräte* in trying to exploit the differences within the Nazi bureaucracy does not testify to their submission to that bureaucracy in the sense of lack of will to find a way out. It rather testifies to a realistic attempt in the circumstances they were confronting to find a way of defending the communities over which they had been put in charge.

Now let me turn specifically to Isaiah Trunk's book on the *Judenrat*, which is a truly great book, but which—as I noted in my paper—has some weaknesses. My main issue with Trunk is that although he professes to eschew generalization, he implies generalization about the *Judenräte* that is factually incorrect. For his analysis encompasses only a certain part of Eastern Europe: not Western Europe, not the Balkans, not (except for brief mention) the areas of the Soviet Union invaded by the Nazis after June 22, 1941. And even in the part of Eastern Europe that it does cover, his analysis, as my paper indicated, tends to disguise differences among ghettos because it is always a "horizontal" analysis.

The reactions of the Jewish bureaucracies were simply very different in different cases. For even though they did not know and could not have known they were facing absolutely unexpected, unpredictable, and unprecedented developments, the adjustment of some, though not all, was quite amazing and out of the ordinary. Nor can the differences between the reactions of different *Judenräte* be explained solely by internal or German developments.

Consider Kovno and Vilna, to give an obvious example, where the *Judenräte* acted under different assumptions, different kinds of what Trunk calls "strategies," and yet were composed of individuals with the same background, who acted in communities with the same kind of structure, and in similar environments. Or consider the Netherlands and Belgium: adjacent countries likewise with similar Jewish communities, where one national *Judenrat* manifested complete submission and executed those tasks for which it had been set up by the Nazis, whereas the other did exactly the opposite. This means that Trunk's implicit generalization is invalid, but also that there can be no counter-generalization. In other words, the Jews neither acted uniformly in the way that his book implies nor uniformly in the opposite way, but rather the reactions of different *Judenräte* and different Jewish communities varied even within the same geographical area and under the same conditions.

Such is my main criticism. Another is that the book fails to take account of the varied reactions of non-Jewish communities in which the Jews lived. The *Judenrat* in Trunk's book is very much an isolated entity in an environment where only the Germans exist and nobody else, which is certainly a wrong way of putting it.

Trunk's book has tremendous importance because it gathers together— and this already has been said by Professor Hilberg—a fantastic amount of knowledge, factual description and most interesting footnotes. But it is weakened by its disregard of the environment and by being wholly "horizontal": it deals with the subject matter always topic by topic, something that Professor Hilberg finds positive, but I find rather negative because I see in the description of a health program in Shavli, in Lodz, and in Warsaw three completely different things. The program may look the same, and yet its significance can be quite different depending upon the idea behind it.

In conclusion, I do not think that we should go from one extreme to the other. I do not believe that we should now describe the ghettos, the people in the ghettos, or the *Judenräte* exclusively in idealistic terms in reaction to earlier descriptions denouncing their "passivity." Rather we ought to describe as best we can the grim horror of Nazi rule, where there was no possibility of meaningful resistance in most places. At the same time, we should realize that there are two sides to the story and that the second side is no less important than the first.

SAUL FRIEDLÄNDER: Although I am not a specialist in this field, I have the impression, since the polemics started some years ago, that there is recurrent confusion between two levels of analysis. The first level is the objective function of the *Judenräte* and the ghetto in Nazi schemes. The second level is the intentions of the actors involved, especially the Jewish leadership. Throughout the debate the two levels have been confused.

Isaiah Trunk and Raul Hilberg have concentrated on the first level: the objective function of the ghetto and the *Judenräte*. But my impression is that Professor Hilberg moves intermittently from that level to the intentions of the Jewish leadership. His conclusion gives that impression and so do some parts of his paper: for he begins on the objective level with a careful analysis of the function of the ghetto and then suddenly an opinion is thrown out about the real intentions of the actors.

It is exactly the other way around with Yehuda Bauer, who in seeking to determine the intentions of the Jewish leadership shows that they often imagined they were doing their best for their communities, but implies then, that it was also the objective function of the *Judenräte* to be a kind of cushion and safeguard for the communities.

Could we not separate these levels and keep them apart? Could we not say (as I remark in my paper) that *objectively* the *Judenrat* was probably an instrument in the destruction of European Jewry, but that *subjectively* the actors were not aware of this function, and that even if they were aware, some of them—or even most of them—tried to do their best according to their very limited strategic possibilities in order to stave off the destruction? The separation of the two levels seems to me a fundamental methodological necessity.

URIEL TAL: I agree that we have to separate these two levels and I would like to suggest another aspect of our conceptual framework that needs clarification. Do the terms that we habitually use in historical studies dealing with other situations, have the same meaning when applied to the situation of the ghetto under Nazi rule? For example, when Professor Hilberg said that the people in the ghetto understood that their situation was merely temporary, my question is: what does "temporary" mean in this unique historical or psychological situation? Is each duration of time—each day—in that situation to be considered the way the same duration of time in a different situation would be considered? Is there not one long moment with much agony and pain and confusion, and another very short moment? When we say "temporary," what is the concept of time to which we are referring?

Similarly, when Professor Hilberg and others speak of "rumors" my question is: what is your methodological approach to the dynamics of information and rumors? If I hear a bit of information, when do I *know* what I hear, when am I *aware* of what I know, when am I aware of the awareness of this knowledge, and when do I consciously or subconsciously repress it? I may establish that people had enough evidence to know what might happen the next day, but did such evidence in that situation mean that they "knew," and wanted to know, and were capable of knowing, or did they repress or suppress knowingly or unknowingly this bit of rumor?

The same with the terms "leadership" and "self-government." In a normal situation, we understand self-government to mean "autonomy," literally that there is a certain law—a *nomos*—existing in its own right. But how applicable is this definition to the situation at hand? If we say that leadership means autonomy, what was the *nomos* involved? Was there a *nomos*?

And what about economic activity? Judged in normal terms, the economic activity of the ghetto can be understood as "exploitation." That is how Professor Hilberg understood it. But it can also be understood as a certain Jewish way of achieving physical survival, of putting up—as Yehuda Bauer correctly put it—a certain resistance. For economic activity also means a certain way of asserting your very existence, of self-realization. If people were capable of economic activity, no matter what the motive, it meant that, contrary to what the Nazis expected, they were realizing their own self, their own existence, their own survival. They made clear to themselves: I act economically, *ergo*, I still exist, which is one of the main ways of survival.

Whether it was for a moment or a day or a year does not matter at all because, as some of Himmler's documents show, the Nazi regime deliberately tried to confuse patterns of thought, feeling, and action among Jews and non-Jews alike. On the information we have, however, it seems that Jews somehow made a psychological effort to resist Nazi policy, the main aim of which was to confuse their own self-knowledge, their self-understanding. These few examples suggest that we need a conceptual framework that clarifies the meaning of terms used in regular historiography as applied to those unusual psychological and historical surroundings.

JACOB KATZ: A short comment on the problem raised by Bauer and Hilberg about the two kinds of possible presentation: whether to examine how a given function was performed by different *Judenräte* (the approach of Trunk's book), or to examine how a given *Judenrat* performed its various functions. I think that both are legitimate approaches, but that we are dealing with a different genre of historiography in each case. If we write in the second way, we may offer a full description of how certain people lived and acted, but it happens very often in such a case that we have no perspective. On the other hand, if we do everything in terms of comparative analysis, then we lose, of course, the total picture of any individual, the possibility of empathy with acting persons in their real life; but we do gain a perspective.

Now, this is not a question that concerns just this subject matter, but a very common problem of historiography. We can take Jewish communities through the ages and find the same problem. And the choice we make between the two approaches will depend on the definition of our objective, but also on the state of research in the field. Given where we were in the field of Holocaust studies, it was more important to do first what was done by Trunk, who set out to obtain a perspective, a description of the basic situation. From now on, if anybody wants to write the history of one given *Judenrat*, he will be assisted by the findings of Trunk because he will be under pressure to compare; and even if he does not mention the other communities, he will keep those findings in mind, and his judgment, his reconstruction, and his perspective will be much more alive than it could be without such a framework.

Of course, in the last analysis I would say that real history is particular history describing one case, or perhaps even only one person and one community. For even if you are dealing with this last, you will reach the individual person whose motivation and actions you are trying to understand and interpret. Yet even historians who set out to deal only with individual cases inevitably generalize, occasionally without self-control and without knowing what they are really doing. So it is better to generalize with an intention and with methodological self-control than to pretend to avoid anything that goes beyond the individual case.

SAMUEL ABRAHAMSEN: While grateful for the masterly analysis of

Professor Hilberg, I would like to raise a question about his statement, in almost as many words, that the ghettos were one of the major instruments, if not *the* major instrument, of the destruction of Jewish people in Europe. Even in countries where there were absolutely no ghettos, Nazi hatred was very effective against the Jews. Even those who lived north of the Arctic Circle were not left alone. To that extent, in my own country of Norway, which had one of the highest rates of victimization, it was done without ghettos.

I also think it is worth asking whether the Germans ever looked upon the ghettos as a threat to themselves. And I must come back to something Professor Hilberg claimed without giving any explanation: the complete absence of intelligence gathering. How can you explain that? For instance, it is startling to hear that Czerniakow, a person of the highest professional integrity, a professional engineer, who had access to not only the Jewish sources but to German sources, and I guess also to German sources beyond the ghetto—that a person like this should not have established even some elementary kind of intelligence gathering.

One other minor point: we should abandon once and for all the approach of contrasting the Jews, both the *Judenrat* and the ghetto, on the one hand, with the Germans on the other. At the same time we should include the vast deceptions played not by Germans on the Jews alone, but by Germans on Germans. This kind of doubleplay is startling, especially in Denmark and Norway where the Gestapo and SS were often completely successful in misleading the occupation authorities as well as the Jews. And I guess this pattern was followed throughout Eastern Europe as well as Western Europe.

EMIL FACKENHEIM: As a philosopher, I would like to ask the historians a question arising out of some assertions that I have made and also out of some lay historical knowledge that I think almost everyone has. For I think the main issue raised by Professor Hilberg is not whether the *Judenräte* were traitors or courageous, or even intelligent and full of foresight, but whether or not the Nazi system was one of an unprecedented diabolical nature, which tried and succeeded very often, perhaps indeed for the most part, in using even Jewish heroism and courage for their own nefarious purposes. That is a question that has haunted me for many years, of which I will give you random examples.

I seem to remember a speech by Goebbels when I was still in Germany, the gist of which was: "We know how we shall deal with the Jews. Of course it would be a criminal thing or seem to be a criminal thing to have virtuous citizens locked away, but first we shall reduce the Jews to poverty, then we shall drive them to crime, and then, of course, we have a way of treating them as criminals." Well, when I hear historians talking about the black market necessarily arising in the ghetto . . . there seems to be a very close connection.

Another example, which takes us from individuals to communities—which we are really concerned with—is suggested by Professor Feingold's reference to the *kahal*. This was a traditional Jewish organization, geared to life, with power that was limited but that could have one presupposition: that even though the enemies outside were enemies, they could be bribed, they could be dealt with in one way or another; they were never after genocide, let alone using the very institution of the *kahal* as an instrument to this end. Now the Nazis had an "Institute for Research on the Jews" and they had real experts in Jewish history; some were experts as great as some of our own, except with a diabolical purpose. So I ask: what was their real purpose? Were they deliberately investigating one thing all those years: how can we divert those very institutions which Jews have generated and developed throughout their history toward their destruction?

Now, I know there is today a great controversy among scholars: was the Nazi system a successful totalitarian system, or was it—as one description puts it—a totalitarian anarchy? There are all kinds of books, even if not convincing ones, arguing that there were limits to the power of Goebbels, or even Hitler, and there was competition and infighting. Yet one thing I do know is that the road to Auschwitz, however twisted by all those anarchies, led there inevitably all the same. And somebody has to investigate how this inevitability came about. Did the Nazis plan it all along with their "Institute for Research on the Jews," or did they slide into it by some kind of diabolical dynamics, which the theologians ought to know more about than anybody else?

HELEN FEIN: I concur with Saul Friedländer's distinction between levels of analysis. Trunk, without being conscious of it, is a structural functionalist: his book describes the *Judenrat* as an organization whose structure was devised for its basic function of controlling the Jews. Such control includes every stage of processing the Jews: definition, expropriation and stripping of social relations, segregation, isolation and ghettoization. (I have elaborated the concept of stages from Hilberg's analysis in *The Destruction of the European Jews* [Chicago, 1961].) We have to acknowledge that this was the intended function of those organizations *(Judenräte)* and that they worked successfully in the great majority of cases. There are indications that they would also work with other groups subjected to the same threat if offered what they perceived to be an opportunity for personal survival. Donald Kenrick and Grattan Puxon in *The Destiny of Europe's Gypsies* (New York, 1972) tell how the Germans recognized a rival contender as "king of the gypsies" in Poland—a man defeated in a prewar contest—who then offered to point out Gypsies in hiding in exchange for passes to exempt his family (p. 171). They also attempted (p. 88) to induce SS-appointed representatives of two tribes "to make lists of those to be saved" (certain "pure" members of those tribes whose preservation elicited Himmler's ethnological interest).

Now to Uriel Tal's question about what "knowledge" and "awareness" mean when we are talking about the psychological situation in the ghettos. The situation does have parallels when considered in terms of human reactions to disaster. In the social sciences we have little experience in investigating responses to human-made disasters, but we do know something about reactions to impending natural disasters such as tornados and earthquakes. Studies of disaster-warning have revealed a common tendency to deny that danger is at hand. Difficulties in public warning often start with the persons or agencies responsible for detecting the danger and issuing the warnings. They are usually reluctant to issue a specific warning unless they are reasonably certain that danger will actually materialize. Waiting for this degree of certainty has sometimes delayed the dissemination of the warning until it is too late.

Even where the existence, the nature, and the time of the danger can be adequately forecast, it is difficult to secure public acceptance of warning messages. People tend to pick upon any vagueness, ambiguity, or incompatibility in the warning message that enables them to interpret the situation optimistically. They search for more information that will confirm, deny or clarify the warning message, and often they continue to interpret signs of danger as familiar, normal events, until it is too late to take effective precautions. Only when danger is recognized as imminent and personal do people seek safety of escape; generally, their behavior is adaptive. The success of their actions will depend to a large extent upon the possibilities available in the situation and the adequacy of the information that they possess. Flight is one means of escaping danger; it is often the only rational choice if one is to survive.

Now, I would suggest, if we have to go back to the level of animal metaphors, that instead of talking about the Jews of Europe going to their deaths as sheep to the slaughter, we talk about them as goats in a stockade, trying by every means conceivable to escape when they could no longer repress the awareness of danger. But this point was usually reached only long after the segregation of the Jews from the rest of the population when there was virtually no possibility of escaping.

Here the important question, in terms of the chain of causation, is: what was the effect of the *Judenrat* in segregating the community? And there are two instances in the literature of a clearly coherent opinion among survivors—informed survivors—and historians that the *Judenrat* leadership was indeed a causal agent, namely, the Netherlands and Salonica (Thessaloniki). In both places there were certainly possibilities for defense.

As to Trunk's questionnaire on survivors' opinions, I questioned Trunk about this. Although I am professionally trained in the construction of such questionnaires, I was unable to tell from the questionnaire tallies in his appendix whether these were 300 survivors of two ghettos, opinions of survivors of 300 ghettos, or whether they were 100 survivors of each of three ghettos. Trunk had no idea how the sample was constituted. We thus have no way to assess how "representative" it is. The interviewers were not trained to avoid interjecting their own expectations in the situation—to avoid any bias. In other words, the interviewees may have been constrained to give as positive an evaluation as possible, so I would reject that part of Trunk's work as completely valueless for the questions we are trying to answer. Trunk himself spells out other sources of their retrospective bias.

What then could the Jewish leadership have expected in terms of the impending disasters? Here I think we have to understand not what they failed to anticipate but their working assumptions, which were perhaps the working assumptions of many Jews, or even of the overwhelming majority. Let us consider the more general question of victimization. Jews were being killed in France and in the Warsaw Ghetto a year before any deportations. It was understood that Jews were going to die. But what did they understand by that? I would hypothesize that they thought *some* Jews would die. Now, what does that mean, if one says *some* of category X are going to be killed? This knowledge elicits psychological defenses from other potential victims: when any group is singled out, others may try to normalize the situation by establishing boundaries around the victim, by disassociating themselves from the victim, reducing any potential cost to themselves, because identifying with the victim, doing anything to aid the victim, might raise the cost for them.

Now, the *Judenrat* and all the other institutions provided exemptions, instituting special categories or classes among Jews. Abba Kovner knows their signs as colored slips of paper, other people know them as stamps or as numbers. But all these mechanisms served to establish classes among Jews, which gave them the illusion that some were protected. Then on the assumption that some will die, the most rational next step is to say: in order not to be among those who are going to die, I will be inside the protected class if I can. Seeking to be a member of the protected class means reducing any incentive to build a defense movement, to create links with the national leadership, to aid the others. And this is a disaster, but it is implicit, of course, in any competitive class structure including that which existed in most of Europe before the Holocaust.

So, I think the most serious charge raised by Hilberg about the *Judenräte,* in Poland specifically, has not yet been stated. It was not the failure to anticipate the total destruction of the ghetto, but the failure to protect the more vulnerable members of the ghetto, those without status and without connections. Ringelblum said this himself, that "the people who are feeding from our soup kitchens are dying in the streets." The Warsaw Ghetto was like Calcutta in 1943: there were beggars and skeletons knocking on the doors. And it was this regressive social structure, based upon the assumption that some would survive and others would die, that was the root of the widespread failure consciously to attempt any social defense system.

HENRY HUTTENBACH: I too feel that if Isaiah Trunk's book is seen as a pioneering work rather than a definitive study, one that stands as a model with perfections and imperfections, it can lead to the next level of work, which is the task ahead of us: to get away from the implied generalizations—

perhaps one could even call them simplifications—and move to the individual level, the local level, because there one is closer to the historical truth.

And secondly, there is a point that I want to make about the questionnaire, or the interview, as a means of gaining primary source material. Here, of course, the historian is faced with a most painful methodological dilemma. Somehow or other, the experience that is memory in the survivor must be translated into reliable information; and by its nature, of course, the historian must be exceedingly wary of this. If the information corroborates documentation few problems may exist. But if it negates the documented information we have the painful task of saying that the survivor may be wrong. The survivor's memory after ten, twenty, thirty years is distorted and not as valuable. And clearly, one reason why we are here now is that memories are becoming vague and dying, though the emotions are sharp, strong, and very much alive, impossible to forget.

GEORGE MOSSE: Since it is part of our business to identify unresearched areas of the field, let me start with one mentioned by Emil Fackenheim—the Nazi *Institut für Judenforschung* or the "Institute for Research on the Jews." So far as I know, no research has been done on the Institute. Still, there are two things I think one can say about it. First of all, as elsewhere, the Nazis wanted to make myth reality. So the Institute's publications were to a great extent about the Middle Ages, and especially about medieval ghettos. But I wonder whether this vast ghetto literature produced by the Institute had some connection with the ghettos that were eventually set up. When you read the publications—and I certainly have read them—it is clear that their primary aim was to demonstrate the nonhuman characteristics of Jews.

The second thing about the Institute's work is that it therefore tried to prove the unprovable. Here it ties in with the Nazi bureaucracy. For there was a department in this bureaucracy whose task it was to investigate the universal Jewish conspiracy that did not exist. In other words—how shall I put it?—to make the myth confirm the reality.

So this is an unexplored area of research and one to be done in Jerusalem. Because, believe it or not, there we have the library of that *Institut für Judenforschung,* or most of its books, in the Hebrew University library.

Next the issue raised by Yehuda Bauer and others: whether the Nazi bureaucracy was monolithic or anarchic. Now, as everything in life, it is both, but in a peculiar way. I would say the situation was as follows: there was a great deal of disorganization on relatively minor matters because there were many subdivisions of the Nazi organization that worked against each other. But in the goals, in the final goals, especially on the Jewish question, Hitler knew what he wanted from the beginning.

To take one such minor matter, at the start of the Nazi era there was some interrelationship between the Berlin Nazi party and the Jewish organizations.

The Hitler youth in Potsdam played football with the "Black Flag" Jewish Youth organization. And so on. And this became pretty widespread; there are some interesting documents—they are not public because they embarrass people still living who organized those football games. Anyway, it is a fact that in part of the party, especially the Berlin party, in the early years there was some confusion. Until it came to Hitler's notice and he laid down the law.

So what we have here is this: on the one hand, in administrative matters, confusion; in the long-range goal on the part of Hitler, none. But remember that this was on the part of Hitler; that Himmler is supposed to have been astonished when the "Final Solution" was put forward. It was a goal determined by a peculiar racism of Hitler rather than by racism in general. Because racism is very differentiated, and that part of German racism which went into the eugenics movement regarded Jews as Aryans. If that sounds surprising, it is because nobody ever reads the journals. Hitler imbibed a peculiar racism, which he picked up from certain circles in Vienna. While the mainstream of racism was rather those who did so-called social biology. The latter eventually became Nazis indeed, but until 1933 they could still write about blond Jews and Aryan Jews.

This brings us to a second unexplored area: the history of racism. Here there is surprisingly little being done, apart from—dare I say it—some current work of my own. And a third area of vast importance is the changing attitude toward death. When did people become accustomed to mass death? Now, there were some massacres in the 1890s, but that is not crucial. Much more happened in World War I. I think myself, for what it is worth, that the Japanese invasion of China was also important, when for the first time in Germany or elsewhere over the radio there came inconceivable figures of Chinese killed.

Lastly, we need more basic research on something else very simple: the Holocaust could not have taken place, in my opinion, had it not been for the growth of a certain stereotype, a certain picture of "the Jew." There is very little research on that, though I have done a certain amount by tracing ideas of beauty and ugliness. In other words, one thing underlying the Holocaust was an idea of beauty. Now, there is nothing more important than this in facilitating, together with the bureaucracy, the mass deaths. So two preconditions of the Holocaust have not yet been considered: a change in the concept of death and the stereotype of the Jew.

RICHARD RUBENSTEIN: I have to say some things that are painful and may be offensive. So I hope you will understand that they will in no sense be said in a spirit of justifying what took place or in anything less than fundamental moral outrage. Nevertheless, I believe that the act of comprehension always involves a bracketing of moral sentiment.

To begin with, I have sadly come to the conclusion that the Nazis committed absolutely no "crime" in the Holocaust. The reason is that a crime can take place only in a political community. Where there is no universe of moral obligation, there can be no crime. Now we still are the heirs of earlier doctrines of law and criminality such as the natural-law theory of the Roman Catholic church, which maintains that there is, in fact, a universe of moral obligation that is not coextensive with the national state. Nevertheless, whether or not we can theoretically defend the proposition that human beings are part of a common universe of moral obligation, pragmatically what we have seen in the twentieth century is that the universe of moral obligation has shrunk drastically in times of stress. And, in extremity, the Jews of Europe found to their misfortune that, with the exception of a very small number of non-Jews, their universe of moral obligation was one in which they participated only with other Jews.

My second point is that it is only possible to have an effective universe of moral obligation in a shared political community. I use the term in the sense that Max Weber did when he defined the State as that institution which has a monopoly of the instruments of coercion within a given territory. Regrettably, even thirty years after the birth of the State of Israel, many Jews still lack a fundamental understanding of the relationship between the State as having a monopoly of the means of violence and their resultant predicament of both the Holocaust and the Diaspora. And one reason why the problem of the *Judenrat* is so serious is that the *Judenrat* did have precedents within Diaspora Jewish attempts at self-governance. Moreover, if we are to be accurate about it, those of us who live outside of Israel are still faced with institutions that have a common origin with the *Judenrat* and could conceivably behave in similar ways if placed under similar conditions of stress.

I think it must therefore be said that at no time from the destruction of the Second Temple until the reconstitution of the State of Israel did Jews ever have a public life. In order to have a public life, one must be a free participant in an institution with a monopoly of the instruments of violence within one's territory. Obviously, the *Judenräte* did not have that. They were agents of those who did have a monopoly of violence. Unless we understand this fundamental fact, then all of our excuses, reflections on what the *Judenräte* may or may not have done, will be devoid of comprehension.

We should also understand that there may have been wisdom in Aristotle's idea of man as a "political animal." If Aristotle is correct, no person is fully human unless he has a public life. In ancient times, the slave who participated in the metabolism of nature, that is, in the running of the household, did not have a public life. Only those who had a share in the instruments of coercion, that is, only those who were able to put their lives on the line to defend their territory and their communities, had a public life.

Now, there have been some crucial analyses of the problem of servile consciousness, of the "slave mentality," notably those of Hegel. But one area in which philosophical rather than historical research needs to be done is the extent to which the religion, the culture, and the symbols of Diaspora Judaism have been expressions of and objectivications of a servile consciousness in the Hegelian sense; that is, a consciousness that was excluded from public life, that knew nothing about the active use of force, a reality that today is probably understood by almost all citizens of the State of Israel. Thus, we understand that the destruction of the State of Israel and its replacement by a binational state could easily lead to genocide. It would mean that Jews would once again be at the mercy of others. Instead of bargaining with the other side with instruments of coercion in their hands, Jews would once again be compelled to seek the approbation of overlords possessing all the instruments of violence.

This relates to the question of the death of God, which I still feel is completely misunderstood by most Jews. The death of God is as much a political and a sociological question as it is a question of "Where was God during the Holocaust?" As a matter of fact, that may be the least significant aspect of the issue. The death of God is in a sense a corollary of the breakdown of public order and public life. Where one has no common universe of moral obligation, any symbol that might legitimate a universe of moral obligation must of necessity collapse. And that is basically what the death of God is all about—the legitimating symbols of moral obligation have collapsed.

I might add that there is also much that can be said about the problem of the bourgeois order as inherently destabilizing and inherently destructive of any genuine conception of a public life. The bourgeois order is therefore one that also destabilizes any conception of a common universe of moral obligation among people of different political communities. This brings me to Saul Friedländer's point: the distinction between the objective function of the *Judënrat*—which was misperceived—and the subjective interpretation of it. That distinction is entirely correct. But where people have a public life, it is the function of leadership to perceive the objective nature of their situation and to act accordingly. Where leadership cannot perceive the objective nature of its situation, it has failed in its fundamental responsibility. I suspect that a similar failure is likely to occur in the Diaspora should such a crisis again take place, because Jewish leadership in the Diaspora is not chosen on the basis of qualification for leadership in public life, but on the basis of bourgeois economic criteria that are implicitly destructive of public life.

This also means that talk about the "irrational hatred" that led the Nazis to genocide is a total misreading of their situation. Consider the perspective of the Nazis' objectives, given the fact that they did not regard the Jews as a part of their universe of moral obligation and that they did not wish to permit the Jews to participate in their public life; consider, too, the remark of Richard Barnet at the end of his book *The Roots of War* (New York, 1972), that half the people in the world today are superfluous and that there are not enough 20-cent-an-hour jobs to go around for them. When one concludes that the world is full of superfluous people, given the structure of things, then what the Nazis did was completely rational from their point of view. Admittedly, theirs was an instrumental rationality that none of us can accept, but they had the power to define their political reality and we were powerless to stop them. Theirs was not a capability of creating a decent human order. But that is where we are. Unfortunately, there are going to be more and more superfluous people, and, in that kind of superfluity, some people may be tempted to see what the Nazis did as goal-directed, purposive and—whatever bureaucratic inefficiencies and contradictions there were—eminently rational and efficient. They did what they set out to do and from their point of view they did it well.

Finally, all this puts today's Diaspora Jewry in question too. I do not see how anybody can read the history of the *Judenräte* and understand the issue of public versus private life and still ask whether Diaspora Jewry is viable.

HENRY FRIEDLANDER: First, a comment on Saul Friedländer's distinction between the objective function of the *Judenräte* and the intentions of their members. I think one cannot separate the two completely, and I am sure he did not mean to do so. They are interrelated, in the sense that one must measure the degree to which those intentions conformed to some form of objective reality. If we compare the ghetto—though I hestitate to use this comparison—with a sinking ship, we have definite rules as to how we behave in the latter situation: women and children first into the lifeboats. If the captain should instead decide that it is cold outside and it is best to keep the women and children warm inside the ship, his intentions may be very humanitarian and concerned, yet obviously he is so far away from the reality of the situation that he must be judging it in a bizarre way. And yet this is somehow the framework in which we just judge the intentions of the Jewish leadership in World War II. To what degree, in that sense, were they aware of the situation?

This takes us to a second point: leaving all intentions aside, how was one indeed to decide who the "women and children" were—who were to be the victims for deportation? It has been suggested that an equitable way would have been to choose them by lot whereas the way actually used to choose the victims, those who would go into the lifeboats and those who would remain, was not by lot, not by some just and equitable system, but by giving preference to those who had jobs or friends in positions of power or those who were more agile than others.

I would suggest that this had an effect upon the entire spirit of the ghetto community. For instance, if you pick by lot, then indeed you are facing something that is similar to a natural disaster like a shipwreck. And if you have a natural disaster, then people do indeed coalesce, they combine and help each other. It seems to me that in tornados and hurricanes and whatever, the community cooperates, it stands together. So by letting those other criteria dominate the selection process you divide the community. You not only create the illusion of "if I have a job I will be saved," an illusion that with selection by lot could not have existed, but you also make everyone fight everyone else; you divide the community and turn bitterness inside and inward. Consequently, the decision as to how to pick the victims had a real influence on the question of resistance. You are not going to have resistance in a divided community in which everyone is fighting everyone else to stay alive, rather than taking the attitude of "it is hitting us all equally."

In closing, I would like to question a detail of Henry Feingold's presentation. He made the very accurate observation that the German Jews—and I can vouch for that in many ways—were so caught by their legalism, by their legalistic tradition, that they reported voluntarily for deportation, for instance, unlike Jews from communities in which this kind of legalism did not exist. But does this not to some degree underline the point made by Hannah Arendt that he set out to demolish? Which is that if those people had not persisted in the fiction that an actual legal order existed, then would they not have been forced to consider escape in some way? What I am saying is that the maintenance of "life must go on," as she argues, can itself be a means of preventing victims from thinking out a way to escape from their dilemma.

LENI YAHIL: I also think that while the distinction between the objective situation and the subjective intention is theoretically of great value, it is not always possible to separate those two categories. Intention was itself an objective factor not only on the part of the Jews, but also on the part of the Germans, who reacted to the intentions of the Jews, who intended to survive and did everything to save life. The Germans found ways to overcome this sort of unarmed resistance, as Yehuda Bauer called it. In time they were able, as Henry Feingold pointed out, to transform the intention of the Jews to save life into its opposite; that means, into the opening of the way to death.

As for Hannah Arendt, I think we have now reached a level of research where we are no longer required to defend ourselves against the kinds of accusations she made. We have got beyond apologetics; instead we have to try to understand the situation as it was without polemics.

The whole question is, of course, one of evaluating the situation and interpreting the sources. Take, for instance, something mentioned by Professor Hilberg: the struggle of Czerniakow against the organization of Abraham Gancwajch, an institution that was actually a Gestapo fifth column, meaning a Nazi intelligence in the ghetto. Czerniakow tried to abolish it and in the end he succeeded. Now, Professor Hilberg sees in it a struggle over different power positions in the ghetto, while my evaluation is that he was trying to get rid of the Nazi intelligence. This, of course, is a very different evaluation.

Also, the whole question of whether Czerniakow had intelligence of his own is difficult, because if he had sources of intelligence he certainly would not have written about them in his diary, which was, as he well knew, open to the Nazis. So, there are things that are difficult to judge and evaluate today with respect to the then-prevailing situation.

JACOB KATZ: The remarks of Professor Rubenstein should not pass without comment because he uses a set of notions unsuited to the analysis of the problem confronting us. To take one example, he quotes Max Weber's definition of the State as an organization having the exclusive right of violence. That is indeed a famous definition of Max Weber. But what did he mean by it? That any individual or body other than the organs of the State is absolutely not permitted to use force, but not that the State can use whatever force for whatever purpose it contemplates. Weber thought, of course, that the State has to use force, but only on the basis of legal institutions. Now, which legal institution decided upon the extermination of European Jewry? The decision was taken, as we all know, clandestinely. The Nazis did not even publish it because they did not want it known to their own people. So Professor Rubenstein's attempt to show that the Holocaust was not a crime is based on a misuse of a definition by Max Weber.

He also mistakenly tries to explain the Holocaust in Darwinian terms: there are too many people in the world and consequently a struggle between groups, so if you decide that a certain group is superfluous you just exterminate it. Now first, we do not live in such a world. Although there is, of course, an urge to exterminate groups and sometimes governments give way to it, there are also inhibitions and horror and struggle against such tendencies. More specifically, the Holocaust cannot be explained in terms of this ideology, not even where the Nazis are concerned. Even they knew that it could not be justified in this way. And clearly, they did not do it because they thought that there was a superfluity of people, that the Jews were superfluous, since we know they indeed used Jews very profitably in SS factories. Sometimes the Germans running those factories tried to postpone the deportation of their Jewish workers, arguing that they were indispensable to the war effort—far from superfluous—but they were overruled and the workers were taken away and killed.

HENRY FEINGOLD: I have just two brief corrections and one question to ask our historical experts on the panel. First, in answer to Henry Friedlander, I was not disparaging the German Jews, but merely speaking to a point made by Trunk, that it is very difficult to generalize about the populations of the ghettos because they were so disparate in their reactions owing to differences in their cultural conditioning. And to Leni Yahil: I hope I am not guilty of apologetics. On the contrary, I expressly regard Trunk's work as a refreshing departure from polemics contrasting an opportunistic leadership on the one hand with heroes and martyrs on the other.

Now for a question that I think lies at the very heart of our discussion about Trunk's book. It is a question that was raised in 1967 at a colloquium sponsored by YIVO, when Isaiah Trunk was asked about a key supposition that applies to the whole of his book: the supposition of continuity. The question is this: was the *Judenrat*, as Trunk maintains, an example of Jewish governance in keeping with the *kahal*, rather than some "unique and queer" episode? Trunk maintains that it was on a continuum, that there was nothing basically different. So I would like to ask the historical experts: to whose history does the *Judenrat* belong? Does it belong to German history, or does it belong to Jewish history, or does it belong to both?

ABBA KOVNER: I hope that the only difficulty between you and myself will be the difficulty of language, but I am not so sure about that. For although I came here to listen, after half a day something strange happened. An almost compulsory thought occurred to me: suppose the door opened at this moment and Jacob Gens, head of the *Judenrat* of the Vilna Ghetto, came in and sat down here and began to explain that he had received an order from the Germans to supply, by tomorrow morning, a list of 10,000 Jews for deportation. If the list was not delivered they would choose the people themselves, but if the list was delivered it might be reduced to 8,000 and maybe he could give them old people and weak people.

Just such an incident is recorded in the diary of Zelig Kalmanovitch, which you can read in English in the *YIVO Annual of Jewish Social Science* 8 (1953). He relates how Gens came to a meeting in the ghetto and said: "To be sure, our hands are stained with the blood of our brethren, but we had to take upon ourselves this dreadful task. We are clean before the bar of history. We shall watch over the remaining. Who knows if any more victims will be demanded from us here, as they were demanded there. We shall give them only the old and the sick. Children we shall not give them. They are our hope. Young women we shall not give them. There came a request for workers. I replied: 'We shall not give. We need them here.' Thereupon they went out into the street, seized a thousand Poles and sent them to Riga. Who can guarantee the future?" Kalmanovitch comments that a heavy dread hung over the assembly while Gens spoke. Yet he prefaces his account by saying of Gens: "Praised be the God of Israel who has sent unto us this man."

Read between the lines there is an anguish so deep in the extract from this diary that the more you read it, the less you understand. And the meeting at which Gens spoke was, if I may say so, similar to our meeting here. It was a meeting of cultural and intellectual workers in the Vilna Ghetto, to whom he presented the situation in order to hear their response. Gens had already made his decision but he wanted to hear the response of intellectuals and writers hoping that they would share the responsibility. As he put it, from that day on all of us had our hands stained with blood. So I ask myself the question after thirty years: only those who were in the Ghetto, only the generation that went through the Ghetto, or later generations as well?

It has been asked here today whether the *Judenrat* was a continuation of the Jewish community and its organization before the Holocaust. Yes, in the same way that the crematorium is a continuation of a baking oven. It has the same basis but a completely different quality. How does one describe a completely different quality? A historian's task is to collect facts. How does he describe facts that are of a completely different quality? Everything is in the historical description except the abyss. Whoever thinks after thirty or fifty years that he is still dealing with open facts does not understand a thing. How does one understand an abyss? It is not just a geological description, it is also the readiness to fall into it without the certainty of coming up again.

I was once shown a model of the Treblinka death camp, and told that it was an "accurate and authentic picture" of Treblinka. But it was not; it was the buildings without the anguish and the horror. Treblinka was not the buildings and the fence; without the horror it was just another youth camp. What is the ghetto in socio-historical accounts without the horror?

The destruction that we, for lack of any other word, call "the Holocaust," brings every rational one of us back to the basis of human existence. There is no understanding. For instance, what was collaboration? People were brought to the pits. They were told to undress and they did. They were told to remove their last bit of clothing and they did. And then one of them was out of the line and the other ones told him to move back into the line because "you are making all of us unhappy." Is that collaboration? Is it choice? Is it power? Is there even a community here? After reading Kalmanovitch—the man who praised God for giving them such a man capable of making such decisions—any rational person will ask himself: what kind of community is it that hands over decisions of that kind to any person? Is it possible to speak about a group of people like that as a community?

In one of my poems, I describe a thousand people within a fence, and that of course is the ghetto. At the end of the poem the one man who had seen and tried to rebel enters a river on a horse. It is not clear whether he passes across the river, or whether both the man and the horse drown. After fifteen years in Israel, in a Hebrew edition, I changed the ending, which is more or less like this, that when all is said and done, we were all defeated, the dead and the living. My students asked me why I changed the ending of the poem. And I did not know how to answer them. But when I sit here now, or in a similar get-together, where people deal with clear minds about those days, I almost know the answer: we are talking about the total defeat of man, the total defeat of civilization. It is not just certain places where certain individuals failed, but a total defeat such as has never happened before. And we are part of that defeat. Only if we realize that, can we begin climbing up out of the abyss. We do not understand the dead; the dead did not understand us.

One evening, I opened the door of a room in the ghetto unwittingly and found an empty room with frost on the walls and a man was sitting next to an old sewing machine. He was sewing not cloth but empty white paper. And there was no thread in the needle. I asked him what he was doing. And he said, "I'm writing." On a sewing machine? "I'm writing the history of the Ghetto." Without thread? "I will thread it later. When we survive this, I shall put the thread into the holes."

Our problem is really that of taking the white paper and trying to thread the holes without going mad. We have to stand modestly before a challenge that we must not suppress. There is something in common between the poet and the historian, and that is the element of consolation, which is hidden from view, and which both employ. The question is how to carry on. How to find the consolation. By suppressing the horror, you will desecrate it. And that horror is part of history: you cannot run away from it, nor can you ignore the warning. It is easy to be deluded by signals and to find them when no danger exists. You have to have the courage to see and to look into the abyss, and not to build rationalizations as people did then. It was not a question of when they knew or what they knew; it was a question of what they should have done when they knew. What were the alternatives? What conclusions can be drawn when there was no choice?

One personal note: it was I who wrote the famous phrase "like sheep to the slaughter"—a phrase that haunts me now wherever I go. I must put it into context. For it was written in December 1941 as the heading of a leaflet that called for rebellion. The aim of the leaflet was to shake ghetto inhabitants out of their conviction that they were standing before a situation of total destruction. Not just in Vilna and not just in Lithuania, but all over Europe. And that the only way out was to go to their death with honor. The phrase that I used then must not be taken out of context. For thirty years I have never repeated it. I never thought afterwards that a woman whose child has been taken out of her arms had gone to her death like a "sheep to the slaughter." There was only one occasion, or type of occasion, afterwards when I thought that, and it was during the fighting when there might have been sheep. But that was a different situation altogether, and I have never thought that the sheep had anything to be ashamed of.

RAUL HILBERG: Perhaps I could begin by concentrating on the point made by my colleague Yehuda Bauer, that for the Jews in the ghettos and for the Jewish Councils time was too short—the time for deciding, for reacting, and for resisting. I have no quarrel with this observation because it is perfectly true. But as with so many statements that are true one must ask: why was time too short? Here a discipline in which I serve, political science, may perhaps contribute something. In many contexts, particularly in the realm of international relations over the last two or three decades, there has been much concern with what is generally called crisis management: how to react quickly to unprecedented, unexpected, drastic events.

The problem is well recognized, even understood to a certain extent. And almost invariably the clue is the mental framework with which one begins. We see in the detailed accounts of events like the Cuban missile crisis, but many others as well, something that I suspect would occur even in the life of an individual faced with impending disaster. Namely, that under the impact of an unexpected event, the alternatives that present themselves immediately to the decision-maker are almost always two extremes: submission or resistance, quitting or fighting. It is only with the passage of time that one discovers what in sociology is called the latent structure of the situation, that one sees the total perspective, the full range of alternatives, and that one examines them one by one to assess the rationality of choices.

How can anyone do this under pressure? The answer is that there has to be an institution, machinery, or preparation to that end. One cannot start thinking when a crisis arrives; even thinking has to be prepared for and planned, in certain contexts institutionally.

Admittedly the Jewish Councils had little time to consider matters, not so much because a few weeks or months or years are inadequate in the face of an event of such magnitude, but mainly because all of the Councils were spending nine out of ten working hours on immediate problems. This is what we must never forget—that they had to solve immediate problems. Anyone the least bit familiar with any kind of bureaucratic apparatus knows that matters of utmost importance are almost always dealt with last. But this is not to say that there were no indications of danger. I will not go into the extreme example of Hungary. Let us take an apparently less clearcut case, that of Poland or Belgium or Holland or wherever deportations began in 1942.

Everyone in Poland knew the one overwhelming fact that Germany assaulted the Soviet Union on June 22, 1941. Everyone knew that only one of two things could possibly happen: either the Soviet Union would collapse, or else it would not and there would be a relatively long war. And if that were the case, German armies would be fighting deep in Russia, so that the Polish Jews would be very deep behind German lines, inaccessible to armed rescue from the Allied powers. This much everyone knew even without detailed reports. All the same, the ghettos were treated as temporary institutions. The problem is that a temporary institution meant one thing to the Germans and another to the Jews.

When the ghettos were formed, by and large in 1940, the only question from the Nazi point of view was whether or not the Jews would be sent somewhere—let us say to Madagascar. If there was to be no Madagascar, then in the German view there would have to be a "territorial" solution, whether that meant working people to death or shooting them, or sending them to gas chambers. For the Jews, on the other hand, the ghettos were temporary in the sense that the war could not last forever. All wars must end, even this one. The problem is that the Jews ran out of time long before the end of a war whose duration, as I just remarked, should have been clear to everyone. This was a fundamental, basic miscalculation.

Uriel Tal asked us: what exactly are rumors? How does one deal with rumors? Rumors are indicators of danger. Even when they are not totally factual, they can still alert people to danger. One of the most widespread rumors in Europe—with the least basis of fact—was that out of the corpses of dead Jews the Germans were making soap. The rumor was widely believed. And it alerted a great many people, including non-Jews, to potential danger. But as has been shrewdly observed, in a disaster situation that calls upon leaders, in particular, to make drastic decisions, the tendency will be to maintain whatever there is, to be governed by inertia, to depart as little as possible from routine, and thus to discount the rumors. This is after all what Czerniakow was trying to do in the last days of his life after he knew that deportation was not merely impending, but actually beginning.

It is a fact that at the end of 1942 the U.S. Department of State spent many months asking for checkups to make sure that the reports were true. It was not going to publicize the fact of the Final Solution in Europe until after there was enough proof, as it were, to satisfy a court of law. Such conservatism in the treatment of information is a rather crucial element that we must examine very carefully. A modern social scientist would approach the matter differently. He would not ignore anything, which is not to say that he would attribute false importance to things that are not important. Here I do not minimize the fact that in situations of danger, the inevitable result of taking everything seriously and reacting to everything is paranoia. This again means that one must be very careful and judicious when faced with an apparent choice between extremes. There are things that can be done short of the employment of brute force, but short also of total compliance with perpetrators.

Now for the question of whether Jews would have been better off without the Jewish Councils. I think it is fairly well accepted that the Councils were not good organizations for planning any kind of resistance and that where resistance took place, though it may have involved some Council member, it was almost invariably the product of newly formed organizations. Resistance was led by what we call emergent leaders, not those who had traditionally been in charge of the Jewish community; it involved new tools and new thinking. There simply is no question that the Councils were obstructions to all such attempts to turn the community around, to put it on a different path. This is not to condemn the Jewish Councils, it is simply to recognize the historical facts for what they are. The Councils opposed resistance much more often than they acquiesced in it, let alone participated in it.

We must remember that the German machinery of destruction was staffed by part-timers essentially, with a few exceptions like Eichmann. By and large it was improvised, which is not to say inefficient. A great many officials were concerned with Jewish matters only every other day or every other week, whether in the finance ministry, the transport ministry, or even the SS and the police. For the local implementation of their measures they required considerable input from some non-German apparatus. If, as in the case of Hungary, the local administration was available for this purpose, the *Judënrat* did not have to become greatly involved. But in several other areas, and particularly in the Polish ghettos, the *Judënrat* became an appendage, an arm of the total bureaucratic machine. It was relied upon—through its registration of data, its police, and many other activities as well—for the final implementation of German measures. That the Council was reluctant we know. That the Council was pained we are convinced. That in desperation Council members committed suicide is a matter of record. But that notwithstanding all of these things they went on doing what they were asked— that is a matter of record, too.

Let us not forget the common excuse of German defendants before war crimes tribunals: "I just had to do my duty; I was never an antisemite." Or: "I hardly remember. When was this you say? Well, if it says that here it must have been so; I must have done it." Let us not fall into the trap of applying the same kind of reasoning to Jewish leaders. To become somewhat legalistic: in the analysis of intentions in law we do not ask about the mental reservations of someone who puts his signature to a contract, to a statute, or to another public document. What we do ask is whether he intends at the time he signs the document to perform the stipulations. And that is the important question. The fact is that Jewish Councils, however reluctant, did draw into the dragnet women and children, so that those who—as was pointed out by Henry Friedlander—should have been the first concern of such Councils, who should have been most protected by them, were delivered to the German perpetrators ahead of others.

We have heard from Abba Kovner about how even Gens admitted the importance of not handing over children or young women, who represent the protected elements of a community and its future. But we have avoided any systematic study of the decisions made by the Councils, insofar as they had power to make decisions—as to who was going to be deported last, who next to last, and so on. If we see in that kind of decision-making a segmentation of the Jewish community into privileged and less privileged, an attitudinal pattern, a social structure, then I believe we are going to learn a great deal about the communities during the Holocaust. Or, for that matter, about Jewish communities as such.

I must end with a point that is most critical of all. It has to do with the comment made by Abba Kovner and others: that no matter what kind of research we do, no matter what kind of findings we arrive at, there is a point at which we cannot approach reality. We cannot see into the bottom of the abyss, we cannot feel it. The replica, the buildings of Treblinka—that is not Treblinka in the absence of the horror. How and what can we do? There is an intimation here, perhaps, that certain research ought not to be done; an intimation that not only are there some things that we will never know, but that we ought not to know. I cannot offer any prescriptions in this matter. But I do know that the physician treating a cancer patient need not acquire cancer in order to treat him. The social scientist who looks at aberrations and malfunctions in society, or simply at extreme events, does not, in order to study these events, experiment on himself. He cannot and he should not.

We either have an optimistic view of life or a somewhat pessimistic one. The optimists say that the Nazis are unique—that what they did could never happen anywhere again. Or they say, even if we cannot be sure of that, we can at least marshall whatever equipment we have—intellectual, organizational—and prepare for whatever contingency may arise. The optimist, in short, takes hold of the phenomenon, recognizes it, studies it as far as it can be studied, and goes on from there. To that extent I am an optimist.

ISMAR SCHORSCH: The subject with which we have been wrestling is the quality of Jewish leadership. In a sense, there was almost no work on this subject prior to Trunk. Jewish historians have not addressed themselves to the quality of Jewish leadership in the Middle Ages or antiquity, apart from occasional remarks in studies involving the larger Jewish community. It is extremely difficult to talk about continuity or discontinuity in Jewish leadership, because we know so little about the nature, the origins, and the policies of the Jewish leadership in the medieval Jewish world. Our discussion of Trunk's work and of the *Judenräte* is taking place perforce in a vacuum.

There is one forerunner of this discussion and, interestingly enough, it followed a calamity of comparable dimensions: the expulsion from Spain. It took the Jews many generations to digest and reconcile themselves to that expulsion. And one of the early responses to the Spanish expulsion came from Ibn Verga, who was himself expelled. He wrote a rather impassioned denunciation of the quality of Spanish Jewish leadership in which he found much of the cause for the Spanish expulsion. I think it reflects a rather natural tendency to personify an overwhelming catastrophe. Somewhere someone with responsibility must be sought. Here the parallelism between Ibn Verga and Hannah Arendt is marked for both wrote after tremendous crises, both denounced the Jewish leadership as being responsible, in part, for the calamity.

In this regard, I would like to take the opposite tack. For even though the argument of Ibn Verga and Hannah Arendt has been widely accepted, it is a distortion of medieval Jewish history. I would argue that the Jews survived the period of Diaspora not because of a servile consciousness or lack of political astuteness, but precisely the opposite: because of an enormous amount of political sagacity, which we have yet to study. If our discussion has any merit, any significance, it ought to make us reexamine the political sagacity of the Jews in the ancient and medieval world. Their survival was not an accident, but the result of conscious policy capable of enormous adaptability. Since we have no Jewish political history and no study of Jewish leadership, it is so easy to make generalizations about the "servile consciousness" and "passivity" of the Jews. They are generalizations based on ignorance.

To argue that the Jews would have been better off without a Jewish community is to argue that men facing the Nazis would have been better off had they not been married. Or that the Jews in the Middle Ages would have been better of had they not been Jews. In the Middle Ages, Jews survived precisely because they were able to create communities, which served as a surrogate homeland and which appeased the deepest spiritual and physical needs of their existence. To expect these communities or institutions to disappear is to expect the impossible. The response of the Jews emanated from their political experience, and that was to rely on the instrument of the Jewish organization.

In this discussion of the quality of that organization, I am struck by a paradox. It is precisely Jews living outside of Israel who are in a sense continuing the old Zionist attack against Jewish passivity. The attack was understandable in the context of the political struggles within the Jewish community early in this century. But it is paradoxical that the charge of Jewish passivity, or lack of political wisdom, continues to be levelled by Diaspora Jews while a Jew living in Israel, Yehuda Bauer, is more sympathetic to the political sagacity of the Jews than Raul Hilberg or Richard Rubenstein or Hannah Arendt.

Like Bauer, I think that one of the lessons of Trunk's book is precisely the caution not to generalize. Take the variety of functions delineated by Trunk. The problem facing the *Judënrat* was not the single question of whether or not to fight. The ghetto was a city, and if it had not functioned as a city, the Jews would have starved and died of disease at a much faster rate than they did. It was a state within a state. In that regard, there is a return to the medieval terms of accommodation. But had the *Judënrat* not undertaken those functions, the Nazis would have exterminated the Jews through starvation, which was one of their policies. Actually, the existence of terms and the variety of functions performed by the *Judënrat* suggest a broader context for discussion than the simple question of physical resistance or its absence, which is all that interests those who talk of Jewish "passivity."

The other thing to emerge from Trunk's study is the diversity of response. And here I must again identify myself with Bauer's position: it is impossible to ignore not only the variety of the functions but the diversity of the response. There is a certain poetic justice in Professor Hilberg being the one to comment on Professor Trunk's book; for it modifies some of the harsh judgments found in his (Hilberg's) original monumental work. It is entirely appropriate that he himself treats Trunk's book with enormous sympathy. Yet he makes a subtle attempt to distill from it a kind of paradigmatic ghetto, and that ignores the evidence in Trunk's book, which shows that no paradigm can be extracted. Trunk's book is enormously difficult to read, precisely because it is so difficult to generalize. But that is the state of the field at the moment, and I think we would be much better served by abandoning the natural inclination to generalize and confronting the diversity.

I also think that the remark at the end of Professor Bauer's paper ought to be taken seriously: the State of Israel was produced by the same Ashkenazi culture that met its end in Eastern Europe. For it suggests that the response is not attributable solely to historical experience, but is greatly determined by the context in which it is formed. Passivity, I would hazard a guess, is a characteristic of a middle-class urban population. Solzhenitsyn's *Gulag Archipelago* is a polemical work that drives home the extent of passivity within the Russian masses and denounces *their* passivity in the face of the Communist assault. All the conservatism in the handling of information was present there; and it suggests that there was nothing unique about the Jewish response, but that it was a function of an urban population.

Lastly, despite my criticism of the Hilberg and Rubenstein position, my view of the causes of Nazi antisemitism lies in their direction. Nazi antisemitism must be understood in the context of the modern world, not as a continuation of medieval Christianity, and we must take into account the phenomenon of secularization. By arguing that Christian antisemitism played a key role, we are attributing a power to Christianity that it simply did not have in the modern world. How many Christians were praying in churches on a Sunday morning in Germany in 1905? A small minority of the population. Indeed, the church exercised so little influence over the masses by the 20th century, that we must look for the causes of Nazi antisemitism in the constellation of modernity and not in the vestiges of medievalism.

RICHARD RUBENSTEIN: While I am greatly indebted to the eminent scholarship of Professor Katz, he has totally misunderstood what I meant. When I said that the State was an institution that had a monopoly of violence within its borders, I was not justifying the State's use of violence. On the contrary, precisely because the State has the monopoly of violence, Jews can only be safe in a Jewish State where they are not powerless before the exercise of violence on the part of others.

This raises the whole question of Jewish-gentile relations in the Nazi period, in medieval Europe, or whenever. The crucial point here is that gentiles always had the power and, had they not been impeded by their own psychological, moral, or religious inhibitions, they could at any time have exterminated every last Jew. What Professor Hilberg has shown in his analysis of the progress of anti-Jewish measures, comparing Nazi measures with earlier ones, is that as time passed the impediments to radical action tended to disappear. I would add that once radical action has been shown to be not only feasible but profitable, it invites repetition, though not necessarily against the same victim immediately. Our century has been filled with radical actions of an exterminatory character. Gil Elliot's work, *Twentieth Century Book of the Dead* (London, 1972), suggests that a hundred million people have already been murdered by one or another form of human violence in this century.

To pass on to something that Abba Kovner said, again I think that we are dealing with a misperception. And I say this respectfully, but nevertheless emphatically. Abba Kovner speaks—as I believe many Jews speak—of the Holocaust as a break, or as a failure in civilization. What must be understood is that the Holocaust was not a break in civilization but an expression of civilization as are Leicas, Mercedes, and intercontinental ballistic missiles. Civilization is also the context in which we must see advances in the organization of human beings and the ways in which they are treated. Civilization is ultimately an organic process with polarities of creativeness and destructiveness that include the mechanisms of extermination.

This is especially important for understanding the process of secularization, which in no way indicates the weakness of churches. All the research that has been done in the sociology of knowledge suggests, on the contrary, that secularization is in reality secular Protestantism, and actually represents the triumph of the Protestant world over all other forms of political and religious consciousness in the 20th century. The triumph is so great that even secular Jews are, in fact, culturally secular Protestants. That is one of the reasons that so many Jewish communities failed in their response to the Holocaust: they did not know who they were, not through any evil on their part or malice; they were simply a part of a cultural process they did not understand.

To speak of the rationality of the Nazi project, is in no sense to justify the project. It is only to suggest that it was a solution to the problem of social cannibalism arising from an overpopulated world in which technological advances make more and more people superfluous. The question of which people will be defined as superfluous, however, is a political matter, and in Germany it received a political definition that overrode or ignored the usefulness of the Jews, who comprised the first category named, but not the last.

Related to the problem of superfluous labor is that of multinational corporations exhibiting a continuity and rationality in their behavior. Consider, for example, the relocations of factories from Massachusetts to Taiwan because the government there will supply people for 20 cents an hour instead of $3.30 and guarantee the absence of union problems. The logical expression of this is what IG Farben—one of the most gigantic and powerful such corporations—did in realizing that slave labor in a death camp was the ideal unskilled labor force. In eliminating superfluous labor, IG Auschwitz was very profitable, indeed.

ALICE ECKARDT: It seems to me that the Jews and their various leadership groups—not only the *Judenräte*—failed to perceive the Germans' full intentions because the latter were not proceeding from accepted norms or values in carrying out their program. They were not simply violating generally-held standards but turning them on their heads. How could the *Judenräte*, or any of the other groups, have grasped this and reacted appropriately to a complete transvaluation of values? Such a transvaluation was the barrier to awareness, despite evidence that now seems so obvious.

This is relevant to another issue that we have been discussing: the question of the rationality or irrationality of the Holocaust, which is a most central question, whether the Holocaust is approached historically or philosophically or theologically. We cannot simply jump to the conclusion that it was irrational, as we are tempted to do, because it violated accepted norms. I must confess that I used to jump to that conclusion, but now—after wrestling with the problem for some time—I can see a certain rationality, though not the precise rationality that Professor Rubenstein claims.

Of course it was illogical to waste manpower, trains, fuels, etc., to kill Jews if winning the war was the most important issue. Of course it was irrational to destroy valuable manpower and even more valuable knowledge and skills, to dissipate those "natural resources" by turning them into products like soap, cloth, mattress stuffing, and fertilizer—none of these being really essentially needed items—if one is thinking in normal economic terms of conservation and maximum use of resources. But if winning the war, maximizing economic gains or the like were not all-important goals of the Nazi regime, then we have to reexamine the question of whether the Nazis in fact acted irrationally.

If the primary aim of the Nazis, or even just of Hitler, was or came to be the destruction of European Jewry because it was perceived as an absolute menace to humanity or as the obstacle to a liberated European civilization, then the actions taken to destroy them at all costs were not irrational. Hitler and the Nazi ideologists could logically conclude—as some statements of Hitler and other spokesmen may indicate—that even if the German people must bear a terrible sacrifice to destroy the Jews, it was worth it because Germany and Aryan Europe, once rid of the "corrupting presence" of Jews, could rise from the ashes of destruction and reach previously impossible heights. This argument, it seems to me, is paralleled in the Arab world today by some Arab spokesmen, who say they can and are willing to sacrifice millions of their people in order to wipe out Israel because they can overcome that loss in the freedom and glory of an Arab civilization no longer threatened by Zionist "imperialists and gangsters."

The Nazis, in fact, perceived the Jews not simply as superfluous—and here I agree with Professor Katz as against Professor Rubenstein—but as an absolute hindrance, a virus, a cancer, and all the other descriptions they used. Given a certain perception of a people as the incarnation of evil, it was not illogical or irrational to destroy them. Consider a question raised by one of my students: if someone had the fate of six million guilty Nazis in his hand, would not a death sentence be at least one logical choice?

With the technological devices at our command, the mass destruction of a people is becoming ever easier. The limits have been passed already, the inhibitions removed. So once another leader or regime comes to the ideological conclusion that extermination of some group is for that regime's own good or for the alleged good of humanity, then the logic can set in motion the machinery of death. Only by recognizing the rationality of the Nazi Holocaust can we begin to meet the threat of future Holocausts based on other "rational ideologies."

ZVIE BAR-ON: What was the nature of the crime committed by the Nazis against the Jews? Professor Rubenstein has tried to argue that there was no crime. But he is mistaken, and his mistake lies in an erroneous conception of the relation between moral obligation and inalienable rights on the one hand and political power or the use of it on the other.

As I understand the political condition of man, it is a gross misconception to think that political power alone creates moral obligation or basic human rights, and can therefore deprive people of them. Political power does not create rights, though it may be needed to give them effect. If the Jews in the ghettos, or for that matter the inmates of the death camps, had no public life in the proper sense of this term, it does not follow that they did not have rights, which neither the Nazis nor any other power—good or evil—could rightfully take away from them. Nor are these rights innate. They are a matter of the basic status of man, deliberately chosen by us, and also I think by the Allies when laying down the legal foundation of their anti-Nazi jurisdiction. If we consider them basic and inalienable, then at worst they can be ignored or violated, not taken away. Ignored or violated along with all the other basic rights: the right to exist, to move freely on the earth, to education, to religious belief, to family life, and so on.

Unfortunately, the violation of basic rights is not without precedent. But Nazi ideology and action did break new ground: first, they claimed arbitrarily the right to decide the fate of whole nations; and second, they managed to convert the State with its system of positive law and its resources—human, economic, technological, scientific—into an instrument for implementing this super-arrogant and quasi-divine claim. Compared with that, the precise criteria chosen for the identification of the groups doomed to be permanently enslaved or instantly exterminated are of less fundamental importance. Though the criteria were indeed irrational in the extreme, a mixture of prejudice and obsession—racial, chauvinistic, religious, pseudo-religious, or anti-religious, and social or anti-social.

I would like to add a remark on the problem of generalization. I think there is no contradiction between the positions of Jacob Katz and Yehuda Bauer, but rather on both accounts historical research is completely impossible without a certain degree of generalization. We should beware of unfounded generalizations, of course, and in the present stage of investigating the Holocaust premature generalizations can and are being made. Still, we have reached a stage where certain general questions can be raised.

For example, based on the ghettos thus far investigated, we know that their history divides into two clearly distinct periods: before mass extermination, and from the moment mass extermination began. From now on, therefore, it will be natural for anyone tracing the history of a ghetto not yet investigated to ask whether it, too, divides into two periods. We know that in most of the ghettos so far investigated at least two leaderships existed: the official one—the *Judenrat*—and the underground. And from many of these ghettos we know that some kind of dialectical relationship went on between the two leaderships. It would consequently be unwarranted for a historian not to ask, when investigating a new ghetto, about them. Thus, a certain generality is already emerging as reflected in the questions that historians now ask.

SHLOMO AVINERI: I find myself in a quandary. Often I am very much in agreement with Richard Rubenstein's work, which I admire. However, on this occasion I have difficulties similar to those of Jacob Katz. I think the problem with Rubenstein's argument is that he is basically a functional structuralist. So Nazi policy toward the Jews has to be explicated within a structure. And if it does not fit a structure that is universally applicable, something is wrong with it. Take, for example, his comments about the relationship between Nazi antisemitism and surplus population.

Now, it is a conceivable hypothesis that the Nazi attitude toward the extermination of the Jews was premised on the universal Darwinian conception of surplus population; that there was a general picture of the world as such, and then, through a process of rationalization or, if you like, of elimination, the Jews were chosen as a target for that conception motivated by technological and scientific advance. But it is not enough to propound a conceivable hypothesis. One must also produce supporting evidence, historical evidence to show that this was indeed part of the Nazi outlook. Professor Rubenstein does not produce such evidence and I think, frankly, that no such evidence exists. On the contrary, Nazi antisemitism was not instrumental to Nazi aims but basic and immanent to them. It was part of their policy *per se.* The anti-Jewish policy had to do with their perception of Jews.

It is here, of course, that the remnants of traditional Christian attitudes toward Jews fit in. I wholly agree that Nazi antisemitism can be viewed only in terms of secularism, and that only with secularism were some of the defensive mechanisms to which Professor Rubenstein himself alluded stripped away, allowing mass murder to be conceived. But the fact that the victim of mass murder was the Jewish people had to do with preconceived notions about the role of Jews and the image of Jews; in this way the gap which Professor Schorsch finds between traditional Christian attitudes to the Jews and modern, racial, secular Nazi antisemitism is bridged. Even many of those people who did not go to church had, or could easily form, a certain diabolic image of Jews that helped the Nazis to propagate their own antisemitism.

For this reason, I have great difficulty in going along with what I consider to be Professor Rubenstein's main point. I agree that the Holocaust cannot be divorced from the very same culture of modernity that produced two World Wars and Hitler. Obviously, it is somehow part of that culture of modernity. But I cannot keep company with him when he goes on to regard the Holocaust as a necessary, immanent expression of the most significant

political, moral, religious, and demographic tendencies of Western civilization, as if there were a deterministic element in modernity that necessarily
leads to genocidal policies.

My contention is that Nazi rule generally, and Nazi policy toward the
Jews, have to be understood not in terms of the modernity of Germany but in
terms of its *retarded* modernity. Nazism was not a crisis of modernity—of
successfully achieved modernity—but a crisis of retarded, regressed, unsuccessful modernization. It has to be viewed in terms of the tension between
the modern world and a traditional culture that is trying to be modern and
cannot manage it. I am not saying that it is therefore the exception rather than
the rule, since obviously there could be further cases of arrested modernization—and arguably already are—amongst the newly emergent states. I am
just saying that it is functional within the crisis of achieving modernization,
rather than within a successful already modernized society.

This is where I would see differences between Nazism and modern
Western civilization, which has problems of modernity but not the problem of
arrested modernization. Nazism based its anti-Jewish policy on myth. It was
reverting to a pagan or quasi-pagan ideology because that is part of arrested
modernization, whereas totally secularized modern societies do not have
those myths. They can speak a rational language, which may be catastrophic
in Vietnam, if you wish, but it is not the same myth, it is not the same
symbolic language that was so "irrational" in the Nazi experience.

Those are my main arguments regarding Professor Rubenstein's theory.
But I also disagree with him on the issue of state power. Jacob Katz pointed
out that the Nazi extermination of Jews was not carried out within the legal
framework of a state. I would go one step further and suggest that it *could
never have been carried out within a legal framework.* Suppose a government within a political state publicly tried to promulgate—I think Richard
Rubenstein and I agree that a political state is public—a law saying that
everybody who is Jewish or of Jewish extraction, according to these or other
criteria, will be physically murdered. Now, that law simply would not work.
Because if there is a public law like that, there must be some recourse to some
sort of justice or courts of justice. Before killing anybody under that law you
would have to prove before a court, some kind of court, that he was indeed
Jewish, or there would have to be some tribunal before which he could
attempt to prove that he was not Jewish. It has to go through a mechanism of
law, even if it is truncated law, and therefore a legally conducted extermination of six million people cannot be carried out.

To give a completely different example, some of the problems the Soviets
are having now in their system arise precisely because they have reverted,
with destalinization, to some sort of semi-legalism, so that there is a gray
zone of semi-legality that lets somebody like Sakharov speak in terms of civil
rights. The latter obviously do not exist in the Soviet Union, but there is some
legal framework. Therefore Nazism, to me, is not in that respect an

expression of totalitarian state machinery; it is in a way the complete transcendance of what we call a state, a legally constituted authority. It was basically an illegal machinery, and it could not have done what it did within a legal framework.

Incidentally, this disposes of the whole defense of Nazi officials—be it at Nuremberg or at the Eichmann trial—that they were "merely obeying orders." There were no such legally constituted orders, nor could there have been.

GEORGE MOSSE: The suggestion that somehow modern antisemitism had nothing to do with Christianity is, of course, totally wrong. Do not forget that the last ritual murder accusation was made a few years before World War II in Czechoslovakia, supposedly a modern state, and that the accused was indicted by the state prosecutor of Czechoslovakia.

Now, it is true that, on the one hand, the Nazis were pioneers in modernity, pioneers in new factory buildings and factory conditions, pioneers in the beauty of work. So National Socialism was certainly a very important stage in modernizing in every way. On the other hand, it is vital not to overlook what you might call popular culture. All the inquiries—and I have made some of them—into German popular literature, for instance, have a very odd result. It was actually a liberal literature. The Jew is generally a good figure; those novels where he is a bad figure being on the fringe, as you can establish by circulation figures. Nor has the literature changed from 1820, let us say, to today. In it you find a great deal of liberalism, a great deal of toleration. But you also find, of course, traditional Christian attitudes and sometimes the Jewish stereotype, if only in a very secondary rank.

If you examine the Nazi cult, for example, it is obviously based on Christianity. I would go so far to say that nobody can really understand National Socialism who does not know about Schleiermacher's liturgical reforms: he introduced a liturgical rhythm and a liturgical form into Protestantism that were adopted by German public festivals all along, especially nationalist festivals from the 1880s on. After all, where were they going to get a liturgy from? Where did National Socialism get the stereotype? No modern mass movement would work if it were something thoroughly new. People do not like to change their liturgy, including their political liturgy. So, obviously, the traditional and the modern are mixed in all recent antisemitism. National Socialism was a stage in modernity, but it did not cut loose from popular culture. Because the Nazi regime was a popular regime, it was a democratic regime, so popular culture was extremely important.

Of course, I am not talking about "democratic" in the sense of parliamentary democracy, which went out with the nineteenth century so far as I am concerned—in any meaningful fashion. By "democracy" I mean that people believed that they were exercising a democratic right when they participated in the modern mass movement. This is how the majority of people after 1918 saw their democratic participation.

In addition, we have to treat things comparatively if we want to see the German picture correctly and to ask the right questions. If you had lived in 1914, you would certainly have said that if Jews were going to be exterminated, it would be the French who would do it. It was not in Germany but in France that National Socialism first arose, that it had a depth, that it had a large following amongst workers, for example. And we have to remember that everything in life is relative. In the West—I cannot talk about Eastern Europe—and in Central Europe it is a fact that popular culture is tolerant and liberal. The only explanation for what happened is one I once gave, that people wanted to realize a liberal and cultural and tolerant society, but thought they would need a Hitler to get it. They needed him to make the fairy tale come true. In other words, things are not simple. You cannot simply say that these were evil people. Genocide is not a simple problem.

Earlier I pointed out that racism is more complicated than it is made out to be. So is the question of genocide, so is the question of motivation. But it seems clear to me that everything is a mixture of modern and traditional, and that you cannot have mass politics or a mass movement which is not traditional. Myths and symbols—that is what modern politics is all about. But myths and symbols in which people can participate have to be traditional. And what does traditional mean in our civilization? It means that we have to have Christian analogies.

BEREL LANG: Listening to this discussion as a philosopher amongst historians, I have noticed what appear to be some continuing conceptual confusions that I would like to try to clarify. First, the matter of generalizations. It seems to me to resolve itself into the truism that sometimes generalizations, if they are not wild ones, are good, whereas if they are unfounded then they should be excluded. Moreover, for history to proceed—this is what some speakers were basically saying—generalization must be a possibility, and what Trunk did in his work was to raise the possibility of generalization about the ghetto.

Second, the distinction between the so-called objective function and the subjective intention made by Saul Friedländer. Although the distinction needs to be made, the two aspects are so obviously intertwined that I am surprised that historians should find it a matter for dispute and a matter of unclarity in their procedures. One can see that the subjective and objective aspects are intertwined from the way one speaks about individual intentions and actions. If one attempts to assess a person's intentions, it is not only his words—such as his estimation of his own intentions—that are relevant, but also the actions which follow. It is not enough to be told what he thinks he is doing, one also needs to know what in fact he does. He himself may not be aware of the intention until the action is, in fact, completed.

This holds true both for individual intentions and what one might speak of as corporate intentions. If one asks, for example, what the intentions of a *Judenrat* were, one would have to learn what was said by people involved on both sides, the Jews themselves and the Nazis, but also the procedures they followed, and the actions that ensued, which may or may not have been consonant with what was said. In particular, the objective function is itself a part—and an important part—of the *evidence* for determining the subjective intentions of the actors.

A further important feature was highlighted by the publication in America some years ago of the Pentagon Papers revealing the workings of the American government during the war in Vietnam. Intentions, whether individual or corporate, need not be formulated prior to an action or at any single moment. They may simply unfold in the course of events, and the figures involved may or may not be aware of them. Conceivably, *no single individual* involved in a corporate action will have a clear conception of the intention—let alone the function—of the events in which he is participating.

I would make a similar point in connection with the notion of rationality. The question has been raised as to whether or not events in the historical period that we are attempting to interpret were rational or not. Here again a distinction seems to me necessary. Are we asking whether individuals who participated in those events, again on all sides, were rational in what they did? This is a question concerning the individual; and it is a question that would have to be answered in terms of what remains a psychological and social category of rationality or irrationality.

It is quite different from the question as to whether or not one can provide a *rational explanation* for the events that ensued. The second question is, of course, much larger; the question of the nature or the possibility of historical explanation is a general problem extending well beyond the Holocaust. And it requires a distinction familiar to philosophers between reasons and causes: that is, between the reasons operating in the minds of the individuals involved and the causes acting upon them. It may be, in fact, that no historical explanation of any event provides an adequate explanation of the particularity of that event. Moreover—and this does specially concern the Holocaust—it may be that the case of evil or evildoing raises peculiar problems; in the Platonic tradition, for example, evil ultimately has no explanation. It may also be that if this thesis were carried to the level of corporate actions, it would be the basis for saying that no explanation could be adequate to the set of events which are the focus of our present attention.

Professor Rubenstein's explanation is certainly inadequate. When he points, for example, to the superfluity of a certain proportion of the population, he hardly begins to explain why certain specific people were picked out as superfluous. Nor does he explain the method used to eliminate this so-called superfluity. When he further claims that Nazis did not commit a crime, because crimes can be committed only within a political context, his argument presupposes what one might call a Hobbesian conception of government and moral obligation. Now the Hobbesian view may be correct, but it is not self-evidently correct. Professor Rubenstein quoted the close connection asserted by the Greeks between the individual and political life.

But Aristotle, the philosopher whom he cited with respect to that former statement, also stated that there is a distinction between the good citizen and the good man. This is quite a different answer to the question of whether crimes can be committed outside the domain of a political organization.

MARIE SYRKIN: On the question of "knowledge" and "awareness," I can say something with regard to American Jewry. In November 1942, when I was editing *The Jewish Frontier,* we published the first full-scale English report on what happened to the Jews of Europe. But why only in November, when we already had the catastrophic news in August? Was it because the Jews of America circumspectly kept a dark secret? In August Leon Kubovitzki came to tell a group of us who were active in Jewish life that Jews were being massacred in Europe. We left the meeting unconvinced, not because we were people of ill will or because we were imbeciles, but because we did not believe him. We had not yet reached the stage at which it was psychologically possible to accept so awful a revelation. In September an account of the Holocaust came in Yiddish from the Bund. It was sent to *The Jewish Frontier* and no less a person than Hayim Greenberg, our editor-in-chief, said, "Well, this can't really be, what shall we do with it?" And as an act of ultimate idiocy—in retrospect—we printed it in small type in the back. We were afraid to throw it out and we were afraid to publicize it.

It was in the following month, October, that we "knew," and then of course we did everything to publicize the truth, publishing whatever information could be gathered, in large print, in black letters. I say this only to show that in accusing a group of passivity one fails to take into account the enormous moral inhibitions or the impossibility of believing. If American Jews could not believe it, certainly I am not going to press the question of what the Jews of Europe ought to have thought or felt or believed.

As for the credibility of oral witness as opposed to documentary evidence, in 1945 I was collecting information in Palestine on the Holocaust from survivors. Among other people whom I met was Joel Brand. I sat with him in a café in Tel Aviv; he told me the story of his Eichmann negotiations and I believe that mine was the first report to appear in printed form at the time. When he spoke to me he made not a single accusation against the Jewish Agency or Sharett or any of the stuff that was to be put out ten years later. Which was the true story? The story told to me, in all good faith, in that café in Tel Aviv by Joel Brand, a few months out of the Egyptian jail? Or the story which, after years of simmering, now appears with regard to everything that "really went on" and the villainies of the Jewish Agency?

Lastly, the question of the legality of the destruction under the Nazis. Aristotle reports that in Sparta the ephors annually declared war against the helots, so that they would have a legal reason for destroying helots whenever they wished. The entire question of the legality and morality of such actions is so old that there are precedents for it. There are even precedents in our own century: take what happened to the kulaks in the time of Stalin through legally-decreed collectivization. Nobody here can foretell what forms legality will assume to destroy a given group once it seems desirable to destroy that group

Closing Statement by **ISAIAH TRUNK:*** Several of my colleagues have analysed and sometimes criticized my book *Judenrat*, whether in their papers or in their contributions to this discussion. I will start with Professor Raul Hilberg, whose analysis in depth is generally favorable. I agree with most of what he said about the Jewish Councils; I disagree only with his characterization of the ghettos and the Councils as a "self-destructive machinery." Here he comes very close to Hannah Arendt's absurd supposition that without the Councils annihilation would not have been so total. This misconception has already been refuted many times; for instance, the mass slaughter of the Jewish population in the Soviet territories and the Baltic countries where no Jewish Councils were functioning in the short period after the German invasion, is a most convincing rebuttal of Hannah Arendt's thesis. While I will not repeat what I wrote in the chapter of my book on "The Strategy and Tactics of the Councils toward the German Authorities," one thing should be clear: the ghettos were a Jewish terrain from which incarcerated Jews could, for a shorter or longer period, wage very limited war against the German machinery of destruction by means of self-help and the Jewish historically conditioned ability for adjustment.

From our perspective and hindsight today, the ghettos were of course a lost position. But in that *unpredictable* situation the ghettos were the only places where the tragic endeavors for survival and adjustment could manifest themselves. Without the ghettos and the Councils, the end would have come sooner. They created the conditions of temporary life—of *hayei sha'ah*—torturous as they were, but still infusing some dim hope of survival. As Professor Hilberg himself aptly remarks in his paper, "Jewish Councils everywhere came face to face with the basic paradox in their role as preservers of Jewish life in a framework of German destruction." He rightly assumes that "many times the meager resources at the disposal of the Councils were strained for the benefit of the community. There were occupational training programs, workshops, rationing systems, housing authorities, hospitals, ambulances and other services in a large number of ghettos." Without all this Jews in the ghettos would have died much sooner, as was the hope and the disappointment of Nazi authorities, when the anticipated disappearance of the Jews by "natural" means did not come about as quickly as they expected.

---

*Professor Trunk, who was unable to partake in the original discussion due to illness, kindly agreed to answer some of the points raised, though regretting (in his words) that his delayed answer would be "therefore devoid of the immediacy of a live discussion, to borrow an expression from the television vocabulary."

For Professor Bauer my book served as a point of departure for an ambitious attempt to synthesize an overall view of the Jewish Councils, whatever their official names, throughout occupied Europe, East and West. I will limit my remarks to the main region of Eastern Europe, which constitutes the geographical area of my book. Professor Bauer maintains that in the book, of which he has a high opinion, I committed the methodological sin of incorrect generalization, and that (as he puts it in his contribution to the discussion) my analysis "tends to disguise differences between ghettos, because it is always a 'horizontal' analysis." I am puzzled to know how Professor Bauer came to such a conclusion, which is at complete variance with the conceptual idea of my approach to the problem of the Councils.

In my book I clearly stated that "the entire Council phenomenon cannot be analysed in general terms. It has to be discussed with a view toward local conditions and personalities, the activities of individual Councils and their attitudes toward the German authorities. . . . The researcher has to beware of the temptation to simplify or generalize, trying to evaluate the attitudes and actions of individual Council members in given situations" (pp. xvii–xviii). I am quite sure that I did not deviate, throughout my book, from this methodological conception. In vain I searched Professor Bauer's paper and his contribution to the discussion for any factual evidence that I was lured by the temptation of generalizing (maybe with the exception of my discussion of the difference between collaboration and cooperation in the "conclusions" of the book). Throughout *Judenrat*, I emphasized the fact that "although the ghettos as a rule were similar, if not identical, in their formal framework of German repressive restrictions and in the role they were destined by the Germans to play in the 'Final Solution,' they were far from homogeneous in their internal demographic and economic structure; nor were the history and traditions of their communities similar, and neither was their geographic and economic position identical. All these circumstances left their mark on the Councils" (p. xviii).

The fragmentary character of the majority of the sources at my disposal prevented me from giving a "vertical" analysis of the history of the ghettos mentioned in *Judenrat*. This would also be rather unnecessary. But the attentive reader will find such analysis dispersed topically throughout the book when such analysis was possible on the basis of more comprehensive sources. For instance, with regard to major ghettos such as Warsaw, Lodz, Vilna, Kovno, Lublin, and Bialystok.

In his contribution to the discussion, Professor Bauer also sought to refute the assumption (which in fact I did not make) that "the differences between the reactions of different *Judenräte* can be explained solely by internal or German developments." To this end, he compares the *Judenräte* in Kovno and Vilna, which acted differently in spite of the fact that they were composed, in his opinion, of individuals having the same background. But one can doubt whether Dr. Elkhanan Elkes and Dr. Leyb Garfunkel of the Kovno Ghetto had the same background and social prestige as the former officer of the Lithuanian army, Jacob Gens, and the rather obscure Anatol Fried of the Vilna Ghetto. Their biographies do not support such a contention.

Lastly, Professor Bauer sometimes formulates his correct observations in such a language as to convey the impression that they contradict my observations and conclusions, which is not a very convincing polemical method!

Professor Henry Feingold posed, in the course of the discussion, the question: "To whose history does the *Judenrat* belong? Does it belong to German history, or does it belong to Jewish history, or does it belong to both?" For a historian the answer is unequivocal: the *Judenrat* belonged to both histories in the same way the Holocaust itself is part of both the Jewish *and* the German history of the fateful period 1933–1945.

By the way, I would like to correct Professor Feingold's misconstrual of Ringelblum's observation regarding "the passivity of the Jewish masses, dying without a whimper." It pertains chronologically *not* to the phenomenon of passivity during the deportations to Treblinka in Summer 1942, but to the meek attitude of the mass of refugees in the Warsaw Ghetto (about 150,000) in the face of their ordeal. This is evident from his explanations. Of course, some of his explanations (the continous hunger, the ubiquitous and relentless German terror) also have bearing on the behavior of the general Warsaw Ghetto population during the deportations of Summer 1942.

This brings us to the problem of resistance, upon which Professor Hilberg dwelled at length in the discussion, but still one-sidedly, limiting his remarks solely to the question of physical, armed resistance. However, he asked pertinent questions regarding lack of intelligence and weapons in the ghettos. In answering them I am reluctant to repeat myself, since I have already devoted two studies to the problem of Jewish resistance: the chapter on Jewish resistance in the Nazi period in my book *Shtudies in yidisher geshikhte in Polin* (Buenos Aires, 1963), pp. 298–312, and the chapter entitled "The Attitudes of the Councils toward Physical Resistance" in *Judenrat*, pp. 451–74. So I will only state two things. First, in the broader meaning of the notion "resistance," including cultural, religious, economic, sanitary, and political resistance, Jews in the ghettos, and to some extent in the camps, were defying and resisting the oppressors almost constantly. As the late Mark Dvorzhetsky put it: the sole fact of staying alive longer than the German calculations predicted was an act of resistance.

Second, the objective and subjective circumstances for armed resistance on the part of the ghetto Jews, who were rendered physically, demographically, and mentally weak by constant hunger, disease, and relentless terror, against the well-oiled Nazi machinery of destruction, were most unfavorable, to say the least. It suffices to cite the behavior of non-Jews during the Nazi actions of "pacification" or retaliation, or the millions of Soviet prisoners of war in the internment camps, who were massacred without any attempt to resist, to get a correct measure for evaluating the degree of Jewish resistance or lack of it. (Similar points are made by Professor Bauer in his paper.)

Rightly, Professor Hilberg concluded his opening remarks in the discussion with the statement: "The Jews were prepared for pogroms, for sporadic acts of violence against them. But they were not prepared for the death blow from the nation of Goethe and Schiller that struck them in 1942 and 1943."

Only a brief remark about Dr. Helen Fein, who questions the value ("completely valueless") of the material on the Council members derived from oral statements and subsequently from written questionnaires submitted to survivors in the United States and Israel. In view of the clear and unambiguous information in my *preface* to the book that "ninety-nine ghettos of all sizes were discussed in the questionnaires, giving certain personal information on 740 Council members and 112 Ghetto policemen in the ghettos in Poland and the Reichskommissariate Ustland and Ukraine" (p. xv), it is no objection that she was unable to tell from the *appendix* "whether these were 300 survivors of two ghettos, opinions of survivors of 300 ghettos, or whether they were 100 survivors of each of three ghettos."

One can only wonder how such misunderstanding of a clearly written text is possible, and from where Dr. Fein derived the information that "the interviewers were not trained to avoid interjecting their own expectations in the situation—to avoid any bias." Why is she so sure of that? The two pollsters were trained and experienced members of research institutions (YIVO and Yad Vashem) and well aware of the pitfalls of "interjecting their own expectations in the situation." In addition, they were properly instructed on the matter of objectivity in polling, and those interviewed were assured of strict confidentiality. I very much regret that a questionable objection with regard to this type of source was "interjected" in the discussion; I was aware of both the strong and the weak aspects of such a source and analysed them in the corresponding appendix of my book.

Postscript

Nathan Rotenstreich

I really wonder whether I am qualified to attempt the impossible: to restate by way of integration the richness of what my colleagues have said. The fact that I am interested in the history of ideas, in philosophy, and in the meeting between Jews and the non-Jewish world in modern times, is possibly an explanation for my venturing to undertake the attempt. But to offer that explanation is not to imply that even somebody better qualified could achieve the impossible, that is, could do justice to the wealth of our deliberations. The very attempt to bring things together can at most integrate some aspects of our discussion, but not the nuances and all the individual contributions.

Let me start with a comment on the scholarly analytical pursuit of a phenomenon having the magnitude and horror of the Holocaust. I think we have to reintroduce the concept of *passion* in the literal sense of that term. Passion as suffering, passion as related to pathos, in the strict sense of the latter. We do not cease to be involved in passions, in this particular sense, even when we attempt to analyse such a phenomenon. We are aware of the fact that intellectual pursuits are only one level of human activity and response to situations, whereas the basic level is that of an encounter, that of an experience, that which can be described in terms of this particular concept of passion as involving suffering.

All the same, any reflection—and we have been engaged here in a continuous process of reflection—is an attempt to articulate the passion, to articulate the basic involvement, to spell it out. This we do, not in order to replace the basic involvement, but to provide room for interaction between that involvement, our reflection upon it, and the hypothetical or tentative outcome, and room for absorption of that outcome again on the level of encounters.

Reflection connotes here also an attempt to learn something. Not that we should say, in a simple-minded way, that history is a teacher of life. The point, rather, is that historical consciousness cannot remain solely on the level of taking in experiences. Historical consciousness eventually has to be at least in part an articulated consciousness. Here the rhythm of Jewish history certainly serves as a paradigm: in that rhythm certain events became focuses of historical consciousness, and this has been the case from time to time, from generation to generation. Our attempt to interpret the Holocaust "a generation after" is probably an inadequate attempt, one that will be reconstituted in the generation to follow; but it is still necessary, because sheer silence toward the phenomenon is also not adequate. Reflection is closer to memory than silence. Mere silence can easily be taken as the first attempt at suppression, and such an attempt can easily be taken as readiness to forget.

We move, then, simultaneously on three levels: the basic experience of our encounter; memory, the retaining of traces; and reflection, including historical and ideological analysis.

Next I would like to make a methodological comment on a problem that came up frequently in our discussions, namely, the problem of generalization. There are at least two meanings to the concept of generalization, and they have to be kept separate. One is generalization as an attempt to provide explanation through laws, through what in contemporary philosophy of history are called "covering laws," whereby events are viewed as cases of a general rule. The second meaning treats the general as a type or a structure—as a *Gestalt.* In this case the general is a composite of ingredients. And since such ingredients are exchangeable, and thus particulars of a universal, but the structure maintains its singularity, we may term the structure a *novum,* to use Professor Katz's term.

Inasmuch as we are looking into the Nazi phenomenon as it manifested itself in the destruction of the Jews, we have to look into the impact of that phenomenon both on history in general, and also on Jewish history in particular. We must consider these two perspectives from the point of view of the singular structure, and from the point of view of the exchangeable ingredients.

The difficulty for us, in dealing with the phenomenon in this double-edged way, is due to the issue of the "whole" as opposed to the "parts": the "whole" of the structure or the *Gestalt* as opposed to its parts. Somehow we take over from traditional modes of interpretation the view of a "whole" as being a *benign* concept because we regard a whole as *more* than the parts. The phenomenon that easily comes to mind here is an organism, and many philosophers try to show that the organism is more than the sum total of its parts. But it is difficult for us to transpose even a neutral concept, let alone a benign concept, and apply it to something that is so clearly evil.

Yet we have to see that the concept of the *Gestalt* or the whole can be applied to different kinds of historical situations and phenomena, and it is not bound to have the immediate humanistic connotation of something nobler created out of the parts and outgrowing the parts. And this, I think, is what we find in the Nazi phenomenon. For the Nazi phenomenon indeed absorbed, as parts within the ignoble whole, the main streams of opposition to the Jews that were present in European or Western history. Those main streams can be listed, perhaps, under four headings, which have emerged in the course of our discussion, and especially in Saul Friedländer's opening paper. So I shall list them, the four ingredients creating the background, in a kind of historical, chronological, and thematic order.

First of all, Christianity was always aware of the Jews, never indifferent to them. Jews are part of the Christian consciousness, both theological and historical. Christianity, mainly in the Augustinian trend, rejected the Jews, but rejected them to the border line of history, making them Cain; the killer of the brother became the killer of God. Jews, as was explained by Professor Katz, had to be maintained as negative witnesses to the victory of Christianity. They had to be maintained, though, in a precarious condition. Now, Christianity did not create Nazi antisemitism, but the effects of an attitude can transcend the meaning of the attitude, and it created a possibility, a horizon for what developed later. We can also express this in terms of what German pedagogical thought in the early twentieth century called the "perceptive mass": a child at school receives a mass of perception, which accumulates and forms a kind of filter through which it sees the world, and in Western society Christianity is part of this perceptive mass.

The second ingredient was the concept of the "soul" of a people (*Volksseele*) or "spirit" of a people (*Volksgeist*), which in a sense is a pluralistic concept. Different peoples have different "souls"—different psychic motivations, psychic syndromes, biases. The French are supposed to like elegance, the English wit and sobermindedness. Let us not forget that Herder used the concept in his appreciation of the poetry of the Hebrews, so that essentially it did not have to have negative connotations in its application to the Jews. But it could also be used as a polemical and antithetical concept when the demand was made that the character or psyche of the German people had to be preserved. In the 1840s the "historical school of jurisprudence" (*Rechtsschule*) in Germany favored removing the influence of Roman law on German jurisprudence because of the antithesis between the "souls" of the two peoples. There was also a tendency to elevate Germanic, Teutonic, or Western culture to the level of the highest manifestation of human creativity. This is, again, not yet identical with the Nazi concept, but it is an essential part of the background.

The third ingredient is the concept of race, which in the later nineteenth century was to some extent a biological transformation of the concept of the "soul" or character of a people. There is a diversity of human races, it was held, but the characteristic feature of a race is not essentially psychic or spiritual creativity, but precisely biological descent. Yet here, too, we have to be very careful because racist thinking is an attempt to classify the varieties of mankind, and even when it leads to positive or negative evaluations of the varieties, it does not necessarily lead to placing the Jews *outside* the historical realm, outside the human species altogether. It is always possible to reach that transformation of the concept when we see the possibility retrospectively. But we can still maintain a distinction between the original idea of race and the particular way in which it became an ingredient of Nazism.

The same applies even to the fourth essential ingredient, which was mentioned, for instance, by Saul Friedländer: the concept of the international conspiracy. Even before the Nazis, anti-Jewish polemics had claimed that Jews were engaged in a conspiracy against mankind. Yet even conspiracy can be viewed—indeed ordinarily is viewed—as involvement in human affairs, an invidious or hostile involvement, but still an involvement in human affairs. Whereas bacteria—which is what the Jews became in Nazi eyes—are not engaged in conspiracies. They bring about epidemics, not conspiracies.

As contrasted with these four ingredients already present in the background to Nazism, the unique aspect of the Nazi phenomenon lies in two facets. First, in pushing the conclusion up to its bitter, horrifying end; and second, in bringing about the sum total of its ingredients, since there is the absurdic structural element in the *Gestalt* that appeared with the Nazis. Here there is a difference between background and consequences, which makes it difficult to provide an *explanation* of the Nazi phenomenon in terms of any structure of history or any application of the principle of causality. On the other hand, we do not lack tools to *explicate* the Nazi phenomenon. The difference has to be maintained between explanation and explication. For even if there is no way to explain the phenomenon without being reductionist—all explanations invoke a precedent phenomenon or a preceding event—there are several ways of explicating the phenomenon. The explication of the phenomenon is, I think, obtained by identifying first the ingredients, and then identifying their unique configuration in the structure they formed or the total *Gestalt.* This was the approach used by Uriel Tal in his paper, which breaks so much new ground.

The importance of the distinction between the ingredients and the total *Gestalt* is also brought out by another consideration. Since the Nazis absorbed various components of opposition to Jewishness and Judaism, and these components were present in their own ideology, they could address themselves simultaneously to different audiences. The receivers could pick up and identify themselves, if not with the total *Gestalt,* then with certain layers of the *Gestalt*. This made the communication like any communication, even a verbal communication: out of the total texture in a verbal communication, each of us picks up only certain information, according to the resonance of the receiver.

Therefore, if we are considering the issue of an ideology and its impact, it is somehow misplaced to ask whether or not the ideology is an autonomous factor, because the context in which an ideology arises and operates does not lack convictions. It is not as if the context were an opaque situation in which human beings are driven by forces, and the ideology were a secondary phenomenon superimposed on codes of behavior. Ideologies, not only when they are an invidious phenomenon, but in many other cases, are rather themselves articulations of codes of behavior, which are themselves imbued with convictions. Moreover, what on the level of convictions is the apparent cause of things that happen may be rather insignificant, because the code of behavior has its own total structure. Therefore, ideology will not be a weapon in propaganda or attempts to convince without the precondition that such ideology "rings a bell"; that is to say, that on the level of behavior people are already influenced by certain convictions. Ideologies are not conceived in a vacuum. So we have to look into them as belonging to the context and articulating the context. This is, I think, the position of any reflective attitude.

Let me now say something more about the novelty of the Nazi phenomenon, after having stressed the various previously existing ingredients in it. As some contributors pointed out, there have been only too many attempts—by scholars as well as by political ideologists—to treat the destruction of European Jewry as a manifestation of "fascism" or economic forces. All such attempts lead at best to half-truths. I myself recently saw a memorial to Jews in Germany that refers to them simply as "the victims of violence and injustice." This kind of generality, which fails to say anything about what specifically characterized the Nazi phenomenon, completely misses the point and trivializes what happened.

The Jews, in the Western tradition, were constantly assigned an antithetical position. They were part of history, but an antithetical part; this is how Christianity, again conspicuously in the Augustinian trend, regarded them. They were dealt with as the predecessors of Christianity in the line of continuity. The Church replaces the Jews as the chosen people; thus the Church belongs to the line of continuity while the Jews have to be preserved within history as an antithetical phenomenon. Traditional antisemitism is an emphatic expression of the rejection of the Jews as an antithetical phenomenon. We are also aware that in contemporary ideologies, too, Jews are used as an antithesis in ways that vary according to the context. They are "rootless cosmopolitans" when the emphasis is on belonging to a national or ethnic group; they are incurable nationalists when the emphasis is on a cosmopolitan, "universal" ideology.

But these are all antithetical positions that nonetheless remain within the historical process. What happened in the Nazi phenomenon was that Jews were transposed from their frequent position as an antithetical *historical* entity to an antithetical *extra-historical* entity. They were moved outside the boundaries of mankind. One way of putting it was the infamous Himmler address recalled by Saul Friedländer: this removed the Jews to the low-level organic world by treating them as a kind of bacteria. But there was another way of putting it, which was to remove them to the realm of the mere material. Jews became a kind of clay; the eventual outcome of their existence was soap. So long as they were accused of bringing about epidemic disease, they were somehow attacking the human realm from an extrahuman position; they were still somehow loosely connected with that realm. But if they are clay they are outside the human realm altogether.

One aspect of this that has to be emphasized is the doom of genetic belonging. Jews cannot "uproot" themselves from being the descendants of Jews. No consciousness, no awareness, no repentance, no conversion can change that. Within the human realm, even when it is viewed from a very racist orientation, there is still provision for interpretation in terms of individual human beings and individual human awareness. Within the realm of nature lying outside human history, there is no room for such awareness. Nobody can change the causally predetermined situation there. The Jew, according to Nazi ideology, had a nature totally determined by the chain of events, by inheritance in the simplest biological-genetic sense of that term.

Yet not only the deterministic aspect of the Nazi ideology imposed on the Jews is important here, but also its metaphysical aspect, which concerns the concept of evil. So I should like to say a few words about the concept of evil as I see it in this context. Namely, if we understood good or goodness as a state of being forthcoming, of granting, of being open, and this is certainly one of the warranted interpretations of the concept of good and goodness whether in the guise of mercy or of justice (both of which are in a sense ways of giving and being forthcoming), then evil amounts to inhibitions, to not letting a thing be or develop. Evil amounts to hampering, to encroachment.

Although these are rather formal definitions of good and evil, they have a relevance to the specific essence of the evil of the Nazi phenomenon, providing we take account of two further points which are, I believe, most important for our attempt to delineate the evil aspect of that historical situation. One is that we must (as always in moral philosophy) decide the question of *what* is to be evaluated here as good or evil—the deed, its outcome, or its motivation? The answer is in this case connected with the motivation. Killing as such, unfortunately, including Hiroshima, is a widespread human phenomenon. But there is a basic difference between a killing, even a massacre, in a war situation where the enemy is destroyed, and a killing that takes place because the enemy is not a human being. In this case the motives leading to the killing are not strategic or tactical, low and cruel as the latter may be, but a certain evaluation of the object to be annihilated. Thus, although in moral philosophy it is a moot point whether good can be described only in terms of motivation, here at least we have a historical phenomenon in which evil can be described in terms of motivation rather than merely as the visible overt act.

The second point is that we have to do with evil as an inhibition, but an inhibition of a totalistic character, which is expressed not only in motivation, but in an articulated attitude. The articulated attitude in question should be termed the notion of total superiority. By this I do not mean merely totalitarianism as a structure of a regime or a bureaucracy; the totalitarian structure, rather, was devised to implement the notion of total superiority. The point is that the notion of superiority could only be truly total through having its negative counterpart, which was the negation of the humanity of the Jews. The total superiority could be, as it were, safeguarded, expressed, made visible and explicit, precisely through denigrating the Jews to a position of being only objects, of being only clay. Otherwise that superiority would still have had some inbuilt inhibiting factors; but if there was no inhibiting factor, the way was open to manifesting the total superiority.

Here evil ceases to be an encroachment, evil ceases to be a non-adherence to principles or commandments, and becomes in the historical situation an imposed transformation of human beings into non-human entities. This is a new phenomenon. We cannot come to grips with it by saying that it is only a certain kind of motivation on the one hand, and encroachment on the other, because normally encroachment is a means through which you want to achieve some further end, which will be to inherit somebody's advantages, to take his position, whereas in a total phenomenon the action is an end in itself. And probably we have to cease, regarding that phenomenon, to use the traditional distinction between ends and means; we must rather see it as one conglomerate in which ends and means were no longer distinct.

Turning now from the Nazi phenomenon itself to the reaction of the Jews, we heard many comments on the *Judenräte* and the whole issue of Jewish leadership. This is a very haunting discussion. We certainly would like, not only—and perhaps not mainly—for the enhancement of our own pride, but for the honor of those implicated, to see the Jews as having faced the Nazis as activists. I mean activists in the day-to-day sense, not activists expecting the coming of the Messiah, not activists constantly exposing themselves to martyrdom (*kiddush ha-Shem*), but activists in the sense of people willing to take initiatives on their own behalf—the kind of Jewish activism we like to see today (and I shall come back to that).

Probably it is impossible to affirm that such activism was the rule, rather than the exception, but is it enough to say this? I would suggest some trivial things in this context. Above all, we have to try to grasp the way things looked to those who lived in Europe in the thirties and forties. We have to see the limitations of their time perspective in two senses. In the narrowest sense, we may remark that they inherited the traditional Jewish strategy of adjustment to situations: not to initiate situations, but to adjust to them and see where there were loopholes that could be exploited. It was to seek the loopholes in society where Jews could still find ways and means of adjusting themselves and maintaining themselves.

More generally, our attempts to explicate the Nazi phenomenon are all of them hindsights, as Professor Katz brought out in his paper. Every historical exploration is a reconstruction, a hindsight; even when we take the view that history is a world tribunal, it is not the historian who is the judge. There is a difference between his knowledge *now* and the knowledge available to those who were *then* in the position of being historical agents. The historian has to be aware that he knows what resulted from the actions of the agent, results that the agent did not know and often could not know. In the case of a Jew living under the later stages of Nazism, his perspective was limited because of the total compulsion of the environment, because he did not have the means of handling that environment. A Jew then did not even know whether there was a future. Any planning has to take into consideration the horizon of the future. I would like to remind you of a paper written by Kurt Lewin on the German Jews of the early thirties. There he said that in the early thirties, because their time perspective had on its horizon the possibility of emigration, the German Jews had shown courage, flexibility, and initiative. There is a correlation between the time horizon and flexibility: if there is no time horizon—as there was none in the later stages—flexibility is curtailed and perhaps ceases to exist.

I am saying this because it seems that we shall continue to be engaged in a sort of dialogue between historical agents of the past and historical observers of the present. Historical agents had their own perspective, historical observers have a different one. Even if the latter tries to show empathy toward the perspective of the earlier agent, he has the advantage of knowing the effects of an action, of seeing the global context of that action, which the historical agent could not see. And this sort of relativism of perspectives is essential here in order to do justice to the phenomena studied, in order to be aware of the virtues and the limitations of any reflective attitude that studies events long after they took place.

Let me now say a few words on the post-Holocaust experience. There is, to begin with, certainly a moral question involved. To what extent are we permitted to turn precisely such catastrophic events into teachers of the present? Are we, perhaps, failing to express full respect to the martyrs by turning their experience into a reservoir of human lessons? We sometimes seek a rescue device in this moral dilemma. In Hebrew we are used to invoking the saying *be-motam tzivu lanu ha-hayyim* ("in dying they bequeathed us life"), which again we sometimes impose on those who cannot speak, and which may have an innuendo from which we should refrain. But, since life goes on, we are inclined, in spite of many hesitations about learning from the past—and especially from that particular past—to learn from everything and to incorporate the experience.

There are two or three major lessons that we may articulate, however hesitatingly. First of all, there is a basic difference between a possibility that looms large *in advance of* an actuality—which is still a hypothetical possibility—and a possibility that became an actuality, and is a possibility *after* an actuality. There is something in the dialectic of historical events whereby a possibility once realized becomes part and parcel of the infrastructure of our experience. We are then less shocked if it recurs. We are less obsessed with the horror of it. The real question, therefore, is not only not to let the possibility became an actuality again, but not to let the possibility become a *triviality.* This is especially so in view of a strange phenomenon character-istic of Western society in general, namely, the shrinkage of the time horizon. Since things are changing so rapidly in the Western world, lines of continuity are steadily undermined. We should be aware that especially today it is easy for the possibility to become a triviality.

The second aspect is related to changes that occurred in Jewish history, changes that were elicited by the Holocaust. In our discussions here it was pointed out that Jewish behavior then was by no means uniformly passive; even if the majority tended to seek adjustment, there were many islands of Jewish activity in spite of the total compulsion. What has hap-pened since is that activity, initiative, an attempt to create our own realm, all those have become leading factors of Jewish life and Jewish experience, not islands of Jewish response in a sea of overwhelming compulsion. There was, of course, previously a continuous effort in Jewish history for the last eighty or a hundred years to give continuous expression to Jewish initiative. But the Holocaust greatly reinforced the impulse toward initiative. We now exhibit a readiness, a willingness, even a compulsion to be active. Perhaps we are even losing an ingredient, because in overemphasizing the aspect of activity we excessively discount the aspect of adjustment. Some of the mistakes we have made in Israel may be related to the creation of an exclusively activity-oriented Jew. Yet even when we try to moderate this orientation in order to provide for the necessary equilibrium, it persists because the memory of the dangers of passivity and adjustment stays with us.

And there is a new phenomenon of Jewish stubbornness. Inasmuch as tra-ditional Jewish stubbornness could be interpreted as an attempt to cling to the past and to maintain the present through the past, what we witness now, and what we are engaged in now, is a stubbornness to be in the present, whether or not that present establishes lines of continuity with the past. This is a stubbornness in maintaining the Jews as an entity in the historical present, and not only as an entity on the periphery of history. We pay for that at a very, very high price, but we incur that price deliberately. We know that we are paying that price, and we know why.

In conclusion, I want to return to the distinction that I suggested at the beginning between passion and reflection. Historical consciousness is not merely an intellectual construct. Historical conscousness is already present on the level of day-to-day reality. An intellectual exploration is a process of making that historical consciousness deliberately self-aware; it does not invent the consciousness. And once such consciousness has made itself aware on the level of our day-to-day existence, it becomes reinforced by intellectual constructs. Eventually, therefore, historical constructs reinforce historical consciousness, while the historical constructs themselves derive their motivation, their subject matter, and their initial impulse from day-to-day awareness. This mutual interaction between historical consciousness and historical constructs applies with special force to our own dilemma, for we are both part of the situation and reflecting on it.

Index